Muslim Slaves

in the Chesapeake 1634 to 1865

Stephen J. Vicchio, Ph.D.

Minneapolis

Minneapolis

SECOND EDITION DECEMBER 2022
Muslim Slaves in the Chesapeake: 1634 to 1865
Copyright © 2019 by Steven J. Vicchio.
All rights reserved.

No part of this book may be used or reproduced in any manner whatsoever without written permission except in the case of brief quotations used in critical articles and reviews. For information, write to Calumet Editions, 6800 France Avenue South, Suite 370, Edina, MN 55435.

10 9 8 7 6 5 4 3 2

Cover and interior design: Gary Lindberg

ISBN: 978-1-960250-71-1

To my students Ray Alsalka and Sarah Ferris,
who helped me learn Classical Arabic.

Contents

Introduction

This study is the result of ten years of research. It began in 2008 when I published a book entitled Biblical Figures in the Islamic Faith. In preparing the manuscript for that book, I learned the classic, Arabic language. Also, during the same time, I learned that the first black man in Maryland, Mattaeus de Sousa, may have been a Muslim slave. I asked myself at the time, if there is one, how many more can there be? The answer to that question is that I have found 106 suspected Muslim slaves in the Chesapeake region from the early seventeenth century to the close of the American Civil War. The study is organized into four parts and expressed in the following way:

Part One: Introduction to Muslim Slaves in the Chesapeake Bay Region (in America)

Part Two: Slave Supply Zones and the Middle Passage (in Africa)

Part Three: Coffles, Slave Traders, slave jails and Slave Auctions (in America)

Part Four: Runaway Slaves in Virginia and Maryland (in America)

Part one consists of the first chapter in America. Part two includes chapters two and three, and the events that happened in Africa. Part three encompasses chapters four, five, six and seven, and is back in America. The fourth and final part includes chapters eight, nine and ten, a chapter that sketches out the major conclusions of this study. In addition, I have supplied four appendices. Appendix A gives a summary of suspected Maryland Muslim runaway slaves. Appendix B is a catalog of suspected Virginia Muslim runaway slaves. Appendix C is a summary of the tribal scars that were possessed by about two dozen of the 106 suspected Muslim captives in the Chesapeake Bay region from the seventeenth century to the nineteenth century.

In Appendix D, we have provided a catalog of the number of prominent Muslim slaves throughout the United States in the seventeenth century to the mid-nineteenth century. In that catalog, I enumerate twenty-one prominent Muslim slaves in America, and then I discuss each of them in Appendix D.

Throughout working on this project, I have incurred debts from many friends, scholars, students and other people. Sarah Ferris and Ray Alsalka, two of my former students, both Syrians, helped me tremendously in our reading of Al-Qur'an together.

Unfortunately, this is not an illustrated version of the book, so the paintings I describe are not present in the text.

Chapter One:
Muslim Slaves in Colonial Maryland and Virginia

There are three categories of people against whom I shall myself be a Plaintiff on the Day of Judgment. Of these three, one is he who enslaves a free man, and then sells him and eats the profit.

—Al Bukhari, *Hadith* (Author's translation)

He learned so much of our language that he was able to understand most of what we communicated in conversation; and we became used to his manner of speaking, which we could shift well to understand him tolerably well.

—Thomas Bluett, On Traveling with Job Ben Solomon Diallo

An act of freeing a slave will make those people who do such a deed to be categorized as the Companions of the Righteous.

—The Holy Qur'an 90:18 (Author's translation)

Introduction

The primary purposes of this first chapter are the following: First, to explore what we know of West African Muslim slaves brought to the New World in general, and the Chesapeake Bay region, in particular. Secondly, we will make some brief comments on the history of African slavery in the Chesapeake from 1600 until 1865.

Successive sections will follow these sections of the chapter on prominent Muslim slaves in Maryland, and then a separate section on prominent Muslim slaves in Virginia. We will conclude this opening chapter with some very general remarks about the practice of African slavery in the Chesapeake Bay region from that same period. First, however, we shall give an important catalog of notable Muslim slaves in America in the seventeenth to nineteenth centuries. We will refer to these prominent American Muslim slaves throughout the remainder of this study.

Prominent Muslim Slaves in America: Seventeenth to Nineteenth Centuries

From the seventeenth century to the nineteenth century, approximately two dozen or so prominent Muslim slaves have been the subjects of several contemporary historians and other scholars. Among those scholars are Michael A. Gomez, Sylviane Diouf, Muhammad Al-Ahari, Allan A. Austin, Terry Alford, Philip D. Curtin, Douglas Grant and many others.

1. Ibrahim Abd ar-Rahman (1762–1829)
2. Abu Bakr as-Saddiq (1790–1841)
3. Salih Bilali (1772–1855)
4. Lamine Kebe (1775–1855)
5. Man Who Prayed Five Times a Day (born ca. 1800)
6. The Moor on the Mississippi (?)
7. Mohammed Ali Ibn Said (1833–1882)
8. Umar Ibn Said (1770–1864)
9. Phillis Wheatley (1753–1784)
10. Selim Aga (1826–1875)
11. Bilali Muhammed (1770–1857)
12. Boyrereau Brinch, aka Jeffrey Brace (1742–1827)
13. Sambo Makumbo (?)
14. S'Quash (?)
15. Muhammed Sinei (1788–1838)
16. Dorugu Kwage Adamu (born ca. 1820)
17. Hamet Abdul (Tennessee slave, mid-nineteenth century.)
18. Charles Ball's South Carolina Muslim (?)
19. The Moorish Slave

20. Mohammad Abdula (Fulbe from Kano. Slave in Bahia, Brazil).

21. Anna Mousa, aka Benjamin Cochrane (Jamaican slave in late eighteenth century).

Abd ar-Rahman was born in Guinea and was captured on the Gambia River and placed in the hold of the British slave ship *Africa* at the Freetown Harbor of Sierra Leone. *Africa* was a 110-ton brig with two masts built in the Shoreham Shipyards. Rahman was brought to the British West Indies and subsequently shipped to New Orleans, where he again was sold. Then he traveled by riverboat to Natchez, Mississippi, and once again sold into slavery. After more than forty years in slavery, Abd ar-Rahman returned to Africa.

Abu Bakr as-Saddiq was born in Timbuktu and a member of the Mandinka Tribe in what today would be Ghana. After his voyage on the Middle Passage in 1807, he became a slave in Jamaica, where he wrote a sixteen-page autobiography in Arabic in 1831. Abu Bakr as-Saddiq later became a slave in Charleston, South Carolina, until he escaped and moved to Fayetteville, North Carolina. In Jamaica, he experienced a forced baptism, though there is evidence he remained a Muslim his entire life. London scholar George C. Renouard translated his autobiography into English.

Salih Bilali was born in present-day Mali or Ghana among the Fulbe Tribe. He was abducted at the age of twelve and taken to the Bahamas and became the slave of William Brown Hodgson of Georgia. Later, he was sold to James Hamilton Couper, who wrote several descriptions of Bilali and his work on Couper's St. Simons Island plantation in the Georgia colony. Mr. Couper's son said of Salih Bilali, "He is the most religious man I have ever known."

Lamine Kebe was born in Senegal near the Senegal River. In America, he was known as "Old Paul." Kebe befriended Theodore Dwight, who suggested, "He was a great source of knowledge of Africa," although he is quoted as saying, "There are good men in America, but all are ignorant of Africa." For a while, Kebe worked for the American Colonization Society in New York City. In Africa, before Kebe's abduction, he taught Qur'anic studies. In fact, in America, Kebe was the first African to publish in an American journal titled the *American*

Annals of Education and Instruction.

The Man Who Prayed Five Times a Day was born around 1800 in either Nigeria or the Bight of Biafra. He became a slave in South Carolina in the New World, where he also was described as being "aloof" and did not interact socially with the other slaves. Little else is known of his biography. Similarly, the man known as the "Moor on the Mississippi" was said to pray openly on his voyage down the Mississippi River. Not much is known of him, either. We do, however, know he refused wine and pork when he became a slave on the Mississippi, which is another common trait among Muslim slaves coming to America during this time.

Mohammed Ali Ibn Said, also known as Nicholas Said, was born in the Kingdom of Borneo. He is mostly known from an 1867 article in the *Atlantic Monthly*. Said appears to have attended the Harvard Divinity School and in 1873 wrote a rare and nearly three-hundred-page autobiography called *The Autobiography of Nicholas Said*. This slave also fought as a corporal in the Union Army of the American Civil War.

Phillis Wheatley was born in Senegal and kidnapped at the age of eight. After the Middle Passage, she was brought to Boston and taught to read and write by her master Mr. Wheatley. Later, Phillis Wheatley became the first African American poet in New England and possibly in America. In 1773, Wheatley completed *Poems on Various Subjects: Religious and Moral*. It brought her acclaim in both America and abroad.

Selim Aga was a native of Sudan and thus the African Interior. He was kidnapped there at the age of eight and brought to Scotland. There, he received a first-rate education. Therefore, he was raised as a free man. Selim wrote an autobiography as well as some poetry, such as his "Ode to Britain." Later, he returned to Africa, where Grebo Insurgents killed him in 1875.

Bilali Muhammad was born in Guinea in the Sierra Leone Supply Zone. After being kidnapped and taken across the Middle Passage, he became a slave on Sapelo Island in the Georgia Colony. He is also the author of the "Bilali Document," a hand-written, Arabic manuscript of sixteen pages that gives a summary of the tenets of the Muslim faith. The manuscript is housed at the Hargrett Rare Book and Manuscript Library at the University of Georgia.

Boyrereau Brinch, also known as Jeffrey Brace, was born in present-day Mali. Later, after becoming a slave in Virginia, he served in the Continental Army under General George Washington. After the war, Jeffrey Brace became the first African American citizen in Vermont. In his later years, Brace became blind and published his memoirs called *The Blind African Slave*: *The Memoir of Boyrereau Brinch.*

In the eighteenth century, a slave known only as "S'Quash" was brought to Charleston, South Carolina, and forced into slavery. There is little else known of the man's biography. Sylviane Diouf, in her *Servants of Allah*, suggests that S'Quash could read and write Arabic, as well as Greek and had been to Cairo. He may be part of a married couple of slaves owned by George Washington, Deborah and Henry, or Harry Squash. The couple escaped Mount Vernon in 1781 and joined the British in New York, where they were declared free in 1783.

Muhammed Sinei was a Mandingo Gambian born near the Gambian River. He was first taken to the French fort on Goree Island and then transported to Trinidad in the New World. Later, he was involved in the manumitting of other Mandingoes in Trinidad by buying them back from their owners. Several contemporary Scholars have written accounts of the life of Sisei, including Carl Campbell, as well as an article in the 1838 edition of the *Journal of British African Geographical Society of London.*

Dorugu Kawag Adamu, of Central Sudan, was abducted in 1839 near his home. He was purchased by a German diplomat named Adolf Overweg in 1851 and taken to Europe. He was later freed and returned to Central Sudan in 1864.

Tennessee slave Hamet Abdul was obviously a captive, who insisted on retaining his African and Muslim name, was first noted in 1834 when he sought to raise money so that he might return to Africa. In his autobiography, Charles Ball supplies a nineteen-page slave narrative from a Muslim man he discovered in South Carolina. Ball's Muslim was most likely a member of the Tuareg Tribe in present-day Mali. Ball says he was captured on the Gambia River and brought to Charleston, South Carolina, around 1807.

A Mississippi slave, known only as the "Moor," was brought to the Mississippi River around the year 1812. He was interviewed by a white American ten years later. He claimed to be a Muslim prince from the Niger River Valley. He was captured there by an enemy clan and placed on a Spanish ship and brought to New Orleans. The Moor was forced to eat pork for survival, but he never touched any spirits in his time in America.

Mohammad Abdullah, a slave from Kano, was enslaved in Bahia, Brazil, sometime in the 1840s. Abdullah fulfilled his obligation of the *Hajj*, or Pilgrimage to Mecca, and appears to have been a member of the Fula Tribe in Nigeria. Anna Mousa, or Benjamin Cochrane, was the son of a Mandinka priest as well as a skilled physician in Kingston, Jamaica. He also appeared to have been a native Arabic speaker and was familiar with and befriended Richard Robert Madden (1798–1886), an Irish writer, physician and abolitionist historian. Madden first arrived in Jamaica in November of 1833.

Finally, Samba Makumbo was a Senegalese slave who became a captive in Trinidad in the late eighteenth or early nineteenth century. He appears to have been a Mandingo and received his freedom shortly after arriving in Trinidad. Afterward, Makumbo formed a Mandingo redemption society whose aim was to buy slaves out of captivity. By August of 1834, all slaves in Trinidad were given a free status.

In the final, conclusive chapter of this study, we have included an appendix on these prominent Muslim slaves in America. In addition to the slaves mentioned above, there more specifically were a number of prominent Muslim slaves in the Chesapeake Bay region. The remainder of this first chapter is dedicated to those slaves in Maryland and then in Virginia.

The History of West African Slavery in the Chesapeake

A man named Mattheus de Sousa, one of nine indentured servants working for Father Andrew White, a Catholic Jesuit priest, arrived at Saint Clement Island, Saint Mary's City, in southern Maryland in 1634, on the ship the *Ark* along with Father White and other European settlers of the seventeenth century.

Andrew White (1579–1656) was an English Jesuit missionary who helped with the founding of the Maryland colony. He was an early chronicler of the colony, and his writings are one of the primary extant sources for interpreting the colony, the Native Americans in southern Maryland and on the Eastern Shore. For his efforts in converting the native people, Father White sometimes was called the "Apostle to Maryland."

The first West African individual to set foot on the colony of Maryland, then, is Mattheus de Sousa. He was, most likely, originally a slave of a European man from a Portuguese colony of East Africa, perhaps from Mozambique. In his first few years in Maryland, de Sousa, along with the other indentured servants of the Jesuits, helped to build churches, parish buildings, houses, as well as the planting and harvesting of tobacco on the Jesuits' property in southern Maryland.

There is also some evidence that de Sousa traveled by boat to the Eastern Shore of Maryland, where he and Father White traded with Maryland Native Americans. Although information about de Sousa is scanty, there are a number of things about him about which we can be certain. First, he came to Maryland as an indentured servant, not as a slave. Secondly, we know that de Sousa was of mixed races, probably European and African, for in some of the extant literature on him, he is referred to as a "Molato."[1]

Thirdly, the *Ark* landed on Saint Clements Island in southern Maryland, and de Sousa arrived on that voyage. Fourthly, de Sousa was elected to the Maryland General Assembly in 1641 and served that assembly until the close of the following year.[2] Fifthly, it appears that de Sousa finished the provisions of his servitude in 1638 when the Jesuits declared him a free man. He also appeared to have continued to work for the Jesuits earning money in trading British goods for animal furs and food from the Native Americans.[3]

Sixth, it is clear that de Sousa sailed small boats for the Jesuits and other early settlers of the colony. And finally, de Sousa may well have been a Muslim indentured servant or slave from the Portuguese colony in Mozambique in the East African Supply Zone discussed in Chapter

---

1 Thomas Hughes, History of the Society of Jesus in North America 1 (Cleveland: Burrows Brothers Company, 1907), p. 281.

2 "Mattheus de Sousa," Maryland State Archives, SC3520-2810. "Freemen in attendance at Legislature," (1642).

3 Ibid.

Two to follow.

Indeed, many slaves and servants from East Africa originally were the property of Muslim traders who brought these captives from Arabia to places in East Africa, including the Portuguese colony of Mozambique.

We know from colonial records that in 1641, de Sousa commanded a small boat on a two-month voyage to trade with the Susquehannock Indians, and a year later, he sailed a ketch belonging to the provincial secretary, a man named John Lewgar.[4] de Sousa is also recorded as having voted in the election of 1641 in Maryland, so he was no longer an indentured servant by then.

Mr. Lewgar (1602–1665) was the first attorney practicing law in the Maryland colony. He was also the first clerk of the House of Burgesses, as well as the first attorney general of the colony. Thus, Lewgar is considered to be the "Father of the Maryland Bar." He was born in London and educated at Trinity College, Oxford, receiving his B.A. in 1619.

While at Oxford, Lewgar met Cecil Calvert, the Second Baron of Baltimore. Lewgar arrived in Maryland on November 28, 1637, along with his wife. In 1638, they built a new home at St. Mary's City on a tract of land they called "Saint John's." The Lewgar home became the unofficial center of the colony, a place where many of the earliest meetings of colonial leaders took place in Maryland.

We also know that the Maryland legislators met there in 1642. Lewgar was instrumental in Mattheus de Sousa becoming the first black man to vote in America. Six years later, a woman named Margaret Brent (1601–1671) attended another meeting at Saint John's, suggesting that she be allowed to vote, as well. Although she was denied by those assembled, Ms. Brent became the first woman in America to ask for "voyce and vote" in the government.[5]

Mr. de Sousa, as we indicated earlier, captained a ship for Mr. Lewgar in the late 1630s. During his voyages, the black man became indebted to Mr. Lewgar. In 1642, when the Susquehannock attacked the

---

4 Ibid.

5 David S. Bogden, "Mathias de Sousa: Maryland's First Colonist of African-American Descent," Maryland Historical Society Magazine 96, no. 1 (Spring, 2001).

English settlement in southern Maryland, he also became indebted to a southern planter named John Hollins.[6]

Other extant court records indicate that de Sousa owed money to two other wealthy planters in Maryland, Lord Leonard Calvert and Captain Thomas Cornwayles. It appears as though de Sousa had trouble meeting his expenses, so he borrowed money from these gentlemen, and when he did not pay them back, they sued the Molato, as he was called.

Thomas Cornwayles was born around 1600 and died in Norfolk, England, in 1676. He was a commander of the British Navy and Lieutenant Governor in Maryland in 1641. His manor was known as "Cornwayles Cross" at the head of the Saint Mary's River. Cornwayles returned to England on June 2, 1659.[7] John Hollins (1616–1657) came from England and worked as an attorney in the early colony, as mentioned earlier in this chapter.

Sir Leonard Calvert (1606–1641) was the first proprietary governor of Maryland. He was the second son of George Calvert (1579–1632). His elder brother, Cecil (1605–1675), inherited the colony and the title upon the death of their father in April of 1632. Leonard Calvert was appointed governor in George's absence. The father, George, was also known as "Leonard Calvert of Yorkshire." This is the Leonard Calvert who lent money to Mattheus de Sousa.

In the historical record that is extant, Mattheus de Sousa was first referred to as a "Molato" by a priest who mentions him in an old spelling for "Mulatto" defined in the seventeenth century as a person of mixed African and European descent. It is sometimes quite difficult in the seventeenth century to determine someone's race. Mulatto could also mean a person's color or complexion. At any rate, Mattheus' surname was a common one in seventeenth-century Portugal, as it is today in Portugal and Brazil.

Information we have from Maryland government records and court cases show that Mattheus de Sousa was well-treated compared to black people who followed him in the Chesapeake Bay region. He voted, stood for public office and was elected, carried on a sailing busi-

6 Maryland Land Office Records, 1646–1657. Liber. ABH, fol. 65. MSA S920-4.

7 Ibid.

ness, paid his taxes, and was taken to court a few times. Most early Maryland black men had little or no chance to achieve their freedom. It was not a crime for masters to beat and punish their slaves. de Sousa had to work for the Jesuits for four years. In 1638, the Jesuits manumitted him, and he began to make a living as a ship captain and a fur trader.

The final mention of Mattheus de Sousa in the historical record is an order from a 1642 Maryland court requiring that de Sousa reenter indentured servitude so he could pay off the debts he owed to Mr. Lewgar.[8] No record of de Sousa is extant after 1642. But a year later, some Native Americans killed a number of colonists, and several other settlers died of disease and starvation at that time. At any rate, Mattheus de Sousa appears to be the first African man to set foot in the Maryland colony, and he may have been a Muslim from the Portuguese colony of Mozambique and brought across Africa by way of an inland slave coffle to Angola. Mozambique was in the East African Supply Zone, as outlined in the next chapter.

One of the things we do not find in the extant record of Mattheus de Sousa is any mention of the servant/slave's religion. This may be because he had none, or it may be due to the fact that he was reluctant to reveal to the Jesuits that he actually was a practitioner of the Islamic faith. At any rate, there nothing in the extant record of de Sousa's religious practices and faith if he had one.

Meanwhile, in the colony of Virginia to the south, the first Africans arrived in 1619 on the Dutch ship *White Lion*. Twenty Africans had been captured in a battle with a Spanish ship. The *White Lion* landed at Jamestown, Virginia. The Dutch ship traded the Africans for foodstuffs and supplies, but they were traded as indentured servants, not as slaves. A couple of years later, in 1621, a British ship named the *James* also brought Africans to the Virginia colony.[9]

This is significant for our purposes because a man named "Antonio" was among those Africans on the *James*. Antonio had been captured in his native Angola by an enemy tribe and sold to Arab slave traders. At this point, Antonio was likely forced to convert to the Is-

8 John Mack Faragher, The Encyclopedia of Colonial and Revolutionary America (New York: Facts on File, 1990), p. 257.

9 Ibid.

lamic faith. At any rate, after arriving in the Virginia colony, he served his indenture to a white planter named Bennet. After serving the seven years of his indenture, Antonio became a free man.[10]

A year after his arrival, Antonio met a woman named Mary, who also had gained her freedom from indenture. She arrived on the English ship the *Margaret*. By 1635, Antonio changed his name to Anthony Johnson. He first enters the historical record in 1647, when he purchased a calf. Johnson was granted a large plot of farmland and bought the contracts of five indentured servants, four white Englishmen and one black man. The land of Johnson's was on the Naswattock Creek in Northampton County, Virginia.[11]

In 1642 an unfortunate fire caused great losses to the Johnson family. Johnson applied to the Virginia court, asking for tax relief. On February 28, 1652, the Johnsons were granted that relief. In 1653, Johnson's black indentured servant, a man named John Casor, approached an English captain named Goldsmith and claimed his indenture had expired seven years earlier. As a result, Casor sued Johnson, and Johnson won.[12]

A neighbor planter of Johnson, named Robert Parker, offered Mr. Casor work, and he signed an indentured contract to Parker. Johnson then sued Parker for the return of Mr. Casor. The court initially found in favor of Parker, but Mr. Johnson appealed the case. In 1655, the court reversed their ruling, finding that Johnson "owns" Casor and that the court costs were to be paid by Mr. Parker.[13]

Eventually, Anthony Johnson moved his family to Somerset County, Maryland, where he negotiated a lease on a three-hundred-acre plot of land for ninety-nine years. Johnson developed the property as a tobacco farm and called it "Tories Vineyard." Apparently, he died on that farm in 1670.[14]

Slavery in the Maryland colony developed along many of the

10 Ibid.

11 Ibid.

12 "Africans in Maryland: Slave and Free," Maryland State Archives. Document dated 6/3/11.

13 Ibid.

14 Suzanne Ellery Greene Chapelle, Maryland: A History of its People (Baltimore: Johns Hopkins University Press, 1952), p. 77.

same lines as Virginia. The early settlements in both colonies were established along major waterways that empty into the Chesapeake Bay. The economies of both colonies were centered on the growing of tobacco for sale in European markets. The cultivation of tobacco required cheap labor to harvest and to process the crop. As these colonial farms became larger, they also became more efficient.

By the close of the seventeenth century, in both colonies, the indentured servitude of white English labor-class servants was on the wane, so now both colonies had to rely on the labor of black African and African American slaves. By the eighteenth century, both colonies of the Chesapeake had become plantation economies requiring vast amounts of slave labor. In 1700, Maryland had a population of 25,000. In 1750, it had risen to 130,000.[15] By 1755, about 40 percent of Maryland's population was African American. Indeed, by the middle of the eighteenth century, Baltimore had become the second-largest port along the Atlantic, trailing only Charleston, South Carolina.[16]

The first historical record of African men, after de Sousa, entering the colony of Maryland is in 1642 when thirteen Africans arrived in Saint Mary's City. It is not clear, however, whether these black men were indentured servants or slaves. Governor Leonard Calvert negotiated with the ship captain in 1642 to purchase the thirteen to work on his Saint Mary's plantation. After that time, the Africans in the colony were on the rise, with British merchants bringing them in large numbers. Between 1675 and 1695, about three thousand Africans entered the Chesapeake Bay colonies to work on tobacco plantations.

By 1685, indentured servitude was over in both colonies. We also know that at this time, indentured servants who were not Christians often were given their freedom if they converted to Christianity. These Africans, as we shall see in Chapter Two of this study, came from various West African ethnic groups from the coast and as far inland as Nigeria.

In Chapter Two, we will explore the nine principal supply zones from which most West Africans came to the Caribbean and British

---

15 Ibid.

16 Matthew Page Andrews, History of Maryland (New York: Doubleday, 1929), p. 192.

North America in the seventeenth to the nineteenth centuries. As well as the two supplemental supply zones of North Africa and South Africa, as we shall see.

By the turn of the eighteenth century, Maryland and Virginia were beginning to get a new generation of black folks in the Chesapeake Bay region who were African Americans—people born in this country. Scholar Allen Kulikoff uses records of several Chesapeake planters to show the gradual change from African-born slaves to African Americans. On the Edmund Jennings plantation, for example, in 1712, nearly all the workers were African born. By 1750, however, 90 percent of black men on that plantation were born in America.[17]

Early on at Robert Carter's farm in Maryland, to cite another example, most slaves were African born. By 1730, the labor population there was now a mixture of African-born and African American. In just a few generations, Africa became simply a distant memory to any slave living on a tobacco plantation in the Chesapeake.[18]

The legal status of black people at the beginning of the two colonies was not always crystal clear. Courts in both colonies disagreed about whether an African who accepts Christianity should be freed. In 1661, the Maryland Assembly passed a law specifically forbidding what was known as "Miscegenation," a word that meant marriages between people of different races. Three years later, in 1664, Governor Charles Calvert directed the assembly to rule that all slaves in the colony should remain "Slaves for Life" and that the children of slaves are to be enslaved *durante vita*, as well.[19]

Included in this 1664 Act was the following passage:

> Be it enacted by the Right Honorable, the Lord Proprietary, by the advice and consent of the Upper and Lower Houses of this present General Assembly, that all

17 Edgar J. McManus, Black Bondage in the North (Syracuse: Syracuse University Press, 2002), p. 6. Edmund Jennings (1659–1727) was an Englishman from Yorkshire. He also settled in York County, Virginia.

18 Ibid. Robert Carter III (1727–1804) left Virginia in 1754 and married Frances Ann Tasker, the daughter of former Maryland Governor Benjamin Tasker.

19 Ibid.

> Negroes or other slaves to be hereafter imported into the Province shall serve *durante vita*. And all children born to any Negro or other slave shall be as their fathers were for the terms of their lives.[20]

This Maryland law made the institution of slavery a perpetual phenomenon in the early colony. Indeed, the number of slaves in Maryland and Virginia grew exponentially until the practice's eradication during the Civil War. The wording of the 1664 Act suggests there may have been other slaves besides Africans early on in Maryland. There is no direct evidence, however, that Native Americans were made slaves in the Chesapeake Bay region, though there appears to have been in the Massachusetts Bay colony.[21]

The exact date of the first African slaves in Massachusetts is not known, but by the year 1642 in the records of a man named Samuel Maverick, there is evidence that he owned black slaves.[22] In 1638, there are records that several Native Americans prisoners were taken during the Pequod War and exchanged for African slaves in the West Indies.[23]

The Pequod War (1634–1638) was an armed conflict between the Pequod Tribe and English colonists in Massachusetts. By the end of the conflict, seven hundred Pequod had died or were taken into captivity. Many were sold in the West Indies or exchanged for African slaves.[24]

At any rate, by the year 1700, the number of slaves imported to the Chesapeake region greatly increased as the tobacco industry began to dominate the economy of the region. In 1753, the Maryland Assembly passed a law that prohibited any slave owner voluntarily to free his slave. This meant that slave masters in Maryland, even if they wished

---

20 Andrews, p. 191.

21 Jason Rhodes, Somerset County: A Brief History (Charleston: The History Press, 2007), p. 59.

22 Peter Kolchin, American Slavery 1619–1877 (New York: Hill and Wang, 1993), pp. 81–82.

23 Ron Field, The Confederate Army: 1861–1865 (Oxford: Osprey Press, 2005).

24 The Pequod people were a North American Native Indian tribe that inhabited much of what today is the state of Connecticut, beginning in the seventeenth century.

to free their slaves, were prohibited from doing so.[25]

During the Civil War, Maryland remained in the Union to the regret of many slave owners on the Eastern Shore and in southern Maryland. Thus, when a bill was presented in December 1861 to Congress that called for the emancipation of slaves, it was passed. When the "Emancipation Proclamation" followed in 1863, Maryland could not follow it because they had remained in the Union. The Proclamation, however, did affect Virginia.[26]

This brings us to an analysis of several prominent West African Muslim slaves in the colony/state of Maryland, the topic of the next section of this first chapter.

Prominent Muslim slaves in Maryland

Perhaps the three most well-known slaves in Maryland were all descended from Muslim West-Africa: Harriet Tubman, Frederick Douglass, and Kunta Kinte, the ancestor of Alex Haley, the author of *Roots*. Robert Moss, in an essay entitled "Harriet Tubman and the Ashanti Traditions of Dreaming," suggests that the Tubman family may have originated among the Ashanti People of Central Ghana in the rain forests of West Africa about one hundred and fifty miles from the coast.[27]

Robert Moss quotes from a 1907 edition of the *New York Herald*, where the memories of Tubman are quoted. She speaks of her grandmother telling her stories as a child. She tells us:

> "The old mammies to whom she told dreams were not wont to nod knowingly and say, 'I reckon you are one of dem Shantees, chillen.'"[28]

This suggests that some of Tubman's ancestors may well have been Ashanti, whose religion is a mixture of spiritual and supernatural powers. The Ashanti hold a form of Animism with respect to animals,

---

25 Ibid.

26 For more on the Ashanti, see Robert Edgerton, The Fall of the Asante Empire (New York: Free Press, 2002).

27 M. W. Taylor, Harriet Tubman (New York: Chelsea House Publishing, 1991), p. 17.

28 Robert Moss, "Harriet Tubman and the Ashanti Tradition of Dreaming," http://bit.ly/2qYnPzS.

plants and trees possessing spirits. They also place a central emphasis on ancestor worship and on a High God known as Nyame.[29] A number of Ashanti villages in North-Central Ghana remain Muslim to this day. It may be that some of Harriet Tubman's ancestors were among these West African Muslims.

Harriet Tubman was born into slavery in Dorchester County, Maryland, sometime around 1820. By the age of six, she began to work as a house slave, and seven years later, she was sent to work in the tobacco fields. In her early teens, she suffered a serious injury that plagued her for the remainder of her life. An overseer threw a two-pound weight at another slave, and it struck Tubman in the head.[30] We cannot be sure if any of Tubman's ancestors were Ashanti, or were Muslims for that matter, but Robert Moss has, at least, suggested that possibility.[31]

In another essay about Tubman by Robert Moss, he suggests this about Harriet Tubman's ancestry:

> The shipping records of the Chesapeake slave trade suggest that Harriet Tubman's ancestors were brought to America from this part of West Africa. Nearly all the slaves brought to Maryland ports came directly from Africa, and the vast majority came on big London vessels that picked up their cargoes along the Gold Coast or from Upper Guinea. Maryland planters were constantly asking for slaves from the Gold Coast.[32]

In Chapter Two of this study, we shall examine nine major supply zones from which African slaves came to Virginia and Maryland. The Gold Coast and the Sierra Leone area, as we shall see, are two of those supply zones. Robert Moss goes on in both these essays to say that Harriet Tubman inherited the Ashanti practice of out of body experiences and other paranormal behavior common, even today, among the Ashanti People. Moss writes:

> Harriet said she inherited these special gifts—including

29 Ibid.
30 Ibid.
31 Ibid.
32 Ibid.

> the ability to travel outside the body and to visit the future—from her father, who could "always predict the future," and who "foretold the Mexican War."[33]

Harriet Tubman's ancestors, then, may well have been Ashanti Muslims living in a central Ghana village in the eighteenth century. Robert Rattray, a British anthropologist, lived among the Ashanti in the early twentieth century. In his 1927 book, *Religion and Art in the Ashanti*, he also speaks about the Ashanti notion of dream travel. He relates:

> Flying is a common experience in Ashanti dreams. If you dream that you have been carried to the sky—and then returned to the ground—that means you will have a long life.[34]

Some scholars have mentioned the similarity of these Ashanti practices with what has been called the *Miraj*, or the "Night Journey," in 621 in the City of Mecca. The Prophet Muhammad had gone to the Ka'baa at night, and, being weary, he fell asleep. He then was awoken by the Angel Jibril and transported across time and space, much like what the Ashanti report. This may be another connection that Harriet Tubman's family had to Islam.

Other scholars, like Sylviane A. Diouf, for example, in her *Servants of Allah*, also suggests that Tubman had Muslim ancestors. In fact, Diouf traces the common practice of African American women wearing handkerchiefs, rags and bandanas around their heads to West African Muslims always wearing a skullcap, turban or fez, including many Ashanti.[35]

William S. McFeely, in his *Frederick Douglass*, says that Douglass may also have been descended from Muslims. He points out that Douglass' great-great-grandfather was named "Baley," and his grand-

---

33 Ibid.

34 Robert Rattray, Religion and Art in Ashanti, quoted in Moss, "Tubman and Dreaming." Robert Sutherland Rattray (1881–1938) was an early British Africanist and expert on the Ashanti people.

35 Sylviane A. Diouf, Servants of Allah (New York: NYU Press, 1998).

parents, Betsy and Isaac Bailey of Talbot County, Maryland, were slaves on the Eastern Shore. Betsy's daughter, Harriet, gave birth to Frederick Augustus Bailey. About the possible Moslem connection to Frederick Douglass, McFeely writes:

> In the nineteenth century, on Sapelo Island (where Baileys still reside), there was a Fulfulde-speaking slave from Timbo, Futa Jallon, in the Guinea highlands who could write Arabic, and who was the father of twelve sons. His name was Belali Mahomet. Belali slides easily into the English "Bailey," a common African American surname along the Atlantic coast. The records of Talbot County lists no white Baileys from whom the slave Baileys may have taken their name, and an African origin on the order of Belali is conceivable.[36]

Again, Sylviane Diouf and others agree that the Douglass family name Bailey may, in many cases, derive from the common Arabic name Belali or Ben Ali. Indeed, earlier, we mentioned a Fairfax, Virginia, slave named Yusuf Ben Ali, or Joseph Benhaley, who fought for the Americans in the Revolutionary Army. This makes the connection between the names Bailey and Ben Ali, or "Son of Ali" in Arabic, even stronger. At this point, however, there is little evidence to support this claim.[37] Nevertheless, like Harriet Tubman, the ancestors of Frederick Douglass may very well have been members of the Islamic faith, as well.

Kunta Kinte (1750–1810) was a member of the Mandinka Tribe in Juffreh, Gambia, in northwest Africa. Kunta is a name that resembles several male Arabic names. Most people in the Senegal-Gambia region in the late eighteenth century were Muslims, although several critics have cast doubt about Alex Haley's family tree. If his ancestors were Gambian, then they were most likely Moslems.[38]

There is, however, some evidence that Kunta Kinte fought hard to

---

36 William S. McFeeley, Frederick Douglass (New York: Norton, 1991), pp. 3–5.

37 Diouf, pp. 47–51.

38 Trans-Atlantic Slave Trade, http://bit.ly/37UtBmL.

keep his Islamic heritage. Having learned the Qur'an as a boy, he used to scratch Arabic phrases in the dirt. He also tried to pray several times every day after he arrived in America. Kunta Kinte was Alex Haley's forbearer, a Mandingo of whom he speaks of in his book and television movie, *Roots*. Haley says that Kinte was one of ninety-eight slaves brought to Annapolis aboard the *Ligonier* in 1767.[39] If this is correct, then the young Gambian was sixteen or seventeen years old at the time. The *Ligonier* was built in New England in that same year. The ship had six decks in all—four of those carried slaves and the other two spice, lumber and tobacco. The *Ligonier* could carry 170 slaves if packed tightly, only 140, if not.

At any rate, as we have indicated, Harriet Tubman, Frederick Douglass and Kunta Kinte all appear to have had Muslim ancestors going back to the eighteenth century and further. Many other prominent Muslim slaves came to Maryland and Virginia in the seventeenth to nineteenth centuries. It is to an analysis of these that we now turn.

Other Muslim Slaves in Maryland: Eighteenth and Nineteenth Centuries

In this section of this first chapter, we will describe and discuss three other significant Muslim slaves in the state of Maryland in the eighteenth and nineteenth centuries. Their names were Job Ben Solomon Diallo, Loumein Yaos and Yarrow Mamout. The first of these, Job Ben Solomon Diallo, was born as Ayyub Ibn Sulayman ibn Ibrahim around 1702 in what is now Senegal. He came from a religious family and was the co-Imam of his community, along with his father. While on a trading expedition for his father, Job was captured in enemy territory and then subsequently sold to the British. He then traveled to Annapolis, Maryland, by way of the Middle Passage. Job did not, however, convert to Christianity as many African slaves did, but prayed openly while still adhering to his Islamic dietary regulations while in America, as well as the Muslim requirement of five daily prayers called *Sallat* in Arabic.

Of all the Muslim slaves in Maryland, we have more information about Job Diallo than anyone else. His original first name was either Ayyub or Ayuba, the two Arabic names for the Biblical patriarch Job.

---

39 Ibid.

He was born in Boundu in Senegal. His memoirs were recorded by an English attorney named Thomas Bluett in his *Memories of the Life of Job, Son of Solomon, High Priest of Bounda in Africa: Who was Enslaved About Two Years in Maryland, and Afterwards Being Brought Back to England, Was Set Free, and Then Sent Back to his Native Land in the Year 1734.*[40]

Thomas Bluett (1690–1749) was an attorney, judge and minister in the colonial Chesapeake region. By 1722, Bluett was a minister working for the Society. In 1731, Bluett gained some renown when he met Ayyub Ibn Sulayman Diallo, who had just been brought from Gambia. Douglas Grant published a second biography of Job published by the Oxford University Press in 1968. Grant's text is called *The Fortunate Slave: An Illustration of African Slavery in the Early Eighteenth Century.*[41] From these two sources, as well as several other early American documents, we can piece together an outline of the life of Ayyub Ibn Sulayman Diallo as he was properly called.

Job came from a prominent family of Fulbe religious leaders. His grandfather was one of the founders of the village of Boundu. In February of 1730, Job's father sent him to sell two negro slaves, and to buy paper and other necessities. Job's father also told his son not to cross the Gambia River, where the rival Mandingo Tribe was in control of the land.[42] The Fulbe People, Fulla or Fulani are the largest ethnolinguistic group in Africa, numbering more than forty million people. The Fulbe are also the most widely spread people in Africa. They are bound together by the Fulfulde language, as well as some very basic cultural elements, such as a code of conduct that is called *Pulaaku*, a word that means righteousness.

Apparently, Captain Pike, the skipper of the English vessel the

40 Thomas Bluett, Some Memories of the Life of Job, the Son of Solomon, the High Priest of Boundu, Africa; Who was a Slave About Two Years in Maryland; and afterwards Brought to England, Was Set Free, and Sent to His Native Land in the Year 1734, Maryland State Archives, vol. 842, pp. 266ff. This text is also reprinted in Five Classic Slave Narratives, Muhammad al-Ahari, ed. (Chicago: Magribine Press, 2006), pp. 37–64.

41 Douglas Grant, The Fortunate Slave (Oxford: Oxford University Press, 1968).

42 Ibid., pp. 61–65.

Arabella, did not strike a deal with Job on the two slaves, so Job proceeded on with a man named Loumein Yoas, who understood the Mandingo language. Together, against the wishes of Job's father, the two crossed the Gambia River. They sold the two slaves in exchange for some cattle. When he began to return home, Job lingered for a while at the house of a friend. He hung his arms on the wall, and a short time later, a band of plundering Mandingo brigands captured Job and his interpreter Yaos.[43]

The Mandigo people of West Africa, also referred to as the Mandinka or Malinke, are the direct descendants of the Mandinka Warriors from Guinea who conquered large territories in areas to the north and east of present-day Sierra Leone. The Mandingo are ninety-eight percent Muslim, as Islam became the basis of the Mandingo cultural and religious lives in the early seventeenth century.

The Mandingo thieves shaved the heads and beards of Job and Yaos. This made them appear as though they were slaves captured in battle. In February 1730, the two captives were carried to Captain Pike, and on the first of March, placed aboard the English ship the *Arabella*. Some short time after that, Job told Captain Pike that he was the same man trying to sell him two slaves just days before.

The captain then gave Job leave to secure a ransom from his father. Job sent an acquaintance to his father with word of Job's capture and a plead to ransom him. It appears that it was common in West Africa, in the seventeenth and eighteenth centuries, that when a member of a well-to-do family was captured and sold into slavery, that person was often ransomed, or, bought back if you will, so that the slave's sale to Europeans would not take place.

In Job's place, the messenger, having not arrived back in time, the *Arabella* sailed a week later, bound for Annapolis, Maryland. Job and Loumein arrived in Annapolis in the spring of 1734, whereupon Job became the property of one Vachell Denton, an agent of the Englishman Henry Hunt.[44] Mr. Denton sold Job to Mr. Alexander Tolsey, a tobacco farmer on Kent Island. Job, at first, was put to work in the fields, but it soon became clear that he was not suited to farm work. Eventually, Job

43 Ibid.
44 Ibid.

was put in charge of tending the cattle, but Bluett says he left the cows unattended so he could enter the woods to pray.[45] On one occasion, Bluett tells us, a young white boy saw Job praying, and the boy mocked him and threw dirt in Job's face.[46]

From this experience, as well as similar slights, Job attempted to escape Mr. Tolsey's farm by fleeing north to Delaware. Job eventually was arrested and taken to the Kent County Court House in Delaware, which was also a tavern that doubled as the county jail. It was there, at the tavern, where Mr. Bluett met Job. The Englishman described that initial encounter this way:

> This happened about the beginning of June 1731, when I, who was attending the Court there and I had heard of Job, and I went with several gentlemen to the Jailer's House, being a Tavern, and desired to see him. He was brought into the Tavern to us, but he could not speak one word of English. Upon our talking and making signs to him he wrote a line or two before us, and when he read it, pronounced the words *Allah* and *Muhammad*, by which, and he refused a glass of wine that we offered him, we perceived that he was a Mohametan [Muslim], but we could not imagine what Country he was from, nor how he got hither; for by his affable Carriage and the easy Composure of his Countenance, we could perceive that he was no ordinary slave. When Job had been sometime confined an Old negro man who lived in that neighborhood and could speak the Jallof Language, which Job also understood, went to him and conversed with him. But this Negro, the Keeper, was informed as to whom Job belonged and what was the cause of his leaving his master. The Keeper whereupon wrote to his master, who soon also fetched him home and was much nicer than before, allowing him a place to pray in and some conveniences in order to make his

45 Ibid.

46 Ibid.

> slavery as easy as possible.[47]

Upon returning to Mr. Tolsey's farm, Job was allowed to write a letter in Arabic to his father back in Boundu. The letter was sent to Mr. Denton so that Captain Pike might take it to Africa before the letter arrived to Mr. Hunt. Eventually, the letter was seen by James Oglethorpe, the founder of the Georgia colony, who took compassion on Job and gave his bond to Hunt upon the delivery of Job to London.[48]

James Oglethorpe (1696–1785) was a visionary, social reformer and military leader during the colonial period. He was also instrumental in the establishing of the Georgia colony in British North America. In 1733, Oglethorpe led an expedition of colonists that landed in Savannah. He spent the next several decades directing the economic and political future of the new colony, defended it militarily, and continued to generate support and to recruit settlers into the colony from England and other parts of Europe.

At the time, Oglethorpe was the director of the Royal African Company. After he received a letter from Job that was authenticated by John Gagnier, the Laudian Chair of Arabic at Oxford, Oglethorpe purchased Job for forty-five pounds sterling. According to his own account, Oglethorpe was moved with sentiments upon hearing of the suffering Job had endured. After Oglethorpe's purchase of Job, he sent him to the London office of the Royal African Company.

In March of 1733, Job went aboard the *William*, a ship captained by George Uriel. Mr. Bluett was also on the voyage. During the trip, Bluett taught Job English so that by the end of the voyage, he could converse adequately in the new language. Bluett says about it:

> He learned so much of our language that he was able to understand most of what we said in common conversation, and we who were used to his manner of speaking could make a shift to understand him tolerably well.[49]

47 Bluett, pp. 47–48. Thomas Bluett (1690–1749) was a British minister, attorney and judge in Annapolis, Maryland.

48 Grant, p. 84.

49 Bluett, pp. 47–48. James Oglethorpe (1696–1785) was born in London. He conceived, planned and implemented his establishment of the Georgia colony in America. George Uriel was the son of George Uriel

Bluett suggests Job was "very constant in his devotion" during the voyage to England. He adds, "He won't eat a bit of pork, it being extremely forbidden by Law." Bluett also speaks about how agreeable Job was with sailors on the voyage, and as they moved up the channel, the sailors called out the names of certain locations that Job dutifully wrote down in his Arabic script.[50]

Since Mr. Oglethorpe had gone to the Georgia colony, when Bluett and Job arrived in England, Mr. Hunt provided lodging for them at Lime House. While in London, Job is said to have written down the entire Qur'an from memory three times, one copy of which stayed at the British Museum. This indicates that Job was a *Hafiz*, an Arabic term that indicates a believer in Islam who has memorized the entire text of the Holy Book, usually at a very early age.

Job was also introduced to various members of the British royalty, including Sir Hans Sloane, the Duke of Montague, as well as some other nobles who were pleased to make his acquaintance. Bluett also suggests that Job met the Queen, who gave the African a number of lavish gifts, including a gold watch from Queen Christina herself. Bluett writes extensively about these gifts. He tells us:

> I may say that in general the goods which were given him and which he carried over with him were worth upwards of five hundred pounds, besides which he was well furnished with money in case any accident should oblige him to go to shore, or incur particular charges at sea.[51]

Perhaps the most noteworthy aspect of the life of Ayyub Ibn Sulayman Diallo is that he was able to return to Africa. Through the aid of the Royal African Company, Job returned to Senegal-Gambia. Mr.

Crocker (1796–1887) of Massachusetts. The younger George Uriel was a New England ship captain in the 1730s in the trans-Atlantic slave trade. He was the skipper of the ship called the William.

50 Ibid.

51 Ibid. Sir Hans Sloane (1660–1753) was an Irish-born British physician, naturalist, nobleman and collector. "Lime House" was a gentleman's club and hotel on the north shore of the Thames River in the eighteenth century. Today it is owned by Holiday Inn.

Bluett says this about the voyage back to Africa:

> About the latter end of July last, he embarked on board one of the African Company's ships, bound for Gambia, where, we hope he safely arrived to the great joy of his friends, and the Honour of the English Nation.[52]

Job's wives and children greeted him upon his arrival, but much had changed since he left Africa. Futa Toro had conquered Boundu. Job's father had died, and one of his wives had remarried. Job continued to work for the Royal African Company in their keeping abreast of the slave trade and the acquisition of gold until the company disbanded in 1752.[53]

The Imamate of Futa Toro was a pre-colonial West African, theocratic state of Fula-speaking people settled in the middle valley of the Senegal River. This region came to be known as Futa Toro, and the strips of land along both sides of the river were part of Futa Toro when Job returned to Gambia.

Job's return to his life in Africa mostly went unrecorded. One exception is in June of 1736 when it appears that Job was imprisoned or held captive by the French. He may have been targeted because of his affinity with the English. He was held captive for a year when his own countrymen secured his release by paying a bounty. Job's death is recorded in the minutes of the Spalding Gentlemen's Society of London in 1773.[54]

In Mr. Bluett's work, he speaks specifically about Job's religion. He informs us:

> As to his religion, it is known that he was a Mohametan, but more moderate in his sentiments than most of the religion are. He does not believe in a sensual Paradise, nor many other ridiculous and vain traditions, which pass generally among the Turks. He was very constant in his devotion of God, but said that he never prayed to

52 Ibid., p. 60.

53 Ibid., p. 51.

54 The Spaulding Gentlemen's Society was formed in London in 1710 by Maurice Johnson (1688–1755). At the time, Job belonged to the society, so did Isaac Newton and the poet Alexander Pope.

> Muhammad, nor did he think it was lawful but to address God Himself in prayer. He was so fixed in the belief in one God, that it was not possible, at least during the time he was here, to give him any notion of the Trinity; so that having a New Testament given him in his own language, when he had read it, he told me he had perused it with a great deal of care; but he could not find one word in it of Three Gods, so some people talk. I did not care to puzzle him and therefore answered in general terms, that the English believe only in one God. He showed upon all occasions a singular veneration for the name of God, and never pronounced the word *Allah* without a peculiar accent, and a remarkable pause: And indeed, his notions of God, Providence, and a Future State, were, in the main, very just and reasonable.[55]

From this account of Job's religion, five separate points must be garnered from Bluett's description. First, although he is a Muslim, Job is moderate in his religion, as opposed to more conservative hardliners. Second, Islam was seen by Britons in the eighteenth century as a militant and violent religion. Third, he does not believe that those who die a *Shahid*, or Martyr, will be met by the *Houris*, or young maidens in a sensual paradise.

Fourth, Job Diallo prayed directly to Allah. Muhammad was simply a mediator or conduit to the Divine. And finally, Job had difficulty understanding the Christian notion of the Trinity, and it appears that Mr. Bluett was somewhat reluctant to explain the idea to Job.

English painter William Hoare (1707–1792), born in Bath, painted a portrait of Job Diallo. Hoare's original painting of Job was believed to have been lost, but in August of 2010, the National Portrait Gallery in London purchased the painting where it is now on loan from the owner, the Qatar Museum Authority. Hoare's painting of Job is the earliest known portrait of a freed slave and the first African subject of modern British art. In Hoare's painting, Job is dressed in traditional African garb. His Qur'an hangs around his neck from a chain.

---

55 Bluett, pp. 51–52.

Another image of Ayyub Ibn Sulayman Diallo was published originally in a 1750 edition of *Gentlemen's Magazine* in London. This second engraving of Job was based on the Hoare painting. Like that painting, in this second image in the *Gentlemen's Magazine*, Job wears a traditional Islamic headdress, and a copy of the Qur'an hangs around Job's neck.[56]

The only other source of information about the life of Ayyub Ibn Sulayman Diallo comes from Francis Moore's *Travels into the Inward Parts of Africa*.[57] Segments of this work have been widely republished in the second half of the twentieth century by Grant, Curtin and Austin, among others.[58] But missing in all of these texts are details of what Job's life was like in slavery, as well as his life when he returned to Africa.[59]

Francis Moore was a clerk, and later a factor, in the Royal African Company. He lived on the Gambia River from November 1730 until May 1735 and represented the commercial interests of the company there. Moore's work consists of a personal journal that he kept during his time in West Africa. This book remains an important primary source of information about British activities in West Africa in the first half of the eighteenth century, as well as the life and times of Job Diallo.[60]

Moore's journals include discussions about natural history, as well as the different ethnic groups living in Gambia at the time. They also include accounts of slave trading, and in particular, an account of Ayuba Ibn Sulayman Diallo. Moore's journal also contains an account of the voyage of Captain Bartholomew Stibbs up the Gambia River in 1732, as well as several English translations of African geography documents from the sixteenth-century Moroccan explorer, Leo Africanus, and the twelfth-century Arab geographer and historian Al-Idrisi.

All we know of these periods in Arab history are the few pages in

56 Gentleman's Magazine 20 (1750). William Hoare (1707–1792) was an English portrait painter and printmaker.

57 Francis Moore, Travels in the Inland Parts of Africa (London: Gale Ecco Print Editions, 2010).

58 Ibid.

59 Ibid.

60 Ibid. Francis Moore (1730–1775) was born in Worcester. He was appointed writer in residence for the Royal Africa Company's Fort James on the Gambia River.

Moore's book in a section where he discusses the expansion of the British gum trade that ultimately was a failure. Likewise, we find nothing of the experience of the Middle Passage, Job's voyage from Africa to the New World. We do know that Job appears to have been very fervent in his religion, and he seems to have placed his life in the determining of Allah, or *Qadar*, in Arabic.[61]

Douglas Grant, in his book, *The Fortunate Slave*, does make a few other observations about both Job and Loumein Yoas, while on the Middle Passage. Grant writes in this regard:

> But taking the figures as a whole, Job ben Solomon and Loumein Yoas stood a better chance of surviving than their predecessors along the route and were the beneficiaries of experience, provided that the *Arabella* was sound and was not becalmed or storm-tossed in the frightening Middle Passage.[62]

In summary, then, Job returned to West Africa under the auspices of the Royal African Company in 1734, just four years after traveling on the Middle Passage to the New World. This was also the year that British Semitic scholar George Sale published the first edition of his English translation of Al-Qur'an.[63] In fact, it may have been the case that Job assisted Sale with the translation, for both were members of the prestigious Spaulding Gentlemen's Club in London, as were Sir Isaac Newton and Alexander Pope at the same time.

61 Ibid. Captain Bartholomew Stibbs was dispatched by the British government with orders to navigate the Gambia River as far as he could in search of gold. By October 17, 1723, he arrived at Fort James on the Gambia. Leo Africanus (1494–1554) was a Berber Andilusi diplomat and scholar. Muhammad Al-Idrisi (1100–1165) was a Muslim geographer, cartographer and Egyptologist, who settled in Palermo, Italy.

62 Douglas Grant, The Fortunate Slave (Oxford: Oxford University Press, 1968), pp. 5 and 146.

63 George Sale, The Koran (London, 1731). This text has recently been reissued by Forgotten Books in 2015. George Sale (1697–1736) was born in Canterbury in Kent. He was an early British Orientalist and practicing solicitor, best known for his English translation of the Qur'an. The Spaulding Gentleman's Society was founded at Number Nine Broad Street in London in 1710. It was established by Maurice Johnson (1688–1755) of Lincolnshire.

Job finally returned to Bounda in 1738. His father had died, and one wife had remarried. Since so few slaves ever returned, she assumed that Job had died. Nevertheless, Job appears to have resumed his former life, as best he could. He lived until 1773 when he died in Africa. This brings us to Loumein Yoas, Job's companion and translator, who made that voyage on the Middle Passage from West Africa to Annapolis, Maryland, in the winter of 1730.

Loumein Yoas, also called "Lumane Joy," "Lahamine Joy," "Lahmine Jay" and "Lamine Ndiaye," was captured on February 27, 1730, along with Job, and sold to Captain William Pike, the skipper of the *Arabella*. Little is known about the life of Loumein, far less than the other West Africans mentioned in this section of the chapter. In 1730, Loumein came from Futa Toro, near the Senegal River in West Africa. He was captured along with Job, while the two were trading on the lower part of the Gambia River. Upon his arrival in Annapolis, Loumein was also made an indentured servant or slave on the Eastern Shore of Maryland. After five years, it appears he was able to secure his freedom from his indenture with the help of his friend Job. The exact location of the farm where Loumein worked is unknown.

We do know that Loumein was something of a linguist, for he quickly picked up English and knew several West African languages. Indeed, as we indicated earlier, Loumein acted as a translator when the two passed over the Gambia River because he spoke the Mandingo language.

The *Arabella* was the flagship of the Winthrop fleet. From April 8 to June 12 of 1730, the ship sailed from England to the Massachusetts Bay Colony in New England.[64] The ship was originally called the *Eagle*, but the vessel's name was changed to honor Lady Arabella Johnson, a member of Winthrop's company. Lady Arabella was the daughter of Thomas Clinton, the Third Earl of Lincoln.[65]

On the same day that the *Arabella* arrived in West Africa, another vessel, the *Elizabeth*, under the command of a Captain Caruthers, came

---

64 Grant, pp. 61, 69, and 71–72. Captain William Pike, the skipper of the Arabella, although he worked for the Royal Africa Company, was actually an American.

65 Ibid., p. 195.

down the river with its complement of slaves. As Douglas Grant put the matter, "Trade had been brisk, it was a good season."[66] After Job had returned to his homeland, he immediately convinced the Royal African Company that, in the future, whenever the company bought a Muslim slave, he should be allowed to redeem himself upon application, in exchange for two other good, non-Muslim slaves.[67]

Douglas Grant picks up the story from there. He writes:

> The Company's rather surprising agreement to this request was not merely nominal and intended to placate Job, backed up as he now was by powerful friends; but they sent instructions to the agents in the Gambia that this arrangement should be put into effect.[68]

Grant says that Job immediately thought of his unfortunate companion and translator, Loumein Yoas, who had remained a slave in Maryland. Again, Grant picks up the story:

> When Job told him of his servant's plight, the Duke of Montague agreed to arrange for his release and to pay the price of his redemption. Strange, that a man's fate should depend on such a set of improbable chances, linking such distant and different places as the burnt savannahs of the Gambia, the Plantations of Maryland, and the drawing-rooms at Boughton, whose architecture copied the splendors of Versailles and whose treasure in pictures and furniture was immense.[69]

A short time later, through the courtesy of the Duke, Loumein was found by Thomas Bluett on his return to Maryland. Bluett put Loumein on a ship bound for London, where he was received and boarded by the company. He arrived in London toward the end of 1737, and the company at once began to make arrangements to return Loumein to his

66 Ibid.

67 Ibid., p. 108.

68 Ibid.

69 Ibid. The Rouse-Boughton Baronets referred to here is the Boughton family in London and elsewhere in England that owned enormous properties in the country.

African homeland.[70] Grant speaks of Bluett finding Loumein in Maryland. He observes:

> But good news was about to come, at least for Job. Thomas Bluett had found Job's servant Loumein Yoas—or Lahamin Joy—as his name appeared in the Company's records, on his return to Maryland and, with the funds so generously supplied by the Duke of Montague, had redeemed him and put him on a ship bound for London, where he was received and boarded by the Company.[71]

The company arranged for Loumein's passage in a man-of-war to set sail for James Fort in West Africa. The company wrote to Charles Orfeur, the chief agent at the fort in February 1738, with instructions on how they were to treat Loumein Yoas. A copy was also sent to the Duke of Montague, reassuring him that the African was to be properly repatriated.[72]

Grant reproduces the order about Loumein. It tells us:

> The bearer, Lahamin Joy, a black man, is the person who was taken and sold with Job and carried with him to Maryland; and by the great goodness of his Grace, the Duke of Montague, he being redeemed from his slavery and brought from thence hither, he now takes his passage for your place in the [blank] Man-of-War, in order to return Joy to his Country; and his Grace having desired that he may be recommended from the Company to you; I am therefore directed particularly to recommend him at the Company's expense and to treat him kindly, until you can send him up.[73]

There is nothing in the extant record about how or when Loumein finally arrived back to his homeland in West Africa. We can be sure,

70 Bluett, pp. 48–49.

71 Ibid.

72 Grant, p. 196. Charles Orfeur (1697–1758) worked for the Royal Africa Company in the 1730s and 1740s in Africa.

73 Ibid.

however, that he did return, and but for the help of his friend Job and the kindness of the Duke of Montague and his wife, he may not have returned at all.

The only other mention of Loumein is the story of a pistol that Captain Pike gave the king who had sold Job and Loumein as payment for the two slaves. The king was said to have worn the pistol around his neck and apparently kept it loaded. One day, or so the story goes, it went off accidentally, and the ball lodged in his throat, killing the African king instantly. When Job and Loumein heard this, they instantly fell to their knees and thanked Allah for using the king's ill-gotten gains as a means of bringing justice, or so Francis Moore tells us.[74]

Job is reported to have said to Francis Moore, "You see how God Almighty was displeased at this man's making me a slave, and therefore died by the pistol for which he sold me."[75] There are no extant images of Loumein Yoas, so one is not included at the end of this chapter. This brings us to our final noteworthy Maryland Muslim slave, Mamout Yarrow, whose story has been related to us by an artist who painted his portrait, Charles Wilson Peale. Little is known of Yarrow's early life in Africa, but his good and well-mannered behavior made it so that he could be manumitted after laying the bricks for his master's home. As a free man, he bought his own home in Georgetown and was known for praying in the streets and for his abstaining from liquor and his rejection of pork.

Yarrow Mamout (1736–1824), then, was another enslaved Muslim man from West Africa. He was born in Guinea, probably from the Fulani or Fulbe Tribe. Like Job and Loumein, Yarrow was kidnapped from his native homeland and brought to Maryland. Guinea was part of what we will see in Chapter Two of this study of the Sierra Leone Supply Zone in West Africa. In Maryland, Yarrow was purchased by Colonel Samuel Beall, Jr. of Montgomery County, Maryland, which had recently been formed after splitting-off from Frederick County farther west.

Little is known of Yarrow's personal life, though we do know he had one son who was named Aquilla or Quilla Yarrow. Mamout's son was also owned by a Montgomery County master, a woman named Ann

74 Ibid.

75 Moore, p. 131.

Chambers.[76] Perhaps the most significant fact about Yarrow Mamout is that he was the subject matter for two prominent, nineteenth-century painters, James Alexander Simpson (1805–1880) and Charles Wilson Peale (1741–1827.) The latter painted Yarrow's portrait in 1819, the former in 1822. Yarrow was seventy-seven years old when Peale completed his painting of him, and eighty-one when he sat for Simpson.

James Alexander Simpson was born in England around 1805 and came to America settling in Frederick, Maryland. Subsequently, he moved to Georgetown, where he became an instructor in art at what was then called Georgetown College in 1825. Simpson, then, must have been seventeen or eighteen when he painted Yarrow and around twenty when he began teaching. Simpson's painting of Yarrow now hangs in the Peabody Room at the Georgetown branch of the District of Columbia Library.

In 1860, Simpson moved to Baltimore, where he died twenty years later. Several of his other works still can be seen at Georgetown University. His painting of Commodore Stephen Decatur, for example, once hung in the University President's office. Charles Peale's portrait of Yarrow was taken by the artist back to Philadelphia when he completed it. The slave obviously did not pay for the portrait. There is no record of the painting's whereabouts until Peale's grandson, Edmond, came across the painting and mistakenly labeled it "Billy Lee" thinking his grandfather had painted a faithful slave of George Washington named Billy Lee.[77]

This identification of the painting continued until 1947. At that

76 "Yarrow Mamout," Maryland State Archives, SC5496-050568. Further information on Yarrow Mamout can be found in James H. Johnston's "Every Picture Tells A Story," Maryland Historical Magazine (2008), and Charles C. Sellars, "Charles Wilson Peale and Yarrow Mamout," Pennsylvania Magazine of History and Biography.

77 James Johnston, From Slave Ship to Harvard: Yarrow Mamout and the History of an American Family (New York: Fordham University Press, 1984), particularly Chapter Four. Charles Peale (1741–1827) was an American painter, soldier, scientist, inventor and naturalist. James Alexander Simpson (1805–1880) was born in Georgetown in Washington, DC. He taught art at Georgetown College. He later moved to Baltimore, where he died.

time, Peale's biographer, Charles Coleman Sellers, carefully matched the painting with Peale's diaries and concluded that the portrait was that of Yarrow Mamout. Sellers wrote at the time of the proper identification, "It is not reasonable to suppose that Peale painted Billy Lee in his old age, for despite his services to George Washington, Billy was a drunkard and a cripple in his final years at Mount Vernon."[78] Nevertheless, even as late as 1994, a *New York Times* reporter, writing about an exhibit that included the painting, was still justifiably confused when she identifies the painting as that of "Yarrow Mamout, a Slave of George Washington."[79]

Captain Willem Bosman (1672–1703), a merchant captain in the service of the Dutch West India Company, as well as an early eighteenth-century Dutch slave trader, describes the slaves from Bissau, part of the Sierra Leone Supply Zone—the zone from which Yarrow Mamout came. He writes:

> Not a few of our Country fondly imagine that parents here sell their children, men their wives, and one brother, another. But those who think so, do not deceive themselves; for this never happens on any other account but that of necessity, or some great crimes; but most of the slaves who are offered to us are prisoners of war, which are sold by their victors as their booty.[80]

Bosman points to what he considers the lax morals of the Africans and to the fact that most of the captives were prisoners of war. Captain Bosman continues his analysis of the Sierra Leone Supply Zone:

> The invalids and the maimed being thrown out, as I have told you, the remaindered are numbered, and it is entered into the record who delivered them. In the meantime, a burning iron, with the arm or the arms of

78 Ibid.

79 Ibid.

80 Willem Bosman, A New and Accurate Description of the Coast of Guinea (Cambridge: Harvard University Press, 2011). Bosman (1672–1703) was an important Dutch captain who traveled the Middle Passage, mostly from the Sierra Leone Supply Zone.

> the Companies, lies in the fire, with our mark on their breast. This is done so that we may distinguish them from the slaves of the English, French, or others (which are also marked with their marks), and to prevent the Negroes from exchanging them for worse, at which they have a good hand. I doubt not, but this trade seems very barbarous to you, but since it is followed by mere necessity, it must go on; but yet we take all possible care that they are not burned too hard, especially the women who are more tender than the men.[81]

Here Bosman tells us that the invalid and the maimed were thrown overboard, that the Dutch slaves were marked with a branding iron, and that these activities may seem barbarous, but they are necessary.

Captain Bosman completes his description of the Dutch buying slaves in Bissau this way:

> When we have agreed with the owners of the slaves, they are returned to their Prison, where from that time forward, they are kept at our charge, costing us two pence a day per slave, which serves to subsist them, like our criminals on bread and water, so that to save charges, we send them on board ship with the very first opportunity, before which their masters strip them of all that they have on their backs, so that they come to us stark naked, both men and women; in which case, they are obliged to continue. If the Master of the ship is not so charitable (which he commonly is) as to bestow something on them to cover their nakedness. You would really wonder to see how these slaves live on board, for though their numbers sometimes amount to six or seven hundred, yet by the careful management of our Masters of Ships, they are so well-regulated, that it seems incredible. And in this particular, our nation exceeds all other Europeans, for as the French, Portuguese, and English slave ships are always foul and stink-

81 Ibid.

> ing; on the contrary, ours for the most part are clean and neat. The Slaves are fed three times a day with indifferent good victuals, and much better than they eat in their own Country. Their lodging place is divided into two parts, one of which is appointed for the men, the other for the women, each sex being kept apart. Here they lie together as close as possible for them to be crowded.[82]

Captain Bosman speaks here of the separation of the two hulls on Dutch slave ships, one for men and one for women. He also refers to what is sometimes called the "Tight-Packing" method for loading slaves on a ship in the eighteenth century, as close together as possible, as we shall see in Chapter Two. Bosman also maintained that the Dutch slave ships were cleaner than those of other European powers, the British, French and Portuguese and that the Dutch captives were fed three times a day, one more than the British and French captives. Captain Bosman was born in Utrecht and sailed as an apprentice on the Gold Coast when he was sixteen years old. He is best known for his descriptions of the Gold Coast in a book he called *Nauwkeuirge beschrijving van de Guinese Goud Tan den Slavekust.*[83] This Dutch title may be translated as *A New and Accurate Description of the Coast of Gold, Divided into the Gold, the Slave, and the Ivory Coasts.*[84] The book of Captain Bosman remained the most authoritative description of the area for more than a century and provided significant details of the Komenda Wars, in which Bosman took part. In fact, the surname "Bossmann" in Ghana is thought to have originated from the many children of Willem Bosman who had a number of black mistresses.[85] It appears it was under similar conditions that Yarrow Mamout was brought to America in 1752. Yarrow was a member of the Fulani Tribe of Guinea, and thus what we will call the Sierra Leone Supply Zone in

82 Ibid.

83 Ibid.

84 Ibid.

85 Ibid. The Komenda Wars were a series of conflicts between the Dutch West India Company and the British Royal African Company from 1694 until 1700.

Chapter Two of this study. The Fulani are a West African people from Senegal and Gambia to Chad in the east, to Sudan and Ethiopia in the southeast, and in Senegal, Gambia, Nigeria and Guinea on the west coast of Africa. The total Fulani population today numbers around six million. We know that Yarrow Mamout was educated in Arabic and Islamic studies before he came to the Maryland colony. When his ship arrived in Annapolis, he was purchased by Colonel Samuel Beall, Jr., of Montgomery County. Mr. Beall died in September of 1777, and his son, Brooke Beall, acquired Yarrow. Little else is known of his personal life in Maryland. We know that he was married and had at least one son, Aquilla, or Quilla, mentioned above. We also know that Quilla was seven years old when Yarrow was freed by the Bealls.[86] Upton Beall manumitted Yarrow on August 22, 1796. We also know that later, Aquilla was a slave for Ann Chambers, also of Montgomery County, in Maryland.[87] "Manumission" was a legal term in the late eighteenth century. It was employed to describe the freeing of a slave in Maryland and other areas in America. The earliest manumissions were recorded by deed in county land records. Between 1752 and 1790, the deed was the only legal record that could free a slave, but before and after that time period, manumissions were recorded in wills, chattel records. In some counties in Maryland, like Anne Arundel and Harford counties, there were separate records recorded called "Manumissions."[88]

The actual wording of Yarrow Mamout's manumission from Upton Beall is recorded by him when he was the clerk of Montgomery County. The document reveals:

> At the request of Yarrow, the following manumission is recorded on this 22nd day of August 1796, to know that all men by these presents [sic] that I, Upton Beall of Montgomery County, Maryland, do manumit and set free Negro Yarrow from this day forward to act for himself as a Free Man in all things. Given my hand and my seal this 22nd day *Anno Domini*, hundred seventeen and

86 Montgomery County Records, LRC No. 385 (1796).

87 Ibid., p. 26.

88 Montgomery County Court Records, Liber G, folio 285 (1796).

> ninety-six years.[89]

Although Mr. Beall did free Yarrow, he did not do the same for all of his slaves. The Beall family of Georgetown, and later of Rockville, owned several slaves, many of whom (like Yarrow) were passed down through the family as inherited property. Brooke Beall, Upton's son, owned twenty-five slaves in his Beall-Dawson House in Rockville when Brooke Beall died in 1827. Thanks to family records, we know the names of most of these slaves and something of their lives before the Civil War.

We know that Quilla, or Aquilla, married a woman named Mary Polly Turner, who, like her husband, was a free black person. The couple bought a piece of land near his employment at the Antietam Iron Works along the Potomac River. Aquilla died young, but his widow lived a long life and had a village that sprang up near their cabin that is now called Yarrowsburg, Maryland. The town is located in Washington County, whose closest city is Frederick.[90]

We also know that Yarrow Mamout worked as a bricklayer at the Georgetown home of Brooke Beall. Other records indicate that Yarrow was hired out at times by his master to work in various places, mostly in the county. Brooke Beall died on July 11, 1795, and a year later, his manumission came in August of 1796. Four years later, Mamout purchased his own property in Georgetown at 3224 Dent Place.

After being informed of the historical significance of the house and property on Dent Place, the city of Washington recently began archeological excavation at the address. After several weeks of digging, nothing of Yarrow Mamout was found. Writing for the *U.S. Capitol Historical Society Magazine*, James Johnston tells us what Yarrow did after arriving at Dent Place. He reveals:

> As a free man, he became a jack of all trades, loading boats at the wharf during the day and at night making baskets for sale. He could turn wood into charcoal and had no equal as a brick maker. He commanded wag-

89 James Johnston, "The Man in the Knit Cap," Washington Post, October 24, 2011.

90 Johnston, "Every Picture," p. 18.

> es that were one and a half times more than those of white laborers. Athletic, he was said to be the best swimmer ever seen in the Potomac River at Georgetown. He saved his earnings and became a financier. He loaned money to merchants and even bought stock in the Columbia Bank in Georgetown. Of course, the Tavern, where the Bank held Stockholders' Meetings, also served as a site for the sale of slaves in Washington.[91]

Near the property on Dent Place, on Q Street, there was an African American cemetery in Georgetown. Some believe Yarrow's body may rest there. Ruth Trocolli, Washington city's archeologist, excavated the site that included the remains of five African American adults. The designs of the coffins, the absence of grave goods, and the position of the bodies within the coffins were all consistent with graves from the early nineteenth century. Yarrow Mamout died and was interred in 1824, so it is conceivable that he was buried in the cemetery on Q Street.

In the fall of 2011, a tree fell on the house on Dent Place, crushing the entire second floor. The tree crashed into the house during Hurricane Irene. The property again went through a tax sale in the spring of 2012. The new owner applied for a permit to raze the building, and the Georgetown Commission of Fine Arts signed the application and sent it to the city of Washington's government.

At any rate, Charles Wilson Peale painted the portrait of the now elderly Yarrow Mamout in 1819.[92] The Philadelphia Museum of Art owns this portrait. In the image, Yarrow is seated and bundled in a heavy overcoat, a high-collar jacket and a knit cap. He has a look of serenity and frankness on his face.[93] Although Peale owned slaves, by that time, he had become in favor of abolition.

Three years later, Yarrow was painted by James Alexander Simpson. In this portrait of Yarrow Mamout, which hangs in the Georgetown Branch of the District of Colombia Public Library, the slave is also

91 Johnston, "Man in the Knit Cap."

92 Charles Wilson Peale, Portrait of Yarrow Mamout, Philadelphia Museum of Art.

93 James Alexander Simpson, Yarrow Mamout, Georgetown Branch of District of Columbia Library.

seated. He is dressed in a red and white shirt, khaki jacket with silver buttons about the size of quarters. He holds a brown pipe in his right hand, his left arm by his side. In Simpson's portrait, Yarrow looks very old, deep lines around his eyes and mouth.[94]

This brings us to an analysis of prominent Muslim slaves in the Commonwealth of Virginia, the topic of the next section of this first chapter.

Prominent Muslim Slaves in Virginia

In addition to these Muslim slaves in Maryland discussed above, there also have been many prominent Muslim slaves identified in various places in Virginia, including the Great Dismal Swamp, George Washington's Mount Vernon home, and several other places throughout the state. The Great Dismal Swamp in Virginia contained a number of people called "Maroons," who most likely were freed and escaped slaves who inhabited the marshlands in southern Virginia and northern North Carolina in the eighteenth and nineteenth centuries.

Harriet Beecher Stowe told the story of these Maroons in her 1856 novel, *Dred: A Tale of the Great Dismal Swamp.*[95] One of the Maroons was a man named Osman, who is spoken of in Allan D. Austin's *African Muslims in Antebellum America.*[96] Austin says of Osman:

> I am assuming an Islamic identity for the Runaway Osman (probably Usuman)...encountered in the 1850s, he quickly slid back into his Virginia Swamp after being visible for only a moment. But the artist, David H. Strother, had clearly been moved by him.[97]

Austin goes on to quote from Mr. Strother's vision of Osman when he tells us:

> About thirty paces from me, I saw a gigantic Negro man

94 Harriet Beecher Stowe, Dred: A Tale of the Great Dismal Swamp (Chapel Hill: North Carolina University Press, 2006).

95 Allen D. Austin, African Muslims in Antebellum America (Oxford: Routledge, 1997), p. 37.

96 Ibid., pp. 37–38.

97 Ibid., p. 38.

> with a tattered blanket wrapped around his shoulders and a gun in his hands. His head was bare, and he had little other clothing than a ragged pair of breeches and boots. His hair and beard were tipped with grey, and his purely African features were cast in a mold betokening, in the highest degree, strength and energy. The expression on the face was of mingled fear and ferocity, and every movement betrayed a life of habitual caution and watchfulness. He reached forward his iron hand to clear away the brier screen that half-concealed him while it interrupted his scrutinizing glance. Fortunately, he did not discover me but presently turned and disappeared.[98]

Austin then goes on to quote from an article in the *Raleigh News and Observer* from August 3, 1913, in which it said that:

> Osman was a famous African Chief, who was sold into slavery, but escaped into the Great Dismal Swamp. He then led a reign of terror during the fifties. He obtained firearms and became half-wild.[99]

We do know that prior to the American Civil War, a Captain Moses (or Musa) Osman had the highest rank in the Union Army of any recorded Muslim before and during that conflict. This Osman may well have been the man seen by Strother. In that case, he may have been a deserter from the Army and then settled in the Dismal Swamp.

In the 1880s, American artist David Edward Cronin painted a series of works that depicted the *Fugitive Slaves in the Dismal Swamp.*[100] One of these paintings shows six black people—one woman and five men—dressed in Islamic headdresses. It may well have been that within the Dismal Swamp in the mid-nineteenth century, a community of Islamic Maroons resided there, and at one time, Osman was their lead-

---

98 Ibid.

99 David Edward Cronin (1839–1925) completed the series called Fugitive Slaves in the Dismal Swamp, Virginia in 1888.

100 Craig Considine, "Saluting Muslim-American Patriots," Huffington Post, June 10, 2015.

er. Another leader of these Islamic Maroons was a man named Captain Mingo, who presided over a community called Black Mingo Pocosin. The name "Mingo," from the Spanish "Domingo," was given to many West African boys born on Sunday. Thus, it may well have been that the Black Mingo Pocosin Community was an Islamic group, as well, or perhaps the same group.

Another early Virginia Muslim slave, Bampett Muhame, joined the Revolutionary Army and served as a corporal in Virginia from 1775 until 1783. We do not know whether Bampett Muhamed was a runaway slave or a free black man, but it is quite likely he was a member of the Islamic Faith.[101] Another early Virginia Muslim was a man named Salim, the Algerian, who claimed to be from a royal family in Algeria. Salim is said to have studied in Constantinople, from which he was captured by a Spanish ship and sold into slavery, and then to French New Orleans. Eventually, Salim became free, and after running away from slavery, he settled in Virginia.[102]

Salim was found dressed in rags and nearly naked in Virginia. It was eventually determined he knew Greek, for he was given a Greek New Testament he could read. Salim befriended several influential people in Washington and later converted to Christianity. Salim decided to return to Africa in order to preach the Gospel, but when he did, was shunned as an apostate, so he returned to America.[103]

In his second stay in America, Salim met Thomas Jefferson, attended the First Continental Congress, and appears to have spent some time in an insane asylum. While Salim was at Congress, Congressman Page is said to have introduced him to Charles Wilson Peale, who later painted Salim's portrait. It is said that at the end of Salim's life, he regained his sanity and renounced his Christianity. Others say he died a Christian at the Page Estate. Still, others say he died at the insane asylum, or so says *Graham's Magazine* in an 1857 edition.[104] In Peale's drawing of "Old Selim," the slave is seated. He has a full beard and a white hat with a dark ribbon. His coat may be from the Continental

101 Ibid.
102 Ibid.
103 Ibid.
104 Ibid.

Army. On Selim's face is a mixed look of serenity and curiosity.

Perhaps the most prominent of Virginia Muslims was a slave of George Washington, known as Sambo Anderson. The name "Sambo" among various West African peoples was given to a "Second Son," particularly in Senegal, Gambia, Sierra Leone, and parts of Nigeria and Niger. It is not entirely clear when Sambo Anderson arrived in America and at Mount Vernon. We do know, however, that he trained as a carpenter by William Bernard Sears, an Englishman who came to America as a white indentured servant. If Sambo Anderson was, in fact, from Guinea, then he also was from the Sierra Leone Supply Zone back in Africa, as outlined in Chapter Two, as we shall see.

We also can be certain that Sambo Anderson was among seventeen slaves of Washington's—fourteen men and three women—who attempted to flee their captivity in April of 1781, when the British warship, the *Savage*, anchored in the Potomac River, off the coast of Mount Vernon. At the time, Sambo was described as, "A man of about twenty years of age, stout and healthy."[105] Anderson and his colleagues appear to have gotten as far as Philadelphia before being recovered along with four other of Washington's runaways. Whereupon, he was brought back to Mount Vernon.

We also know that Sambo Anderson was manumitted, along with 122 other slaves owned by Washington, on January 1, 1801. As a free man, Sambo took the name Anderson and made his home in Little Hunting Creek, Virginia. There he supported himself hunting game and wildfowl that he then sold to private customers, as well as to hotels in Alexandria.[106]

There are two separate descriptions of the life of Sambo Anderson. The first was penned by "An Old Citizen of Fairfax County." It

105 Anonymous, "Uncle Sambo," Alexandria Gazette, January 18, 1786.
106 Ibid.

was published in the *Alexandria Gazette* on January 18, 1786. The article tells us:

> Sambo Anderson, as he called himself, but was better known by the name Uncle Sambo, belonged to George Washington. He informed the writer that he was brought to this country five years before Braddick's Retreat. He was a genuine Guinea negro and claimed to have come from a royal family. He was a bright, Mahogany color, had high cheekbones, and was stoutly made. His face was tattooed, and he wore rings in his ears, which, he informed me, were made of real, genuine Guinea gold.[107]

Both the rings in his ears and the tattooed face suggest that Anderson was a member of the Krio Tribe of the Sierra Leone Supply Zone of West Africa. In the eighteenth century, in both the Sierra Leone and the Windward Coast Supply Zones, men wore earrings. This was particularly true of both the Mende and the Krio Peoples. Sambo Anderson could easily have been a member of either of these tribes.

The other account of the life and character of Sambo Anderson also comes from the *Alexandrian Gazette* on January 22, 1876, and appears to have been written by the same person as the first account. This second description adds one fact about Anderson that was unusual for Virginia slaves in his time. This second account tells us:

> In my last entry, I mentioned that Sambo Anderson, an old manumitted slave of George Washington, was allowed to keep a gun, and a very good flint it was. I remember, at the time of Nat Turner's Rebellion, I was ordered out as the Captain of a patrol to collect all the firearms, etc., from the Negroes in the lower part of Fairfax County. Among the rest, I called upon Uncle Sambo. But the old man did not want to part with his gun. Indeed, I felt sorry for him to take it from him, for I believe that this Sambo would have shot Nat Turner

107 Ibid., January 22, 1876.

had he come upon him.[108]

The author here, of course, refers to Nat Turner (1800–1831), the African American slave in Southampton County, Virginia, who led a slave rebellion there, beginning in August of 1831. The rebellion led to the killing of fifty-five to sixty-five white, Virginia settlers.

This brings us to an analysis of other Virginia Muslim slaves, the topic of the final section of this first chapter. In the second chapter of this study, as we shall see, we shift locations from North America to Africa and the nine major supply zones from which African slaves came to the Americas, as well as the route by which these slaves traveled. This route has come to be known as the "Middle Passage."

Other Virginia Muslim Slaves

In addition to the prominent Muslim slaves in Virginia mentioned in the last section of this chapter, there were also two other places where it was likely to find Muslim slaves—the Continental Army and at Washington's Mount Vernon residence. Among the former were Peter Salim, mentioned earlier, as well as Yusuf Ben Ali, and Francis and Joseph Saba. Peter Salim served in the Revolutionary Army and is said to have fired the shot that killed John Pitcairn at the Battle of Bunker Hill.[109]

Yusuf Ben Ali was a North African Arab who worked as an aide to General Thomas Sumter during the war against Britain.[110] The Saba brothers—Francis and Joseph—were also North Africans who were sold into slavery in Annapolis, Maryland, and later served together in the Continental Army.[111]

Finally, there is also some evidence that at least three other slaves at Mount Vernon may well have been members of the Islamic Faith. A woman named Fatimer and her daughter, Little Fatimer, as well as another woman named "Nila," that may have been a derivative from the common female name in West Africa, *Naaliah*, may have been Moslems. Naaliah means "one who acquires something" or "someone gets

108 Considine.

109 Ibid.

110 Ibid.

111 Mary V. Thompson, "Islam at Mount Vernon," in Digital Encyclopedia of George Washington.

what she wants." The name Fatima, of course, was the name of the Prophet Muhammad's favorite daughter.

In an article entitled, "Islam at Mount Vernon," researcher, Mary V. Thompson, says of the young woman Nila, at Washington's farm:

> Even if no one was practicing Islam at Mount Vernon by this time, this child's name provides evidence that some knowledge of Islamic traditions or a familiarity with Arabic still could be found in the larger African-American Community in Fairfax County, if not at Mount Vernon itself, at the beginning of the nineteenth century.[112]

This brings us to the major conclusions we have made in this first chapter of this study on Muslim slaves in early Maryland and Virginia, followed by the notes of this chapter. In Chapter Two to follow, as indicated earlier, we shall explore the phenomena of slave supply zones in Africa and the Middle Passage, the route by which most Africans came to the Chesapeake Bay region.

Conclusions

We began this opening chapter with a discussion of twenty-one prominent Muslim slaves in America from the seventeenth to the nineteenth centuries. These twenty-one, as we shall see, will make several appearances in the other chapters of this study to follow. In fact, at the close of Chapter Ten, we will return to these same twenty-one offering some further comments on them.

In this first chapter, we have made some general remarks on the history of West African slavery in the Chesapeake Bay region. In this section of the chapter, we introduced and discussed various laws in both Maryland and Virginia in regard to slavery. We also described and discussed the first known African man to set foot in Maryland, an African named Mattheus de Sousa, who may well have been a Portuguese Muslim slave from the Mozambique colony in the East African Supply Zone. In this opening section of this chapter, we also have suggested that the three most famous Maryland slaves—Harriet Tubman, Frederick Douglass and Kunta Kinte—all had Muslim an-

112 Ibid.

cestors.

In the third section of this opening chapter, we also introduced three other prominent Muslim slaves in early Maryland: Job Diallo, Loumein Yoas and Yarrow Mamout. Each of these three, as we have shown, led prominent lives in Maryland. One, Yarrow, bought a house in Georgetown. Two of the three—Job and Loumein—were repatriated back to Africa. All three left their servitude within seven years.

In the fourth section of this first chapter, we described and discussed a number of other prominent Muslim slaves in Virginia. We spoke of Osman the Maroon, Bampett Muhamed, Salim the Algerian, the Saba brothers, and Sambo Anderson, perhaps the Virginian Muslim slave about whom we have the most information.

In the final section of this chapter, we explored what we know of several other Muslim slaves in the Commonwealth of Virginia. In this section, as we have shown, our primary materials were the Continental Army and the farm at Mount Vernon. In the former, we have pointed out the participation of many Muslim soldiers. These included Peter Salim, Yusuf Ben Ali and Francis and Joseph Saba, a pair of brothers from North Africa.

In addition to Sambo Anderson, we introduced the work of Mary V. Thompson, who suggests at least three other female slaves at Mount Vernon may well have been Muslims. The names of these women were Nila, Fatimer and Little Fatimer. This brings us to Chapter Two, in which we will explore the phenomena of slave supply zones in Africa, as well as some comments on the Middle Passage.

Chapter Two: Slave Supply Zones and the Middle Passage— Sixteenth to Nineteenth Centuries

When I looked around the ship, I saw a large furnace of copper boiling, and a multitude of Black People of every description, chained together, every one of their countenances expressing fear, dejection and sorrow.

—Olaudah Equiano, *The Interesting Narrative of the Life of Olaudah Equiano*

Show kindness to your parents and to your new near kindred, and to orphans, and to the needy, and to those of your neighbors who are kin to you; and to the fellow traveler and the wayfarer and to the slaves who are property that you own.

—The Holy Qur'an 4:92 (Author's translation)

There is no *Zakat* to be paid either on a horse nor or a slave that belongs to a believing Muslim.

—Sahih Bukhari, *Hadith*, 3:44, no. 667 (Author's translation)

Introduction

In this second chapter on Muslim slaves in Maryland and Virginia, we shift our focus from America to West Africa in the fifteenth to nineteenth centuries. Our principal aims in this chapter are to explore four separate and distinct issues. First, we will look at the major supply zones in West Africa from which many of the Maryland and Virginia Muslim slaves originated. As we shall see in this next section, there are eleven separate slave supply zones in fifteenth-to-nineteenth-century Africa—nine principal supply zones and two supplemental zones, which will become clear later in this chapter.

In the second portion of this chapter, we will describe and discuss what has come to be called "The Middle Passage," the route by which many West African slaves came to North America, in general, and to the Chesapeake Bay region, in particular, from the sixteenth to the nineteenth centuries.

The Middle Passage was the stage of the triangular trade in which millions of African slaves were brought to the New World by way of the Atlantic Ocean. Ships departed Europe for African ports with manufactured goods that they traded for human cargo, slaves in Africa. Voyages on the Middle Passage were large financial undertakings either by European governments or by private companies. The Europe to Africa leg was called the Outward Passage, Africa to the New World was the Middle Passage, and the New World back to Europe was known as the Return Passage—so the three legs make a triangle and thus is known as the "Triangular Trade."

In the third section of this chapter, we will make some observations about several tribes and peoples of West Africa and how they were treated and judged by Europeans and by the American planters who owned these slaves in America. Indeed, some tribes were prized by North American planters, and some were disdained by them, as we shall see later in this chapter.

In the fourth section of this second chapter, we shall look at a number of pieces of historical and contemporary art depicting the Middle Passage and supply zones. We will bring the chapter to a close, as we shall with all of the chapters in this study, with the major conclusions we have made in it. We move, then, to African supply zones.

African Supply Zones for Transatlantic Trade: 1480 to 1850

In the period from 1480 until 1850, there were nine major supply zones from which slaves came to the New World, in general, and to the Chesapeake Bay region, in particular. We will list these nine African supply zones here and then speak of each one individually. These nine supply zones were the following:

1. Senegambia
2. The Niger River Valley
3. The Sierra Leone Zone
4. The Windward Coast
5. The Gold Coast

6. The Bight of Benin
7. Angola
8. The Bight of Biafra
9. Mozambique and East Africa[113]

The first eight of these zones were in West Africa, the final zone in East Africa. The first of the West African zones, the Senegambia Supply Zone, extended from the Senegal River to the Casamance River in the north and south, and from the Atlantic Coast to the Upper Niger River Valley, west to east. This supply zone also included the area on either side of the Gambia River, as well as the River Senegal in northwest Africa.

Indeed, European ships would dock at settlements on these two rivers, the Senegal and Gambia, where slaves were brought to be sold in the seventeenth to nineteenth centuries, and then transported to the New World across the Middle Passage. In this time, Senegambia was ruled by the Wolof Tribe, an ethnic people found in Senegal, Gambia and Mauritania. Most Wolof by this time had become members of the Islamic Faith.

Today in Senegal, the Wolof consists of about 45 percent of the population. In Gambia, 15 to 20 percent. In Mauritania, about 10 percent of the population are still members of the Wolof Tribe.[114]

Indeed, most of the major rivers of West Africa, at least those that had connections to ports on the Atlantic, had European settlements, as we shall see in more detail in Chapter Three of this study. The Gambia, Senegal, Niger, Congo, Volta, and Benin rivers and many others had these ports.

The second supply zone in West Africa was on the western edges of the Niger River Valley, including such fabled cities of Ja, Jenne and Timbuktu. In the early seventeenth century, the area was a mixture of Muslim and non-Muslim peoples. The Empire of Songhay, which lasted from 1464 until 1591, eventually fell to the armies of the militant

113 Michael A. Gomez, "Muslims in Early America," Journal of Southern History 60, no. 4 (1994), pp. 671–710.

114 Terra Wolf and Ally Summers, Seize: the Tribe Series (Amazon Digital Services, 2016).

Fulbe People, who had become Muslims by that point.[115] This was also true of the Yoruba, the Igbo and the Ibibio, who all had significant numbers of Moslems by the eighteenth century.

The Fulbe, or Fulani People, are one of the largest ethnolinguistic groups in Africa. They are also among the most widely dispersed people on the continent. About forty million Fulbe live throughout Africa. About thirteen to fifteen million of these are nomadic people, many in the desert of North Africa. They spread over several countries in West and Central Africa.[116] The Mandinka was a second West African tribe with significant numbers of captives who were brought from this supply zone by the Tenda People. By the eighteenth century, the Mandinka Tribe was also principally Islamic.

The third West African supply zone was Sierra Leone, or what is now Guinea-Bissau, Guinea, Sierra Leone and portions of Liberia. The zone spans the west coast from the Casamance River in the north, to Cape Mount in the south. From the middle of the sixteenth century to the end of the seventeenth century, the major slave traders in this area were members of the Tenda Tribe.[117] Many of the slaves from this supply zone spoke Dutch, with whom they often traded. For the most part, however, the Tenda people did not become Muslims, though members of some of the other tribes mentioned above were Muslims shipped from this supply zone.

The Sierra Leone Supply Zone also included the Portuguese colony at Bissau, established in 1765. Between 1757 and 1777, 25,000 slaves were imported from the "Rivers of Guinea" to Grao-Para in the north of Brazil. The Portuguese also built a fort on the Cape Verde islands, beginning in the mid-fifteenth century, starting around 1455 and

115 David C. Conrad, Medieval Empires of West Africa (New York: Chelsea House, 2009), pp. 49–50. Also see: M. Alpha Bah, Fulbe Presence in Sierra Leone: A Case History (New York: Peter Lang, 1998). Ja and Jenne, or Djenneas as it is now called, were cities in the inland Niger Delta in Central Mali. Caravans stopped in these cities on their way to Timbuktu. The Songhai Empire dominated the western Sahel in the fifteenth and sixteenth centuries. It was one of the largest states in the history of Africa.

116 Ibid.

117 See the article on the "Tenda" in the World Heritage Encyclopedia (New York, 2014).

continuing through the 1880s.

For three centuries, the Cape Verde islands were the setting for much trans-Atlantic slave trading by the Portuguese. The mining of salt also took place there. By 1843, on the island of Bon Vista, an attempt was made to abolish slave traders on the Cape Verde islands. This was not actually accomplished until 1870—fairly late in the slave trade.

At the same time, the British built a fort on the offshore island of Bolema. The Portuguese first established claim to Bolema in 1687. It became the capital of Portuguese Guinea from 1877 until 1943. When the British took over in 1792, the island was uninhabited. The ruins, complete with Greek pillars, are now in disrepair. Britain finally relinquished its claim to the island in 1870, when it declared its independence from Britain. More will be said about slave forts and castles in Africa in Chapter Three of this study.

The French dominated the trade of the Sierra Leone Supply Zone in the first fifty years of the eighteenth century. They were succeeded by the British in the second half of the century. Scholar Walter Rodney, in his *A History of the Upper Guinea Coast, 1545–1800*, estimates that 75 percent of the Africans sent from this supply zone in the eighteenth century came from the interior of Africa, and not the coastal areas.[118]

The Windward Coast, our fourth supply zone, stretched from Cape Mount to the city of Assini near the present-day border of Ghana and the Ivory Coast. This zone also encompassed what is now most of Liberia and much of the Ivory Coast. Centers in Kankan, in Guinea, and Kong in the Ivory Coast, indicate that some of the slaves were sold in the area. We also know that many of the slaves from this zone spoke French, as they still do in those areas of West Africa.[119]

118 Walter Rodney, A History of the Upper Guinea Coast 1545–1800 (New York: Monthly). Walter Anthony Rodney (1942–1980) was a prominent Guyanese historian. Grao-Para is a municipality in the state of Santa Caterina in the southern region of Brazil. "Bissau" was a fifteenth-century Portuguese colony established in what today would be Guinea-Bissau. Bissau is the capital of Guinea-Bissau on an estuary of the Geba River. Approximately half a million residents live there. Bolema is one of the nine regions of Guinea-Bissau.

119 Roger Gocking, The History of Ghana (Santa Barbara: Greenwood

Kankan is the largest city in Guinea, in terms of land area, and third in population with approximately a quarter of a million people. Kong, in the Northern Ivory Coast, was the center of a pre-colonial Muslim state, centered in the northeast portion of the country. The "Kong Empire" lasted from 1710 until 1898.

The commercial activity in this supply zone, from Kankan in Guinea to Kong in the Ivory Coast, combined with the theocracy expanding in the Futa Jallon region, indicates that it is likely some Muslim captives reaching the Windward Coast must have been believers in the Islamic Faith.

The Gold Coast, our fifth supply zone, occupied much of present-day Ghana. Early on, Ghana was a great exporter of gold, and thus the name of the zone, going all the way back to Europeans arriving there in the fifteenth century. Ghana was also an exporter of other precious metals. In the opening decades of the eighteenth century, Ghana supplied slaves at a rate of 2,500 to 3,000 slaves per annum. By the 1740s, that figure had increased and peaked at a rate of ten thousand slaves a year.[120]

One reason the Gold Coast Supply Zone was significant, as we shall see in the next chapter, is that there were more slave forts and slave castles in this zone than in all the others. Indeed, of the roughly one hundred of these structures in colonial Africa, nearly half of them were in Ghana, as we shall see in Chapter Three to follow. Today, approximately thirty of these slave forts and castles survive on the coast of Ghana. The Portuguese, French, British, Swedes, the Spanish, the

---

Publishing, 2005), particularly chapter two. Professor Gocking teaches at McMaster University in Ontario, Canada. In terms of land area, Kankan is the largest city in Guinea and third largest in population. It borders both Mali and the Ivory Coast. The Kong Empire, which lasted from 1710 until 1898, also known as the Wattera Empire, was the name of a pre-colonial Muslim state in Africa.

120 See: Stanley B. Alpern, Amazon's Black Sparta (New York: NYU Press, 1998) and Paul L. Dunbar's In Dahomey. Reprinted in 2003 by the Alexandria Street Press, Alexandria, Virginia. The Dahomey was an African kingdom that existed in southern Benin from about 1600 until 1894 when their final king, a man named Behanzin, and his army were defeated by the French.

Danes and the Germans, as we shall see in Chapter Three, all built slave castles and forts there.

The Bight of Benin in the Gulf of Guinea, the sixth West African supply zone, extended from the Volta River to the Benin River and corresponds to the present-day lands of Togo, Benin and Southwestern Nigeria. During the Atlantic slave trade, the Bight of Benin was known as the "Slave Coast," and slaves from there were known as "Bite Negroes."

In the seventeenth and eighteenth centuries, the wars in the Bight of Benin between the Yoruba and the Dahomey of that region produced a great many captives from this supply zone sent to the New World. The Yorubans are a large tribe in South Nigeria. The Dahomey were a pre-colonial West African kingdom in South Benin. The kingdom existed from 1600 until 1904 and was ruled by an absolute monarch.[121]

There is some evidence that a significant number of slaves came from Nigeria and the southern part of Benin, particularly to Virginia. Many of these captives were members of the Igbo Tribe, one of the largest tribes in this portion of Africa. Indeed, between 1790 and 1860, somewhere between 30 and 50 percent of all slaves who came to Virginia were members of the Igbo Tribe. Ambrose Madison, the grandfather of President James Madison, was murdered on his Montpelier estate by his own Igbo slaves, as the recent book by Douglas B. Chambers, *Murder at Montpelier,* points out.

There were also a significant number of Igbo slaves who came to Alexandria, Virginia, to Galveston, Texas, on the Gulf of Mexico—an area saturated with Igbo in the eighteenth century. Olaudah Equiano, who we discussed in the first chapter of this study, came from the Niger Valley Supply Zone, and he may have been an Igbo, as well, or possibly Yoruban or Ibibio.

The supply zones of Angola and Mozambique sent very few slaves to North America. The former consisted of areas around the cities of Luanda, and later Benguela, as well as a few independent towns over which Portugal had some claims. The most noteworthy of these is the town of Ambriz, a fishing village in the northeast corner of Angola.

121 John Thorton, "The African Experience of the Twenty and Odd Negros Arriving in Virginia in 1619," William and Mary Quarterly (July 1998).

Ambriz is in the Bengo Province of Angola, about 125 km from Caxito. It borders the Nzeto Province of Zaire. Ambriz is significant because it was from there, in 1619, that the first African slaves were brought to Port Comfort, Virginia, the first Africans to arrive in the Chesapeake Bay region—and some of the first in America.[122]

The city of Cabinda in Angola at the mouth of the Congo River also had a slave fort from the sixteenth to the nineteenth century. During that time, the Portuguese shipped thousands of slaves to the New World, including many that came to Annapolis and Baltimore in the first sixty-five years of the nineteenth century.

On a stormy night in August of 1619, at the English colony at Jamestown, Virginia, "twenty or soe Africans" were not slaves but servants. We know this because they are described as "Servants" in records a few years later in 1623 and 1624. Under "Black Inhabitants of the Colony," these twenty are listed as "Black Servants."[123]

There is also evidence that the first eleven Africans to be brought to New Amsterdam, or New York City, in 1625, were mostly Angolans. By the end of the century, as Michael Gomez contends, between 1675 and 1698, a significant number of Africans came to the city from Madagascar, another Portuguese colony in East Africa. He also suggests some slaves from Senebegambia also came to New York in that period.[124] Antonio, or Anthony Johnson, introduced in Chapter One, also was from the Angolan Supply Zone. Mattheus de Sousa, as we have seen, may have originated there, as well, though both may originally be from Mozambique or elsewhere in the East African Supply Zone and traveled inland to the Angolan Supply Zone.

In the Planalto region, or High Plains of Brazil, the most important slave states were Bie and Bailundo, that was also known for food growth and the production of rubber. From 1764 on, in Brazil, there was a gradual shift from a slave-based economy to one based on the domestic production of goods. After the independence of Brazil from Portugal in 1822, far fewer slaves were brought to the New World by

---

122 Ibid.

123 Gomez, p. 685. Philip D. Curtin, The Atlantic Slave Trade: A Census (Madison: University of Wisconsin Press, 1972), p. 157.

124 Gomez, p. 685.

the Portuguese.

When slavery was abolished in 1836 in Portugal, it stopped completely. Slavery had gone on in Brazil for over three hundred years by that time. All tolled, four million slaves were brought from Africa to Brazil in the sixteenth to nineteenth centuries, far more than any other place in the New World.

Mozambique, and East Africa, for the most part, sent very few slaves to the New World in general and to the Chesapeake Bay region, in particular. Both Curtin and Gomez estimate that less than one percent of slaves sent to the New World were from Mozambique and East Africa.[125] We also have suggested that both Mattheus de Sousa and Antonio, alias Anthony Johnson, may have come from the Portuguese colony of Mozambique, and thus the East African Supply Zone.

As we have maintained, they may have been sold by Arab traders from Arabia to the east coast of Africa, and then on to India and other places. Although Gomez suggests that fewer than one percent of Muslim slaves who came to North America were from this East African Supply Zone, in our study at least seven of the one hundred and six suspected Muslims in the Chesapeake Bay region were from this zone, as we shall see later in this study.

Southeast Mozambique and Madagascar together shipped nearly one million slaves or about 7 percent of captives sent to the New World. The Portuguese built Fort Lourenco Marquis on the coast of the small coral island located at the mouth of the Mossuril Bay in the Mozambique Channel. Until 1898, the island served as the capital of Portuguese East Africa. There were slave trading centers in Tanzania and Somalia from the seventeenth century on, in the East African Supply Zone, as well. More will be said about this in Chapter Three.

Our ninth and final supply zone was the Bight of Biafra. It made up what is present-day southeastern Nigeria, Cameroon and Gabon. From this ninth supply zone, large numbers of captives were procured in many small-scale raids upon the densely populated areas of this region.

There appears to have been some Muslims living in the northern portions of this zone, but those arriving at the coast for export appear to

125 Ibid.

have been minimal in number. Perhaps the most significant slave trading post in this ninth supply zone, as we shall see in Chapter Three to follow, was in Bimbia in Limbe, Cameroon. The enormous stone ruins of the slave fort at Bimbia still can be visited.

Nevertheless, the Bight of Biafra supplied a significant number of slaves that came to the New World, as we shall see shortly, perhaps as many as twenty-five percent to the Chesapeake Bay region. Bimbia, in Cameroon, was an independent state that was annexed by the Germans in 1884, and then incorporated into the "Colony of Kamereun." There are extensive stone ruins of the slave fort there that still can be visited.

In addition to these original nine supply zones sketched out by Michael Gomez, there are two other zones that will play some part in this chapter, and in this study in general. The tenth zone is that of North Africa. In Chapter One, we have shown that a number of Africans came to the Chesapeake from North Africa, like Selim, the Algerian, for example, or Yusuf Ben Ali, or the Saba brothers, also spoken of in Chapter One.

The other additional slave supply zone is that of South Africa and, more specifically, the southwest African nation of Namibia, where the Germans built three separate slave prisons at the beginning of the twentieth century. In fact, one of our suspected Muslim slaves, a female in Maryland named Elinor, was from the Colony of Namibia but may originally have been a member of the Wolof Tribe of the Senegambian Supply Zone because of the tribal mark on her right hand, as we shall see in Chapter Nine.

Altogether, then, we now have outlined eleven different supply zones we shall speak of in this chapter. These are:

1. Senegambia
2. Niger Valley Zone
3. Sierra Leone Supply Zone
4. The Windward Coast
5. The Gold Coast
6. The Bight of Benin
7. The Bight of Biafra
8. Angolan Supply Zone
9. Mozambique and East African Zone

10. North African Supply Zone
11. South African Supply Zone

Michael Gomez estimates the percentages of slaves coming to North America in each of the first nine supply zones. His estimates are the following:

1. Senegambian Zone: 13.3%
2. Niger River Valley Zone: 7.0%
3. Sierra Leone Supply Zone: 5.5%
4. The Windward Coast Zone: 11.4%
5. The Gold Coast Supply Zone: 15.9%
6. The Bight of Benin Zone: 4.3%
7. The Bight of Biafra Zone: 23.3%
8. Angola Supply Zone: 1.0%
9. Mozambique/East Africa Zone: Less than 1.0%
10. North African Zone: Less than 1.0%
11. South African Supply Zone: Less than 1.0%[126]

The estimates of the tenth and eleventh zones above are those of the author of this study. Thus, half of the slaves coming to North America were from the Senegambian, Niger Valley, Sierra Leone, the Windward Coast, and Gold Coast supply zones. One quarter came from the Bight of Biafra Zone alone, mostly members of the Igbo and Yoruban Tribes.

Michael Gomez suggests that Curtin, in chapter four of his *Atlantic Slave Trade*, had earlier outlined similar numbers for the various supply zones.[127] The estimates listed above are those of Gomez based on this work of Curtin. He (Gomez) goes on to point out that 73.7 percent of the slaves exported to North America came from Senegambia, the Niger River Valley, the Sierra Leone Zone, the Windward Coast, the Gold Coast, the Bight of Benin, and the Bight of Biafra.[128]

If we eliminate the Bight of Biafra, we would be left with slightly

126 Ibid.
127 Ibid.
128 Ibid.

more than half of the slaves imported to North America. If somewhere between 400,000 and 525,000 Africans came to North America, then at least 200,000 came from areas of Africa influenced by the Islamic Faith. Moslems came to America, then, not by the thousands, nor tens of thousands, but more likely by the hundreds of thousands.[129]

Gomez goes on to point out that Muslim trading networks, through which Juula, Yarse and Hausa merchants supplied captives to disparate West African communities, and these traders were another source of the Muslim slaves that arrived in North America.[130] Gomez says that Muslim clerics across West Africa were also a source for members of the Islamic Faith that wound up in North America.[131]

Finally, Michael Gomez also makes four major conclusions about the Moslem slaves he has studied who arrived in North America. First, the numbers certainly reach into the thousands, if not tens or hundreds of thousands. Second, Muslim believers seem to have made persistent efforts to observe their religion. Third, Islam and ethnicity were important in regard to the issue of social stratification within the larger African American community. And finally, as he puts it:

> Cultural phenomena as found in segments of the African American Community, such as ostensibly Christian worship practices and certain artistic expressions, probably reflect the influence of these early Muslims.[132]

Gomez seems to suggest that the religious convictions of some Muslim slaves may have been altered when a significant number of them converted to Christianity in the New World. They also very well may have been affected by the Baptist and then the Methodist movements of the First and Second Great Awakenings, beginning around 1720 and continuing to the end of the eighteenth century. There is significant evidence, however, that many of the prominent American Muslim slaves mentioned in Chapter One, held fast to their Muslim tenets

129 Ibid.

130 The edition of Equiano's autobiography used here is The Interpretation Narrative and Other Writings, revised edition, published by Penguin in 2003.

131 Ibid., p. 7.

132 Ibid.

in America, as we shall see in Chapter Ten of this study.

Earlier in this chapter, we suggested two other slave supply zones, independent than those outlined by Michael Gomez. We have called these the "North African Supply Zone" and the "South African Supply Zone."

In the second section of this second chapter, we will move to a description of what has come to be called the "Middle Passage," that is, the routes by which Africa slaves journeyed from Africa to the New World, from the fifteenth to the nineteenth centuries.

The Middle Passage and Slavery

As outlined earlier, the Middle Passage refers to the part of the trans-atlantic slave trade, in which densely packed European ships crossed the Atlantic Ocean to the West Indies, and to North and South America. The voyage took three to four months, and during that time, slaves mostly were kept lying on the floor of the hold or on planks that ran around the inside of the hull.

Nowhere in human history has a people experienced such a long and traumatic ordeal as the continent of Africa during the Atlantic slave trade. Over the nearly four centuries of the trade—which continued until the American Civil War—millions of African men, women and children were savagely torn from their homelands in Africa and herded onto European ships. Then finally dispersed all over the New World, mostly to the Caribbean, Brazil and ports on the Atlantic in America.

There is no way to compute the final numbers in the Atlantic slave trade. Some estimates suggest as many as thirty to sixty million Africans were subjected to the misfortunes of this horrendous triangular trade system. As pointed out earlier in this chapter, the system was so named because the ships embarked from European ports, stopped in African ports to gather up their captives, after which they set out for the New World to deliver their human cargo. They then returned to their ports of origin, usually with raw materials or foodstuffs. The Middle Passage, then, was that leg of the triangular slave system that brought this human cargo from mostly West Africa to North American ports from Boston to South Carolina, and to Brazil in South America, as well as to the Caribbean.

Traders from the Americas and the Caribbean received the captive slaves in the New World. European powers such as Portugal, England, Spain, France, the Netherlands, Denmark, Sweden, from Norway and from the Brandenburgs, as well as traders from Brazil, the British Caribbean, and North America, all took part in the Atlantic slave trade. The name "Middle Passage" then refers to the aspect of the African slave trade, where captives were densely packed onto ships and then transported across the Atlantic Ocean to the West Indies, as well as to North and South America.

European slave ships ranged in size from the 10-ton *Hesketh*, which sailed from Liverpool to St. Kitts in the 1760s, to the 566-ton *Parr*, another Liverpool ship, active in the 1790s.

The *Hesketh* could accommodate only 30 slaves, plus the crew. The *Parr*, on the other hand, carried about 700 slaves across the Atlantic on the Middle Passage. The average African cargo on the Middle Passage voyages was somewhere between the two. American traders preferred smaller ships than their British counterparts. Two-masted brigs of 25 to 75 tons and schooners, which carried 30 to 150 tons, were the preferences of the Americans.

All tolled, there were over one hundred African ports from which slaves were transported across the Middle Passage. Nearly half of those were on the Gold Coast. The others were spread out from Senegal and Gambia in the north to Angola and Namibia in the south, as well as ports in the East African Supply Zone, such as Mozambique, Ethiopia, Somalia, Zanzibar and Egypt. There were slave ports in Senegal, Gambia, Nigeria, Sierra Leone, Guinea, Guinea-Bisseau, Ghana, Ivory Coast, Liberia, Toga, Cameroon, Benin, Namibia, and Angola.

The voyages on the Middle Passage took anywhere from a month to four months, depending on the prevailing winds. During this time, the captives mostly lay in chains in rows on the hulls of ships or on shelves that ran around inside the sides of the hull. The first leg of a voyage was known as the "Outward Passage" from Europe to Africa. This was followed by the "Middle Passage" from Africa to the New World, followed by the "Return Passage" where ships returned from the New World to their home ports in Europe bearing raw materials, foodstuffs, whiskey, cotton, sugar, as well as other cargo.

Several slaves who traveled along the Middle Passage wrote about the conditions in the hulls of these slave ships. Sylviane A. Diouf tells us about them:

> The filthiness of the slave holds can hardly be imagined. Four hundred men, women and children were aboard Keledor's ship and seven hundred aboard Eisami's.[133]

The two figures to whom Diouf refers here are the slave hero of a French novel called *Keledor* by Jacques Francois Roger, and Ali Eisami, a slave from the Sierra Leone Supply Zone, who dictated his story to German writer, Sigismund Wilhelm Koelle, around the year 1850. The Mr. Roger, to whom Ms. Diouf refers, was the governor of the French involvement in Senegal in the eighteenth century.

Diouf goes on to quote a slave named Mohamad Baquaqua, who remembered the "loathsomeness and filth of that horrible place," and that they were allowed to bathe only twice during the entire voyage, the final time just before arriving. Indeed, before they arrived, the captives were bathed, shaved and covered with a mixture of ash and oil to give the slaves a sheen.

Again, Baquaqua summarized the frame of mind of many of the Africans when they arrived in the Americas. He observes:

> When I reached the shore, I felt thankful to Providence that I was once more permitted to breathe pure air, the thought of which nearly absorbed every other. I cared very little then that I was a slave, but having left the ship, that was all I thought about.[134]

Mahommah Gardo Baquaqua was born in West Africa in the city

---

133 Ibid., p. 8. Jacques-Francois Roger (1787–1849) was a French attorney, politician, and explorer of Senegal for two decades in the nineteenth century. Ali Eisami was born around 1780 in an Islamic state in northeast Nigeria, in the Niger Valley Supply Zone. Sigismund Koelle (1820–1902) was a German missionary and pioneer scholar of African languages. More is said about Ali Eisami in Chapter Ten.

134 Mohomah Gardo Baquaqua, The Biography of Mohomah Gardo Baquaqua (New York: Create Space, 2012). p. 17.

of Zoogoo, in what is now Benin, around the year 1830. Thus, he was from the Bight of Benin Supply Zone, as discussed earlier in Chapter Two. Baquaqua attended college in New York and later wrote an autobiography entitled *The Biography of Mahommah G. Baquaqua: A Native of Zoogoo, in the Interior of Africa.*[135]

On the Return Passage, slave ships needed far fewer sailors for these voyages back to Europe. Indeed, many of the ports in America and the Caribbean contained sailors who were no longer employed by the European powers on the return voyages. The ships usually carried raw materials from the New World back to their European home ports. This mostly included tobacco, sugar, cotton and whiskey, among other staples.

These shelves on the ship's hull mentioned above were under a meter high, so most times, the slaves could not sit up in place. The largest of the ships on the Middle Passage carried up to seven hundred captives, but usually, these voyages brought between three hundred and four hundred captives to the New World. Slaves from different places in Africa were mixed together, making it more difficult for them to communicate, and thus to plan rebellions.

Two separate philosophies could have dominated the loading of slaves in the Middle Passage ships. They could use a "loose packing system," in which case fewer slaves could be transported in any shipment. Or they could employ a "tight packing system," in which situation more captives could be carried. For the most part, the "tighter" system was the one used. This allowed the captains of these ships to move more slaves in each shipment, but it also meant the casualty rates were much higher in the "tight system," due to the spread of disease and other malefactors on the Middle Passage voyages.

Seasickness was much more severe for the captives than the captain and his European crew. Smallpox, measles, syphilis, dysentery, scurvy, and a condition known as the "Bloody Flux," a severe stomach bug accompanied by high fever, were the biggest killers of captives who died on the Middle Passage voyages.

Women and men were kept in separate compartments on these ships on the Middle Passage. Women also had considerably less space than the men on these journeys. In both compartments, however, the

135 Ibid.

slaves were packed quite tightly with little room for each captive. Doctors would inspect the slaves before purchase to determine which of the captives were more likely to survive the voyage. "Tight packing" captains believed that more slaves, despite higher casualties, would also yield greater profits when they arrived at the trading block in the New World.

Indeed, as we shall see later in this study, somewhere between 20 and 30 percent of both captives, as well as crew members, did not survive the hardships of the Middle Passage voyages. Some died of disease, some committed suicide by throwing themselves overboard, and some captives were thrown overboard by the crew in the morning when slaves died overnight.

At any rate, many first-person accounts of the Middle Passage are extant. We move to some of those now in the next section of this second chapter.

First-Person Narratives of the Middle Passage

Mahommah Gardo Baquaqua (1842–1897), mentioned above, a native of present-day Benin, writes of first encountering his enslavement of the Middle Passage. Baquaqua writes:

> In the morning, when I awoke, I found that I was a prisoner, and my companions were all gone. Oh Horror! I then discovered that I had been betrayed into the hands of my enemies. Never shall I forget my feelings on that occasion. The thought of my poor mother and the loss of my liberty grieved me with the greatest of sorrow. I no longer would be the ruler of my own life.[136]

Earlier, we mentioned Olaudah Equiano (1744–1797), also known as Gustavus Vassa, who was a prominent African leader in London in the late eighteenth century. Equiano came from Nigeria, or the Niger Valley Supply Zone, and was kidnapped and placed on a slave ship bound for the New World. Eventually, Equiano became a freed slave who supported the British movement to abolish the slave trade at the

136 Ibid., p, 23.

close of the eighteenth century.[137]

Equiano was captured on the West African Coast in 1755, in what is now Nigeria, when the boy was only eleven years old.[138] He may have been a Yoruban, an Igbo, or a member of the Ibibio Tribe, all of Nigeria, or the Bight of Benin.

In 1789, Equiano wrote a widely read autobiography that he called *The Interesting Narrative of the Life of Olaudah Equiano, or Gustavus Vassa, the African.*[139] He was among the ten to twelve million Africans who were sold into slavery and then transported to the New World, from the sixteenth to the nineteenth century, across the Middle Passage.

In his narrative, Equiano describes his experiences on a voyage of the Middle Passage. He observes:

> At last when the ship we were in got all its cargo, they made ready with many fearful noises, and we were all put under deck, so that we could not see how they managed the vessel... The stench of the hold, while we were on the Coast, was so intolerably loathsome...The closeness of the place and the heat of the climate, added to the numbers on the ship, which was so crowded that we hardly had room to turn oneself. It was also suffocating us. This produced copious perspiration, so that the air became unfit for respiration because of a variety of loathsome smells. This brought on a sickness among the slaves, of which many died...thus falling victim to the improvident avarice, as I may call it, of their purchases.[140]

Equiano describes clearly the filth present in the hulls of the slave ships of the Middle Passage. He also points to a persistent problem that arose during the Middle Passage Voyages—that it was very difficult to get fresh air on those voyages. Thirdly, Equiano hints at the

137 A discussion of the device called the Speculum Orum appears at the end of Chapter Two.

138 Equiano., p. 25.

139 Ibid.

140 Ibid.

various diseases that often festered aboard the Middle Passage voyages mentioned earlier in this chapter. And finally, by using the expression "improvident avarice," he hints at the possibility of a theological interpretation of the experiences he endured across the Atlantic—that all things happen by the Decree, or *Qadar*, of Allah, a word that also means "Destiny" in Arabic.

Near the close of Equiano's biography, he informs us, "I believe there are few events in my life that have not happened to many people."[141] Presumably, the "many" he refers to here are the Africans taken as free people and then forced into slavery in the Americas or the Caribbean. Along the west coast of Africa, from the Cameroons in the south to the ports of Senegal in the north, as well as the rest of Africa, the Europeans built some one hundred forts that served as European trading posts from the fifteenth to the nineteenth centuries. The next chapter in this study is dedicated to these slave forts and castles, mostly in West Africa during this time, where we will examine nearly sixty of these forts and castles in Chapter Three.

European sailors who sought riches brought rum, cloth, gums and other goods to these forts. In turn, they traded these goods for human beings. This human cargo was transported across the Atlantic by way of the Middle Passage and then sold in the New World. Closer to the opening of Equiano's narrative, the Nigerian slave describes more about his conditions under captivity on the Middle Passage. In a quotation used as an epigram for this chapter, Equiano tells us:

> When I looked round the ship, I saw a large furnace of copper boiling, and a multitude of Black people of every description, chained together, every one of their countenances expressing dejection and sorrow. I no longer doubted my faith, and, quite overpowered with horror and anguish, I fell motionless on the deck and then fainted...I asked if we were not to be eaten by those White Men with horrible looks, red faces and long hair.[142]

---

141 Ibid., pp. 26–27.

142 Ibid., pp. 25.

The furnaces on the decks of slave ships appear to have had several functions. One has to do with the branding of slaves. Indeed, the slaves of the Middle Passage were sometimes branded with hot irons and restrained with iron shackles. Faced with these nightmarish conditions, many Africans preferred to die. But even the choice of suicide was sometimes taken from them. Nets were often placed along the sides of ships for those who contemplated jumping overboard. A contraption known as the "Speculum Orum," which forced the mouth wide open, was employed for those who refused to eat.[143]

Equiano also hints at an ambivalence concerning religion and faith when, on the one hand, he suggests he may have lost his faith, while on the other hand, he speaks of putting his fate in the "hands of Allah." He also tells us in the above passage that he and some of the other captives feared they were to be eaten by their white captors.

Another first-person slave narrative of the Middle Passage is that of Nigerian-born Ali Eisami, born around 1787. He tells us this in his autobiography:

> The people of the great vessel were wicked. When we have been shipped, they took away all the small pieces of cloth which were on our bodies; and they threw them in the water. Then they took chains and fettered us together, two by two. We in the vessel, young and old, were seven hundred whom the White Man had purchased. We were all fettered across our feet, and all the oldest died of thirst, for there was no water. Every morning, they had to take many and throw them overboard in the water.[144]

Ali Eisami makes five points in this passage. First, the European captors are "wicked." Secondly, the clothes of the slaves were tak-

143 William Saint Clair, The Door of No Return. (Waynesville: Blue Ridge Books, 2007.) William St. Clair of Roslin, who died in 1778, was the Grand Master of the Grand Lodge of Scotland. He was elected to that office on St. Andrew's Day, 1736.

144 Ali Eisami, who was born around 1787, was kidnapped from his home in present-day Benin and sold into slavery. He crossed the Atlantic by way of the Middle Passage and became a slave in Brazil.

en away and thrown into the sea. Thirdly, they were placed in chains. Fourth, there was not enough fresh water for the captives. And finally, the dead were often thrown overboard.

European traders such as Nicholas Owen, who died in 1759, waited at these African forts for slaves to arrive, often from farther inland. Equiano and Eisami, and others like them, found themselves sold or traded, sometimes more than once, often at these slave markets on the west coast of Africa, as well as at ports in the New World. African merchants, the poor, royalty—anyone—could be abducted in the raids and wars that were undertaken by Africans to secure those captives brought to the European ships on the coast.[145] Often slaves were made captives in the scuffles that ensued between two rival clans.

After being kidnapped, merchants forced the slaves to walk in captive caravans, or "coffles," to the European ships on the coast so the captives could be loaded. Sometimes these slaves walked long distances, as much as a hundred miles to the coast. They were shackled and underfed. Only three-quarters of the captives survived the journey. Those who were too weary or too sickly to keep up with the queue were often thrown overboard or left to fend for themselves or to survive by their own devices. A later chapter of this study is dedicated to an exploration of slave coffles and Goree sticks.

Those captives who reached these coastal forts were often placed in underground dungeons where they would remain until they were boarded onto European ships. Sometimes these slaves waited in these dungeons for a very long time. Some reports say even up to a year, but most no more than three months.[146] As we shall see in the next chapter, many of these slave forts and castles, primarily on the west coast of Africa, had separate dungeons for their male and their female captives.

Most of the major slave forts and castles in Africa, as we shall see in Chapter Three, were equipped with two separate slave dungeons,

---

145 Ibid.

146 John Newton, Messiah: Fifty Expository Discourses (London: Gale Ecco, 2010). Newton (1725–1807) was shipwrecked in 1748 and was eventually rescued and returned to England. Nicholas Owen was an Irish sailor who went into the slave-trading business. He is the author of Journal of a Slave Trader, 1746–1757.

one for men and the other for women. Usually, the male dungeon was underground and the female dungeon on the first floor at ground level. Administrative offices and officer living quarters were generally on the second floor at most slave forts and castles in the period. Sometimes the governors of these slave areas in Africa resided where there were third floors of these facilities, as in the Cape Coast Castle, for example.

Just as horrifying as these marches to the coast was the Middle Passage itself. On the "Middle Leg," ship captains such as John Newton, who later became a foe of slavery, loaded their empty holds with human beings. Newton (1725–1807) was an Anglican clergyman and former slave ship captain.[147] It took him a very long time to speak out against slavery, but he was greatly influenced to do so by William Wilberforce (1759–1833). Wilberforce was an English politician and a leader of the abolition movement in Britain in the first half of the eighteenth century.[148]

A typical voyage of the Middle Passage took sixty to ninety days, but some trips lasted as long as sixteen weeks due to the prevailing winds. Upon arrival in the New World, captains sold their cargo and in turn, purchased raw materials to be brought back to Europe on the return leg. Often, they brought back tobacco, cotton, sugar or whiskey.

Sometimes slave ship captains sold their cargo on-board while still in port. At other times, slaves were sold to local slave traders in auctions, in the North American sales. In all, it has been estimated that Europeans ships took some fifty-five thousand journeys across the Middle Passage.[149] The overwhelming majority of these Middle Passage voyages were conducted by the Portuguese, British, French, and Dutch slave ship captains, more than 70 percent from those four nations alone.

Several slaves wrote about the Middle Passage. Steven Mintz of the University of Houston, for example, has compiled a collection of these narratives entitled *Excerpts From Slave Narratives.*[150] One of the

147 Tom Feelings and J. H. Clarke, The Middle Passage: White Ships and Black Cargo (New York: Dial Books, 1995). p. 21.

148 Newton, p. 34.

149 Steven Mintz, Excerpts From Slave Narratives, http://bit.ly/2RVJrbj.

150 Thomas Trotter, The Health of Seamen (London: The Navy Records Society, 1965), vol. 107. Trotter (1760–1832) was a Scottish Naval physician educated at Edinburgh. He was also an ardent critic of the British slave

narratives in Mintz's book tells us:

> There is hardly any room 'tween decks, by half.
>
> The sweltering cattle stowed spoon-fashion there.
>
> That some went mad of thirst and tore their flesh
>
> And sucked the blood.[151]

This report, by a slave on the Middle Passage voyage, highlights the lack of space for each of the slaves. He speaks of the "tight-packing" method and the fact that often slaves on the Middle Passage went mad or attempted suicide by starvation or by simply jumping overboard.

A good amount of materials of these voyages are extant: letters, diaries, memoirs, captain's logs, records of shipping companies, and testimony before the British Parliamentary investigations into the treatment of British slaves and sailors, during the passages. Dr. Thomas Trotter, for example, a ship surgeon, was interviewed by Parliament and was asked, "Whether the slaves had room to turn themselves or to lie easy?" Dr. Trotter (1760–1832) responded:

> By no means. The slaves, when out of irons, are laid spoonways and closely locked to one another. It is the duty of the First Mate to see them stowed in this manner every morning...and when a ship has much motion at sea, they were often bruised against the deck or against each other. I have seen their breasts heaving with all those laborious and anxious efforts for life alone.[152]

---

trade. Nicholas Owen (died 1759) was an Irish sea captain who was taken prisoner and served a term of four years before the British government secured his release.

151 Ibid.

152 Alexander Falconbridge, Accounts of the Slave Trade on the Coast of Africa (New York: Forgotten Books, 2012), p. 39. Falconbridge (1760–1792) was a British ship surgeon. He accompanied four voyages to Africa from 1780 until 1787. Later, he became an abolitionist and a follower of Wilberforce.

Dr. Trotter refers to the "tight-packing" method to slaves lying on their sides in a spoon-like fashion, to the peculiar duties of the first mate aboard the slave ships, and to the bruises that slaves sometimes got when the wind and seas were not calm.

During Parliament's investigation, which took place from 1783 until 1787 as provisions of the Dolben Act of 1788 that put limitations on the number of persons on British slave ships, also included other witnesses such as Robert Norris, a representative of a shipping company, who also was called to testify before Parliament. Mr. Norris made these observations:

> The slave ships were delightful. The Captives had sufficient room, sufficient air, and sufficient provisions for the trip. When the slaves were on deck, they made merry with dancing and singing. In short, the voyage from Africa to the West Indies was one of the happiest periods in the slaves' lives.[153]

Norris and Trotter point to the vastly different economic involvements from the point of view of the trading companies and the slaves and ship surgeons. Norris gives a white-washed, almost delightful, picture of the Middle Passage, while Trotter concentrates more on the pain and hardships of the captives.

Other British eyewitnesses were used in supporting the anti-slavery movement in Britain in the eighteenth century. Alexander Falconbridge, for example, another former ship's surgeon, wrote a narrative entitled *Accounts of the Slave Trade on the Gold Coast of Africa.*[154] His narrative, published in London in 1788, describes the loss of life, the state of the holds below deck, or the tight-packing system, and how severely distraught some Africans were that they chose to take their own lives by starvation or by jumping overboard. Dr. Falconbridge remarks about one female slave this way:

> A woman appeared dejected from the moment she

153 Ibid.

154 Trotter, p. 73. Robert Norris, who died in 1791, was also a slave trader operating in the West African kingdom of Dahomey. His testimony to Parliament was both as a slave trader and as an official of the shipping companies.

> came on board, and she refused both food and medicine; being asked by an interpreter what she wanted, she responded, "Nothing but to die," and that is precisely what she did a few days later.[155]

Other captives chose to behave more violently. "A man was sold with his family for practicing witchcraft," testified Dr. Trotter at the Parliament's proceedings on slavery.[156] The man refused any sustenance after coming aboard. Early the next morning, it was discovered that the slave cut his throat with a sharp knife. Dr. Trotter sewed up the wound, but the next evening the man had not only torn off his sutures. He also made a similar attempt on the other side of his throat. Dr. Trotter reported:

> He declared he would never go with a White Man. He died of hunger eight or ten days later.[157]

The slave in question did not ultimately go "with a White Man," nor did he become enslaved by a white man when the ship arrived in the New World. Dr. Falconbridge gives this description of slaves kept below deck during the Middle Passage. He tells us:

> They were frequently stowed so close, as to admit no other position than lying on their sides. Nor will the height between decks permit the indulgence of an erect posture, especially where there were platforms that were generally the case. These platforms is a kind of shelf, about eight or nine feet in breadth, extending from the side of the ship to the center. They were placed nearly midway between the decks, at a distance of two or three feet from each deck. Upon these, the Negroes were stowed in the same manner as they were on the deck underneath.[158]

Again, the lying on one's side like spoons and the hardship of

155 Ibid.
156 Falconbridge, p. 40.
157 Ibid.
158 Ibid., pp. 41–42.

the tight-packing method, as well as the planks that lined the hulls of the slave ships, are all mentioned by the English ship surgeon. He also comments on the diet of the slaves on the Middle Passage. He observes:

> The diet of the Negroes, while onboard, consisted chiefly of horse beans boiled to the consistency of a pulp; of boiled yams and rice and sometimes a small quantity of beef or pork. The latter was frequently taken from the provisions laid for the sailors. They sometimes made use of a sauce composed of palm oil mixed with flour, water, and pepper, which the sailors called "Slabber-Sauce." Yams are the favorite food of the Eboe or Bight Negroes, and rice or corn of those from the Gold or Windward Coasts; each preferring the produce of their native soil.[159]

Falconbridge points out here that slaves from the Niger Valley and the Bight of Benin, or what he tells us the Crew refers to as "Eboe" and "Bites," prefer yams as a staple of their diet. In the Gold Coast Zone and the Windward Coast Supply Zone, slaves much more preferred corn or rice. What is true of these three zones was also true for the other eight. Slaves preferred food grown in their native soil to staples grown elsewhere.

Here Dr. Falconbridge even describes what happened when a slave refused to eat. He observes:

> Upon the Negroes refusing to take sustenance, I have seen coals of fire, glowing hot, placed on a shovel and brought close to their lips as to almost scorch or burn them. And this has been accompanied with threats of forcing them to swallow the coals, if they still insisted on not eating. This means generally that the desired effect was met. I also have been credibly informed that a certain Captain in the Slave Trade, poured melted lead on such of his Negroes who obstinately refused to eat.[160]

---

159 Ibid.

160 Ibid., p. 44.

Although this technique described by Dr. Falconbridge may seem to be outrageous, there is absolutely no evidence elsewhere in the literature about this practice actually having taken place in the eighteenth century. Dr. Falconbridge also alludes to a second function of furnaces on the main deck of slave ships. They serve as an incentive for those captives who rebel by refusing to eat. Falconbridge continues his analysis. He even comments on the ventilation on the slave ships. He writes:

> The hardships and inconveniences suffered by the Negroes during the Passage are scarcely to be enumerated or conceived. They are far more violently affected by seasickness than are Europeans. It frequently terminates in death, especially among the women. But the exclusion of fresh air is among the most intolerable. For the purpose of admitting this needful refreshment, most of the ships in the Slave Trade are provided between decks, with five or six airports on each side of the ship, of about five inches in length and four in breadth.[161]

Falconbridge mentions seasickness, death that often comes from starvation on the Middle Passage voyages, and the often lack of fresh air on these voyages. Dr. Falconbridge continues his analysis. He observes:

> Thus, fresh air is being excluded from the Negroes, and their quarters begin to grow intolerably hot. The confined air is rendered noxious by the gasses exhaled from their bodies and being repeatedly breathed, soon produce fevers and fluxes [dysentery.][162]

Amoebic dysentery and scurvy, then, were the cause of the majority of deaths among slaves and crew on the voyages of the Middle Passage. Additionally, there were also deaths to be attributed to measles, syphilis and smallpox. This was true of slaves as well as crew members on the Middle Passage voyages, as we have indicated earlier

161 Equiano, p 17.

162 Falconbridge, p. 45.

in this chapter.

In another place of his *Narrative*, Olaudah Equiano writes about those slaves contemplating jumping overboard. He observes:

> One day, when we had a smooth Sea and moderate wind, two of my wearied Countrymen who were chained together, preferring death, to such a life of misery, somehow made it through the netting and jumped into the Sea. Immediately, another dejected fellow, who on account of his illness was suffered to be out of his irons, also followed their example.[163]

Equiano points out that nets often were employed on the sides of slave ships to keep captives from jumping overboard. He also indicates that at times when slaves were ill, they were often permitted to move about or remain inclined without their chains. Dr. Falconbridge continues his description:

> And I believe that many more soon would have done the same if they had not been prevented by the ship's crew, who were instantly alarmed. Those of us who were the most active were in a moment put down under the decks, and there was a noise and confusion amongst the people of the ship that I had never heard before. However, two of the Wenches were drowned, but they got the third and afterwards flogged her unmercifully for attempting to prefer death to slavery.[164]

Olaudah Equiano points here to the desire for suicide among many of the slaves kept aboard European slave ships during the Middle Passage. Indeed, statistics suggest that a quarter of all African slaves who embarked on the Middle Passage did not make it to the New World, mostly due to disease, starvation or suicide. Similarly, between 20 and 25 percent of the crews on these voyages did not survive, mostly due to disease or lack of fresh water.

In reality, the life of the slaves during the Middle Passage brutalized

163 Ibid.

164 Ibid.

both slave and sailor. In fact, the sailor experienced sub-par conditions as bad as those of the captives. Sailors were often recruited through coercion. They were signed on in port towns where recruiters and tavern owners conspired to get sailors drunk and indebted, and then offered to relieve the debt if they signed a contract with a slave ship's captain.

Those who refused were usually imprisoned. Sailors out of prison often had tough times securing work outside the slave trade. Most maritime businesses would not hire convicted felons, so they were forced to return to the slave ships.

On the Middle Passage, the captain had total authority over his ship, including what went on in it. He was answerable to no one except the Crown. Captives on slave ships out-numbered the crew about ten to one, up to as many as fifty to one on larger ships.[165]

Slaves were punished on slave ships by being put in thumbscrews or flogged by the crew when they were rebellious. Despite this fact, resistance and rebellion were still quite common. The death toll was quite high. Between 1680 and 1688, for example, of every one hundred slaves taken aboard, twenty-three died in transit.[166] When diseases like dysentery began to spread, as indicated earlier in this chapter, the dying and the dead were usually thrown overboard.

Douglas Grant, in his *Fortunate Slave*, points out that on a 1694 voyage of the British ship, the *Hannibal*, with a full complement of seven hundred slaves, had a mortality rate of 46.9 percent. The British Committee of Privy Council, in an investigation of the death-rate on British voyages of the Middle Passage, found that by 1789, the death rate had dropped to 24 percent.

In November of 1781, to cite another example, 470 slaves were crammed aboard the slave ship *Zong*. During its passage to Jamaica, many captives became ill. Seven crew members and sixty Africans died on the trip.[167] The captain, a man named Luke Collingwood, ordered

---

165 James Walvin, The Zong: A Massacre, the Law, and the End of Slavery (New Haven: Yale University Press, 2011). Walven is professor of history at York University in England.

166 Ibid.

167 Charles James Fox (1749–1806) was a Whig statesman from Midhurst, Sussex. He served in Parliament for a total of thirty-eight years.

that the sick be thrown overboard. Only one survived. When the ship arrived back in England on the return leg of the Middle Passage, the owners filed an insurance claim for the value of the drowned slaves.[168] And they, in fact, won their claim.

Interesting enough, Captain Collingwood was called as a witness for the shipping company in the case, which was known as Gregson V. Gilbert (1783). Collingwood told the court that there was not enough drinkable water on the voyage—something pointed out earlier in this chapter by Dr. Thomas Trotter—compounded by the existence of sickness. The court held that in some circumstances, the deliberate killing of some slaves might be legal, and insurers could be required to compensate for their loss.[169]

The shipping company argued that there was not enough drinkable water for the voyage and that the sick Africans posed a danger to the health of the white crew, and to other slaves, as well. This tells us a little of what value was placed on the lives of the white sailors, as opposed to the black slaves. By 1783, the owners of the *Zong* won their suit in court, but the case did much to show the many horrors experienced on the Middle Passage, from the sixteenth to the nineteenth centuries, both in Britain and in America.[170]

The death toll among sailors was equally high. Some estimate as high as 25 percent of each of the crews during the passage. Fewer sailors were needed on the return voyage back to Europe. It was not uncommon to see deserted sailors living in the Caribbean, or in port towns of North and South America, at the time of the European slave trade.

In late 1788, the British Parliament passed a law called the Dolben Act, introduced above. The law fixed the number of slaves a British ship could carry. The debate over the act was precipitated by a general debate on whether the United Kingdom should give up slavery completely. Charles Fox, an MP, denounced the "disgraceful traffic that

---

168 The Dolben Act was also known as the "Slave Trade Act of 1788." Sir William Dolben (1727–1810), the sponsor of the act, was born in Finedom, Northamptonshire. He was educated at Christ Church, Oxford.

169 Ibid. One interesting fact about Captain Luke Collingwood is that he never commanded a ship before the Zong episode, nor afterward.

170 Wilberforce on the floor of Parliament, September 22, 1788.

should not only be regulated but also destroyed."[171]

William Dolben, the MP associated with the act, describes the shipboard horrors of slaves chained hand and foot, and stowed "like herring in a barrel."[172] This is obviously another reference to the "tight-packing" method. Dolben put forth the bill, and it passed fifty-six votes to five. Later, it went on to receive royal assent on July 11, 1788, when the act became law.[173]

A short time later, in a speech to the House of Commons, William Wilberforce, who by now was an MP himself, quoted evidence that, "Not less than 12 1/2 percent of enslaved Africans perished in the Middle Passage, and another four and a half percent died on-shore, before the day of their sale."[174] Mr. Wilberforce's estimates, as we have seen earlier in this study, actually fall short of the real numbers.

He also gave extensive descriptions of the conditions aboard the slave ships. Wilberforce (1759–1833) became the voice of the British abolition movement in Parliament, and beyond, in the late eighteenth century. From 1789 on, he regularly introduced bills in Parliament to abolish the slave trade entirely in Britain.[175] Wilberforce, however, was heatedly opposed by owners of the shipping companies, for they were making fortunes from the Middle Passage voyages.

At any rate, the transatlantic slave trade was the largest movement of human beings in history. Somewhere between ten and twelve million Africans were brought to the New World by way of the Middle

---

171 William Wilberforce (1859–1833), a native of Yorkshire, was a British politician philanthropist and an abolitionist. He served in the House of Commons from 1784 until 1812. Charles Fox (1749–1806) was a prominent Whig politician whose Parliamentary career spanned nearly four decades, thirty-eight years, to be precise.

172 Brian Lavery, The Ship of the Line: A History of Ship Models (London: Naval Institute Press, 2014).

173 Robert Parthesius, Dutch Ships in Tropical Waters (Amsterdam: University of Amsterdam Press, 2010). An outstanding account of the history of the Dutch East India Company.

174 Mariano Sennewald, El Jardin de la Amistad (Amsterdam: Gisela Sawin, 2014), p. 100. Sennewald is a modern Dutch scholar.

175 Ibid. The technical legal name of the Zong Case was Gregson V. Gilbert, which was decided in 1783.

Passage, but only about 500,00 to 600,00 to North American ports. The Atlantic slave trade, however, was not the only slave trading going on in Africa in this period.

Many African slaves were transported across the Sahara Desert, the Red Sea and the Indian Ocean, from the beginning of Islam in the seventh century until around the year 1900. Much of the slave trade with India was carried on from the East African Supply Zone. The Arabs also conducted slavery from East Africa to West Africa using the six principal slave caravan routes across the continent. Indeed, slave caravans moved from slave forts in Mozambique, Madagascar, Tanzania and Somalia, across the continent east to west, by way of six traditional caravan routes. Many of these overland routes were instigated and organized by Arab slave traders from Oman and Yemen.

Indeed, slave caravans, or coffles, in Africa traveled by land from ports in Ethiopia and Mozambique, across the Sahara to the Mali Empire, and from there to slave forts and castles on the Gold Coast, the Windward Coast, the Sierra Leone Supply Zone, to the Senegambian Zone, and to Marrakech, or other ports of the North African Supply Zone.

The destinations for the slaves traveling on the Middle Passage were the Caribbean, Brazil and the British ports of North America, from Boston to South Carolina. European powers such as Portugal, Britain, Spain, France, the Netherlands, Norway, Denmark, Sweden and Brandenburg all participated in the Atlantic slave trade in the fifteenth to the nineteenth centuries. These enslaved Africans came mostly from the eleven supply zones we have mentioned earlier in this chapter.

By the late eighteenth century, the need for greater profits gave rise to new ship designs, as well as new ways of handling human cargo. Improvements in airflow on the slave ships helped to decrease the high mortality rates on the ships. Ventilation ports became standard on these new designs. These air ports often were placed next to cannons. They also allowed the ships to travel faster and to venture farther into inland ports, such as along the Niger, Gambia, the Congo, and Senegal rivers.[176]

By the 1780s, another improvement in the slave trade in the late

176 Ibid., p. 132.

eighteenth century was the new knowledge about diseases and illnesses and the medicines to treat them. The Dutch East India Company was the first to realize that the inclusion of surgeons and other medical staff aboard slave ships may be a great aid in controlling sickness on the voyages of the Middle Passage.[177] So after 1780, the Dutch, French, British and Portuguese slave ships all carried ship surgeons and other medical personnel.

Although slave rebellions appear to have been quite common, very few of them were successful. One key exception is the revolt on a ship named *la Amistad*.[178] In February of 1839, near the end of slavery in the west, Portuguese slave hunters abducted a large number of slaves from the Sierra Leone Zone. They then shipped these slaves to Cuba. By July 2 of the same year, a rebellion took place on the ship near the coast of Cuba.[179]

The mutineers were captured and then tried for desertion in the United States. In 1841, in a surprise decision, the US Supreme Court ruled that the rebels should be set free. This case had many repercussions for the Anti-Slavery Movement. In the US American President John Q. Adams argued the side of the mutineers before the Supreme Court. Eventually, thirty-five of the rebels were returned to Africa, and others died in prison while awaiting trial.[180]

One of the surviving mutineers described the mindset on the day of the mutiny. He wrote:

---

177 Ibid. The Dolben Act was part of the "Slave Trade Act" of 1788, introduced by MP William Dolben.

178 Gomez, p. 706. More is said about the Amistad in a later chapter of this study.

179 Wilem Bosman, in his An Accurate Description of the Coast of Guinea, published in 1705, speaks of the sharks following his slave ship. He observes, "I have sometimes, not without horror, seen the Dismal Rapaciousness of these animals."

180 See article on "Middle Passage," in Dictionary of American History (2003). Also see James A. Rawley, The Transatlantic Slave Trade: A History (Boston: Little Brown, 1981). This is one of the lesser known aspects of the career of John Q. Adams. He regularly did pro-bono legal work after his time as president. Adams had been recruited by abolitionists to represent the Amistad captives. At the time, he was a seventy-three-year-old congressman.

> When we found ourselves at last taken away, death was more preferable than life, and a plan was organized among us, that we might burn and blow up the ship, and to perish altogether in the flames.[181]

This mutineer points out that the *Amistad* revolt was planned long beforehand, and that they had contemplated burning, or even blowing up, the ship and perishing in the accompanying fire. At any rate, it was clearly an organized affair.

The number of mutineers varied greatly in these insurrections. Often the rebellion would end with the deaths of a few slaves or crew members, and the surviving rebels were punished or executed or were made examples of to the remaining slaves left on-board, as well as the crew. By the year 1820, about nine million slaves had been brought to the New World. Portugal took between three and four million to its colony, Brazil. The Spanish brought one million slaves to the New World; the French and the Dutch, about two and a half million apiece. The British brought about three million slaves to the New World, but only between 500,00 and 600,00 to British ports in North America, such as Boston, Philadelphia, Baltimore, Annapolis, Washington, Alexandria, Richmond and Charleston, among other ports.[182]

While on the Middle Passage, slaves were usually fed twice a day, except on Dutch ships who fed their slaves three meals a day. Some captains made vain attempts to clean the hold when their captives were eating on the main deck. Somewhere near a quarter to a third of the captives did not survive the voyage, as outlined earlier in this chapter. The bodies of the dead were most often thrown overboard. The survival rate of the sailors was only marginally better. About twenty percent of the crew succumbed during the Middle Passage, as well. Indeed, in the middle of the middle five decades eighteenth century, there were reports of schools of sharks following European slave ships for some distance hoping for a meal or two from the castoffs.[183]

One final statistic concerning the Middle Passage is the percent-

181 Gomez, p. 707.

182 Ibid.

183 Terry Alford, Prince Among Slaves (Oxford: Oxford University Press, 1977), p. 42.

age of the total voyages made along the route. Of the 55,000 estimated voyages across the Middle Passage, these statistics can be summarized thusly:

The Portuguese	42.3% of Total	Britain	23.6%
Spain	14.5%	Denmark-Swe-den	5%
France	11.4%.	Brit. North America	2.7%
Holland	4.5%		

From these figures, we may make several conclusions.[184] First, the Portuguese, who made the largest percentage of Middle Passage voyages at 42 percent, nearly doubled the percentage of the second-highest percentage of Middle Passage trips, the British, at 23.6 percent. The Portuguese tripled the voyages of Spain (14.5 percent) and made four times more Middle Passage trips than France at 11.4 percent. Denmark-Sweden at 5 percent and Holland at 4.5 percent were distant players at the fifth and sixth positions. Portugal, with the greatest percentage of Middle Passage voyages, may have been because they were involved in the Atlantic slave trade earlier and as long as any other European power.

This brings us to the next section of this second chapter, in which we will discuss the attitudes of North American planters to various peoples of West Africa. As we shall see, these perspectives varied greatly from place to place in America, as well as to our different supply zones mentioned earlier.

184 Ibid.

Attitudes of American Planters Toward African Supply Zones

In this section of the chapter, we will make several observations about what Maryland, Virginia and elsewhere in the early colonies of America thought about slaves coming from the various supply zones. We will begin by pointing out that many English-speaking North Americans thought that some Africans, such as the Igbo and Ibibio of southeastern Nigeria, and thus the Niger Valley Supply Zone or the Bight of Benin, were thought to be surly, unruly and suicidal. Thus, they were not highly prized in the colonies.[185] Terry Alford, in his book *Prince Among Slaves*, says of what he calls the "Iboes," "They were the least popular Africans at Natchez."[186] Alford goes on to observe:

> They were thought [to be] poor workers, inclined to despondency and suicide. While the planters disliked them by name, they made few fine distinctions between Africans based on their ethnic groupings.[187]

Professor Alford goes on to add:

> Most of them [slaves] were sorted into great clumps, like "Gold Coast" and "Congo." Muslims were termed "Mandingoes," the Fulbe being considered a Mandinka "tribe." They were admired for their intelligence, but believed to be less capable of sustained labor than "Guiney Negroes" from under the West African bulge.[188]

At any rate, the North Americans did not highly prize the Igbo Tribe. Indeed, this tribe, as well as the Ibibio, were seen as malcontents by most of the European captains of the Middle Passage. Even in America, slave traders in New Orleans and Natchez, Mississippi, found members of the Igbo Tribe to be the "least popular Africans in these locales."

---

185 These are all peoples of the Sierra Leone Supply Zone. The Krio are significant because they are the descendants of freed African American slaves.

186 Gomez, p. 708.

187 Ibid.

188 Alford, p. 42. The Akan People are a tribe of southern Ghana and the majority tribe in the Ivory Coast.

On the other hand, Akan speakers from the Gold Coast were regarded as industrious and hard-working. In fact, planters in Maryland much preferred slaves from Ghana, or the Gold Coast in their slave trading, and secondarily, those from the Senegambian Supply Zone in the North.

In the Senegambian and Sierra Leone zones, the slaves were collectively called "Mandingoes." They were generally believed by the North American planters to be preferable to others. In Senegambia, these people were Fulbe, Mandinka and Wolof. In the Sierra Leone Zone, in places like Guinea, the most significant peoples were the Temne, the Mende, the Mandingo, the Krio, the Kurakot People and the Fulbe Tribe.[189]

The preference for Mandingoes is reflected in the activity of the eighteenth-century North American shipping companies. Indeed, many European companies only imported certain kinds of slaves. In Georgia and South Carolina, especially along the coast, the planters also preferred people from Senegal and Gambia. Those growers of Louisiana preferred the indigo and rice-growing slaves of the Sierra Leone Supply Zone.[190] The Chesapeake tobacco planters of Maryland, as well as those of South Carolina and Georgia, also had a distaste for slaves originating in the Bights of Biafra and Benin, called collectively "Bites" or "Bytes" by North American planters. The Virginia planters, however, were not nearly as discriminating.[191]

A significant number of African slaves in North America were thought to be "harbored by Indians." Indeed, the relationship between Africans and Native Americans were, for the most part, cordial. Many Mustee children were among runaway slaves all over the colonies in the eighteenth and nineteenth centuries.[192] A "Mustee" was a term em-

189 The Oxford English Dictionary defines a "Mustee" as "A person of mixed European and African descent, sometimes a person with one white-skinned parent and the other one black." Merriam Webster's Dictionary says a "Mustee" is the "offspring of a white person and a Quadroon."

190 We have in mind here Job Diallo, Yarrow Mamout, Sambo Anderson, Kunta Kinte, and others from Maryland and Virginia in the eighteenth century.

191 Dr. James Collins, Practical Rules for Managing the Treatment of the Negro Slaves (London: Vernon and Hood, 1805).

192 Gomez, p. 708.

ployed for the children of an African and a Native American union. In fact, three of the suspected Muslim slaves outlined in Chapters Eight and Nine are reported to have been Mustees.

One fact that has become clear in the last twenty years is that people from the Senegambian Zone, like the Fulbe and the Mande speakers, are much closer genetically to white Europeans than are other African peoples. Dr. David Collins, a British ship surgeon, was among the first to point out that the tall, muscular Senegambians look more like Europeans than other Africans.

Another fact that seems to be true is that many of the slaves from this zone saw themselves as superior to other Africans, particularly the Muslims who felt that way. In that regard, many of the Muslim slaves who can be identified, like the prominent ones in the opening chapter of this study, were from prominent backgrounds in West Africa, and thus thought themselves to be a "cut above" other slaves around them.[193] More will be said of this phenomenon in Chapter Ten.

Another observation about the Senegambians is that they rarely seem to be suited for agricultural work. Dr. Collins, in his book *Practical Rules for Managing the Treatment of Negro Slaves*, reveals that "Slaves from Senegal are excellent in the caring for cattle and horses, as well as domestic service, though little qualified for the ruder labors of the field."[194] Indeed, both Job Diallo and Loumein Yoas, among others, were two slaves from Senegambia who, quite early on, showed their shortcomings in doing farm work, so Job Diallo tended cattle instead.

Again, later, in the final chapter, we say more about this tendency of prominent Muslim slaves in early America not to be very useful at manual labor, as well as eleven other core characteristics. This brings us to the final section of this second chapter, an exploration of pieces of art that depict the Middle Passage, slave ships and the supply zones. Indeed, Job Diallo and Loumein Yoas, among others, were two slaves

---

193 Ibid. Dr. Collins was a British physician and planter who spent fourteen years traveling, working, and ministering to the sick and injured on Middle Passage voyages.

194 "An Illustration of Fort de Maures," in Pieter van der Aa, La Galerie du Agreable du Monde (Leiden, 1729).

from Senegambia who, quite early on, showed that they were nearly useless when it came to farm work.

Michael Gomez, as well as Austin, with whom we began this chapter, suggest that:

> Vis-à-vis other Africans, Muslims were generally viewed by slave owners as a "more intelligent, more reasonable, more physically attractive, and more dignified people.[195]

They suggest one reason for this phenomenon is that captives from the Senegambian and Sierra Leone supply zones, the Fulbe and Mande-speakers, for example, "were believed to be phenotypically closer to that of Europeans than are other Africans."[196] One reason that these captives were preferred, then, well may be that they most look like Europeans compared to other Africans.

Other participants of the Atlantic slave trade also spoke of the self-pride of Senegambian captives, as well as how much they resemble Europeans. Richard Madden, for example, Irish physician, writer and abolitionist, who took an active role in trying to impose abolitionist rules in Jamaica on behalf of the British government, suggests that the Mandingos "are said to be superior to the intelligences of other classes. Many of them read and write Arabic."[197] Dr. Madden, as well as many other white Europeans in the eighteenth and nineteenth centuries, thought that Africans from the Senegambian Supply Zone were superior, both physically and intellectually, to other Africans.

British naturalist, George Gardiner, who traveled to Brazil from 1836 until 1841, was also of the opinion that:

> Africans from the northern part of Africa are by far the finest races...Both the men and the women are taller

---

195 Ibid.

196 Quoted in Diouf, p. 131. Richard Robert Madden (1798–1886) was an Irish physician, writer, abolitionist and historian. He was active in slavery issues in Jamaica, as well as the United Irishmen Movement.

197 Gomez, pp. 708–710. George Gardiner (1821–1891) was a British scientist and Irish recipient of the Victoria Cross.

and more handsome than elsewhere in Africa.[198]

Earlier, we stated that British ship surgeon, Dr. David Collins, made the same point about slaves from the Senegambian Supply Zone. This brings us to the final section of this second chapter, in which we describe and discuss several artistic depictions of supply zones and the Middle Passage.[199]

Supply Zones and Middle Passage in Artistic Depictions

Several pieces of art related to our supply zones are extant in various history of art publications in the west. An analysis of some of these is the subject matter of this section of the chapter. An illustration of "Fort de Maures" on the Island of Moyella in Ethiopia from 1729 shows an engraving of Europeans purchasing slaves on the coast of East Africa. Two Europeans bargain over the price of slaves under a palm tree to the right, while three European sailors and another slave wait on the left.[200] The engraving comes from a book published in Leiden in 1729 by Pieter van der Aa called *La Galerie du Agreable du Monde*.[201] Vander der Aa (1659–1733) was a Dutch publisher who specialized in maps and atlases.

In the engraving, several Europeans are purchasing slaves on the east coast of Africa. A few slaves stand beneath a palm tree accompanied by a European trader. To the right, on a hill can be seen a city of some size. In the distance on the left is an awaiting slave ship, offshore. The original of this print is twenty by fourteen and a half inches on hand-laid paper. It was drawn on Moyella Island of contemporary Ethiopia. In this sense, image one is a representation of a slave fort from the East African Supply Zone.[202]

198 Ibid.

199 Ibid. Pieter van der Aa (1659–1733) was a Dutch publisher known mostly for his maps and atlases.

200 Francis Spilsbury, "A View of a Slave Yard at Goree," in An Account of a Voyage to the West Coast of Africa, Special Collections, University of Virginia Library. Francis Brockwell Spilsbury (1784–1830) was born in Plymouth, England. He followed his father as a naval surgeon.

201 Ibid. Francis Spilsbury (1733–1767) was the son of Edward Spilsbury. Francis made a number of voyages on the west coast of Africa.

202 "Holding Pen With Thatched Roof," London News, April 14, 1849.

A second image from Senegal, dated 1805, features a caption that reads "A View of a Slave Yard at Goree."[203] It shows several men, women and children in Senegal. A man on the left appears to be having lice picked out of his hair. Two women have infants on their backs. One is pounding meal using a wooden mortar and pestle. The image appears in Francis Spilsbury's *An Account of a Voyage to the Western Coast of Africa.*[204] This piece is owned by the Special Collections Division of the University of Virginia Library. Francis Spilsbury (1733–1767) was an eighteenth-century British voyager and explorer. This image, of course, is from the Senegambian Zone.

A third image, from the Gallines River in the Sierra Leone Zone, shows a slave holding pen with a thatched roof. Captured slaves can be seen through the bamboo bars of the pen. Guards stand watch outside. The illustration comes from the *London News* published on April 14, 1849.[205]

A fourth image from Richard Drake's *Revelations of a Slave Smuggler*, published in New York in 1860, depicts a slave market on the Kambia River. The image displays a crowd scene with Europeans and Africans, one of the latter being examined by one of the former. Another slave nearby is being whipped by a European. A slave ship coming to port can be seen in the background. The Kambia River

203 Richard Drake, "A Slave Market on the Kambia River," in Revelations of a Slave Smuggler (New York: Barnes and Noble, 1979), with a preface by The Rev. Henry Byrd West. Kambia is also a district in Sierra Leone. Before the Portuguese and the British settled there, a farmer named Kimba Pa settled there on the banks of the river. The city and the river are named after him. The river is also called the River Koleten. Richard Drake operated as a slave trader in Africa from 1807 until 1857. The New York Public Library owns an original copy of this book. He was also known as George Burton Drake (1870–1942). In addition to being a painter, he was also a Congregationalist minister and abolitionist

204 Edward James Glave, "A Captive," in "The Slave Trade in the Congo Basin," in The Century Illustrated Monthly Magazine, November of 1889 to April of 1890, vol. 39, first edition, 1889. E. J. Glave (1863–1895) was an English adventurer, author and journalist. His most famous work is his Six Years of Adventure in Congo Land published in 1892.

205 The Slave Trade by Auguste-François Biard (1799–1882), a French genre painter in the early nineteenth century. This image is dated 1833.

is primarily in the Sierra Leone Supply Zone.[206] Drake (1770–1842) was a British artist and explorer, and early in adulthood was a slave trader.

An illustrated sketch from E. J. Glave's *The Slave Trade in the Congo Basin* is entitled *A Captive*. It shows a black man in a slave shed, or a *Barracoon*. He is being restrained with a hewn log attached around his neck called a "Goree stick." The date of the illustration is 1889–1890. Presumably, the slave remained restrained thusly until he was ready to be shipped to the New World.[207] Edward James Glave (1863–1895) was an explorer and artist on the Congo River in the late nineteenth century. He also describes African slave coffles where the captives are held together by the employment of Goree sticks, as we shall see in Chapter Four of this study.

Another image entitled *The Slave Trade* is a painting by Frenchman Auguste Francois Biard. The painting was completed in 1840. It shows a young child dressed in a white tunic clinging to its mother at the edge of a slave boat on a river. In the boat, slave agents are restraining another slave.[208]

Another painting, also called *The Slave Trade*, was owned by Sir Thomas Fowell Buxton (1751–1812), who was a zealous English abolitionist. The painting can now be found at the Wilberforce House of Kington Upon Hull City Museum in London.[209] Buxton (1786–1845)

206 Thomas Fowell Buxton (1786–1845) was a member of Parliament, a Brewer, and a social reformer. The image is owned by the Wilberforce Museum in London. The word "Barracoon" comes from the Catalan barracca that means "hut." Thus, we get the English word "Barracks."

207 George Morland, The Slave Trade (1791) and African Hospitality (1791). The first painting shows several black captives on the African coast being accosted by five Europeans. The other painting shows the aftermath of a European shipwreck. A white European family, husband, wife, and child, are given comfort by several slaves on the coast of Africa. George Morland (1763–1804) was a London-born painter who mostly painted rustic scenes of country life.

208 J. R. Smith's engraving after the painting by George Morland called The Slave Trade. The original is owned by the Australian National Library. J. R. Smith (1751–1812) was an English landscape painter and mezzo-tint engraver.

209 "Slave Tight-Packing" plan of British slave ship the Brookes. It

was an MP, brewer, and social reformer.

George Morland's 1791 painting *The Slave Trade* is also owned by the Wilberforce House Museum. Another painting of Morland's is called *African Hospitality*. In it, a group of a dozen slaves is huddled on the shore. The stern of a slave boat can be seen on the right.[210] Morland (1763–1804) was a London-born painter.

A hand-colored mezzotint painting by John Raphael Smith (1750–1812) is owned by the Rex Nan Kivell Collection of the Australian National Library. The painting called *The Slave Trade* is based on George Morland's painting by the same title mentioned earlier.[211]

The Harvard College Library owns an image that depicts the Middle Passage. It shows the upper deck of a slave ship that included "about four hundred and fifty native Africans, in a sitting or squatting posture. Most of the many slaves on the top deck have their knees pulled up to their chests, to form resting places for their heads and arms." The image shows more than a hundred captives, all with desolate looks on their faces.[212]

Finally, also included at the end of this chapter three, other descriptions of artistic depictions of the notion of the "tight packing" of slaves on the Middle Passage and an artistic rendering of the *Speculum Orum* mentioned in the body of this chapter. The former shows several slaves sitting on the floor of the hull for male captives. Their arms are across their chests, and knees are bent, allowing room for the slave in front. A caption suggests that the space available for these slaves is

---

shows the stowage and the tight packing of slaves below the main deck.

210 Ibid. John Raphael Smith (1750–1812), English painter and mezzo-tint engraver was the son of Thomas Smith of Derby, a landscape painter, and the father of John Rubens Smith, also a painter, who emigrated to the Unites States.

211 Thomas Clarkson, The History, Progress, and Accomplishments of the Abolition of the African Slave Trade by the British Parliament (London, 1808), two volumes. Clarkson (1760–1846), English abolitionist, was a leading figure against the slave trade conducted by the British Empire.

212 "Speculum Orum" is a device used to hold a slave's mouth open while he is force-fed. Q Magazine at Yale in its October 16, 2014, issue included an interview with M. Lamar by Ron Gregg. The article also contains pictures of the Speculum Orum.

only three feet and three inches.[213]

A schematic drawing of the slave ship the *Brooks* illustrates the tight-packing method. It shows the inhumane conditions under which slaves were kept below deck. This image was published in an 1808 edition of *The History, Progress, and Accomplishments of the Abolition of the African Slave Trade*, written by Thomas Clarkson in two separate volumes.[214] The image shows the incredible number of slaves packed tightly on the *Brooks*. Clarkson (1760–1846) was an English abolitionist and leading campaigner against the British slave trade in the eighteenth and nineteenth centuries.

The final description of a depiction in this chapter is of the *Speculum Orum*.[215] It comes from a nineteenth-century photograph that shows the steel contraption that forces open the mouth of the captive so that he can be force-fed. These devices were frequently employed, as we indicated earlier in this chapter when a slave refused to eat.[216]

This brings us to a summary of the major conclusions we have made in this second chapter, followed by the notes of the same. In Chapter Three of this study, we will describe and discuss slave forts and slave castles, mostly on the coast of West Africa during the Atlantic slave trade period.

Conclusions

We began this second chapter of this study by enumerating the nine major supply zones from which slaves were brought from Africa to the Caribbean and the Americas. We also indicated the percentages that each of the nine zones have contributed to slaves brought to America in general, and to the Chesapeake region, in particular. In addition to the nine supply zones mentioned by Professor Michael Gomez, we also have added two supplemental supply zones—those of North Africa and South Africa—to the original nine zones.

213 Ibid. The Brooks became infamous when prints of her were published in England in 1788 that showed the "Tight-Packing" method of British voyages on the Middle Passage.

214 Image of Speculum Orum at http://bit.ly/2ThtPj2.

215 Ibid.

216 Ibid.

In the second section of this chapter, we have introduced what has come to be called the Middle Passage, that is, the route by which the predominate number of European ships in the seventeenth to the nineteenth centuries brought slaves to America. In this section, we have included first-person accounts from slaves and others by sailors, ship surgeons, and ship captains of these voyages and one by a representative of the shipping companies, Thomas Trotter, who also became a slave trader for the British Empire.

Some of the major views that American planters had of various varieties of African slaves were the subject matter of the third section of this second chapter. As we have shown in this section, some tribes back in Africa were prized, while others were disdained. As an example, we have shown that people of both the Igbo and Ibibio tribes of southeastern Nigeria and the Bight of Benin were thought by some North American farmers to be "surly, unruly, and suicidal." Other tribes, like the Akan from the Gold Coast Zone, for example, were regarded as industrious and hard-working, as were the Wolof, Mandinka and Fulani of the Senegambian Zone.

In the fourth and final section of this second chapter, we introduced and discussed thirteen separate pieces of European and American art, in which the eleven supply zones were depicted. Some of the twelve artists of these paintings and prints were French, some were English, and some were Americans. At the end of this chapter, we described thirteen pieces of art, ten of which pertain to the eleven supply zones discussed earlier in this chapter, while the final three images were representations of the "tight-packing" method and the *Speculum Orum*.

We shall now turn to Chapter 3, in which the slave forts and castles in West Africa, from the seventeenth to the nineteenth centuries, is the subject matter for this chapter.

Chapter Three: Slave Forts and Castles—Fifteenth to Nineteenth Centuries

Evidence of change during the post-European contact period is not confined to Ghana. Archeological data from northeastern Sierra Leone still being analyzed at the present time provide evidence of significant change during the eighteenth and nineteenth centuries. Settlements of Limba, Yalunka and Kuranko dating to this period were commonly surrounded by a variety of fortifications, including earthen walls, entrenchments, hedges, or thorn bushes, and stockades of living trees.

—Christopher DeCorse, *West African Archeology and the Atlantic Slave Trade*

Is it now evident that there is not a man in the Kingdom, who in proportion to his rank in the community, does not more or less partake of the Benefits of the African Company's Forts and Castles in Africa?

—Benjamin Peter Smith, *The Importance of the African Company's Forts and Settlements Considered* (1745)

Whoever frees a Muslim Slave, Allah will save the parts of his body from Hell Fire, in the same way that he has freed the parts of the Slave's body.

—Abu Hurayra, *Hadith*, Vol. I, #694 (Author's translation)

Introduction

The principal aims of this third chapter are the following: First, to make some general remarks about the phenomenon of slave coffles in Africa in the fifteenth to the nineteenth centuries. The coffle, from the Arabic word *Kafila*, which means "caravan," were the queues of African slaves brought to the coast of Africa and then transported to the New World.

The second aim of this third chapter is to explore several dozen slave forts and castles that existed for the housing of slaves until exported to the Caribbean and the Americas. All tolled, European powers in the fifteenth to the nineteenth centuries built approximately one hundred slave forts and castles, fifty alone in the Gold Coast Supply Zone of Ghana. In the main section of this third chapter, we shall speak specifically about fifty to sixty of these slave forts and castles, according to the supply zones from which they came. As we shall see, in each of our supply zones, as outlined in Chapter Two, there were forts and castles built by European powers. Building began in the 1480s by the Portuguese, which continued up to the beginning of the twentieth century when the Prussians built three slave castles in Namibia on the coast of southwest Africa.

In the final section of this third chapter, we shall introduce and discuss several pieces of art that were produced to depict these African slave coffles and slave forts and castles. We move then to slave coffles in Africa.

Slave Coffles in Africa

The slave coffle was a means by which African slaves from the interior were brought to the coast for their transport, by way of the Middle Passage, to the New World. During tribal wars or other kinds of raids, slaves were brought to the coast by the use of what are called "Goree sticks." The Goree stick is a forked wooden stick or yoke that was used to tie together slaves in a queue, or coffle, when they were marched to the coasts of Africa, or to river ports.

The Goree sticks were made of hard, tropical woods, and weighed about seven kilograms. They were about two meters long, which kept the slaves a short distance from each other. The Goree stick was a much cheaper way of transporting slaves than the use of iron chains, as they were moved in America. Large numbers of slaves were accompanied by a small number of guards, or overseers. The coffle walked in a single file, or in pairs, through the forested interior of Africa to the coast.

The guards of these coffles usually carried weapons to keep the slaves in line. They often wore red caps and carried British muskets or swords. One French naval officer, in the Angolan region in the late eighteenth century, described how the captives appeared in their coffles:

> Each was attached to a forked branch which opens exactly to the size of a man's neck, so the head cannot pass through it. The forked branch is pierced with two holes, so that an iron pin comes across the neck of the slave...so that the smallest movement is sufficient to stop him and even to strangle him.[217]

This French officer described the forked Goree stick, the piercing holes beneath the chin joined together by an iron pin, as well as how easily a captive could be strangled in the event of one false movement. Contemporary songwriter, Karl Sanders, also gives a good description of a historical Goree stick. He observes:

> The "Slave Stick" is a tree branch, forked at one end, by which, with the help of a strip of leather, is fastened around a man's neck. It hangs down in front of the wretched creature doomed to carry it. If the branch is thick, the weight is considerable, and if to the end a block of stone could be attached, aiding in effectiveness as an instrument of torture. In some cases, the hands were also fastened, sometimes to the stick.[218]

In fact, many of these African slave traders attached metal hooks at the stem end of the Goree stick to which they could attach weight if a slave were unruly or rebellious. Indeed, Mr. Sanders, in the quote above, suggested that slaves who were unruly during these coffle marches in Africa were forced to carry heavy weights on the ends of their Goree sticks. They also would have their hands fastened behind their backs with hemp or rope.

A Prussian archeologist, Richard Lespius, saw the Goree stick in

---

217 Joseph Roger de Benoist, Historie de Gorree (Paris: Maissonneuve & Larose, 2003), p. 18. Pere Joseph Roger de Benoist was a French missionary, journalist and historian, mostly of French West Africa and the history of the Roman Catholic Church in sub-Saharan Africa, particularly Senegal.

218 Karl Sanders, born in South Carolina in 1963, is a member of the death metal band Nile. This poem is part of a song called "Lashed to the Slave Stick."

a slave coffle in Africa in use. He wrote:

> Each captive carried before him the stem of a tree, as thick as a large man's arm. It was about five or six feet long, and it terminated in a fork, into which the neck was fixed. The prongs of this fork were bound together by a cross-piece of wood, fastened with a strap. Some of their hands also, were tied fast to the handle of the fork; and in this condition they remained day and night. The stick can easily be driven into the ground firmly, for those who are unruly. Then the slave is attached to it, with the arms tied in position. The pain is said to be unbearable.[219]

Again Mr. Lespius emphasizes the weighing down of unruly or uncooperative captives, that the captives' hands were secured behind their backs, and that any slave could easily be driven to the ground, making sure the Europeans and their African agents stayed in control of the coffle.

Vautier Golding, in his book *The Story of David Livingstone*, describes Livingstone coming upon a long file of slaves, or an African slave coffle. Mr. Golding tells us this about Livingstone's discovery of a slave coffle in Africa:

> He [Livingstone] has halted his party in a village for rest and food, when suddenly a long file of eighty-four slaves came around the hillside towards them. The Captives, mostly women and children, were roped together with thongs of raw hide, but some of the men had their necks fixed in a "Goree," or forked-stick. The back of the neck was thrust into the fork, and the two prongs were joined by a bar of iron under the chin, while a Slaver walked behind, holding the shaft of the stick, ready to wring the poor slave's neck at the first sign of escape. Worn out with pain, misery, and fatigue,

219 Richard Lespius, quoted in "Lashed to the Slave Stick" lyrics, mentioned above. Karl Richard Lespius (1810–1884) was a pioneering Prussian Egyptologist and linguist.

> the hapless slaves limped and staggered beneath their loads. The Slavers were decked out with red caps and gaudy finery. They marched jauntily along, blowing tin horns and shouting, as though they had just won some sort of noble victory.[220]

Several points from Golding's account of Livingstone must be pointed out. First, the captives were mostly women and children. Secondly, the men, who were more likely to escape, are attached to Goree sticks. Third, these slaves can very easily be punished if they begin to be out of line if you pardon the pun. Fourth, the slaves carried goods on their heads, or in their arms, which presumably belonged to the African slave traders.

Fifth, overseers wore red caps. Sixth, they played tin horns to announce the arrival of the coffle. And finally, there were very few guards who accompanied the eighty-four captives of the queue, but they did carry powerful weapons.

Gardo Baquaqua, a slave from the Dahomey Kingdom in contemporary Benin, in his autobiography, speaks of being attached to a Goree stick. Sylviane Diouf speaks of this experience of Baquaqua, when she writes, "His first buyer had secured him in a traditional manner: a six foot branch with two prongs crossed the back of Baquaqua's neck and was fastened with an iron bolt."[221] Diouf describes Baquaqua's Goree stick and then goes on to explain about the Goree stick and the coffle:

> In the caravans, each branch was then attached to the neck of the captive in front, ..."so that they formed a single line, a chain in which each one dragged by the head the one who followed him...If a captive tried to escape, he had to carry the long branch in front of him; otherwise, it would be stuck in the ground or the bush-

220 Vautier Golding, The Story of David Livingstone (London: Yesterday's Classics, 2007), p. 77. Arthur Vautier Golding (1828–1888) was a British historian and biographer, including that of David Livingstone.

221 Sylviane Diouf, Servants of Allah (New York: NYU Press, 2013), p. 65. Mohomah Gardo Baquaqua (1828–1857) was a native of Zoogoo in West Africa, a tributary of the Bergon Kingdom.

es, preventing him from walking, let alone running.[222]

Dorugu Kwage Adamu, a Hausa slave born in Central Sudan, was captured in his homeland in 1839 at the age of seventeen. Later, he was taken to Zinder, where a Kanuri slave trader purchased him. German scholar, James Francis Schon (1803–1889), a missionary in Sierra Leone, recorded Dorugu's experience in an African coffle, complete with Goree sticks. The Rev. Schon recorded Dorugu as saying:

> We went along and passed another town near to our own. They took the people there. I think we were then about four hundred; so we went along and they set the town on fire.[223]

Dorugu, whose account was published by James Schon in the latter's *Magana Hausa,* speaks of his coffle picking up slaves as it marched to the coast of Africa. James Frederick Schon also wrote other works, including a grammar of the Hausa language (1842), his *Journals of Explorations Up the Niger* (1841), his *Dictionary of the Hausa Language* (1876), as well as dictionaries of both the Igbo and Mende languages. In fact, Dr. Schon was one of the foremost nineteenth–century scholars of West African languages.

These slave coffles brought the African captives to slave forts and castles on the coast. They were often housed in dungeons there until a ship arrived to transport them to the New World. Generally, there were separate dungeons for men and women. The men were most often kept underground. The women's dungeon was usually on the ground floor.

Officers were housed on the second floor of most of these slave castles and forts, as well as the administrative offices. When there was a third floor, the governor of the colony often lived and worked there, as in the Cape Coast Castle, for example.

Those slaves who misbehaved were placed in what was called "The Hole." It was a dark, damp, cell with poor ventilation and no bathroom facilities. There were no windows, no bathing, and slaves ate and

222 Ibid. Dorugu Kwage Adamu was born in Dawagaram in the Central Sudan. He was kidnapped there at the age of seventeen.

223 Dorugu, quoted in James Frederick Schon, Magana Hausa (London: Society for the Promotion of Christian Knowledge, 1885), p. 43.

slept in the same room. A channel in the floor carried waste away from the hole. The floor was covered with urine and waste. Many times, the slaves kept there starved to death or died from disease.

Judith Graham, of the *New York Times*, describes the state of these rebels. She tells us:

> The fate of those who rebel were sent to the condemned cell, or the Hole, a small black room with a small hole in one wall, where they were starved to death...Women were beaten and chained to cannon balls in the courtyard.[224]

Ms. Graham also describes entering the dungeon at Elmina Castle in Ghana. She tells us:

> We entered an underground tunnel through which slaves passed when they left Elmina. At the end of the tunnel, there is a narrow opening, which led to the beach, where canoes took the captives to ships at anchor.[225]

The ramp to the male dungeon at Elmina goes more than ten feet underground. Below, there are four black rooms with a stale, acrid smell. Under the large arched roofs, bats fly about. Some stones bear circular scratches, perhaps made by a desperate desire to leave their marks in Africa. From here, there was no escape for the fifteen hundred slaves the castle held when it was full.

Many of these European slave forts and castles had a door behind which was a narrow hallway that led to waiting slave ships. A skull and crossbones marked many of these wooden portals. The name for many of these portals was "The Door of No Return," through which captives left the African continent, most for good.

Several pieces of art are extant depicting slave coffles and Goree

---

224 Ibid. James Frederick Schon (1803–1889) was born in Baden, Germany. Later he became an explorer for the British government in Africa. He also wrote a number of dictionaries and grammars on African languages.

225 Judith Graham, "Ghana's Slave Castles," New York Times, November 25, 1990.

sticks in Africa. One image of a slave coffle from western Sudan, from 1879–1881, is published in J. W. Buel's *Heroes of the Dark Continent* published in New York in 1890.[226] The image shows a line of men and women lashed together by ropes guarded by a mounted slave trader. The caption, which is misleading in Portuguese, says, "Victims of the Portuguese Slave Hunters" when, in fact, the image was taken and made by the French.[227]

A second image published in the *Anti-Slavery Reporter* from July to August of 1892 shows a Portuguese coffle from Southeast Africa. Twenty-four slaves, both men and women, are queued together by Goree sticks. Seven guards carrying rifles accompany the coffle. A few of the women carry bundles on their heads. From this site, the Dutch transported thousands of slaves from the second half of the seventeenth century on.

A third image of a slave coffle comes from Central Africa in 1861. The image shows children and adults making their way from the African interior to the coast. It is interesting that although three of the twelve slaves in the queue are small children, they appear not to have received any special treatment by the two guards who carry long spears about the size of a javelin.[228]

David and Charles Livingstone, in their 1865 book published in London called *A Narrative of an Expedition to the Zambesi and its Tributaries* included a sketch of a Goree stick in the text. It is about six feet long and has the typical Y-shape of the device. Another illustration of an African Goree stick appears in an illustration by William A. Aery called *Caravane d'esclaves.* It shows a coffle of five slaves connected by Goree sticks accompanied by one overseer. The overseer is equipped with a knife at his belt and a five-foot-long spear. The slaves are dressed in loincloths.[229]

226 Ibid.

227 J. W. Buel, "Slave Coffle from the Western Sudan," in Heroes of the Dark Continent (New York, 1890). James W. Buel (1849–1920) was an English adventure writer and was the author of over thirty books. He was a professional writer and illustrator from St. Louis. His other books include Land and Sea (1889) and the History of the Human Race also published in 1889.

228 "Portuguese Coffle," Antislavery Reporter, July–August 1892.

229 Coffle in Central Africa, 1861. This image is captioned Gang of

Later in the next chapter, we shall see that slave coffles were employed in the colonies and early states in North America, as well. Some of these, as we will show, were to transport slaves locally from ships to slave jails and slave pens in large towns into the Deep South to places like Natchez, Mississippi, and New Orleans, Louisiana.

This brings us to our analysis of about sixty or so slave forts and castles built by Europeans from the late fifteenth to the early twentieth centuries in Africa.

Slave Forts and Castles: 1483 to 1920

In the next several sections of this third chapter, we shall examine between fifty and sixty of these slave forts and castles that could be found in our eleven supply zones, as well as several that were not in these supply zones. We will begin by looking carefully at the Senegambian Zone. In Senegal and Gambia, from the middle of the seventeenth century until slavery was abolished in the early nineteenth century, there were five separate slave forts and castles in the region. The oldest of these was Fort Bayona on Saint Mary's Island. It was established by the Dutch in 1651 on the Gambia River.[230]

Fort Bayona was built under the rule of Duke Jakob Kettler (1610–1682) of Courlander. The fort was on St. Mary's Island at Dockyard Point, which was formerly known as "Banyon Point on the Gambia River." The fort was situated on an estuary to the Atlantic Ocean in what today would be Gambia.

A second slave fort in Senegambia was located on Goree Island off

---

Captives Met at Mbame's on Their way to Tette by William Anthony Aery. Beginning in 1906, Aery taught art and social science at the Hampton Normal and Agricultural Institute in Virginia.

230 David and Charles Livingstone, A Narrative of an Expedition to the Zambesi and its Tributaries. Also, William A. Aery, Caravane d'esclaves, Digital Public Library of the New York Public Library. David Livingstone (1813–1873) was a Scottish Congregationalist and pioneer medical missionary. Charles Livingstone (1821–1873) was a missionary and traveler and brother of David Livingstone. William A. Aery was a British explorer who eventually settled in Orange County, Virginia, where he married and became a tobacco farmer.

the coast of Senegal. The fort there was built by the British in 1786.[231] Fort James, in Gambia, was first established by the Courlanders and then the British. This is the slave fort from which Alex Haley's ancestor, Kunta Kinte, came in the mid-eighteenth century. In fact, the island is now named Kunta Kinte Island.[232] The name "Goree stick" came from this island. It was developed by a French mariner there, a man named Etienne Goree.

Another slave fort from the Senegambian Supply Zone was called Fort Louis. It existed in northwest Senegal on the mouth of the Senegal River. The French first established the fort in 1659. From that time until 1779, the fort changed hands nine times. The fort is now a UNESCO World Heritage Site.[233]

Another French fort called Fort Saint Joseph also was built on the southern bank of the Senegal River around 1800. By 1825, the fort was in ruin, and it was replaced by a factory built there by the French. Adriano Bilbi, in his *Systems of Vulnerable Geography* published in Edinburgh in 1842, gives a thorough description of Fort Saint Joseph at Bakel on the Senegal River, (p. 855).

Finally, in 1681, the French established a trading post at Albreda on the north bank of the Gambia River opposite James Island and the fort there. This marked the start of the Anglo-Franco rivalry for control over the River Gambia. In 1688, the War of the Grand Alliance broke out, which provided both powers to bring damage to their rival's trade in West Africa. In 1692, the British successfully captured the French settlement of Saint Louis on Goree Island, but the French quickly recovered the island.

Two other island bases on the Senegal River were built by the French, Fort Saint Joseph in the eighteenth century, and Bakel and Medine in the nineteenth. The fort at Bakel, mentioned above, was known

231 Liste Historischer Forts jund Tatos von Gambia. Bayona is now known as "Banjul."

232 James Fort in Gambia was first settled by the Portuguese in 1456. The British built Fort Bullen there in 1826, later to be named Fort James. It is now called Kunta Kinte Island.

233 Ibid. Fort Saint Louis, or Ndar as it was called by the local Wolofs, was a French slave fort near the mouth of the Senegal River in northwest Senegal, about two hundred miles north of Dakar, Senegal's capital.

as Saint Louis. It was heavily Muslim, while the French establishment on Goree Island was mostly Christian. Fort Saint Joseph was a square structure with two large bastions on the northwest and southeast corners of the fort where several cannons were placed. In 1825, Fort Saint Charles replaced Fort Saint Joseph on the site on the southern bank of the Senegal River.

In 1695, after the recapture of Goree Island, a French flotilla of six ships sailed up the River Gambia and attacked British Fort James. The garrison on Saint James Island was weakened by sickness, and the governor surrendered only after the firing of two shells at the fort. The French weakened the strength at the fort, but later the French African Company again occupied the island and planned to make repairs there.[234]

James Island on the north bank of the Gambia River today is called "Kunta Kinte Island." The seventeenth-century fort was about an hour's travel by boat from the capital Banjul. A fort was first established there by the Courlanders, who were dispossessed by Major Robert Holmes of the British Africa Company. Fort James was seized in 1667, after thirty-one of the thirty-two Englishmen of the garrison there were killed.

A pirate named Anderson ransacked Fort James in 1683, and the French reduced the site to ruins in 1695. The British recovered the fort on the Gambia in 1713, and the Welsh pirate Howel Davis plundered it in 1718. Three years later, the British again took control of Fort James. It remained in British hands until the French destroyed the site in 1778. In 1779, Fort James was returned to the British.

In the end, control of Fort James was returned to the British under something called the Treaty of Rijswijjin, also known as the Treaty of Utrecht, in 1797, before any of the repairs could be carried out. Fort James was rebuilt between 1798 and 1801 to the same design as before. War broke out again in 1802, and this put an end to the British repairs. The fort was attacked again and ransomed by the French in 1802, damaged by fire in 1804, suffered a mutiny in 1808, and finally captured

234 William Laird Clowes, The Royal Navy: A History of its Earliest Times to the Present (London, 1898), vol. 3, pp. 173, 187–188. Clowes (1856–1905) was a British journalist and historian. He is best known for his history of the Royal Navy.

and demolished in 1809.[235] In the meantime, France and Great Britain constantly fought over the lands connected to the Senegal and Gambia rivers from approximately 1650 until around 1825.

Once back in the hands of the British, Fort James was again rebuilt from 1714 until 1717. In 1719, it was captured by the pirate Howell Davis, who visited the governor, posing as a merchant. His men took the fort by surprise and looted it. In 1725, disaster struck again on the island when powder magazines exploded at the fort.[236]

Captain Howell Davis, or Hywell Davies, (1690–1719) was a Welsh pirate, although his career as a pirate lasted a mere eleven months from July of 1718 until June of 1719 when his ship was ambushed, and he was killed. Davis had four ships of his own. He commandeered at least fifteen British and French vessels during those eleven months.

After Davis lost Fort James, it was again repaired, and an annex was added called "The Spur." Fort James was a two-story building built on the southeast side of the island. The building also contained storehouses and accommodation for the garrison. The officers slept on the second floor. Their quarters had a beautiful parquet floor. The Spur annex, however, did not last long. It was demolished in 1750. By that time, erosion had begun to take its toll on the island's shore, especially on the south end. The upright battery of cannon was now under water. After the explosion of 1725, the powder magazines were moved to a better place, under the east bastion.[237]

In the mid-eighteenth century, a cistern was built at the fort between the east and north bastions. The new cistern was much larger than the previous facility for water storage, but it affected the fort's defenses. Because it was between two bastions, it blocked some of the flanking fire across those bastions. The new cistern, however, was constructed with angled exteriors so that there was no dead ground. There was also a large parapet around the top by which soldiers could fire

235 See Note 14.

236 The Treaty of Utrecht was signed after meetings in Utrecht on March and April of 1713. The treaty was signed by Spain, Great Britain, France, Portugal, Savoy, and the Dutch Republic.

237 Howel Davis (1690–1719) was a Welsh pirate whose pirating career lasted only eleven months. His ships were called the Cudagan, Buck, St. James, and the Rover.

their arms.[238]

The French built another fort on the Senegal River. It was originally known as Fort Saint Joseph. Later, it was referred to as Fort Bakel, after the name of its location. Bakel was on the left bank of the Senegal River about forty miles from the Malian border. People there were mostly Mandinka in the eighteenth century, with minorities of Wolof and Fulbe. The fort was the site where the upper and lower Senegal Rivers come to a confluence at Bakel.

The Portuguese also built a slave fort on Cape Verde Island, seven hundred miles west of the city of Dakar. The Cidade Velho was constructed in 1462. The city considers itself to be African and European. For many years, the fort at Cape Verde Island acted as a staging area where slaves were brought before the beginning of the Middle Passage voyages.

In the Niger Valley Supply Zone, in the town of Badagry, there was a trading post and then a fort. Olaudah Equiano was likely shipped from this Nigerian port. Badagry is one of the oldest cities in modern Africa. Some say it was founded around the year 1425. It is the second-largest commercial city in the state of Lagos. The city is bordered on the south by the Bay of Guinea and surrounded by lakes, creeks and islands.[239]

This ancient town of Badagry served mainly the Oyo Empire, which comprised of Yoruba and Ogu peoples. Today, the Aworis and Egun are primarily the people who live there. In the 1500s, slaves were transported from West Africa to America through Badagry. Some report that the city exported no fewer than 550,000 African slaves. Slaves from there were also sent to Europe, to South America and to the Caribbean.[240]

Slaves transported from Badagry came mostly from neighboring Benin and Togo, as well as other parts of Nigeria. The Palace of the

---

238 See Note 14.

239 Ibid. The Portuguese discovered Cape Verde Island in 1456 under the direction of Henry the Navigator, a Venetian sailor and explorer.

240 "Badgary," in Wesleyan Juvenile Offering (London: Wesleyan Mission-House, July 8, 2007). The Oyu and Ogu, also called the Egon, are ethnic people of the Niger River Valley.

Akran, which was originally the slave quarters, is still standing. The Vlekte Slave Market was where slaves were bought and sold, and the cannons of war, chains, etc., can be found in a museum there. A plaque, officially commemorating the Badagry slave route, was erected on the site on May 18, 1999.[241] This brings us to the Sierra Leone Supply Zone, where the British established another slave fort in 1670.

The Portuguese also built slave forts at São Tomé and Príncipe on the Bight of Bonny. When the Portuguese arrived there in the late fifteenth century, São Tomé, Portuguese for "Saint Thomas," was uninhabited. It originally grew sugar cane that gave way to coffee and cocoa growing. The fort there was constructed in the 1490s. In fact, the national language is still Portuguese.

In that year, the British Africa Company built a slave fort on Bunce Island located in Freetown Harbor. Thousands of slaves came from farther inland to the Island of Bunce and the slave fort there. This fort was the major slave exporter in the Sierra Leone Supply Zone, mostly from the sixteenth to the eighteenth centuries.[242]

Another slave fortress in the Sierra Leone Supply Zone was the Spanish settlement at Fort Lomboko. It was established by explorer Pedro Blanco who has been called the "Rothschild of Slavery."[243] The fort at Lomboko was featured in Steven Spielberg's 1997 film *Amistad*, which was based on the true story of the 1839 mutiny aboard the slave ship *La Amistad*.[244] At any rate, Blanco built a slave compound with several buildings in the early nineteenth century and then went into the

---

241 Ibid. The Royal Palace of Mobee of Badgary still survives. It is located near the city of Lagos, Nigeria. There is also a museum there. The traditional name of Badgary is Gbagle. It was situated between the city of Lagos and the border with Benin at Seme.

242 Ibid.

243 Joseph Opala, Bunce Island (Historical Summary: Decorse, 2007). Joseph Opala, born 1950, is an American historian, noted for establishing the link between indigenous people of the West African nation of Sierra Leone and the Gullah People of the Low Country.

244 Hugh Thomas, The Slave Trade (New York: Simon and Schuster, 1997), pp. 100–101. Thomas (born 1931) is an English author of history and novels. He is also a member of the House of Lords. See Kirkus Review essay of the "Slave Trade" from September 1, 1997.

slave business.

Two other slave forts in the Sierra Leone Supply Zone were constructed by Europeans, both in the country of Guinea-Bissau. The first is called Cacheu on the northwest coast of Guinea-Bissau. It is called "The place where we rest" in the local Papel language. Cacheu was the center of the Portuguese Upper Guinea from the sixteenth to the early eighteenth centuries. The slave fort at Cacheu was built in the sixteenth century. This site was also used as a place to keep *Degredados*, Portuguese for condemned people, usually who have committed violent crimes. Ironically, there is now an important nature park there at Cacheu.

The other Portuguese slave fort in the Sierra Leone Zone was at Bafata. It was a three-story, white stone building with square bastions. The fort was built there in 1765. Today, it remains a tourist attraction. The fort also has a "Door of No Return" marked by a skull and crossbones. The *Museum of Foreign Literature and Science*, from a January of 1842 edition, volume eight, describes in some detail the fort at Bafata. [p. 221.]

A trading post and slave facility also existed at Port Timbuktu in the Niger Valley Delta. It stood at the northeast end of the delta. From there, the Niger River flows east and then southeast before entering the country of Niger. The Niger River then passes along the border with Benin. Then it flows into Nigeria, where it turns south, eventually meeting the Atlantic.

The Niger Delta, where the river meets the Atlantic, forms an important ecological and commercial zone. The Niger Delta is also an important site for petroleum production in present-day Nigeria. Oil is one of the most important exports of present-day Nigeria. It is the largest producer of oil in Africa and the eleventh largest petroleum producer in the world.

A number of scholars have noted the benign treatment the enslaved people received in Timbuktu in present-day Mali and thus the Niger Valley Supply Zone. Frenchman René Caillé, for example, remarks: "In general, the slaves at Timbuktu were better treated than in other countries."[245] Henri Duvertier, the first European man to make a

245 Ibid. August Rene Caille (1799–1838) was a French explorer who

detailed description of the Tuareg people and their role in enslavement, says of slavery at Timbuktu, "It was very mild and had little in common with the forced labor of the colonies."[246]

The Tuareg are a people who inhabit the Saharan region of North Africa. They can be found in Niger, Mali, Libya, Algeria and Burkina Faso. The word "Tuareg" is an Arabic term that means "abandoned by Allah." They call themselves the Imohag or "Free Men." The most striking attributes of the Tuareg is the indigo veil worn by men, but not by women. Thus, some call them the "Blue Men of the Sahara."

The French built two other slave forts on the Falemme River that arises in North Guinea and flows north/northeast to Mali, forming part of the border between Guinea and Senegal. The first of the two was Fort Saint Pierre of Kaynura, on the east bank of the Falemme. It was erected in 1714 by French engineers and soldiers. The other French fort on the Falemme was called Fort Senudebu. It was built on a small levee overlooking Fort Saint Joseph.

Fort Senudebu was constructed in 1845 but not occupied until 1847. One of the most interesting things about these structures on the Falumme River is that they were made almost entirely of mud. This was also true of another fort built by the Portuguese called Saint Angelo, three kilometers from the city of Kannor in India. Saint Angelo, which faces the Arabian Sea, did business with Arab slave traders beginning in the sixteenth century. The massive triangular fort, replete with moat and flanking bastions, was built by Portuguese Viceroy Dom Francisco de Almeida in 1505.

The Angolan Supply Zone was situated in southwest Africa. At the time, it had a diverse landscape, including beaches, forest, savannah and desert. Angola's current population is mostly of Bantu origin, as the result of an ancient and complex history. The slave trade in Angola was an important part of that history from the fifteenth to the nineteenth century. In that period, Africans were exchanged for arms,

---

left France for Senegal at the age of sixteen.

246 Sudarson Raghavan, "Timbuktu's Slaves Liberated," in Washington Post, June 1, 2013. Raghavan is the Washington Post's correspondent in Cairo. Rene Caille (1799–1838) was a French explorer and first European to return alive from Timbuktu.

gun powder, alcohol, glassware and cowrie shells, originally from the Maldives in the Indian Ocean.[247] Indeed, much of the Angolan slave trade was conducted using overland slave coffles from East Africa to Luanda, Benguela and Cabina in Angola.

Earlier, we have suggested that Antonio, or Anthony Johnson, one of the first black men in Virginia, was from the Angolan Supply Zone—and possibly Mattheus de Sousa, the first black man in Maryland, as well.

The most important Angolan slave fort was the "Fortaleza de Sao Paulo" in Luanda. Constructed in 1576, it became the administrative center of the colony by 1627. For many years, it was like a self-contained town, protected by high walls with cannons. Until 1975, the fort remained the center of the Portuguese armed forces in Angola.[248] The Portuguese shipped over four million captives to Brazil by the end of the Atlantic slave trade.

Many of the Africans taken from the Angolan Supply Zone to the Americas ended their journey in Brazil. The Portuguese presence in that country was concentrated in ports to the north and south of Kwanza. Angola's two main posts on the coast were in Luanda and Benguela, where there were forts and coastal military posts.

A third slave fort was attempted to be built three times by the Portuguese in Angola, on the mouth of the Congo River, at the city of Cabinda, with little success. Finally, the Royal Africa Company did establish a fort at Cabinda, between 1721 and 1723. Cabinda was called "Ngolo" by the local people, mostly the Woyo Tribe. Most of the slaves brought to Cabinda were from the interior of Africa. After the first quarter of the eighteenth century, the British sent a variety of slaves

---

247 Ibid. Henri Duvartier (1840–1892) was a French explorer of the Sahara Desert, where he made observations of the Tuareg people. The Tuareg are a Berber people who traditionally were pastoralists. They mostly live in the Sahara Desert. The Falemme River arises in North Guinea and flows north-northeast to southwest Mali. Fort Saint Pierre of Kaynura was erected by the French in 1714. It is on the east bank of the Falemme, opposite Fort Senudebu. These forts were characterized by cement floors and stone architecture. In addition to slaves, ceramics, glass, beads and metals were exported from these locations.

248 Hugh Thomas, The Slave Trade: The Story of the Atlantic Coast (New York: Touchstone Books, 1997), pp. 200–204.

shipped from Cabinda to several places in the New World, including the Chesapeake Bay region. In fact, the slave ship the *Echo*, also called the *Putnam*, traveled to Cabinda from the city of Baltimore for many voyages in the late 1850s.

Angola's waterways were known as *libambos*. They were crutial in the country's slave-trading history, carrying captives from the interior, by way of Goree sticks and coffles, to the Atlantic.

Slavery in the Angolan Supply Zone began in the 1570s, when Friar Luis Brandao, the head of the Portuguese-run Luanda Jesuit College, wrote a letter to officials back in Portugal who had questioned the morality of enslaving Angolans. Fr. Brandao wrote at the time:

> We have been here ourselves for forty years and there have been many learned men here, and in the Province of Brazil, who never have considered the trade to be elicit.[249]

He goes on to say that some local chiefs may have enslaved some Africans, but at least the Portuguese baptized those slaves and converted them to Christianity. Nevertheless, Angola exported slaves at a rate of ten thousand a year by 1612.[250]

The Portuguese built a new port in Benguela in 1616 to expand the earlier facility of Father Brandao at Luanda. From 1617 until 1621, during the governorship of Luis Mendes de Vasconcellos, up to fifty thousand slaves were shipped from Angola to the Americas.

Slave forts, then, were built at both Luanda and Benguela. A civil war broke out in Angola between the Ndongo and the Portuguese-backed Imbangala. A combined force attacked the Kingdom of Ndongo at Kabasa. As a result, the Portuguese sold thousands of Kabasa residents, with thirty-six ships leaving Luanda in 1619, alone.[251]

From 1764 onwards, there was a gradual change from a slave-based economy to one based on the production of domestic consumption, and thus, the export of goods. By that time, slavery was

249 Ibid.

250 Friar Luis Brandao, Portas Ornamentados (Lisbon: Panorama, 1960), p. 111. Brandao served as bishop at the slave fort on Cape Verde Island in the 1580s, where he presided during the famine of 1582 there.

251 "Benguela," in Encyclopedia Brittanica, vol. 3, 2013, pp. 117–120.

on the wane there and no longer served such a central element of the economy.

In the sixteenth century, Luanda was the center of Portuguese presence in Angola. It was where the slave coffles would end up coming from the interior. Luanda still has many places of memory that were built or created by enslaved Africans. Ports, forts, churches, chapels, market places, government buildings and what were called *Quintaloes*, or "Slave Enclosers," their version of slave jails, all are still extant.

The church called *Igreja do Carmo*, for example, built in the seventeenth century, still stands in the Ingombotas section of Luanda. Many Quintaloes were also in this area to control the captives until transport to the Americas.[252] The *Baleizao* in Luanda, which still stands, was one of the places where Africans were gathered and sold. The *Morro da Cruz,* a chapel built in the eighteenth century, still exists. There is a slavery museum there now, but in the eighteenth century, thousands of enslaved Africans were embarked onto Portuguese slave ships to travel on the Middle Passage.[253]

The chapel still stands alone facing the sea. The area around it is now barren, with no trees and little fertile land there. The area is now a symbol of the isolation and misery caused by the slave trade. In Benguela, the *Nossa Senhora do Populo*, an eighteenth-century church still stands. Benguela also had a number of *Quintaloes* that were employed to hold slaves until their shipment to the New World. The Portuguese built Fort Sao Miguel in Luanda, Angola, in 1576.

After the independence of Brazil from Portugal in 1822, by then four million slaves had been brought to South America. Fourteen years later, in 1836, Portuguese authorities in Lisbon abolished Portugal's overseas involvement in the slave trade.[254] From the 1620s to the early 1830s, Portugal sent thousands of slaves to North America, including

252 The Kingdom of Ndango, or "Dongo," was an early African state, beginning in the sixteenth century. It was one of the most powerful vassal states of the Kongo Empire.

253 The Igreja do Carmo remains one of the most important national monuments of Angola and is a fine example of the Rococco style.

254 Ibid. Fort Saint Miguel was built by Paulo Dias de Novais in 1576. By 1627, it had become the administrative center of the colony. It was a major outlet for slaves traveling to Brazil.

many to the colonies of the Chesapeake Bay region.

Indeed, earlier, in Chapter One, we argued that the Portuguese slave Antonio, who changed his name to Anthony Johnson, was from the Angolan Supply Zone. Earlier, we suggested that Mattheus de Sousa may have been from the Portuguese colony in Mozambique, and thus from the East African Supply Zone, as well.

One final point about these slave forts in Angola is that the Portuguese, in general, brought captives from neighboring Benin and the Congo, in addition to slaves found in Angola. At both Luanda and Benguela, the Portuguese shipped millions of African captives from its African ports to Brazil, to America, and to the Caribbean.

In the East African Supply Zone, slave castles and forts were built in Kenya, Ethiopia, and Egypt. Fort Jesus was built by the Portuguese between 1593 and 1596, on the island of Mombasa. From the air, one can see that Fort Jesus was constructed in the form of a man. Between 1630 and 1870, Fort Jesus changed hands nine times.[255]

Fort Jesus is located on the edge of a coral reef overlooking the entrance to the old Port of Mombasa. The fort was built mostly to protect the trade routes east to India. It was dedicated on April 11, 1596. The sultan of Mombasa was the ruler of the area at the time of the construction of the fort. It was designed by Italian architect Giovanni Cairati. Mombasa became Portugal's main trading center from the East African Supply Zone.[256]

In 2011, Fort Jesus was recognized as a UNESCO World Heritage Site, and as "One of the best-preserved and amazing examples of the sixteenth-century Portuguese military architecture."[257]

Fort Usher in Zimbabwe is a second slave fort built in East Africa. It is on the Mzingwane River, which rises at the fort. The building has 400,000 square kilometers of space. It is located in the Mashonaland Province of Zimbabwe. In the eighteenth century, the fort served as a

255 Portugal was one of the first European nations to ban slavery in 1819 after Spain (1811), Sweden (1813), the Netherlands (1814), and France (1817). Fort Jesus of Mombasa was constructed in 1593. The fort, which still exists, is across the coastline near Old Town. There is now a museum there.

256 Thomas, p. 317.

257 Ibid. Giovanni Battista Cairati (15?–1596) was an Italian military architect from Milan who served in India.

slave fort where captives were shipped to India and sometimes west to the Americas, around the southern tip of Africa, or traveled by land to West Africa.[258]

Three other significant slave forts and castles were constructed in East Africa: two in Egypt and one in Ethiopia. The latter is known as the Fasil Ghebbi Castle in the Gondar region of Ethiopia and built by Emperor Fasilides of Ethiopia, who ruled from 1632 until 1667. In 1979, the site was designated by UNESCO as a World Heritage Site.[259]

In the sixteenth and seventeenth centuries, the Castle of Fasil Ghebbi was the residence of the Emperor and his successors. The castle is in the Amhara National Regional State in the North Gondar Administrative Zone of the Federal Republic of Ethiopia. The castle compound includes eight separate buildings: the castle, a palace, a banquet hall, the bath of the Emperor, the thermal area, and three monasteries and churches.[260] In 1979, the Fasil Ghebbi complex was recognized as a UNESCO World Heritage Site, as well.

The Cairo Citadel, also known as the Qaitbay Castle, is a fort/castle built by Sultan Qaitbay in 1480, on the island of Pharos, near the site of the original Light House of Alexandria. The citadel is located on the eastern side of the northern tip of Pharos, at the mouth of the Eastern Harbor of Alexandria. The structure, after the fifteenth century, has been renovated several times, including efforts by Sultan Al-Ghouri and later by the ruler, Muhammad Ali, when he became head of Egypt in 1805.[261] For a short time, at the close of the seventeenth century,

---

258 Ibid., p. 320. Fort Usher in Zimbabwe is now the Saint Andrew's School.

259 Fort Ussher in Accra, Ghana, was built by the Dutch in 1649. See: Albert Van Dantzig, Forts and Castles in Ghana (Accra: Seduvpug, 1999). Also see: Dantzig, "English Bosman and Dutch Bosman: A Comparison of Texts," in History of Africa, vol. 2, January 1975, pp. 185–216.

260 Richard Pankhurst, "Fasil Ghebbi Castle," in The Ethiopians: A History (Oxford: Blackwells, 2001), pp. 109ff. "Fasil Ghebbi" means "Royal Enclosure" in the language in Ethiopia. It was built in the seventeenth century.

261 Ibid. Qaitbay Castle is an enormous white stone structure built in 1477 by Sultan Al-Ashraf Sayif al-Din Q'ait Bay.

there is some evidence that black slaves were kept at the citadel.[262]

The Cairo Citadel remained neglected until 1904 when the Ministry of Defense restored the upper floors of the structure. King Farouk wanted to turn the citadel into a royal rest house, so he ordered another renovation at that time. After the revolution of 1952, the Egyptian Navy turned the building into a maritime museum. One final restoration was completed in 1984 when the Egyptian Department of Antiquities announced an ambitious plan to restore the structure.[263]

Fort Sao Sebastio was built by the Dutch in Mozambique beginning in 1558, though it was not complete until a hundred years later. This East African fort was near the Nossa Senhora de Baluarte Church or Chapel, which was erected in 1522. The chapel is considered the earliest European building in the Southern Hemisphere. One final East African slave fort was called fort Lourenco Marques after the Portuguese navigator by that name. Along with Antonio Caldeira, they were sent by Portugal in 1544 to explore the area of Mozambique and to build a fort for keeping slaves.

This Mozambique fort was later called Fort de Nosso Senhora de Conceicao. It still stands today in the middle of the city of Maputo, the capital city of Mozambique. The square-shaped fort, with two large bulwarks, was used for storing slaves until they could be shipped from the island, south, around Africa, or east to Arabia and India.

The fort had two dungeons, one above ground for women and the other below ground that housed male slaves. The fort officers and administrators lived on the second floor, as was the case in many European slave forts and castles in Africa in the colonial period.[264] The

---

262 William Lyster, The Cairo Citadel: A History (Berkeley: Palm Press, 1993). William Saurin Lyster (1828–1880) was born in Dublin and became an operetical entrepeneur throughout most of the nineteenth century. In the ancient world, the lighthouse on the island of Pharos was one of the Seven Wonders of the World. In 1909, German illustrator Herman Thiersch completed a sketch of what he believed it looked like.

263 Ibid.

264 Ibid. Maputo, formerly known as Lourenco Marquis, is the capital

Portuguese first arrived at Delagoa Bay in Mozambique in 1502, where they conducted trade in ivory. The Netherlands was the first to establish a fort on the bay in 1721 on the site of present-day Maputo. The Dutch East Africa Company established a trading factory and fort in 1730, but they soon abandoned it shortly thereafter.

Finally, the Portuguese first arrived in Madagascar in 1506. By 1671, the French built a slave fort there called Fort Dauphine on the Dauphine River. In 1703, the French took control of the fort. In Michael Gomez's book, *Exchanging Our Country Marks*, he suggests that a number of slaves traveled from Madagascar to the Virginia colony/state in the early years of the transatlantic slave trade.[265]

Professor Michael A. Gomez also suggests the Malagasy people are "yellowish" and have features that resemble people from Southeast Asia and Indonesia. In fact, one narrative from the MSGenWeb website includes a quotation of one Virginia woman about her roots in Madagascar. This source tells us:

> My grandma was from Virginia. When she died, she was one hundred and ten years old. She said she was a Molly Gasca negro. That was the race to which she belonged. She did look awfully different from any of the rest of us.[266]

Another slave outpost in Madagascar was called Fort de Rocher. This fort did business with Massachusetts ships in 1671, when they

---

and largest city of Mozambique. It is known as the "City of Acacias," for the trees that grow there.

265 Fort de Nosso Senhora de Conceicao was built by the Portuguese at the end of the sixteenth century. It changed hands several times, and then it was rebuilt by the Portuguese from 1701 until 1740, mostly to defend the town there from pirates. Laurenco Marques was a sixteenth-century Portuguese trader and explorer who settled in Mozambique. Antonio Caldeira was a Portuguese Evangelical Christian working in Mozambique.

266 Fort Dauphin, on the southeast coast of Madagascar, is now called Taolagnaro. The French developed their first settlement there in 1642. It was the headquarters of the American Lutheran missionaries who worked in southern Madagascar in the nineteenth century. The fort was located in the southeast of Madagascar.

dealt both with the French at the fort and with the Makos or Masomboka people in northern Madagascar. The chieftain of the Masomboka was called an *Ampenjaka*. He appears to have been the real organizer for slaves leaving Fort de Rocher, in Madagascar, to the New World.

There was also in the East African Supply Zone, the Fort de Maures on the island of Moyella in Ethiopia, The Dutch and then the French built facilities there, beginning in the 1680s. French slave captain, Jean Barbot, at that time, writes of establishing trade with the natives there. He remarks:

> We had a conference with the king and the principal natives of the country about trade which lasted from three o'clock until night without any result. They insisted on having thirteen bars of iron for each male slave and ten bars for the women. They objected that slaves are now scarce because of the many ships that had exported vast quantities of late. Four days later, we had another conference and the next day the trade had been completed.[267]

The French explorer, Mr. Barbot, indicates that he negotiated with local chiefs, that these negotiations were difficult and protracted, and that they finally came to an agreement after four days of haggling.

There is also extant a slave fort in Zanzibar, in Tanzania. The fort is known there as *Miji Mkongwe*, or "Old Town" in Swahili. The fort has an eclectic architecture with Arab, Persian, Indian and European influences. The fort in Zanzibar was built by the Omanis. There was also a brisk slave trade in Somalia from the time of the early Sultanates called Adal and Ifat.

For the most part, the Arabs and Somalis, who were in business together in Somalia, brought their slaves from Sudan in the interior to the coast. By the mid-eighteenth century, most of Somalia was Islamic, and the country remains that way today.

In addition to these twenty or so slave forts and castles from the

---

267 Gomez, p. 17–18. The famous lighthouse at Fort de Rocher in Madagascar still survives. The Fort de Maures is located near the town of Mega, between Mayole and Yabelo in Ethiopia.

supply zones of Senegambia, the Niger River Valley, the Sierra Leone Zone and from the East African Supply Zone, there were nearly four dozen slave forts and castles in Ghana on the Gold Coast. The subject matter of those structures is the topic for the next section of this third chapter.

Slave Forts and Castles on the Gold Coast: Fifteenth to Eighteenth Centuries

Between 1482 and 1786, a myriad of slave forts and castles were erected over a 500-kilometer-long coastline of Ghana, from Keta in the east to Beyin on the west. Back then, Ghana was called the Gold Coast due to its vast resources of the yellow mineral, and these forts and castles served as fortifications against other foreign powers and local tribes.

The Portuguese first arrived on the Gold Coast in 1471. Prince Henry the Navigator sent ships to explore the west coast of Africa as early as 1418. They were intrigued by rumors of large quantities of gold and other minerals in the area, as well as ivory. They also were looking for a southern route to India, so they could circumvent the trading of Akan traders and establish a more direct route to the Orient. Another focus of the Portuguese was their Roman Catholicism and their desire to convert the Africans.

These motives also prompted the Portuguese to develop trade in Guinea. They made gradual progress down the western coast of Africa, with each voyage reaching a point further south than the last. After fifty years of exploration, the Portuguese finally reached Elmina in 1471, during the reign of King Alfonso the Fifth. By that time, Portuguese royalty seems to have lost interest in Africa, mostly because the returns were not what had been hoped. Thus, the Portuguese/African trading in Guinea was placed under the leadership of Fernao Gomes.

When Gomes reached Elmina, he discovered the thriving gold trade of which the Portuguese had been seeking. Gomes established relationships with local chiefs, clan leaders, as well as Arab and Berber traders. Indeed, it was Gomes who established the fortress at Elmina.

Upon its completion, Elmina was established as a proper city. A man named Diogo de Azambuja (1432–1518), a Portuguese nobleman and knight of the Order of Aviz, was named governor of the site. In fact, King Joao added the title "Lord of Guinea" to his noble titles. Elmina took on the military and economic importance of the Portuguese facility at Arguim Island on the southern edge of the Moorish empire.

At the height of the Portuguese gold trade in the early years of the sixteenth century, twenty-four thousand ounces of gold were exported annually from the Portuguese Gold Coast alone. This amounted to about 10 percent of the entire world's supply. The new fort at Elmina signified a permanent presence of European powers on the west coast of Africa. This also had considerable effects on Africans living in those areas. Hostilities among rival African groups arose, particularly after Portugal introduced firearms to the Africans.

These slave forts and castles on the Gold Coast were placed there strategically as links in the trade routes first established by the Portuguese in the late fifteenth century. They were the first Europeans on the Gold Coast. These forts and castles thereafter were seized, attacked, exchanged, sold, and abandoned during nearly four centuries of struggle between European powers for domination over Ghana, or the Gold Coast.

By 1500, the European interests concentrated more on the slave trade in light of the growing demand for labor in the New World. Europeans in the slave forts and castles began to imprison slaves who now were seen as another commodity. These majestic fortresses along Ghana's coast housed dark dungeons, overflowing with misery and despair, right up until the early 1800s when slavery began to be abolished among the European nations.

By the mid-eighteenth century, the height of the West African slave trade, Europeans built more than fifty slave castles and forts along the two-hundred-mile stretch between Ghana's capital Accra and the City of Abidjan in the Ivory Coast. Today, around thirty of these structures are still standing. Some lie in ruins, a few have guest houses, several have become prisons, and one, the Christianborg Castle, has a lighthouse. This latter structure is the seat of government in present-day Ghana, which won its independence from Britain in 1957. Writing in an edition of the *New York Times* on November 25, 1990, Judith Graham introduces slavery on the Gold Coast. She tells us:

> A few centuries ago the African slave trade thrived at the European-built castles and forts clustered on Ghana's southern coast. Today those fortresses reveal some of the horrors of West Africa's past.[268]

Ms. Graham continued her introduction:

> No other stretch of African coastline carries the scars of history as this one does. Along a 156-mile span, more than 25 stone structures remain as testaments to a slave trade that reached across the Gulf of Guinea to the Americas from the mid-1500s to the late 1800s.[269]

From the late fifteenth century to the middle of the eighteenth century, more than four dozen slave forts and castles were built on the coast of Ghana, or the Gold Coast. The oldest of these, the Elmina Castle, was built by the Portuguese in 1482, on the place of a town called *Amankwa* or *Amankwakurom*. This was the first sub-Saharan structure in Africa. The Dutch took over the site in 1640. Local Ahanta people seized it in 1694 and abandoned in 1840.[270]

Elmina Castle, built in 1482, is also called "Feitoria de Mina." Originally, the site was to be a trading post, but the castle eventually became involved in the Atlantic slave trade. It served as a depot for slaves, most of whom were eventually sold to the Americas. In 1979,

---

268 Jean Barbot, Barbot on Guinea (Paris: Hakluyt Society, 1991), p. 31. Barbot (1655–1712) was a French explorer and trader. For many years he worked for the Senegalese government in the Atlantic slave trade.

269 Judith Graham, "The Slave Fortresses of Ghana," New York Times, November 25, 1990. The Christiaborg Castle, also called the Osu Castle, complete with lighthouse, was built by the Norway-Denmark Federation around 1660.

270 Ibid.

the Elmina Castle was inscribed into the UNESCO World Heritage Sites.[271] In 1515, a second slave castle was built by the Portuguese on the Gold Coast at what was called Fort Saint Anthony.[272]

At the height of the slave trade, it is estimated that the Portuguese sent thirty thousand people a year to the New World.[273] The operation at Elmina became a model for future forts and castles. These structures were the final place that millions of Africans would see their homeland. To keep the forts and castles on the coast in operation, the dungeons had to constantly be replenished with a regular flow of Africans.

Elmina was also known as "San Jorge de Mina" or "Saint George of the Mines" because of the rich deposits of gold that existed in the supply zone. The Portuguese thus called the area on the coast of Ghana the Gold Coast. In the late fifteenth and early sixteenth centuries, the Portuguese had a monopoly there despite attempts by the Spanish, and later the French and British, to break that monopoly.

Twenty years after the establishment of the fort of Elmina, the storerooms were converted to dungeons. The building that once housed a Portuguese Catholic church became the slave market. By the eighteenth century, an estimated seventy thousand slaves were exported from Africa per year. Of those, about forty-one thousand came from West Africa, and about ten thousand a year came from Elmina.

A 1987 German film called "Cobra Verde" was filmed at Elmina Castle. It was directed by German-born Werner Herzog and starred German actor Klaus Kinski. The film is about a European slave trader in Africa and the Caribbean.

A second castle on the Gold Coast was called the Cape Coast Castle. This castle had a strategic location being constructed on a sheltered beach. The Portuguese built the first trade lodge there in 1555 and called it "Cabo Corso" or "Short Cape," which later was corrupted to Cape Coast. The Swedes built a permanent fort at the site in 1653. They

---

271 Tony Hyland, The Castle at Elmina: A Brief History (Accra: Department of Architecture, University of Science and Technology, 1971), p. 11. This work was originally a twenty-seven-page pamphlet published by the Ghana Museums and Monuments Board in Accra in 1972.

272 Ibid.

273 Ibid.

called it "Carolusburg" after King Charles X of Sweden. From 1555 to 1567, the Danes, the local Fetu chiefs, and the Dutch, each, in turn, captured Carolusburg for a time.[274]

This first lodge at the site of the Cape Coast Castle was built by Hendrik Caerloff (1621–1691) for the Swedish Africa Company. Earlier, Caerloff had worked for the Dutch West India Company. For them, he had risen to the rank of fiscal responsibility before employing himself with the Swedish under the direction of Louis de Geer.

The Cape Coast Castle was also the site of another "Door of No Return," a portal through which slaves were lowered into boats and then loaded like cargo on to large slave ships further out to sea. They would never set foot on their homelands again—a final goodbye to the African freedom they once knew. The Door of No Return is more like a "window" through which slaves departed and was a very small and narrow space.

Finally, the British fleet, led by Captain Holmes, took Carolusburg. The fort remained in English hands until the late nineteenth century, serving as the West African headquarters of the President of the Committee of Merchants and later as the Head of the Government. The Swedes built the Cape Coast Castle and eventually taken over by the British during the Seven Years War (1754 to 1763). The British made Cape Coast Castle the seat of their colonial government until the year 1877. Later, the site was used as a school and then in 1979 recognized as a UNESCO World Heritage Site.

Between the Elmina Castle, the oldest operating castle in West Africa, and the Cape Coast Castle, perhaps the most famous West African castle, tens of thousands of African men, women and children were taken from their homes. Over multiple centuries, they were sold into slavery, died on the voyage of the Middle Passage or killed.

In both Elmina and the Cape Coast Castle, there were Portuguese churches. The church in the Cape Coast Castle sat directly above the male dungeon, and parishioners could look down at the captives. The church at Elmina was directly at the center of the main courtyard of the castle. It was a two-story building. Services were held on the ground floor, and two priests lived on the second floor. The church was also used as a missionary sanctuary. More recently, the church at Elmina

274 Ibid, pp. 12–13.

was converted into an auction hall and then a museum.

The Elmina Castle was different from the Cape Coast Castle in a number of ways. For one, the Cape Coast Castle had four levels. Secondly, it was originally constructed by cheap African labor. Third, it was planned by the Portuguese to become a warehouse. It only began exporting slaves when the Dutch took over the cape coast site in 1637. The Dutch maintained control of the site until 1871 when it was ceded to the British. Finally, the Cape Coast Castle, unlike Elmina, had a moat to prevent the ocean from washing away the facility.

Another big difference between the two major slave castles was that Elmina had the "Door of No Return," which was not a door so much as a portal or child-sized window through which slaves squeezed through to awaiting slave ships at the harbor, while the Cape Coast Castle did not.

Elimina also had a Christian church on the second floor of the castle. The spacious governor's quarters occupied the third floor and had fancy parquet floors. Finally, the Cape Coast Castle had two eighteen-foot water wells as well as four graves. The first grave is that of Rev. Phillip Quarcoo, the first black Anglican pastor at the castle. Beside him lies the remains of C. B. Whitehead, a thirty-eight-year-old British soldier who was killed by a Dutch soldier in the castle courtyard. Next to these two, are the graves of Letitia Elizabeth Landon and her husband George MacLean, who was the British governor of the cape coast site from 1830 until 1844, where they resided on the third floor of the castle.

There were six other early slave forts and castles built on the Gold Coast between 1515 and 1638. Two of these were Dutch, three Portuguese, and one British. The earliest of these was Fort Anthony at Axim. It is the second oldest slave fort in West Africa. The Portuguese built it in 1515.[275] It was followed by Fort Saint Sebastian, which the Portuguese constructed between 1520 and 1526. The fort is located in Shama, Ghana.[276]

275 William Saint Clair, The Door of No Return: The History of the Cape Coast Castle (Katonia, New York: Blue Bridge Books, 2007), pp. 8–9. The Fetu Tribe, also called the Oguaa People, are primarily found in the area near the Cape Coast Castle in Ghana.

276 Brepong Osei-Tutu, "African-American Reactions to the Restoration

Another slave castle built by the Portuguese in 1555 was Fort Saint John on Ghana's coast. In 1666, the Dutch converted the site to a trading lodge with a tall watchtower.[277] Fort Saint Jago, as it was called by the Portuguese, provided military protection for Elmina Castle, which was within walking distance from Saint Jago.

The two early seventeenth-century Dutch castles were first, Fort Nassau at Mouri. The fort was built in 1612 under the direction of Jakob Clantius.[278] The Dutch had taken control of the site in 1609 after the Portuguese had settled it earlier, beginning in 1598. Clantius reinforced the fort, which turned out to be notorious for its unhealthy conditions. In 1624, the Dutch made it much larger, and it became the capital of the Dutch Gold Coast from its establishment until 1637. During that time, the Dutch also captured Fort Elmina from the Portuguese.[279]

Jakob Clantius was the first governor of the Dutch Gold Coast ruling from 1611 until 1614. Clantius preceded the reigns of A. J. Roest and Arent van Amerstat. Clantius was a significant figure in the Gold Coast Supply Zone at the beginning of the seventeenth century. He was the first Dutch general in the Gold Coast and completed the Treaty of Asebo between the Dutch Republic and local native people. In this treaty of 1615, Clantius sketches out the provisions of an agreement between the Dutch government and tribes in the Gold Coast, such as the Bonoman and the Dagomba states.

The other early trading post of the Dutch on the Gold Coast was Fort Batenstein at Butre, established as a trading post between 1595 and 1600. In 1649, the trading post was upgraded to a fort. Eventually, the fort was ceded, along with the other forts and castles on the Gold Coast, to Britain in 1872. The Treaty of Butre was signed in this fort on August 27, 1656, between the Dutch and the Ahanta people of Ghana, as well.[280]

Fort Amsterdam is the early seventeenth-century British fort built

---

of Ghana's Slave Castles," Public Archeology, vol. 4, 2004, pp. 195–204. Osei-Tutu teaches at the University of Cape Coast in Ghana.

277 Ibid., p. 200.

278 Ibid.

279 Johannes Postma, The Dutch in the Atlanta Slave Trade (Cambridge: Cambridge University Press, 2004), p. 39. This book was first published in Leiden in 2003 by Brill.

280 Ibid., pp. 40–42.

in 1638 near the city of Kormantin in Central Ghana. At that time, it was called Fort Cormantin. The fort was later captured by Admiral Engel de Ruyter of the Dutch West India Company in 1665. It was subsequently made part of the Dutch Gold Coast and remained that way until the fort was traded to the United Kingdom in 1868. The building is still extant. It is at Abandze, on the northeast of Cape Coast, in the central region of Ghana.[281]

Other seventeenth-century slave forts and castles were established by the Dutch, the Danes and the Brandenborgs. The Dutch built Fort Vredenberg in 1682. They had earlier established a trading post there, around 1600. The British occupied the fort between 1781 and 1785, which was ceded to them in 1872. In 1687, English Fort Komenda was built nearby.[282]

Fort Komenda was a British fort on the Gold Coast established between 1695 and 1698. This fort has the most eclectic architecture of all the forts and castles of Ghana and was built in range of Fort Vredenberg mentioned above. It was abandoned by the British in 1816 after the abolition of the slave trade in 1807. The fort had four large bastions around the earlier fourteen bastions that the British built in 1633.[283] The Dutch built the Senya Beraku Castle in 1702. It is a four-sided building that lies on a promontory overlooking a cove and a harbor.[284]

Two other seventeenth-century Dutch forts were built on the coast of Ghana. The first is Fort Orange at Sekondi, initially built as a trading post in 1642 and enlarged into a fort in 1690. British Fort Sekondi joined it in 1682. Fort Orange was sold to the British in 1872, along with Holland's other interests in the Gold Coast.[285] From 1683 to 1684, the Brandenbourgs built a slave fort called Groot Fredericksborg at

281 Ibid., p. 60–67. Jacob Clantius also supervised the building of Nassau Castle, near the town of Moree. The Treaty of Asebo was signed in May of 1611.

282 Ibid. Engel de Ruyter (1649–1683) followed his father and became an admiral in the Dutch Navy. He served gallantly during the third Dutch-Anglo War.

283 Ibid., p. 100.

284 Ibid., p. 111.

285 Ibid. The Senya Beraku Castle in the central region of the Republic of Ghana was the final slave fort built in Africa by the Dutch in 1702.

Princetown, named in honor of Prince Frederick Wilhelm I, Elector of Brandenburg. The fort subsequently became the headquarters of the Brandenburger's interests in Africa. It is one of the only two German/ Prussian slave forts built on the Gold Coast.[286]

The other fort constructed by the Brandenbourgs was Fort Dorothea at Akwida. They established trade there from 1683 until 1720. In the midst of that period, they constructed the fort in 1711 to 1712. Later, the Brandenbourgs sold Fort Dorothea to the Dutch for 7200 ducats of silver. In 1683, the Brandenbourg Africa Company built a lodge at Akwida, east of Cape Three Points in the western region of Ghana.[287] The lodge at Akwida was originally planned to be a small triangular building. It was captured in 1690 and turned into a fort by the Dutch. It was the Dutch who named the structure Fort Dorothea.

The British built one other castle in the Gold Coast Supply Zone called the Annamaboe or Anomabu Castle, ten miles east-northeast of the Cape Coast Castle. Irish trader Richard Brew came to the fort around 1745. He married a woman there, and they lived at the castle, which was then known as Castle Brew. The couple had several Mulatto children, who later acted as excellent translators with the English ships to follow. In 1807, the castle was attacked by the Ashantee, but the fort's defenses held well, and they were spurned back.

In addition to the forts and castles mentioned above, the Danish, Dutch and British constructed another dozen structures in the eighteenth century. Four of these were Danish, six were British and two were Dutch. The Danes built their first fort in 1559 in Accra, Ghana, and called it Fort Christianborg. It was also known as Osu Castle and built on land bought by the Danes from a tribal chief in Accra.[288] The

286 William Saint Clair, The Grand Slave Emporium (London: Profile Books, 2007), p. 221. St. Clair, born in 1937, is a British historian and senior researcher at the University of London. The Grand Slave Emporium is primarily about the Cape Coast Castle of Ghana, or the Gold Coast.

287 Ibid. Richard Brew (1725–1776) arrived in Africa in 1745 where he became the registrar of the headquarters of the British Gold Coast.

288 Laura Murphy, Metaphor and the Slave Trade in West African Literature (Oxford: Oxford University Press, 2002), pp. 169–180. Laura Murphy received her Ph.D. from the African American Studies Department. Her research is mostly on the history of modern slavery in the post-colonial

fort changed hands several times among the Danish, the Swedish and the Portuguese, and back again. In 1824, the British rebuilt the castle, and it became the seat of government for British interests in the Gold Coast Supply Zone outlined in chapter two.

The Denmark-Norway Federation built six different slave facilities on the West African coast. The earliest of these was a trading fort at Fredensborg built in 1658. Fort Fredenborg at Old Ningo was redesigned in 1734. The town of Old Ningo and the fort began as a major port in May of 1743. By the time the British took over the site in March of 1850, the fort was in ruins, so they rebuilt it. The fort became a key player in the British Gold Coast, but strictly for military reasons, not for engaging in the slave trade, which Britain had outlawed decades earlier.

The Danish fort at Ningo was on the Gulf of Guinea, in the Greater Accra Region of Ghana. The fort was once an important site for the Danish slave trade, but with the abolition of slavery, the fort began to decay. By 1835, only one Danish soldier was still stationed at the fort.[289] The Danes built fort Augustaborg at Teshie in 1787. Beginning in 1860, and continuing until 1957, Fort Augustaborg was controlled by the British.[290]

A final Danish fort was called Fort Prinzenstein, built in 1784 and located in the city of Keta.[291] It was originally built for defensive purposes in a war against the Anlo Ewe people and to keep the area safe from other colonial powers. Until 1803, the Danes used the fort as a slave prison, equipped with dungeons. These slaves later, for the most part, were shipped to the Caribbean on Danish ships.[292]

Two other Dutch slave forts constructed in the seventeenth century were at Apam and Sekondi. The former was called Fort Patience, which was built by the Dutch from 1697 until 1702. The latter structure was Fort Orange of Sekondi and established as a trading post in 1670. In 1694, local tribes destroyed it and then rebuilt by the Dutch. Fort

---

period.

289 Ibid.

290 Hyland, p. 119.

291 Ibid.

292 St. Clair, p. 202.

Orange was later occupied by the French, beginning in 1779.[293]

The earliest of the six British slave forts and castles in the Gold Coast Supply Zone was built as a trading post in 1683. It came to be called Metal Cross at Dixcove and later ceded to the Dutch. The Prussians building Fort Gross Frederiksborg Castle prompted the construction of Fort Metal Cross. It was besieged twice by the Prussian ally, John Kanu, but to no avail. The Fort of Dixcove was declared by UNESCO to be a World Heritage Site in 1979.[294]

The British built a lighthouse at Cape Coast under the direction of the English governor, Hope Smith, in 1820. The structure is still employed for that purpose.[295] Fort William at Anomabu was built to honor King William IV in 1753.[296] Fort Victoria at the Cape Coast of Ghana was constructed by the British in 1821 to honor the Queen and was built on the ruins of an earlier fort from 1712.[297]

Fort Vernon at Prampram began as a small British trading post that in 1740 became a slave fort, complete with dungeons and the "Hole." For about a century, Fort Vernon was an important location for shipping slaves, mostly to North America. Altogether, we have examined twenty-six of the slave forts and castles, out of the fifty structures, or so, built on the Gold Coast, from the fifteenth century to the nineteenth century.

Fort Coennraadsburg, also known as Saint Jago, was on a hill opposite the Elmina Castle, also on the Gold Coast. From there it kept watch on its bigger brother that was a house of horrors for the slaves who were brought there. There was also a Door of No Return at the Elmina Castle, that operated right up until 1814 when slavery was abolished by the Dutch, seven years after the British.

One of the most interesting aspects of the slave forts and castles

293 Ibid. The Anlo-Ewe people can be found in South Togo and South Benin, as well as southwest Nigeria.

294 Postma, p. 57.

295 St. Clair, p. 171. John Kanu attacked the fort at Dixcove twice in 1712 with little success either time. Kanu was an ally of the Prussian government.

296 Ibid. John Hope Smith, who died in 1831, was the English colonial governor of the Gold Coast from 1817 until 1822.

297 Tutu, p. 202.

in Ghana on the Gold Coast is how close together many of them are, particularly on the southern coast of the country. In a very short space, Fort Nassau, Fort Amsterdam, Fort Batenstein, Fort Komenda, as well as Fort Vredenburg, Fort Orange, and the Fort at Princes Town, are mere stone throws from each other.

Many slave forts and castles of the Gold Coast, such as Elmina, the Cape Coast Castle and the Ussher Fort, for example, have been turned into museums offering guided tours. These tours are somewhat moving as the tour walks the visitors through the forts and castles, bringing to life the ordeals and miseries that were part of everyday life there in the fifteenth to eighteenth centuries.

Finally, the Portuguese established a settlement at what they later would call Fort Appolonia on February 9, 1691, the Feast Day of Sao Appolonia. The facility began as a trading post but changed to a slave fort between 1768 and 1770. The Portuguese abandoned the site in 1819 after Portugal's banning of slavery. It was later occupied by the Dutch and then the British in 1850. This brings us to the next section of this third chapter, which we shall call "Slave Castles and Forts in Other Supply Zones."

Slave Castles and Forts in Other Supply Zones

In addition to the many slave forts and castles mentioned above, we will also examine three other supply zones that had forts and castles. In the Bight of Benin, the Portuguese built a fort in 1580 called Sao Joao Baptista de Ajuda, or Fort John the Baptist of Ajuda, located in the port city of Ouidah, in the kingdom of Dahomey, which later became Benin. It was situated on the southern shore of the kingdom/country. The fort changed hands seven times between 1580 and 1721 when Portugal again gained control and continued that control until 1961 when Benin declared its independence from Portugal. The Ouidah Empire is also sometimes called the Whyday Empire.[298]

There were several slave holding pens in the Bight of Biafra in the seventeenth to nineteenth centuries. The most important of these was at Bonny and Old Calabar. Bonny is on the southern edge of the river state in the Niger Delta, near Port Harcourt. There was a large building in Bonny that, in the seventeenth and eighteenth centuries, housed slaves

298 Murphy, pp. 154–168.

to be sent to the Americas. Many of the slaves at Bonny were Igbo and Ibibio, many of whom were shipped to the Chesapeake Bay region in America.[299] Portuguese navigators established this slave pen in Bonny in the late fifteenth century. It was a popular place for moving slaves until the year 1800.[300]

From the sixteenth century on, the port city of Old Calabar also had slave pens. Like at Bonny, the slaves brought to Old Calabar were mostly Igbo and Ibibio. After Old Calabar ended its export of slaves, their major export was palm and palm oil. Two other ports towns, at Dockstown and Creektown, also of the Bight of Biafra, had large slave pens, as well.[301]

Perhaps the most significant slave fort in the Bight of Biafra was the one located in the town of Bimbia, in Limbe, Cameroon. Bimbia, at the time, was an independent state of the Isubu people of Cameroon. In 1884, the Germans built a slave fort there. It is in the southwest region, south of Mount Cameroon, and to the west of the Wouri estuary.

About sixty-five thousand Africans were sent from Biafra to the New World. Forty-five thousand of those came to the Chesapeake Bay region. In fact, between 1690 and 1750, this group was the largest ethnic immigration contingent in Virginia and Maryland, followed by Senegambians and those from the Niger Valley Supply Zone.

The Castle of Good Hope was erected by the Dutch, beginning in 1666 and completed in 1679. The castle replaced an earlier structure made of clay and timber. Being constructed in the form of a five-point star, it has five bastions. It is painted pastel yellow to cut down on the heat. Slave labor was used in the construction, but captives were not exported from that spot. Nevertheless, it remains one of the most beautiful castles in all of Africa.[302]

The southwestern African nation of Namibia built three different castles in the Windhoek area of the country. The most significant of these is the Sanderberg Castle built between 1917 and 1919. It was designed by architect Wilhelm Sander to be his private residence. The

299 Ibid.
300 Ibid.
301 Ibid., pp. 139–153.
302 Ibid.

second Namibia castle is called Duwisib, built by Baron Hans Heinrich von Wolf, a German captain. It was designed by Wilhelm Sander, as well, and built earlier, in 1908.[303] The castle is in a remote valley on the edge of the Namib Desert, on the high ground looking south. From a distance, it appears to be a medieval structure with thick walls and square bastions on the corners.

The earliest of the three Namibian slave castles was the "Hohenzollenhaus," built by the Germans in 1904 to 1906. The building is in a Neo-Baroque style. It still stands today in Swakopmund in Namibia. The area was founded by the Prussians in 1892, to serve as the main harbor of German South West Africa.[304] These final three castles, however, were not slave castles, for, by the time they were built, slavery had ceased for over forty years in America and a hundred years in Britain.

There is a slave castle in the Africa nation Zambia, south of Congo and east of Angola, in the district of Lundazi. It was built by the British in 1948, making it the most recent structure in this chapter. It began as a guest house, but it has morphed into a popular hotel, with seventeen rooms and a slave dungeon that still survives.[305]

From our analysis in this third chapter, we have spoken of fifty-eight different slave forts and castles in Africa from the fifteenth century to the nineteenth century. Five of those were in the Senegambian Supply Zone, five in the Niger Valley Zone, two in the Sierra Leone Zone, twenty-four in the Gold Coast, two in the Windward Coast Zone, two in the Bight of Biafra, two in the Bight of Benin Zone, two at the Angolan Supply Zone,

---

303 Ibid. Old Calabar was a Cross-River state in southern Nigeria. Its local name was Akwa Akpa. There are substantial ruins at the slave fort at Bimbia in Cameroon.

304 Dirk Teeuwen, The Castle of Good Hope (Pretoria: Tafleberg, 2007). The Castle of Good Hope, or the "Kasteel de Goede Hoop," is in Cape Town, South Africa. This stone castle was constructed between 1666 and 1679. It replaced a wooden fort there that was built in 1652.

305 K. Gustafsson, "The Trade of Slaves in Ovamsoland," in African Economic History 33 (2015), pp. 31–68. Gustafsson (1888–1960) was a Swedish scholar and football player. Wilhelm Sander (1860–1930) was a partner in the firm Sander and Kock. Hans Heinrich von Wolf (1896–1944) was a German police official and politician.

three from Southwest Africa in Numidia, and six from the East African Supply Zone. These findings may be summarized this way:

Senegambian Zone

1. Fort Bayona
2. Goree Island
3. Fort Lewis
4. Fort Albreda
5. Fort Saint Joseph

Niger Valley Zone

6. Badgery
7. Palace at Akran

Sierra Leone Zone

8. Bunce Island.
9. Fort Lomboko
10. Fort Timbuktu
11. Fort Senudebu
12. Fort at Bafata.
13. Fort at Cacheu

Angolan Zone

14. Fort Saint Paul
15. Fort Usher
16. Luanda
17. Cabinda

East African Zone

18. Fort Jesus
19. Fort Usher
20. Fasil Ghebbi
21. Cairo Citadel
22. Fort Saint Sebastien
23. Fort de Maurier

24. Fort Dauphine
25. Fort De Rocher
26. Freiedersburg at Pricetown Castle
27. Fort Dorothea
28. Fort Annamaboe
29. Fort Christianborg
30. Fort Fredenborg
31. Fort Augustaborg
32. Fort Prinzensten
33. Fort Metal Cross
34. Fort Vernon
35. Fort Lago
36. Fort Ningo

Gold Coast Zone

37. Elmina Castle
38. Fort William Anabau
39. Cape Coast Castle
40. Fort Anthony
41. Fort Nassau
42.Fort Saint John
43. Fort Batenstein
44. Fort Komenda
45. Fort Vredenberg
46. Fort Orange
47. Gold Coast Castle

Bight of Benin Zone

48. Fort John the Baptist

Bight of Biafra Zone

49. Bimbia
50. Bonny
51. Old Calabar
52. Dockstown
53. Creektown

South Africa Zone

54. Castle of Good Hope

Zambian Zone

55. Lundazi Castle

Namibia Zone

56. Sanderberg Castle
57. Duwisib Castle
58. Hohenzhaus

This brings us to the final section of this third chapter, in which we examine a number of pieces of art that depict the West African slave castles and forts.

Slave Forts and Castles in Art

In this final section, we will describe and discuss five different historical images of the slave forts and castles discussed above. The first of these comes from a surveyor's 1755 illustration of James Island and fort in the Senegambian Zone. The illustration shows the outer wall surrounding the island. On the east end are two large towers with cannons. Inside the walls is the fort, which has a central box, where there are administrative facilities surrounded by four large bastions on the northwest, northeast, southwest, and southeast corners of the fort.[306]

A second depiction is of Saint Anthony's Castle at Axim. It is an illustration of the castle, completed in the eighteenth century and drawn from the sea. The castle sits atop a hill. It flies the Portuguese flag. In the background, the town of Axim can be seen, with tall trees illustrated on the edge of the shore, behind the castle. A few small sailboats drift about the harbor in front of the castle.[307]

A third image seen below is also an eighteenth-century depiction

306 Ibid.

307 John Grimoldi, "Africa Forty Years On: Return to Lundazi," in The Economist, December 20, 2005. The first John Baptiste Grimoldi arrived in London from Italy in 1758. The author is his great-grandson.

of Fort Saint Sebastian. In the interior, the plans show several administrative buildings, eight in all. The walled fort includes a series of fifteen bastions, four large and eleven smaller. In the background to the right, a city can be seen. A river winds between the castle and the city.[308]

A sketch of the Castle of Good Hope in South Africa is our fourth image. It shows the seventeenth-century architectural plans for the castle, which flies the South African flag. A man named "Witterbol" completed this illustration in 1680. An outer wall connects four large bastions. Inside the wall are two central courtyards, a larger pentagram to the north, and a smaller triangle on the south.[309]

Finally, our tenth illustration is of the Annamaboe Castle on the Gold Coast. It is a view from the sea. The image is a depiction of a large white stone building that flies the British flag—a two-sail boat sails past the perspective. The illustration is from Thomas Astley's *A New General Collection of Voyages and Travels* published in London in 1745 (plate #64, facing page 608).[310] Thomas Astley, who died in 1759, was a London book dealer who conducted business between 1736 and 1742 at Saint Paul's Churchyard in London.

This brings us to the major conclusions we have made in this chapter, followed by the notes. In Chapter Four, to follow, we again move from Africa back to the Chesapeake region. The topic for Chapter Four is slave coffles in America.

Conclusions

The two main goals in this third chapter have been first, to describe and discuss the phenomenon of slave coffles, or caravans, in West Africa, from the sixteenth century to the nineteenth century. In this first section

308 Illustration in Mungo Park's Travels in the Interior of Africa (London, 1813). Mungo Park (1771–1806) was a Scottish explorer of West Africa. He was the first westerner to visit the Central Niger River Valley.

309 Illustration at Saint Anthony's Castle at Axim in Richard F. Burton's Wandering in West Africa (London, 1863). Richard Francis Burton (1821–1890) was a British explorer, translator, writer, cartographer and Orientalist.

310 The plans of Fort Saint Sebastien were drawn up for Louis XIV on April 16, 1672, and presented to him then.

of the chapter, we have explored the idea of employing Goree sticks used by Africans to transport slaves to the coast in that period. At the close of this opening section of this third chapter, we have described five separate illustrations and depictions of African coffles and African Goree sticks.

In the next several sections of this chapter, we explored the many slave forts and castles built on the African coast from the fifteenth century to the twentieth century. In the second section of the chapter, we introduced and discussed slave forts and castles in the Senegambian, the Niger River Valley, the Angolan, and the East African supply zones. Altogether we have discussed fifteen separate slave castles and slave forts in those four zones.

In the third section of this chapter, we described and discussed about half of the fifty or so slave forts and castles from the coast of Ghana, or the Gold Coast, in the fifteenth to the eighteenth centuries. In this section, we mentioned slave forts and castles built by the Portuguese, the Dutch, the Danes, the Swedes, the Brandenborgs, the French, and the English in this supply zone. About thirty of these slave forts and castles in Ghana are still standing.

In section four, we explored the establishment of slave forts and castles in other supply zones. More specifically, we introduced and discussed structures in the Bight of Benin, the Bight of Biafra, as well as others in the South African and North African zones. Even more specifically, we have shown that slave forts and slave castles existed in Egypt, Ethiopia, and on the Cape of Good Hope in South Africa.

Altogether, we have examined and discussed fifty-eight different slave forts and castles spread over seven of our supply zones, as well as some other areas in Africa not covered by those zones.

In the fifth and final section, we introduced five more historical illustrations and depictions of slave forts and castles, mostly from the nineteenth century. These other five images come from the Gold Coast Zone, South Africa, and from the Senegambian Supply Zone. This brings us to the notes to this third chapter.

In Chapter Four of this study, we remain with a discussion of slave coffles but will change the venue of our discussion. Also, the subject matter of the chapter will switch to slave coffles in America, both in general, as well as specifically in the Chesapeake Bay region, in the eighteenth and nineteenth centuries.

Chapter Four: Slave Coffles in America: Seventeenth Century to the Nineteenth Century

Coffle: A line of animals or slaves fastened or driven along together, from the Arabic *Kafila*.

—*Oxford English Dictionary*

Then have the Trumpet sounded everywhere on the tenth day of the seventh month, and on the Day of Atonement, and sound the Trumpet throughout the year.

—Leviticus 25:9 (Author's translation)

The alms are only for the poor and the needy and those who collect them and those whose hearts are to be reconciled, and to free the captives and the debtors, and for the cause of Allah and for the wayfarers, a duty imposed by Allah, for He is All-Knowing and All-Wise.

—The Holy Qur'an 9:60 (Author's translation)

Introduction

The purposes of this fourth chapter are to accomplish the following goals: To make some very general remarks on how slave coffles operated in America from the seventeenth century to the nineteenth century. In this regard, we shall see that slave coffles operated in the American scene in the first sixty-five years of the nineteenth century in three separate and distinct ways: First, as a way of moving slaves from ships at ports to local American slave jails and prisons, or vice-versa. Second, as slaves who traveled by land in coffles from the Chesapeake Bay region, such as Maryland and Virginia, to places deeper in the South, like Mississippi and Louisiana. And third, by coffles that traveled by sea who were shipped "Down the River" from the Chesapeake ports in Maryland and Virginia to the Deep South in places like Natchez, Mississippi, and New Orleans, Louisiana, along the major waterways such as the Mississippi and Ohio Rivers.

Later in this chapter, as we shall see, slaves also began to be moved from the Chesapeake Bay region to the Deep South by way of the new North American railroads beginning in the early 1840s. So altogether, then, there were four separate ways in the 1800s in America where slaves were moved by slave traders from the Upper South in Maryland and Virginia, to locations in the Deep South, like to Mississippi and Louisiana. There also were slave coffles from ports in large cities of the Chesapeake Bay region to slave jails owned by the major slave traders in the nineteenth century, and sometimes from slave jails to waiting ships at the Chesapeake ports, as we shall see in Chapters Five and Six of this study to follow.

The English word "Coffle" comes from the Arabic term *Kafila*, and its plural form *Kawafil* means a "Caravan" or "Caravans." The word is employed twice in the Holy Book Al-Qur'an at 2:30 and 38:26. It comes from the Semitic root KFL, or Ka-Fa-Lam, that generates words connected to crowding, bundles, or a line of people or animals. *Kafila* is also an Urdu word. It means a convoy of travelers in Arabia, Persia, or even in India.

Scholar William Montgomery Watt, in his biography of the Prophet Muhammad called *Muhammad: Prophet and Statesman*, the Holy Qur'an's 22:39 was the earliest Qur'anic passage permitting Muslims to fight. This passage in translation may be rendered:

> Permission is granted to those of you who wish to take up arms, those who wish to fight because they were oppressed. Allah is certainly able to give help to these people.[311]

Dr. Watt says, however, that Muhammad's followers had a disinclination to fight, but they were given an incentive when they were told that they could keep a portion of the spoils that came in the raids.[312]

In terms of classical Hadith in the Islamic tradition, most references to *Kawafil* come in regard to the earliest "Caravan Raids" by the

---

311 Qur'an 23:39 (Author's translation). William Montgomery Watt, Muhammad: Prophet and Statesman (Oxford: Oxford University Press, 1974), p. 105.

312 Ibid.

forces of the Prophet Muhammad in the seventh century. Most of these were caravans sponsored by the Quraysh tribe. One typical example comes from Ibn Ishaq and Ibn Hisham's *Sirat Rasul Allah*, that relates:

> Go forth against the Caravan [*Kafila*]. It may be that Allah has granted you plunder from it.[313]

Another classical Hadith on caravans comes from *Sahih Bukhari*, volume five, book fifty- seven, number seventy-four, narrated by Qais, that tells us:

> I was the first among the Arabs to shoot an arrow at the Caravan [*Kafila*] in the Cause of Allah.[314]

The word Kafila, or "Coffle" also exists in modern English, French, Spanish, and Portuguese. A single line of camels and men would be called a *Kafila*, in the early Arabic of Islam, but two lines would be referred to as *Kawafil*, in early Islam. An Arabic synonym for the word *kafila* is the term *karwan*, whose plural form is *karawin.* This term comes from the Arabic Root, KWN that is the source of words related to "crowding" and "putting things in order."[315] The English word "Caravan" comes from the Arabic *karwan.*

The Semitic and Arabic root KFl is also the source of Arabic verbs related to surrendering, submitting or guaranteeing, as well as words like "surety" and the verb, "to entrust." The connection to the word *Kafila* is that there is a surety to the fate of the slaves who have "submitted" or have been "entrusted" to the slave traders.

The second goal of this fourth chapter is to describe and discuss several first-person narratives of the activities of domestic slave coffles. Some of these come from black slaves, and some come from white

---

313 Ibn Ishaq, Sirat Rasul Allah, or The Life of Muhammad, translated by A. Guillaume (Oxford: Oxford University Press, 2002), p. 39. The English translation of the Qur'an's 22:39 is that of the author of this study.

314 Abu Bukhari, Hadith, 5, 57, number 74.

315 Abraham Lincoln to Mary Speed, September 27, 1841, and August 24, 1855, in Matthew Pinster, "Lincoln Confronts the Slave Trade," http://bit.ly/2R8v0yy. Joshua Fry Speed (1814–1882) and his sister, Mary, who was born in 1800, were close friends of Mr. Lincoln in his youth. He met Joshua Speed in 1837 in Springfield, Illinois.

Britons and Americans. Indeed, one of these first-person narratives of a slave coffle in America, as we shall see later in this chapter, comes from President Abraham Lincoln in two letters to his friends, Mr. Joshua and his sister, Mary Speed, about traveling on the Ohio River in the early 1840s. Mr. Lincoln saw a slave coffle of a dozen slaves on a steamship traveling on the Ohio River. Another account of a slave coffle traveling in the District of Columbia was seen by a US congressman there, as we shall see later in this chapter.

Finally, in the third section of this fourth chapter, we will explore several descriptions of artistic depictions of American slave coffles, mostly in the nineteenth and twentieth centuries.

Introduction to Slave Coffles in the Americas

American slave coffles were significantly different from those we have discussed in Africa. In America, only 5 percent of male slaves in coffles were thirty years or older, and only 6 percent of the slaves were women. In Africa, those numbers were much higher, sometimes as much as a quarter to a third of the African coffles.

Children under ten years old made up 20 percent of the members of American slave coffles, far more than in African slave coffles. In America, most children were sold along with their mothers, as they were back in Africa. Thus, statistics regarding slave coffles in Africa were significantly different than those in America.

In Africa, slaves did not move to sale by way of the railroad. The African rail system began in South Africa in the 1840s but did not arrive in West Africa until two or three decades later. In America, slaves were transported by rail in the early 1840s, mostly from eastern states to the Deep South, or on steamships on the Mississippi and Ohio Rivers heading to the Deep South.

As in Africa, slave coffles were used in the United States early on in the seventeenth to nineteenth centuries. In America, however, there were other distinct differences from the coffles we have described in Africa.

For one thing, Goree sticks were never employed to attach one slave to another. In the States, the Caribbean, and South America, the Goree stick had been replaced with irons and chains. A long, central line could accommodate a few dozen slaves at a time, or even more, was attached by smaller, two-foot chains connected to that central line. Indeed, some coffles in America had a hundred captives or more, even up to two hundred slaves.

In Africa, coffles rarely contained more than thirty members. In America, there are records of coffles with two to three hundred slaves per coffle. In Africa, there were no overnight sleeping arrangements for the slave chain gangs. In America, when a coffle went by land, it sometimes took up to several weeks to complete the journey. Slaves were fed by local farmers or town folk, along the coffle path. They often slept in tents along the way. If the coffle traveled by sea, it could take several days on rivers like the Mississippi and Ohio, to complete the voyage, so they sometimes slept aboard ship, as well. This was true of the slave coffle Mr. Lincoln saw on a voyage on the Ohio River in 1841.

In Africa, little or no money changed hands between the capturers in Africa and the European captains. African chiefs and the heads of clans were often the sellers of captives. These slaves often were exchanged for other goods in Africa. A good-sized coffle in the United States may have cost between thirty and fifty thousand dollars.

In Africa, the ratio of guards or overseers to slaves was about ten to one. In America, it could be as much as fifty to one or more. In Africa, the guards on coffles often used other dangerous weapons like swords and spears, and occasionally firearms. In the States, coffle guards always carried both pistols and rifles, as well as whips, clubs, swords and other weapons.

In America, many heads or overseers of coffle excursions were mounted. Horses often were part of domestic slave coffles, while that was never the case in Africa. What we do see beginning in the eighteenth century, and in the East African Supply Zone, is the use of camels ridden by slave traders to help transport their captives to Mozambique or India from Arabia. This was particularly true of Arab coffles that originated in Oman and Yemen in the colonial period and sometimes traveled by land from East to West Africa, using the six major trade routes across the continent, by using camel coffles.[316]

316 James Silk Buckingham (1786–1853) was a Cornish-born author, journalist and world traveler. The Rev. James H. Dickey (1780–1857) was a

Slave coffles never traveled by sea in Africa, where slaves were moved from the interior to the coast, except again in the Arab coffles that originated in Yemen or Oman and moved to East Africa or India. In America, some voyages that included coffles of slaves moved from ports in Virginia and Maryland farther south to ports in Mississippi, Alabama, Kentucky, the Carolinas, Georgia and New Orleans, Louisiana.

In September of 1841, Abraham Lincoln encountered a group of chained slaves from Kentucky being taken down the Ohio River on a steamboat to New Orleans. This experience had a great emotional response on Mr. Lincoln. He described his experience in two separate letters, which we shall discuss in a later section of this fourth chapter.

These letters were addressed to a brother and sister, Joshua and Mary Speed, as we shall see at the close of this chapter. At any rate, Lincoln's narrative is an example of moving slaves by ship from the Chesapeake region to the Deep South in the 1840s and 50s.[317]

In slave coffles in Africa, a large percentage of slaves did not reach the coast in the trek from the interior. If stragglers could not keep up in Africa, they were killed or left to die on the side of the road.[318]

In America, slaves who could not keep up were usually women carrying babies, the elderly and the lame. In America, if slaves were unruly in the coffle, they were often outfitted with a ball and chain that they were forced to drag along on the trip or were made to ride in wagons or coaches that accompanied the coffles.

Narratives about slave coffles in Africa were always written by Europeans, either as participants, like James Silk Buckingham, British parliamentarian and temperance advocate, who participated in a coffle, or as witnesses. In the States, narratives of slave coffles were written by the captives themselves, or by sympathetic white folk who came upon the line of slaves, or by one viewed by a US congressman in Washington, DC, as we shall see later in this chapter.

Presbyterian pastor born in Virginia. He was a pastor for many years in a congregation in South Salem, Ohio.

317 Rev. John Rankin, Letters on American Slavery (London: Forgotten Books, 2015), p. 116. Rankin (1793–1886) was an American Presbyterian minister, educator and abolitionists.

318 Quoted by Tim *Talbot*, "A Witness to a Kentucky Coffle," December 8, 2013.

In America, slave coffles were almost always accompanied by music and song, while there is no evidence that was true in Africa. In America, slave coffles were often led by a fiddle player or two, or perhaps a harmonica player, or even by a banjo musician. That did not happen in Africa except in coffles led by a slave or an overseer with a tin horn.[319]

In Africa, slaves often carried goods in their arms or on their heads. In America, that rarely seems to have been the case. Whips were employed on every coffle in America, while there is little evidence that was the case in Africa. Although there was a good deal of misery and degradation in both locales, there appears to have been a far greater sense of community on American coffles than in Africa, mostly because of the music and the singing of the slaves.[320]

In America, flags were regularly carried to identify a slave coffle, but that did not occur in Africa. In Africa, slave coffles mostly were organized by enemies of the captives, or rival clans or tribes. In America, they were organized by farm and plantation owners, or by large slave dealers and Traders, in the nineteenth century.[321]

In both Africa and America, the final destination of a slave coffle was known by the organizers, but not by the captives. In America, handcuffs were often employed in a coffle, but not in Africa. If a captive's hands were bound in Africa, it was always by the use of leather straps or ropes of hemp. In Africa, a slave coffle always proceeded in single file with the use of Goree sticks, while in the States, they traveled in both single and double file, with the use of handcuffs and chains.[322]

If slaves were punished or disciplined in a slave coffle in Africa, they were forced to carry even heavier lumber as their Goree stick, or weight was added to the end of it. Weights could be attached to hooks embedded in the stem end of the Goree stick.

In America, if slaves were unruly in a slave coffle, they were forced to drag a ball and chain, or punished by other means, like whip-

319 Ibid.

320 Ibid.

321 Ibid. Gordon William Featherstone (1846–1873) was born in Montreal, Canada. He studied geology and poetry and wrote a number of songs in Christian hymnals.

322 Ibid.

ping, for example. This brings us to the central section of this fourth chapter, first-person narratives of slave coffles in America. Some of these narratives are of black slaves, some of white abolitionists, and some by other white Americans and Britons, mostly in the nineteenth century.

First-Person Narratives of Slave Coffles in America

One example of these first-person slave narratives comes from the pen of nineteenth-century Presbyterian minister, the Reverend John Rankin, in his *Letters on American Slavery* published in 1836.[323] In the narrative, he sometimes included, in his often lengthy footnotes, a letter penned in 1824 from a fellow clergyman named James H. Dickey.

The letter in question describes the Rev. Dickey's eyewitness account of a slave coffle led by Bourbon County slave trader Edward Stone (1782–1826).[324] Stone was in the slave business in Kentucky from 1815 on. In an 1816 Lexington newspaper, Stone informs us he wishes "to purchase Twenty Negroes, Boys, and Girls, from ten to twenty-five years of age."[325]

Similar advertisements were taken out by Mr. Stone in the early 1820s. His plantation was known as the "Grange." Slave pens can still be seen today in the basement of the Grange manor house in Kentucky.[326]

Mr. Dickey's 1824 account of Stone's coffle reads this way:

> In the Summer of 1822, as I returned with my family from a visit to the Barrens of Kentucky, I witnessed a scene such as I had never witnessed before. Having passed through Paris, in Bourbon County, the sound of music, beyond a little rising of ground, attracted my at-

323 Ibid.

324 Ibid.

325 Ibid.

326 Quoted in Emma Christopher, Many Middle Passages (Los Angeles: University of California Press, 2007), p. 263. John Armfield (1797–1871) was an American slave trader. In 1828, he and his uncle Isaac Franklin formed the company of Franklin and Armfield, whose main office was in Alexandria, Virginia. More is said about Mr. Armfield in Chapter Six of this study.

> tention. I looked forward and saw the flag of my Country waving. Supposing I was about to meet a military parade, I drove hastily to the side of the road; and having gained the top of the ascent, I discovered, I suppose, about forty Black men all chained together after the following manner:[327]

Several points should be highlighted concerning this description. First, the Rev. Dickey considered the lands of Kentucky to be "barren" and uncivilized. Second, Dickey and his family were visiting Kentucky when he heard the sound of music. Third, he believed the source of the sound was a military parade, when in fact, it was the singing and music of an American slave coffle.[328]

Fourth, the singing was accompanied by the playing of violins. Fifth, when he finally came upon the coffle, he discovered forty men chained together, followed by thirty females in the same condition. And finally, the American flag was carried in the coffle.[329]

The Rev. Dickey continues his description:

> Each of them was handcuffed, and they were arranged in rank and file. A chain, perhaps forty feet long, the size of a fifth-horse chain, was stretched between the two ranks, to which short chains were joined that connected with handcuffs. Behind them were about thirty women, in double rank, the couples tied hand to hand. A solemn sadness sat on every countenance, and the dismal silence of the march of despair was interrupted only by the sound of two violins; yes, as if to add insult to injury, the foremost couple were furnished with a violin apiece, the second couple was ornamented with cockades, while near the center waved the Republican flag of the United States, was carried by a hand, literal-

327 Ibid.

328 Thomas William Humes, The Loyal Mountineers of Tennessee (New York: Amazon Digital Services, 2007), p. 219. Humes (1815–1892) was an American clergyman, educator and activist active in Knoxville in the latter half of the nineteenth century.

329 Ibid.

> ly, in chains.[330]

A fifth-horse chain mentioned in the quote above was about two inches in diameter. The "cockades" referred to were ribbons placed on the hats of the leaders of a slave coffle in America.[331]

The Rev. Dickey points out that the slaves traveled chained together in pairs, women followed the line of male slaves, and violins led the men. He also tells us he witnessed a male slave carrying the American flag as they marched.

In the letter, the Rev. Dickey goes on to express his indignation with the scene as being nothing less than disrespectful toward fellow men, an insult to Christianity, and an ironic use of the American flag. Dickey continued his journey and found a place of rest for the evening in Bourbon County, Kentucky. When he described the scene to the homeowner, she said, "Ah, that was my brother."[332]

From this woman, Dickey learned that the owner of the coffle was a Bourbon County slave trader named Edward Stone, and another man named Kinningham, from Paris, also in Bourbon County. Stone's sister continued to tell her tale, as he relates in the letter. She observes:

> A few days before, he [Stone] had purchased a Negro woman from Nicholas County. The woman refused to go with him. He attempted to compel her, but she defended herself. Without further ceremony, he stepped back, and by a blow on the side of her head with the butt of his whip brought her to the ground. He tied her up and drove her off. I learned farther, that besides the drove I had seen, there were about thirty shut up in a Paris Prison. For safe keeping, to be added to the company later, and that they were headed for the New Orleans Market. And for this they are doomed for no

---

330 Ibid.

331 Ship manifest from the Wild Cat, September 1, 1838.

332 Ibid. Following the US presidential election of 1860, some prominent southern leaders, such as Jefferson Davis, wanted to give Mr. Lincoln the chance to sooth the sectional strife over slavery. When he refused, the South's subsequent actions were known as the "Secession Crises."

other crime than that of black skin and curled locks.[333]

Edward Stone's sister begins her tale by telling us that Edward was displeased by a female slave in his coffle, because she refused to accompany him, presumably to his slave jail in Paris, so he beat her unmercifully.[334] Secondly, Stone had a slave jail in which he held his captives in the basement of his Grange manor estate in Paris. And finally, the final destination for Stone's slave coffle was to be New Orleans.[335]

Another white witness to an American slave coffle was English geologist G. W. Featherstone. In 1834, he also happened upon a huge Natchez, Mississippi, coffle led by slave trader John Armfield of the Franklin and Armfield Firm of Alexandria that we will meet in Chapter Six of this study. The Englishman noted:

> The Slave Drivers endeavor to mitigate their discontent by feeding them well on the march, and by encouraging them—encouraging them? To sing "Old Virginia never tire," to the accompany of a banjo.[336]

Mr. Featherstone points out that along the way, farmers and town's people often fed the slave coffles that moved by foot. The slaves in a coffle were sometimes hired out to pick cotton while resting for a few days from the coffle. Featherstone also points out that the slaves in the coffle he had seen were forced to sing and play music, though he does not say why, and that they were accompanied by a banjo.[337]

Thus, in the coffle Featherstone witnessed, a banjo accompanied the singing, not violins. It appears the overseer encouraged the singing. Whether this was to make the slaves more docile, or to encourage their

333 Ibid.

334 Ibid.

335 Ibid.

336 Lyman Abbott, quoted in Princess6, "Will I be White-Washed from History Too?" July 2, 2011. Abbott (1835–1922) was an American Congregationalist preacher, theologian and author. He was educated at NYU and ordained in 1860. He resigned his pastorate in November of 1898 over disagreements with the church.

337 Levi Coffin, "A Slave Coffle," in Chambers Journal of Popular Literature, Science, and the Arts (1826), p. 13–19.

solidarity, is not entirely clear. At any rate, the instruments that accompanied the slaves' singing was not always violins.[338]

Thomas William Humes (1815–1892), an American minister and educator active in Knoxville, Tennessee, saw coffles of Virginian slaves passing through Tennessee, by land on foot, and in shackles on the way to the slave market. He wrote, "It was pathetic to see them march, thus bound, through the towns, and to hear the melodious voices in plaintive singing as they went."[339] Often, these American coffles traveled from cities like Baltimore, Alexandria and Richmond, through Tennessee, on their way to Mississippi and Louisiana.

One of the interesting things about Mr. Humes is that he was an owner of slaves, but he also helped several slaves in Knoxville purchase their freedom in the late 1840s and 1850s. He opened a school for free blacks in Knoxville.[340] For his day, Mr. Humes was quite progressive for a white man of the Deep South.

During the secession crisis of 1860 to 1861, in which southern legislatures were deciding if their states would leave the Union and join the Confederacy, Humes remained fervently loyal to the Union, even though many of his relatives and members of his congregation supported secession.

After Humes refused to acknowledge the president of the Confederacy Jefferson Davis' National Day of Prayer in mid-1861, he was finally forced to resign. After Tennessee seceded in June of 1861, Humes wanted to move north, but a broken leg prevented him from doing so.[341]

Until the late 1830s, slave coffles were the primary means for trans-

338 Frederick Law Olmstead, A Journey on the Seaboard Slave States (New York: Dix and Edwards, 1856), p. 163. Olmstead (1822–1903) was an American landscape architect, journalist and social critic. Voyages of the Thomas Hunter can be found in rolls ten and eleven of ship manifests from 1832 to 1837; the Wildcat was a two-masted schooner guided by a Captain Flint; the Charlotte Reed was a 471 ton, 128 feet long and 29 feet wide ship built in 1845.

339 Manifest of Thomas Hunter, Norfolk to New Orleans, October 17, 1835.

340 Ralph Clayton, Cash for Blood: The Baltimore to New Orleans Slave Trade (Berwyn Heights: Heritage Books, 2002), p. 117.

341 Ibid. James Buckingham (1786–1855) also went by the name James Silk.

porting slaves, but as railroad routes became more extensive, they also were employed. Lyman Abbot, a visitor from the north, also described the slave coffle he witnessed in 1856, while on a train. He tells us:

> Every train South had slaves on board...twenty or more, and has a "nigger car," which is generally also the smokers' car, and sometimes the baggage car.[342]

The fact that these slave cars on these early nineteenth-century trains were often either the baggage car or the smoking car, as well as the use of the N-word, tells us something about the value and worth of these slaves. The air in the smoking car would have been intolerable, and the baggage car crowded. Apparently, these facts were much more accommodating by the slaves than by the white folks.[343]

This also tells us a great deal about what the white railroad officials, as well as the white slave traders of the Chesapeake, thought of the value of the black slaves in these coffles by rail. The slaves were only worthy to sit in the smoking or baggage cars.

In the 1850s, renowned urban planner and landscape architect, Frederick Law Olmstead, in his book, *Seaboard Slave States*, also reports seeing groups of slaves being transported by train to the Deep South from the Upper South.[344]

By that time, slaves were moving from the Chesapeake to the Deep South by land in slave coffles, by sea in steamboats and by rail from the Chesapeake Bay region to the Deep South, as we shall see later in Chapters Five and Six. Indeed, as early as 1810, slaves were being transported from ports in the Chesapeake Bay region to locations in the Deep South.

---

342 Quoted in Ned and Constance Sublette, The American Slave Coast (Chicago: Chicago Review Press, 2016), p. 254. The American Anti-Slavery Society, which existed from 1833 until 1870, was founded by abolitionists William Lloyd Garrison and Arthur Tappan. Frederick Douglass frequently spoke at the society's meetings. Levi Coffin's narrative can be found in the Chambers Journal of Popular Literature, Science, and the Arts (1878), p. 253.

343 Joshua R. Giddings, Journals. Entry from January 29, 1844.

344 Asharaf A. Rushdy, Neo-Slave Narratives (New York: Oxford University Press, 1999), pp. 160–164.

As we have suggested earlier, traders also moved coffles along waterways—the Mississippi River from Saint Louis to Natchez and on to New Orleans, the Alabama River from Montgomery to Mobile, and then by way of the sea to New Orleans. Those slaves arriving by sea came mostly from Chesapeake ports, like Washington, Baltimore, Annapolis, and the Virginia cities of Alexandria, Richmond, Norfolk, and Petersburg, and from Charleston, South Carolina, as well.

These vessels made month-long voyages, carrying up to 150 slaves from these ports to Natchez, Mississippi, and New Orleans, Louisiana, the most common final destinations of American slave coffles.

The names of many of these ships are known from slave manifests of coastal vessels filed in New Orleans from 1807 until 1860, such as the schooner, *Thomas Hunter*, that departed from Norfolk, Virginia, on October 17, 1835, or the schooner, *Wild Cat,* which left from Charlestown, South Carolina, bound for New Orleans on September 1, 1832.[345]

Another American slave ship called the *Charlotte Reed*, a 450-ton vessel built in 1846, regularly traveled from Baltimore to New Orleans from November 17, 1846, until January 2, 1847. It was one of the largest American slave ships of the nineteenth century. The names of other ships owned by Chesapeake traders will be discussed in the next two chapters of this study.

Two significant works that explore the ships that moved from the Chesapeake to the Deep South are Walter Johnson's *Soul By Soul: Life Inside the Antebellum Slave Market* published by Harvard University Press in 1999; and more locally, Ralph Clayton's *Cash For Blood: The Baltimore to New Orleans Slave Trade*, published in Baltimore by Heritage Books in 2002.[346] Clayton points out that in 1807, and 1808

345 Anonymous, Testimonies of a Thousand Witnesses (New York: American Slavery Society, 1839). Charles Ball (b. ca. 1780) was an African American slave from Maryland. He is best known for his Life and Adventures of Charles Ball published in 1837.

346 Charles Ball, Fifty Years a Slave (New York: Dover Books, 2012), p. 74. Charles Ball was born on a tobacco farm in Calvert County, Maryland. He later became a slave in Georgia. When his master died in 1809, Ball walked from Georgia back to his Maryland home to be reunited with his family. William L. Andrew's To Tell a Free Story: The First Century of

to 1818, no Chesapeake slave ships carried slaves to New Orleans. By 1858, however, twenty-five ships made that trip from Baltimore in that year alone.[347] This shows us something of the rapid growth of the slave trade in the Deep South in the first half of the nineteenth century.

In September of 1839, British traveler James Buckingham witnessed a slave coffle a few miles from Fredericksburg, Virginia. He wrote this about the encounter:

> It was in a valley that we met a gang of slaves, including men, women, and children, the men chained together in pairs, and the women carrying their children and bundles on their march South. The gang was under several White drivers, who rode near them on horseback, with large whips, while the slaves marched on foot beside them; and there was one driver behind, to bring up the rear...They were chained together for precaution, rather than punishment; because, when accompanied by one or two white men, they might be tempted to rise against them in any solitary part of the road, or, at the very least, escape from them if they could.[348]

Buckingham speaks of men, women and children being in the coffle he witnessed, that the white drivers were mounted on horses, and that these drivers constantly kept in mind the possibility of an uprising in the ranks of the coffle.[349] They carried dangerous weapons to be well prepared.[350]

Another first-person narrative is advice for those preparing slaves for a coffle. This advice comes from a work entitled *Testimonies of One Thousand Witnesses*. It was published in New York in 1839 by the American Anti-Slavery Society. The ironic advice consists of the following:

African-American Autobiography, 1760–1865, published by the University of Illinois Press in 1986 gives a full treatment of Ball's life.

347 Ibid.

348 Ibid.

349 Ibid. The Congaree River is a short but wide river in South Carolina. It flows for only forty-seven miles.

350 Ibid., p. 79.

> Try him. Clank his chains in his ears and tell him that they are for him. Give him an hour to prepare his wife and children for the life of slavery that is to come. Bid him to make haste, and get ready their necks for the yoke and their wrists for the Coffle Chains.[351]

The abolition pamphlet speaks of slaves bound by yokes and chains and, more importantly, about the separation and the longing that inevitably accompanies what occurred when the captives were taken from their homes and families.[352] It also speaks of the chains and yokes that were outfitted for the captives in American coffles in the nineteenth century.

White farmer Levi Coffin describes another American slave coffle recorded in the 1878 edition of the *Chambers Journal of Popular Literature, Science, and the Arts*. Coffin tells us of his 1826 experience:

> Along the road came a coffle or gang of slaves, chained in couples on both sides of a long chain that extended between them.[353]

Joshua Giddings (1795–1864), a congressman from Ohio, also came upon a slave coffle in the streets of Washington, DC, on January 29, 1844. He says he happened upon this coffle of "Sixty slaves, male and female, overseen by a man on horseback holding a large whip in his right hand."[354] Giddings seems more concerned in his description about the angry countenance of the overseer than he did about the welfare of the captives.

Scholar Asharaf A. Rushdy, in his book *Neo-Slave Narratives*, speaks of adding a slave named Linda in Montgomery, Alabama, on the coffle's way from Virginia to New Orleans, Louisiana, as well as

---

351 Ibid.

352 Ibid., p. 82.

353 Ibid.

354 Ibid., p. 83. Boyrereau Brinch (1774–1817) was a West African slave whose biography was completed with the help of Benjamin Prentiss in Philadelphia in 1774. The Kingdom of Bow Wow was an African kingdom in Mali and Nigeria throughout most of the eighteenth century. Brinch was a member of that kingdom.

the pain and the degradation that came with the coffle. Linda had never seen a coffle before, and now she was in one.[355]

All the narratives about slave coffles we have discussed to this point were written by white men and one black woman, Linda. A significant number of African American slaves also left accounts of coffles they experienced. For the next several pages, we shall look at some of these. Charles Ball, for example, a slave from Calvert County, Maryland, was shipped down south, overland, along with fifty-one other slaves.

Ball was born sometimes in the 1780s, on a tobacco plantation in Calvert County, Maryland. When he was four years old, the slave owner holding his family died, and Ball was sold away from his mother and siblings. Later he walked in a coffle from Maryland to South Carolina, where the slave traders running the coffle sold him to a Georgia plantation owner. In Georgia, Ball learned to pick cotton—a grueling experience he later relates in detail in his autobiography.[356]

In his slave coffle, Ball left Maryland in chains, marching South with thirty-one men and nineteen women. The coffle was directed by a slave trader Ball identified as a Mr. McGiffin. The women were bound together with a halter of rope around their necks. Iron collars with padlocks joined the men. A central chain a hundred feet long passed through the hasp of each padlock.[357] Indeed, in American coffles, men more often than not were in chains, while women rarely were.

The men in Charles Ball's coffle were also handcuffed in pairs with iron staples and bolts; a foot or two iron chain united the pairs alternately by way of right and then left hands. The group was thus secured, as they marched south for four weeks and five days. Later, on Independence Day, Charles Ball was one of fifty-two slaves sold at auction in 1805.

355 Ibid.

356 James Beckwourth, The Life and Adventures of Jim Beckwourth (New York: Gale Sabin Americana, 2012). Another Virginia slave who writes about traveling in a land coffle was WPA interviewee, James Olney, whose narrative is called "I Was Born…" appears in Charles T. Davis and Louis Gates (eds.), Slave Narratives and Their Status as Autobiography and as Literature (New York: Signet, 1985), p. 148.

357 Ibid.

He was sold to a South Carolina farmer. He joined a workforce of two hundred and sixty slaves on the plantation, twenty miles from Columbia, South Carolina, just two miles from the Congaree River.[358]

In September of 1806, Charles Ball was given by his owner as a wedding present to his daughter. Six years later, Ball made a difficult escape from Georgia back to his home in Calvert County, Maryland. Later, he wrote an autobiography that contains his account of the slave coffle in which he traveled.[359]

While on the road in South Carolina, the coffle encountered a thin, white man who wished to buy some slaves. Ball describes the scene this way:

> The stranger, who was a thin man, weather-beaten, sunburned figure, then said he wanted a couple of breeding wenches, and he would give for them as much as they would bring in Georgia...He then walked along our line, as we stood chained together, and looked at the whole of us—then turning to the women asked the price of the two pregnant ones.[360]

Mr. Ball points to the value of possessing female slaves who are capable of producing multiple children. If for no other reason, it meant more slaves for the owner. Charles Ball continues his analysis:

> Our Master replied that these were two of the best breeding wenches in all of Maryland—that one was twenty-two, and the other only nineteen—that the first was already the mother of seven children, and the other of four—that he himself had seen the children at the time he bought their mothers—at that, such wenches would be cheap at a thousand dollars each; but as they were not able to keep up with the gang, he would take

358 William Wells Brown (1814–1884) was a prominent African American abolitionist, writer, playwright and historian.

359 Ibid.

360 Boyrereau Brinch, The Narrative of My Life (Philadelphia: Bejamin Prentiss, 1774), pp. 5–6.

> twelve hundred dollars for the two of them.[361]

Mr. Ball shows that male slaves in his coffle wore chains and handcuffs, while rope bound the women's hands. Ball also makes another reference to the value of the ability to reproduce in this passage. Charles Ball continues his description of his coffle:

> The women were merely tied together with a rope, about the size of a belt around their necks like a halter around the neck of each one; but the men were different. Around their necks were iron collars which were closely fitted by means of a padlock around their necks. Running between all the men was a hundred foot chain to which each of the slaves was attached. The captives were not generally allowed to talk among themselves, as they tramped along, but sometimes, in the midst of their suffering, they were made to sing.[362]

Charles Ball points out that the slaves in the coffle were forced to sing. He reiterates the importance of music in the solidarity of a coffle. Mr. Ball follows this with an accurate description of the slave coffle in which he traveled to the Deep South. He also, however, points to a contradiction that often existed on the American slave coffles. On the one hand, the captives were told to be silent on the marches, while on the other hand they were encouraged to sing and play music to foster solidarity.[363]

---

361 William Wells Brown, The Narrative of William Wells Brown: A Fugitive Slave (New York: CreateSpace, 2016), p. 31.

362 Ibid.

363 Frederick Douglass, Narrative of the Life of Frederick Douglass (New York: Dover Books, 1995), p. 37. Madison Washington was also an American enslaved cook who instigated a slave revolt in November of 1841 while aboard the brig Creole, which was taking 135 slaves from Virginia to New Orleans. Later, Washington was tried and convicted. In the fall of 1841, this same ship, which was owned by Johnson and Eperson of Richmond, was transporting 135 slaves to New Orleans. During the voyage, there was a rebellion and the slaves ordered the crew to sail the ship to Nassau, where they became free. Additional information about Austin Woolfolk (1796–1847) can be found in Chapter Six of this study.

Mali slave Boyrereau Brinch, who was born in the Kingdom of Bow Wow, around 1742, was kidnapped while taking a swim in a river near his home, at the age of sixteen. Benjamin Prentiss published the narrative of his life in Philadelphia in 1774. Brinch speaks of "being marched in a line along with seven other slaves, to a waiting ship not far on the same river." The river was most likely the Niger, and he was most likely from the Niger Valley Supply Zone.[364] It is also most likely that Brinch's slave coffle traveled in Africa with the employment of Goree sticks in the queue.

Another slave coffle narrative was dictated by Virginia-born slave James Pierson Beckwourth (1798–1866). He was born in Frederick County, Virginia, moved by a coffle to Saint Louis, and then settled in Denver. He was known as a mountain man and trapper.[365] Later, he moved to California during the Gold Rush.[366] There, he dictated his *The Life and Adventures of Jim Beckwourth.*[367] This work includes Beckwourth's account of traveling by a land coffle from Virginia to St. Louis, whereupon he then traveled by ship to New Orleans. Later, he escaped, went to Denver, and then California, in the late 1840s.[368]

In American coffles, women with babies in hand were in a particularly cruel situation. Small children were not worth much money, and they often slowed down the rest of the coffle. In fact, in America, child captives were valued according to their height, the taller the child, the

364 Frederick Douglass, The Heroic Slave (New York: Another Leaf Press, 2013), p. 21.

365 Ibid.

366 William Wells Brown, The Anti-Slavery Harp. Originally published in 1849. Facsimile published by Kessinger Books, 2004, pp. 63–64.

367 Ibid.

368 Ibid.

more expensive the child.

Historian and author William Wells Brown tells of a slave trader by the name of Walker, who gave up a baby while still on the side of the road.[369] When Frederick Douglass was a child in Baltimore, he tells us in his autobiography that he heard the sound of chains attached to slaves marching near his house in Fells Point in the city. In fact, Douglass tells us about that experience:

> In the deep, still darkness of midnight, I have often been aroused by the dead, heavy footsteps and the piteous cries of the chain gangs that passed our door, driven to the docks by Woolfolk.[370]

Frederick Douglass refers to the slave coffles in Baltimore that moved from ports in Fells Point to the waiting slave jails of what today would be the Inner Harbor. They were marched west along Pratt Street, usually in chains, until they arrived at the jails of the principal slave traders in the city, or, vice-versa, when moving from the jails to Chesapeake ports, as we shall see in Chapters Five and Six of this study to follow.[371]

The Woolfolk about whom Douglass speaks is Austin Woolfolk, who came to Baltimore in 1815 at the age of nineteen. He was a great entrepreneur in his day, and he became one of the largest slave dealers in the city. Douglass speaks of the sounds of the chains rattling in the slave coffles of Mr. Woolfolk.

In the next chapter of this study on early Maryland slave traders and jails, we will say much more about Austin Woolfolk and his influence on slavery in the nineteenth-century Chesapeake Bay region, as

---

369 Sis Shackleford, quoted in Charles L. Perdue, Weevils in the Wheat: Interviews with Virginia Ex-Slaves (Charlottesville: University of Virginia Press, 1991), pp. 252–253. There is some confusion about Shackleford's slave home. Some say Phoebus, Virginia, others Hampton; still other scholars say Lunenburg, Virginia, or even Brunswick County.

370 Louis Hughes, Thirty Years a Slave (Montgomery: New South Books, 2002). Hughes was born near Charlottsville in 1832. He was the son of a slave woman and white father. His autobiography was published in 1897.

371 Ibid. Benjamin Banneker (1731–1806) was the African American almanac author, surveyor, naturalist and farmer from Maryland.

well as a number of other Baltimore traders.

We also will see in the next chapter that some of the Baltimore slave dealers preferred to transport their slaves through the streets of Baltimore, not in chain gangs or slave coffles, but by using omnibuses and horse-drawn wagons and carriages. Again, more will be said about this phenomenon in the next chapter of this study. Hope Slatter, a Baltimore slave trader we shall see in the next chapter, preferred to move his slave coffles from Baltimore ports to his slave jail at night and in these omnibuses mentioned above.

Frederick Douglass also describes a coffle being transferred from a ship at the Fells Point Harbor through the streets of Baltimore in his novel, *The Heroic Slave,* published in 1853. He speaks about the activity at the harbor on Pratt Street where many slave trading firms were located in Baltimore in the mid-nineteenth century:

> The flesh mongers gather up their victims by the dozen and drove them, chained to the General Depot in Baltimore.[372]

The "General Depot" is the place where they were auctioned and sold in Baltimore. It was situated near the railroad station. In *The Heroic Slave,* the central character named Listwell is in Virginia and staying at an inn. He observes a long slave coffle to be sold. Among the slaves of the coffle is a man named Madison Washington, who Listwell helps escape. Earlier, Washington had spent five years in Virginia's Dismal Swamp, which we introduced back in Chapter One.[373]

Frederick Douglass comments, however, point to another source of information on American slave coffles. In many cities of the Chesapeake Bay region, such as Baltimore, Annapolis, Washington, Richmond, and Alexandria, for example, slave coffles moved from ships at these slave ports to the slave jails and prisons owned by the major slave traders in the nineteenth century. More is said about these American slave coffles in Chapters Five and Six of this study, as we

372 Lawrence Hill, The Book of Negros (New York: W. W. Norton, 2015). The Temne people have been the largest ethnic contingent in the Sierra Leone Supply Zone for many years. They constitute about 40 percent of the current population of the country.

373 Ibid.

shall see.

William Wells Brown, in his book *The Anti-Slavery Harp: A Collection of Songs for Antislavery Meetings*, wrote a song called "The Coffle Gang," which juxtaposes the suffering of the slave coffle against "a better day to come." This song of Brown's has a rhythm and power derived from the repetition of the "Sound the Jubilees," a song based on Psalm 89 and Leviticus 25:9 of the Hebrew Bible.[374] Among the lyrics of the Song of Jubilees are the following:

> And we will sing unto you Lord
> until you break us through.
> It's the sound you heard at Jericho.
> It's the sound you heard in the Philippian Jail.
> It's the sound you will use to set your people free.[375]

The reference to Philippians, of course, refers to the imprisonment of Saint Paul in the New Testament at Philippians 1:12–14 and Acts of the Apostles 16:19ff. Psalm 89, on the other hand, is one of the most evocative Psalms in the Hebrew Bible. It speaks of:

> My steadfast love that I will keep forever, and my covenant will stand firm for Him. I will establish His line forever and His Throne as the days of the Heavens. If his child forsakes my law and do not walk according to my Ordinances, if they violate my statutes and do not keep my commandments.[376]

Other first-person slave coffle narratives were written by Louis Hughes, Emily Edmonson, Sis Shackleford, and Gambian slave Aminata Diallo. Shackleford describes the activity of a slave coffle traveling from Virginia's Five Forks Depot to Natchez, Mississippi. She tells us:

374 Ibid. The word toubah is also used in classical Arabic to designate a "purchasing agent."

375 Ibid. Bayo is a town near Segou in present-day Mali in the Niger Valley Supply Zone.

376 Ibid.

> They had a slave Jail built at the Cross Roads with iron bars across the winders. Soon the Coffle got there and they bring the slaves in two at a time. From the Jail, they are strung together with long chains.[377]

Shackleford points out that the owners of the slave coffle also owned a slave jail at the Cross in the Roads vicinity of Natchez, and that the captives were taken there, two by two, until later they would move "Down River," to New Orleans.

Louis Hughes was a slave born in 1832 in Virginia. He describes the slave coffle he journeyed in from Virginia to Mississippi. He reveals:

> I don't know how far we walked every day, but the irons around my wrist troubled me much. Those in front of me often pulled me along, as though the three guards with rifles did not allow us to talk.[378]

In Mr. Hughes' coffle, the slaves moved in single file, making it more difficult in that they may be pulled along. He also shows that the slaves in the coffle were required to maintain absolute silence while moving in the line. This is ironic, given that they also frequently were encouraged to sing and play music while in the coffles to the Deep South. Mr. Hughes also tells us that the three overseers of this American slave coffle carried rifles.[379]

Later Hughes became a prominent businessman in the north. He paid a Wisconsin printer to publish *Autobiography of Louis Hughes* because the former Alabama slave was now free to write about his experiences any way he saw fit. His autobiography, in many ways, identifies him as a typical southern slave, both before and after the Civil War. In some ways, much more typical than Harriet Tubman, Frederick Douglass and other prominent Maryland slaves, like Benjamin Banneker,

---

377 Sherley Ann Williams, Dessa Rose (New York: William Morrow, 1999).

378 Ibid.

379 Winifred Conkling, Passenger on the Pearl (Chapel Hill: Algonquin Books, 2015).

for example.[380]

The first-person coffle narratives of Aminata Diallo and Dessa Rose are different from the others mentioned earlier because they are both fictional characters. The former is a central character in a novel written by Lawrence Hill entitled *The Book of Negroes*. In the book, Aminata was abducted from her village in West Africa at the age of eleven. Eventually, after traveling across the Middle Passage, she was sold into slavery on a South Carolina plantation.[381]

Aminata falls in love with a fellow West African named Chekura. Coming from Gambia, Aminata and her family are Muslims. In fact, her home is not far from that of both Kunta Kinte and Job Sulayman Diallo, discussed in Chapter One. Indeed, Aminata and Job shared the family name "Diallo," a common name in the Senegambian Supply Zone in the eighteenth and nineteenth centuries.

In the midst of Mr. Hill's novel, Aminata experiences a slave coffle from New York to Nova Scotia. Later, she describes the experience. The book was turned into a television miniseries that consists of six episodes. Aminata's coffle in Africa is depicted in the series, but the one in America is not.[382]

At one point, a coffle is marched right through the town where Aminata was. One of the settlement's leaders, a man named Thomas Peters, loudly opposed the coffle. In the scuffle that ensues, Peters is

---

380 Ibid. Henry Ward Beecher (1813–1887) was the son of Lyman Beecher, a Calvinist minister and one of the best preachers in America.

381 "Emily Edmonson (1835–1895)," Maryland Women's Hall of Fame, Maryland Commission on Women, 2004. Emily and her sister Mary (1832–1853) were born into slavery in Montgomery County, Maryland. On April 15, 1848, they were among the seventy-seven slaves who escaped from Washington, DC, on the schooner the Pearl. They sailed up the Chesapeake to freedom in New Jersey.

382 Silvia King's abduction described in "Captives: Selections from Narratives of Slaves," National Humanities Center, The Making of American Identity, 1, 1500–1865. King claimed she was born in Morocco, and thus was from the North African Supply Zone. She spoke French and was interviewed for the WPA Project in Falls County, Texas, in the 1930s. The Bruin & Hill slave jail in Alexandria was the partnership formed by Joseph Bruin and Henry B. Hill.

shot along with another man.[383] Aminata felt strangely separate from her fellow Africans. The Temna people, who she knew back in Africa, were part of the coffle.

Aminata learns their language and tries to communicate with them, but she is seen as a *Toubah*, or black face. Even so, she tells the Temna that she wishes to return to Bayo, her home in West Africa, and to get there, she has no choice but to travel inland with the African slave trader and his coffle.[384]

Dessa Rose is the title character in a 1986 novel written by Sherley Ann Williams and published by Harpers. Dessa becomes friendly with another character named Jemina. While on their coffle, the two found ways to communicate, despite the silence that their handlers demanded. Nevertheless, the pair always looked straight ahead, forming a very intimate bond.[385]

Despite the fact that these last two first-person narratives were fictional, they are incredibly historically accurate. Dessa Rose also revises the trope of the "Slave Woman," in her interaction with Nemi, a white man who attempts to record her life story and Miss Rukel, her white mistress who attempts to control Dessa's narrative with little success.[386]

Another first-person coffle narrative comes from the historical figure Emily Edmonson who appears in Winifred Conkling's book *Passenger on the Pearl*.[387] In 1848, then thirteen-years-old, along with her five siblings and seventy other enslaved people, were taken aboard the

---

383 Henry Ward Beecher, Lectures to Young Men: On Various and Important Subjects (London: Forgotten Books, 2015), pp. 73–75.

384 Ibid.

385 Ben Simpson, Texas slave narrative on Rootsweb. Simpson was born in Norcross, Georgia, and eventually was moved to Austin, Texas, where he met his wife, Emma, after the Civil War. The pair had thirteen children. Simpson's WPA narrative can be found in John Ernest, ed., The Oxford Handbook of African-American Slave Narratives (Oxford: Oxford University Press, 2014).

386 Ibid.

387 Francis Fedric, Slave Life in Virginia and Kentucky (London: Wertheim, McIntosh, and Hunt, 1863). Fedric was born into slavery in Mason County, Kentucky. At birth he had the name Francis Parker. His autobiography was published in London in 1863.

Pearl. The ship arrived at the port of Washington, DC, and the slaves were brought to the slave jail by way of a slave coffle.[388]

Emily Edmonson (1835–1895) was a light-skin African American woman born in Montgomery County, Maryland. She left on a trade ship from Washington bound for New Orleans. She was returned, however, to Alexandria, Virginia, when an outbreak of yellow fever erupted.

Abolitionist Henry Ward Beecher raised funds for the purchase of Emily Edmonson's freedom that followed on November 4, 1848. Afterward, Edmonson worked tirelessly for the Anti-Slavery Society, mostly in New England.[389]

Henry Ward Beecher (1813–1887), was an Anglican Congregationalist clergyman, social reformer, and supporter of abolitionist causes. Beecher raised money among his parish members to purchase the Edmonson sisters who were being held in the Bruin & Hill Slave Jail in Washington, DC.

Henry Beecher gave the pair, $2,250.00 to secure their release. Eventually, the sisters were freed on November 4, 1848.[390] More will be said about Bruin & Hill in Chapter Six of this study. It is enough now, however, to point out that the Bruin & Hill Firm was one of the major players in the District of Columbia slave trade in the nineteenth century, as we shall see in Chapter Six.

Winifred Conkling chronicles all these developments in the life of Emily Edmonson. In the book, Emily has strong feelings about the coffle she was in, where captives are chained together while marching. Many of those feelings parallel much of what we have seen in the

388 William Wells Brown, "J. Sella Martin," in The Black Man in History and His Antecedents (Boston: J Redpath, 1863), pp. 241–245. John Sella Martin (1832–1876) was a noted Boston abolitionist, author and pastor who escaped slavery in Alabama. William Wells Brown discusses John Sella Martin in this publication, particularly pp. 214–245.

389 Ibid.

390 James Williams, "Rules of the Coffle," New York Commercial Advertiser, June 8, 1827. The Commercial Advertiser was an evening daily newspaper. It was begun by Noah Webster as the American Minerva in 1797. Later the paper's name was changed to the Commercial Advertiser. It was published continuously from 1797 until 1904.

above analyses.

Between 1936 and 1938, the "Federal Writer's Project" completed 2,300 first-person accounts of ex-slaves from all over the South. The database includes those interviews. It also includes five hundred black and white photographs related to the interviews. Silvia King was one of those interviewed for the project.

African-born Silvia King, who, as one of the interviews conducted with slaves in the 1930s and reproduced by the National Humanities Center, describes her abduction, her auction, and her movement in a coffle in the nineteenth century. King relates:

> I know I was born in Morocco, in Africa, and was married and had three children before I was stolen from my husband. I don't know who stole me, but they took me to France, to a place called Bordeaux, and drug me with some coffee, and when I next know anything about it, I was in the bottom of a boat with a whole lot of other Niggers. It seemed like we was in that boat forever, but then we comes to land, and we are put on an auction block and sold. Then we were taken by land from New Orleans to Texas. On the way, we was chained together and walked every day for several hours before we were allowed to get some sleep.[391]

Five important points may be made about Silvia King's narrative of a coffle. First, she claims to have been born in Morocco in North Africa, and thus from the North African Supply Zone. Secondly, she was kidnapped there and taken from her home to France. Thirdly, she sailed across the Middle Passage, and then was taken from the Upper South to the Deep South by way of a French ship. Fourthly, she was placed on the auction block, most likely in New Orleans, and sold. And finally, she traveled by land, by way of a coffle from Louisiana to Texas.

Another slave named Ben Simpson was born in Georgia and sold in Kentucky. He observes this about the by-land coffle he traveled in:

> Then he [the Master] chains all his slaves around the neck and fastens the chains to the horses and makes

391 Ibid.

> them walk all the way. One day on the road it began to snow, but the Massa would not let us wrap anything around our feet. We had to sleep on the ground too in all that snow.[392]

Simpson's account of his slave coffle is significant for at least four reasons. First, it was conducted in the winter months, a rarity for American overland slave coffles. Second, Simpson mentions the snow and how little concern the traders seem to have with the welfare of the slaves on his coffle. Third, the slaves in Simpson's coffle were outfitted with shackles, and finally, they were attached to horses, so there was little dawdling of the captives being pulled along by those horses.[393]

Finally, we suggested earlier that slaves sent by rail in nineteenth-century America frequently were kept in the baggage or smoking cars, and this shows how little value their owners places on their captives. In Simpson's account, we see another aspect of the little value placed on the slaves on the coffle in which he marched. Although it was snowing, the master of Simpson's coffle pressed on, for the cold and snow did not matter.[394]

Francis Fedric, a slave born in Virginia but sold in Kentucky, recalls the scene before his coffle commenced on its journey. He says, "Men and women were down on their knees begging to be bought with their wives and husbands."[395] The experience of separation was traumatic. Traders bought selectively, without any regard to family. They picked individuals only in regard to how much profit they thought they would bring.

392 James Williams, The Narrative of James Williams: An American Slave (New York: Create Space, 2010). Williams' narrative was originally published in New York by Isaac Knapp in 1838. Hank Trent has produced an annotated version of the Williams narrative, which was published by the LSU Press in 2013.

393 Ibid.

394 Ibid.

395 Moses Grundy, Narrative of the Life of Moses Grundy (London: Gilpin Company, 1843). Grundy was born into slavery in North Carolina. Eventually, he bought himself from his master for the sum of six hundred dollars. Late in life, he moved to Boston and became an out-spoken black abolitionist.

Two other first-person narratives of American slave coffles come from descriptions authored by J. Sella Martin (1832–1876) and from James Williams (1805–?). Martin was a noted abolitionist in Boston and a pastor there after he escaped slavery from Alabama. He describes a slave coffle, as his mother had described it to him. He relates to us:

> A long run of men chained together, called a coffle, and numbering somewhere around thirty people.[396]

Another former slave, James Williams, in an edition of the *New York Commercial Advertiser*, from June 8, 1827, sketches out the rules of the coffle he was traveling in. He tells us:

1. Perfect obedience is required of the slave.
2. The authority of the master is absolute.
3. Slaves should maintain absolute silence on the march.
4. Runaways may be shot down with impunity.
5. The masters offer rewards for killing their escaped slaves.
6. The slaves are branded with hot irons.
7. Iron collars, with projected prongs, are fastened to the necks of the women.
8. The lash is the main support of the master on the coffle.
9. Runaways are chased with dogs.
10. Men are hunted like beasts of prey.[397]

Items number one, two and three are about the obedience required of the slave. Six and seven above clearly refer to coffle chains, while items eight, nine and ten refer to punishment that may be dealt to insubordinate captives. Mr. Williams ends this section of his *Narrative of James Williams: An American Slave*, published in 1838, by remarking, "Such is American slavery in practice."[398] Later in his narrative Williams, who was born in Virginia in 1805, writes of coming upon a slave coffle chain while with his master. Mr. Williams describes the experience:

> I saw on one occasion, while traveling with my master,

396 Ibid.

397 Ibid.

398 Ibid.

> a gang of nearly two hundred men fashioned in a single chain. The women followed unchained and children in wagons. It was a sorrowful sight. Some were praying, some were crying, and they all had a look of extreme wretchedness. It is an awful thing to a Virginia slave to be sold for the Alabama and Mississippi country.[399]

Williams points out that his coffle had two separate segments, one for men and the other for women, and that stragglers traveled in wagons. He also points out that it was an "awful and wretched thing" to be sold South in the 1830s, and he points out the anguish and sorrow that accompanies the parting of family members in American coffles.

Continuing his description of the slave coffle, Williams adds, "I have known some of them to die of grief, and others to have committed suicide, simply on account of these marches."[400] He also tells us that children, the elderly and the lame traveled in wagons that accompanied these American slave coffles by land. His mention of suicide recalls the many victims of the Middle Passage who took their lives by jumping overboard or by refusing to eat, as we have seen in Chapter Two when we discussed suicide on some of the Middle Passage voyages.

Moses Grundy was born a slave in 1786 in Camden County, North Carolina. He was hired out by his owner, James Grundy, when he was only ten years old. Moses worked for a man named Richard Furley, who allowed Grundy a good amount of freedom. Grundy transported goods in the Great Dismal Swamp and appears to have contact with the Maroon community there.[401] Indeed, Grundy may have converted to Islam while living among the Maroons in the swamp.

---

399 John Greenleaf Whittier, "The Christian Slave," in The Poetical Works in Four Volumes (Boston, 1892). The same poem was earlier published in Whittier's Poems Written During the Progress of the Abolition Question in the United States, published in Boston in 1837. Whittier (1807–1892) was an American Quaker poet and abolitionist. He was influenced by the Scottish poet Robert Burns.

400 Ibid.

401 William W. Brown, "See the Poor Souls From Africa," in Songs of the Coffle Gang (Santa Barbara: Greenwood Press, 1990). William Wells Brown (1814–1884) was born into slavery in Kentucky. After escaping, he went on to write fiction, plays and an autobiography.

Later Grundy wrote an autobiography entitled *Narrative of the Life of Moses Grundy: Late a Slave in the United States of America* published in London by the Gilpin Company in 1843.[402] At the time of this writing, he was planning to buy back from slavery his wife and five children. In the midst of his autobiography, Grundy describes the slave coffle he was in early in his life.

Mr. Grundy says about his reaction to the coffle, "I was still young yet and had seen a rough go of things, but I was old enough to know that life should not be all brutish, and near starvation and standing on the ceremony and bad habits of white men."[403] Grundy clearly had disdained for the habits of white men.

Mr. Grundy is also very perceptive in his analysis. He knows, for example, that he was too young to understand much about his coffle. Nevertheless, he was not too young to understand the violence and deprivation that comes with the slave coffle. He also clearly had a keen understanding of the starvation that often comes with it.[404]

American poet, politician and abolitionist, John Greenleaf Whittier (1807–1892), wrote about slave coffles in a number of his poems, including this stanza from a poem called "The Christian Slave" written in 1842:

> Oh from the field of cane from the low-
> rice swamp, from the trader's cell,
>
> From the black slave ship's foul and
> loathsome Hell,
>
> And Coffles wearied chain.[405]

402 Ibid.

403 Ibid.

404 Ibid.

405 Eileen Southern, African American Traditions in Song (Santa Barbara: Greenwood Press, 1990), p. 191. There is a vast literature on the relation of music in the American slave coffle. The Library of Congress has published a document called, "Songs Related to the Abolition of Slavery." The University of North Carolina Press also published a collection of slave songs, including interesting comments on the tune, "Come Along Moses," written in 1867 by Lucy Kim Garrison. The Southern Harmony and Musical Companion also includes a number of comments on the relation of the slave coffle to music, including a number of songs written by William Walker

Whittier writes of the sugar and rice fields back in Africa, the loathsome smells on the ships of the Middle Passage, and the coffle chains in America. William M. Brown, a Boston writer, collected poems and essays for his collection called *Song of the Coffle Gang,* published in 1848. One of those poems included begins this way:

See the poor souls from Africa

Transported to America

We are stolen and sold to Georgia.

Will you go along with us?

We are stolen and sold to Georgia,

Go sound the Jubilee.[406]

This connection between the American slave coffle and music was a strong one. Instruments such as violins, banjos, tom-toms, jawbones, triangles and harmonicas often accompanied the march from the Upper South, Maryland and Virginia, to the Lower South, Mississippi and Louisiana, as we have noted many times in this chapter. Many African American spirituals also were identified with the slave coffle.

Among these were "Go Down Moses," the "Thorny Desert," and "Sampson."[407] Eileen Southern, in her book *African-American Traditions in Song*, includes an entry called "A Discussion of Slave Coffles and the Use of Slave Violinists in the Coffle."[408] This essay, among other things, discusses the role of violins and other instruments at the head of American slave coffles.

The entry concentrates on the central place that music and prayer had in the American slave coffle. Music seems to have supplied a way of solidifying solidarity, as well as creating an identity for captives in

in the 1840s. Finally, Saidiya V. Hartman's Scenes of Subjection: Terror, Slavery, and Self-Making in the Nineteenth Century, published by Oxford University Press in 1997, also makes a number of observations about music in American slave coffles.

406 Max Haymes, "Slave to the Blues," https://earlyblues.com.

407 Katrina D. Thompson, Right Shot: Wheel About (Champaign: University of Illinois Press, 2014).

408 See Note 311.

the coffles.[409]

Similarly, contemporary scholar Max Haymes, in his essay "Slave to Blues," suggests that one of the central sources for the origins of the blues is the music of slave coffles.[410] Katrina D. Thompson, an African-American historian, in her book *Ring Shout: Wheel About*, published by the University of Illinois Press in 2014, makes the same connection between the blues and the music of the slave coffle.[411]

A number of other contemporary scholars have begun to suggest that the origins of coffle singing may well have been back in Africa. Among these scholars are German musicologist Gerhard Kubik, whose book *Africa and the Blues*, published by the University Press of Mississippi, makes that connection; and Paul Oliver in his *Yonder Comes the Blues*, published by Cambridge University Press in 2001, makes the same claim about African origins. On page 81 of this text, Oliver speaks of six *Jilli keas* or "Singing men" who were at the head of an African coffle.[412]

Eileen Southern, in her *Music of Black Americans*, also suggests the origins of the blues and American coffle music are to be found back in Africa, though she does not deny the connection between coffle music and black spirituals.[413]

Finally, to return to the issue of Abraham Lincoln and his viewing of a slave coffle in September of 1841, when Lincoln was thirty-two years old, he encountered a coffle of slaves from Kentucky. They were being taken down the Ohio River on a steamboat. Lincoln describes the affect the coffle had on him in two different letters. His correspondents were siblings Mary and Joshua Speed. Joshua Speed was one of Lincoln's oldest and dearest friends. In fact, he was with Lincoln when they observed the coffle.

The first letter was written to Mary Speed, dated September 27,

409 Psalm 6:2, The Holy Bible, Revised Standard Version.

410 Soren Kierkegaard, Tempers the Wind to the Shorn Lamb (Copenhagen, 1843). Kierkegaard (1813–1855) was a Danish philosopher, theologian, poet and social critic. He was also the founder of the philosophical movement known as Existentialism.

411 Ibid.

412 Ibid.

413 See Note 311.

1841, just days after the voyage on the Ohio River. In the letter Lincoln says:

> By the way, a fine example was presented on board the boat for contemplating the effect of condition upon human happiness. A gentleman had purchased twelve Negroes in different parts of Kentucky and was taking them to a farm in the South. They were chained six and six together. A small iron clevis was around the left wrist of each, and this fastened to a main chain, by a shorter one at a convenient distance from the others; so that the Negroes were strung together precisely like so many fish upon a trout-line. In this condition, they were being separated forever from the scene of their childhood, from their fathers and their mothers, and brothers and sisters, and many of them, from their wives and their children, and going into perpetual slavery where the lash of the Master is proverbially more ruthless and unrelenting than any other were; and yet, amid all these distressing circumstances, as we would think them, they were the most cheerful and apparently happy creatures on board. One, whose offense for which he had been sold, had an over- fondness for his wife, and played the fiddle almost continuously; and the others danced, sung, cracked jokes, and played various games with cards, from day to day. How true it is that God, "tempers the wind to the shorn sheep," or, in other words, that He renders the worst of human conditions tolerable, while He permits the best, to be nothing better than tolerable.[414]

The verse of scripture Mr. Lincoln quotes is Psalm 6:2 that says in part, "Temper the wind to the shorn lamb. Be tender and pitiful to a poor withering flower, and break it not from its stem."[415] Soren Kierkegaard, the great nineteenth-century Danish philosopher, also uses "Temper the

414 Ibid.

415 Ibid.

Wind to the Shorn Lamb" as the title of one of his most important, but lesser-known, books.[416] In Kierkegaard's account of Psalm 6, he brings all the philosophical tools to bear that can be found in his other works, like his fundamental beliefs in existentialism and truth as subjectivity, for example.

The other letter of Lincoln's about the slave coffle was written to the man who accompanied the future president on the Ohio River when the pair witnessed the queue of slaves. Lincoln wrote to Joshua Speed on August 24, 1855, fourteen years after the voyage on the Ohio River. Lincoln wrote, in part:

> You suggest that in political action now, you and I would differ. I suppose we would; not quite as much, however, as you may think. You know I dislike slavery; and you fully admit the abstract wrong of it. So far there is no cause of difference. But you say that sooner than yield your legal right to the slave—especially at the bidding of those who are not themselves interested, you would see the Union dissolved. I am not aware that anyone is bidding you to yield that right; very certainly I am not. I leave the matter entirely to yourself. I also acknowledge your rights and my obligations, under the Constitution, in regard to your slaves. I confess Oh I hate to see the poor creatures hunted down, and caught and carried back to their stripes, and unrewarded toils; but I bite my lip and keep quiet.[417]

Mr. Lincoln points out that he and his friend Joshua Speed disagreed about the slavery question, that Lincoln was convinced slavery was immoral by its very nature, that Speed may have been in favor of a dissolution of the Union, and that the rights and obligations to the Constitution should be the measure of the issue. More specifically, Mr. Speed's right to call for a dissolution of the Union, and Mr. Lincoln's obligations to the rights of all in America, white and black, slave or

416 Ibid.
417 Ibid.

free.[418]

Immediately following this, Lincoln mentions that day on the Ohio River and comments about it thusly:

> In 1841, you and I together had a tedious, low-water trip, on a steamboat from Louisville to Saint Louis. You may remember, as well I do, that from Louisville to the mouth of the Ohio, there were, on board, ten or a dozen slaves, shackled together with irons. That sight was a continual torment to me, and I see something like it every time I touch Ohio, or any other slave border. It is hardly fair for you to assume, that I have no interest in a thing which has, and continually exercises, the power of making me miserable. You ought rather to appreciate how much the great body of northern people do crucify their feelings, in order to maintain their loyalty to the Constitution and the Union.[419]

Several other things can be pointed out about these two letters from Lincoln. First, as historian Eric Foner in his book *The Fiery Trial* puts it, "The first letter to Mary Speed is oddly dispassionate."[420] Indeed, this first letter of Lincoln's seems to lack emotion and verve. In fact, it is rather pedestrian in character.

Secondly, that Joshua Speed was an owner of slaves. And finally, by the time of the second letter, the one to Joshua Speed fourteen years later, Lincoln had come a long way to make his claim about the "violation of rights" in the letter. Indeed, in a few short years, he would be elected President of the United States, and in 1863 would preside over the passage of the Emancipation Proclamation, as well as the Thirteenth Amendment making all slaves in America free.

Nevertheless, one of the greatest presidents of the United States also has provided us with a first-person narrative of seeing a slave

418 Eric Foner, The Fiery Trial (New York: W. W. Norton, 2011), p. 220.

419 Fergus M. Bordewich, "Lincoln and Slavery," Wall Street Journal, January 22, 2016.

420 Mark R. Cheatam, Andrew Jackson (Baton Rouge: LSU Press, 2013).

coffle being sold South. Although Lincoln witnessed a coffle first-hand and wrote about it, Andrew Jackson was the only president personally to conduct a coffle of chained slaves. Fergus M. Bordewich, writing in the *Wall Street Journal* from January 22, 2016, refers to this fact,[421] as does Mark R. Cheatam, in his biography *Andrew Jackson.*[422] Indeed, from these two sources, it would appear that Mr. Jackson was the driver of several slave coffles, usually in the summer months.[423]

Before the Civil War, the firm of Franklin and Armfield, of Alexandria, sent slave coffles from Virginia to the Forks in the Road Slave Market in Natchez, Mississippi, where they had an office and a slave jail. These coffles usually began in the summer months and traveled on foot through Tennessee, as we have shown earlier in this chapter.

From central Tennessee, the usual route was down the Natchez Trace. Farmers or town's folk along the way would supply the captives with food. Scholar Betsy Phillips, in an April 28, 2015, essay entitled "The Forgotten Supervillain of Antebellum Tennessee," writes about Isaac Franklin in late August 1833, bringing a coffle from Virginia through Tennessee, and on his way to Natchez, Mississippi, with his charges.[424]

During these overland marches, male slaves were usually in manacles and chained together in single or double file. They were under the supervision of mounted drivers who carried pistols, long guns and whips. Women also walked, usually at the end of a coffle, behind the men. The children and the injured rode in wagons that accompanied the coffle.

Already, we have seen that Franklin and Armfield augmented their movement of slaves from the Chesapeake region to the Deep South with the use of ships. Later in this study, in Chapter Six, we will make mention of a fleet of slave brigs owned by the Alexandrian firm of Franklin and Armfield.[425] The recent book by Ned and Constance Sub-

---

421 Betsy Phillips, "The Forgotten Super-Villain of Antebellum Tennessee," http://bit.ly/2tej0Db.

422 Sublette, p. 271.

423 Ibid.

424 Image of coffle passing US Capitol, http://bit.ly/34k0bLM.

425 Ibid.

lette's called *The American Slave Coast: A History of Slave Breeding*, published by Chicago Review Press in 2015, also gives an evocative description of a mid-nineteenth-century American slave coffle. They begin their description of a slave coffle this way:

> About a quarter of those trafficked were children between the ages of eight and fifteen purchased away from their families. The majority of coffle prisoners were male: boys who would never see their mothers again. Men who never would see their wives and children again.[426]

The Sublettes go on with their very accurate description of the trek from the Upper South, or the Chesapeake Bay region, to the Deep South, or Mississippi and Louisiana, speaking quite provocatively about the misery and suffering that took place on the coffle, but also of some of the joy that was engendered there, as well, such as the comraderie that came with the music and singing in American slave coffles.[427] This brings us to the final section of this fourth chapter—images of slave coffles in American art.

Slave Coffles in American Art: 1815 to 1865

In the period from 1815 until the close of the Civil War, there are many extant artistic pieces depicting slave coffles in the United States. We shall describe and discuss a number of these.

The artist of the first piece is unknown, but the image shows a slave coffle walking past the US Capitol in Washington, DC. Several men stand together. The two men at the head of the line are of a man with a walking stick in his right hand and a shorter black man wearing white trousers and a dark sombrero. The image is owned by the Library

---

426 Ibid.

427 James Buchanan, "A Slave Coffle," in The Slaves State of America (New York, 1842). Buchanan, of course, was the fifteenth president of the US (1857–1861). He was liked by northern Democrats and southern Moderates alike. He considered himself to be a Pacifist and peacemaker, and he was decidedly against the practice of slavery.

of Congress and is dated, as we said earlier, in 1815.[428]

A second illustration is one alluded to earlier. It comes from Alamy Stock. The image shows two chained slaves attached by Goree sticks accompanied by two Arab overseers. One is on horseback and the other on a camel. This anonymous image likely came from the East African Supply Zone, particularly from Oman or Yemen in the colonial period, for the Arabs used camels in conducting their slave coffles in this zone.[429]

A third American image of a slave coffle is in Kentucky in 1836. It shows a line of several dozen slaves led by a man on horseback. The white overseer wears a Panama hat, has a rifle swung over his back, and carries a whip in his right hand. At the head of the coffle are two fiddle players and a man carries an American flag. The queue contains both men and women, more of the former than the latter. Two other mounted guards accompany the coffle, which winds around a grove of large trees.[430]

The next image of American slave coffles is an 1839 illustration from a book by James Buckingham, mentioned earlier, published in London in 1842, entitled *The Slave States of America.*[431] It shows a scene in a clearing where three mounted agents of planters organize a group of about thirty slaves. Four slaves relax on a hill to the left, the woman of the four carries a bundle on her head. In the distance, behind the clearing on either side, are two ominous-looking trees.[432]

The fifth illustration of an American slave coffle was completed in 1849 and comes from a manuscript owned by the New York Public Library. The image shows a coffle of five slaves fastened together with

---

428 "Slave Coffle," in Illustration of the Life of Henry Bibb (New York Public Library, Digital Collection), p. 19. Henry Bibb (1815–1854) was a Kentucky slave who escaped to Canada.

429 Ibid. Henry Bibb (1815–1854) was born into slavery in Kentucky. After escaping, he went on to become a noted author and abolitionist. He also wrote an autobiography entitled The Narrative of the Life of Henry Bibb.

430 Ibid. The J. W. Neal & Company was named after J. W. Neal, who was born in 1887 and conducted a slave-trading firm in Washington, DC.

431 Ibid. This image may be found in the holdings of the Roy Rosenzweig Center in a book entitled History of the National Mall.

432 Ibid.

chains around their necks and wrists. All five of them wear bowler hats.

A slave master accompanies the coffle. He wears a top hat and carries a four-foot-long whip in his right hand. The image comes from an edition of the *Autobiography of Henry Bibb.*[433] Henry Bibb (1815–1854) was the son of white Kentucky State Senator James Bibb and a Kentucky slave woman named Mildred Jackson. Henry Bibb eventually ran away to Canada, where he opened the first black newspaper there. He was also one of the most important figures in the abolitionist movement in Canada.[434] A caption above the illustration reads:

> This idea of utter helplessness in perpetual bondage is all the more distressing as there is no period even with the remaining generation where it shall terminate.[435]

There is an 1836 illustration of a slave coffle owned by J. W. Neal, a nineteenth-century District of Columbia slave trader, as we shall see in Chapter Six of this study. The illustration shows a coffle of a dozen captives, both men and women, most likely on their way to auction.

To the right of the captives is a white man dressed in a white frock and Panama hat. He holds a long whip in his right hand and points to something on the ground with his left. Toward the rear of the coffle is a man on horseback. He holds a long pole in his right hand. Another white man stands behind the horse, dressed as the other two. Some of the slaves in this image carry bundles. One of the captives, which is about five people deep in the line, has his right arm raised above his head.[436] The buildings in the rear of the coffle are most likely the slave jail owned by Mr. Neal. There are three buildings in all. The one on the left appears to be a residence, while the one in the middle of the three

433 Illustration of a slave coffle of J. W. Neal, http://bit.ly/36LxbhT.

434 Ibid. The Abolitionist Campaign of 1835 and 1836 was designed to put pressure on the US Congress to end slavery in the District of Columbia. J. W. Neal was one of the largest slave traders in Washington.

435 Advertisement in The Anti-Slavery Record (New York: R. G. Williams, 1837) 3. The Anti-Slavery Record was published by the Anti-Slavery Society of America from 1835 until 1837. R. G. Williams was the publisher of the paper in New York City.

436 Ibid.

most likely is the jail, for there are bars on the windows.[437]

Mr. Neal was one of the most prominent slave dealers in the District of Columbia. More will be said about him in Chapter Six.[438] Mr. Neal and his company regularly advertised in the early nineteenth century for the purchase of slaves. In one advertisement, he proclaims:

> Cash for Negroes
>
> We will at all times give the highest prices in cash for likely young Negroes of both sexes, from age ten to age thirty.[439]

The depiction of the fifth image, first printed in a broadside issued in 1835–1836, condemned slavery in the District of Columbia. The abolitionist in Washington desired to have Congress pass a law, or a "Gag Rule," that tabled all discussion and debate on petitions related to slavery without reading them. The gag order remained in place until 1844.[440]

Another image from around 1790 from Africa shows a coffle of ten, bare-breasted female slaves, three of whom have children with them. Goree sticks connect the slaves. They are accompanied by one trader, wearing a white hat and carrying a black whip in his right hand. The scene appears as though it is a dance in progress, with the overseer as the conductor.[441] The original of this image is an 1836 engraving owned by the Stapleton Collection in Southwest London, UK.

An image called "Slave Trader Sold to Tennesee" is from Lewis Miller's *Sketchbook,* dated 1853 in Staunton, Virginia. It is a multi-colored illustration of a slave coffle. There are two dozen slaves in all—men, women and a few children. The men are shackled, but the women

---

437 Ibid.

438 Slave Coffle, Africa, ca. 1790, owned by Getty Images.

439 Ibid.

440 Ibid.

441 Lewis Miller, Slave Coffle, Stauton, Virginia, 1853, in Sketchbook. Image is owned by the Abby Aldrich Rockefeller Museum in Colonial Williamsburg. It is dated August 18, 1853. Lewis Miller was born in York, Pennsylvania, in 1796. His father also was an artist. Between 1861 and 1865, Lewis completed several watercolor sketches of Virginia slave life.

are not. The slaves are directed by two white overseers, both on horseback and carrying long, black whips in their right hands.[442]

Lewis Miller (1796–1882) was a Pennsylvania Dutch folk artist, noted for his watercolors of everyday life. He frequently visited Christianburg, Virginia, where he painted scenes of slave life.

The National Museum of the Bahamas owns another image of a New World slave coffle. The artist is anonymous, but it shows a coffle of five black slaves overseen by a mounted European man holding a large whip. The five slaves are fashioned together with rope. The piece is part of an exhibit of slave artifacts owned by the museum.[443] Apparently, slave coffles were employed in the British Caribbean, as well.

Wingman61 on *Deviant Art* produced another image done in pastel inks of an American slave coffle.[444] Several slaves are marched "across the USA." The men of the coffle are handcuffed in front. In this image, two overseers are mounted on horses. One raises a large whip above his head, in a menacing gesture. The original from which this print was copied was most likely produced before the Civil War.[445]

Finally, an image of a five slave coffles, complete with a standing overseer with a long whip, is a piece of art made by someone who identifies himself simply as "Everett." The slaves in this coffle are chained around their necks. The captives carry shovels and pickaxes. A second overseer can be seen bringing up the rear. The image is produced @fine art America.com.[446]

This brings us to the major conclusions we have made in this fourth chapter, followed by the notes of the same. This chapter will be followed by a fifth and sixth that deal primarily with slave dealers

442 Slave Coffle by Wingman61 on Deviant Art website.

443 Ibid.

444 This point about "Go Down Moses" was made in the Continental Monthly, vol. 2, July–December 1862.

445 See Notes 356 and 358.

446 James Williams, "Rules on a Slave Coffle," New York Commercial Advertiser, June 8, 1827. See Note 361. The New York Commercial Advertiser was an afternoon daily newspaper published from December of 1793 until 1904. It was begun by Noah Webster as the American Minerva. After going through several proposed name changes, they settled on the New York Commercial Advertiser.

and slave jails in Maryland (Chapter Five), particularly in Baltimore, followed by the same in Washington, DC, and the colony/state of Virginia, particularly in Alexandria and in the city of Richmond (Chapter Six).

Conclusions

In this fourth chapter of this study, we have had three principal aims. First, to introduce the phenomenon of slave coffles in America, and then compare and contrast with those coffles we saw in Africa back in Chapter Three. The second goal of this chapter and principal aim was to describe and discuss several first-person narratives of slave coffles in the US.

In this second section, we introduced and discussed the first-person narratives of slave coffles in America, written by white men, as well as African slaves, both men and women. In fact, we explored the stories of seven white men of American slave coffles, both Americans and Britons. We also analyzed the first-person narratives of slave coffles from seven slave men and five slave women.

As we have seen, some of the first-person slave narratives are prominent figures, such as Frederick Douglass and William Wells Brown, and some of these narratives were from obscure slaves like Louis Hughes, Moses Grundy and Sella Martin. One interesting feature of two of the female first-person narratives were fictional characters, Amaninta Diallo and Dessa Rose. The other female narratives, those of Emily Edmonson, Silvia King and Sis Shackleford, were far more typical of what women must have experienced on their coffle trips by land, sea, and rail. The third goal of this chapter has been to explore some of the ways slave coffles were depicted in American art during the first half of the nineteenth century.

Among these first-person narratives of experiencing a nineteenth-century American slave coffle, we made some remarks about two letters Abraham Lincoln sent to friends, Mary and Joshua Speed, in 1841 and 1855. In the initial letter to Mary, the older sister, Lincoln seems rather ambivalent about slavery. In the one to Joshua Speed, however, he asserts his conviction that slavery violates the human rights of the slaves.

In the second section of this chapter, we also pointed out that several contemporary scholars suggest that music played and sung on American slave coffles may have been one of the origins of Negro spirituals and the blues, particularly considering that "Go Down Moses" was the most popular song sung and played on coffles in the Deep South.[447] Other contemporary scholars, as we have indicated, suggest that the origin of slave coffle music in America is not the blues, but rather to be found back in Africa.

In the third section of this fourth chapter, we introduced and discussed eleven separate pieces of American art, which show American slave coffles. These seven illustrations are dated from 1790 to 1853 and tell us a great deal about the nature and uses of slave coffles in America.[448] One of the coffle narratives we have seen in this chapter—that of slave James Williams—provides us with ten rules that were observed by slaves traveling in a coffle, whether locally, or to the Deep South. These ten rules, which are sketched out in Mr. Williams' *Autobiography*, tell us a great deal about the misery and hardships of captives in the American coffles. Mr. Williams sums up these rules concerning the captives in slave coffles in America this way: Perfect obedience is required of the slave. The authority of the master is absolute. Slaves should maintain absolute silence on the march. Runaway slaves may be shot down with impunity. Masters offered rewards for the recovery of escaped slaves. Slaves are branded with hot irons. Iron collars with projected prongs are fastened to the necks of the women. The lash is the main support of the master on the coffle. Runaways are chased with dogs. Runaways are hunted like beasts of prey.[449]

This brings us to the notes of this fourth chapter, followed by Chapter Five, in which we will explore the phenomenon of the slave dealer and traders, as well as the slave jails and prisons that existed in the state of Maryland up until the time of the close of the Civil War, particularly in Baltimore.

In Chapter Six of this study, we shall continue on the same theme, concentrating instead on slave dealers, traders, and slave jails in the

---

447 Ibid.

448 Ibid.

449 Williams, "Rules."

District of Columbia and the Commonwealth of Virginia over the same period.

Chapter Five: Merchant Ships and Slave Traders of Baltimore—1800 to 1865

It is a peculiar sensation, this double consciousness, this sense of always looking at oneself through the eyes of others, of measuring one's soul by the tape of a world that looks on in amused contempt and pity. One ever-feels his twoness—an American and a Negro; two souls, two thoughts, two unreconciled strivings; two warring ideals in one dark body.

—W. E. B. DuBois, *Essays*

Greed made strange bedfellows. Many of Baltimore's slave dealers shipped together on the same brigs, barks, ships, and schooners making their cyclic runs to New Orleans.

—Ralph Clayton, "A Bitter Inner Harbor Legacy"

Then a woman said to Muhammad, "Do you know I have freed my slave-girl?" He said. "Have you really?" She replied in the affirmative. Then he said, "You would have gotten more reward if you had given her to one of your maternal uncles.

—Ibn Abbas, *Hadith,* volume III, no. 765 (Author's translation)

Introduction

The interregional slave trade performed an important function by moving slaves in America from places with less need for them to areas with a greater need. With changes in agricultural production in the Chesapeake region, and with lower tobacco production by the mid-eighteenth century, planters there found themselves with a surplus of slaves. Meanwhile, with the invention of the cotton gin in 1792, the production of that plant grew exponentially, while tobacco production waned in Maryland and Virginia.

The cotton gin was invented and patented by Eli Whitney (1765–

1825). It was a machine that revolutionized the production of cotton by speeding up the process that separates the seeds from the cotton fiber. One overall effect was the reduction of tobacco productions and the increase of both cotton and sugar production in the Deep South in America, as well as the cultivation of grains, beginning in the late eighteenth century. The two major causes of the reduced production of tobacco in the Chesapeake Bay region were unstable markets and issues related to quality control of the tobacco, as indicated earlier in this study.

This state of affairs saw two major changes regarding the practice of slavery in the US. First, slaves began to be moved by Chesapeake planters overland in slave coffles to the Deep South. A coffle from the Chesapeake to Mississippi took about eight weeks. Slaves slept in tents along the way. Often, they were fed during the trip by local farmers and town people, who also sometimes hired out their labor for a short period before the coffle resumed.

On many slave coffles to the Deep South, the captives were hired-out to work in the cotton fields, sometimes for several days or even a week or more before they resumed the coffle marches. Stragglers, malcontents and women with children traveled in wagons or carriages, or they were forced to drag a ball and chain on the march, both men and women, particularly male malcontent slaves.

The second effect of the economy shift mentioned above is that at Maryland and Virginia ports, such as Baltimore and Alexandria, for example, captives were now transported by ships from the Chesapeake to the Deep South by the opening of the nineteenth century, or were moved by rail beginning in the fourth decade of the nineteenth century.

In this chapter, we will look at a number of these slave-trading firms, primarily in Baltimore, that moved their slaves by these three methods, land, sea and rail, as outlined earlier. The third method by which captives were moved from the Chesapeake region to the Deep South, from the late 1830s on, was the American railroads. Indeed, in this chapter, we will introduce a few examples of Baltimore slave traders moving captives to the Deep South by rail. Before then, however, we will turn to Baltimore slave traders in the mid-nineteenth century.

In the *Baltimore Directory* of 1850, thirteen firms advertised as slave traders in the city of Baltimore.[450] In the fifth chapter, we have three major goals. First, to make some general remarks about what we know of nineteenth-century merchant ships used for the slave trade, both internationally and domestically, in Baltimore.

Our second goal in this chapter is to enumerate the thirteen slave traders in Baltimore, Maryland, in the 1850s. Then to discuss these businesses in terms of their slave jails or pens, as well as the local coffles to and from those establishments to ports in the Deep South during the first sixty-five years of the nineteenth century.

The third goal in this fifth chapter is to examine works of art that depict Baltimore slave ships, as well as the businesses of Baltimore slave traders, primarily in the middle of the nineteenth century. Chapter Six, as we shall see, has similar aims and goals, but pertains to slave traders in Washington, DC, and the Commonwealth of Virginia, in the same period.

An appendix of manifests of slave ships moving from Baltimore to the Deep South in the first sixty years of the nineteenth century also is included in this chapter. A similar appendix is attached to Chapter Six, as well as ship manifests in the District of Columbia and Virginia. We move, then, to merchant ships in Baltimore, which were engaged in the international and domestic slave trade in Baltimore in the nineteenth century.

Merchant Slave Ships in Baltimore: 1800 to 1865

One of the primary materials for the first section of this chapter is a document called "Lists of Ships Trading in Maryland From April 30, 1689 to 1693." The other primary source is Loren S. Walsh's article entitled "The Chesapeake Slave Trade: Regional Patterns of African Origins and Some Implications," published in the *William and Mary Quarterly*, from January of 2011.[451] A number of other primary sources for the nineteenth-century voyages from Baltimore to New Orleans abound.

The manifests for several slave ships in Baltimore in the first six-

450 Baltimore City Directory 1850, http://bit.ly/35mX1bs.

451 Lore S. Walsh, "The Chesapeake Slave Trade: Regional Patterns of African Origins and Some Implications," in William and Mary Quarterly (January 2011).

ty-five years of the nineteenth century are extant. Some of these ships were built in Baltimore and then were in the slave-trading business, while others mostly moved from the ports of Baltimore to locations in the Deep South to sell captives.

A ship called the *Echo*, for example, and later renamed the *Putnam*, and then back to the *Echo*, was built in Baltimore in 1845.[452] For the next thirteen years, the ship was used to sail to Africa, purchase slaves from Cabinda, Angola, in West Africa, and then return to Baltimore. One typical voyage departed from Baltimore on March 8, 1858. The name of the ship was also changed at this time from the *Putnam* back to the *Echo*.

The *Putnam* had an eighty-foot-long deck, sixteen-foot beams, very heavy raking masts, a ten-foot hold, very high bulwarks, and six guns made for anyone who wished to cause the ship trouble. The ship was a brig of 187 tons, ninety-two feet and two inches overall in length, and twenty-two feet eight inches in breadth. She had a square stern with no galleys and a billet head and a ten-foot depth of hold, or a ten-foot draft.

Originally, the *Putnam* was built for interests in Philadelphia and sailed under a Philadelphia captain with a temporary registry on her first voyage from Baltimore to Philadelphia in June of 1845. The ship went on to operate out of Philadelphia for the next five years, and then was purchased by new owners from Providence, Rhode Island, in June of 1850. A year later, in August of 1851, the *Putnam* was registered in Boston. Later, after 1857, the ship was registered in New York City.

In that same year, on October 9, 1857, the *Putnam* was registered in the port of New Orleans, the major nineteenth-century slave-trading center in the Deep South, as we have seen earlier in this study. Still later, the name of the *Putnam/Echo* changed again to the *Jefferson Davis* after the ship operated illegally in the Atlantic slave trade just before the American Civil War.

From June 30 to July 5, 1858, slaves were purchased by the *Putnam* in the city of Cabinda on the coast of Angola in the Angolan Supply Zone.[453] A few weeks later, in late July of 1858, a slave revolt

452 "The Echo Slave Trader" at http://bit.ly/38A9rPn.

453 Ibid.

broke out on board, with the crew finally gaining control. From August 1 to the 15, the *Echo* narrowly escaped a shipwreck near Great Abaco Island in the Bahamas. The near wreck was 180 miles east of South Florida, but the captain and crew remained in control until that time.[454]

When the *Echo* was not making these international voyages, it was making domestic ones. The ship frequently traveled between Baltimore and New Orleans, mostly carrying slaves to the Deep South and then transported manufactured goods or raw materials back again, such as sugar, cotton, whiskey and other staples.

Later, when they arrived in Charleston, South Carolina, the mutineers from the *Echo/Putnam* were tried as were some select members of the crew under Sections IV and V of an act from May 15, 1820, which stated that an American's participation in the slave trade was an act of piracy. If convicted, the penalty was death. The law did, however, offer potential lifelines to those charged. It said that the case would be heard at "The Circuit Court of the United States for the District wherein the suspect may be brought or found."[455]

This meant that the trials of the *Echo* were to take place in Columbia, South Carolina, the capital and a radically pro-slavery stronghold in South Carolina. Judge James Moore Wayne delivered three indictments against the *Putnam* crew under the 1820 act, but he found no claim of substance against the prisoners. After ninety minutes of deliberation, the jury returned a verdict of not guilty, and all sixteen prisoners, some crew and some slaves, were released.[456]

---

454 Ibid. Cabina is a province of Angola. It was formerly known as the Portuguese Congo, but it is known locally as Tchiowa. The capital city of Cabinda is the city of Cabinda. For more on the Echo/Putnam Revolt, see: "Voyage of the Echo: The Trials of an Illegal Trans-Atlantic Slave Ship," of the Low Country Digital History Initiative at http://ldhi.library.cofc.edu. The Abaco Islands are a group of islands and barrier bays in the northern Bahamas, east of South Florida. The "Land and Sea Park" there is noted for its wildlife, such as pelicans, for example.

455 Section IV and V of An Act from May 15, 1820, State of Maryland Archives.

456 Opinion of Judge James Moore Wayne, South Carolina Superior

A report published in the spring of 1840 revealed a list of twenty-one American vessels engaged in the slave trade, during the spring and summer of 1839. Of the ships listed, eleven of them, or 52 percent, were identified as having been built in Baltimore. Thus, it was not simply the *Putnam/Echo* that made contributions to the Atlantic slave trade, as well as the domestic trade.[457]

In fact, a variety of ships, sloops, packets, schooners, barks, and brigs brought captives from the ports of Baltimore at the Inner Harbor and Fells Point to ports in the city of New Orleans, Louisiana, throughout the first sixty-five years of the nineteenth century. Many of these voyages were conducted and financed by the major slave traders in the Maryland city.

Indeed, Baltimore shipbuilders played a primary role in both the international and domestic slave trades in the nineteenth century. In an appendix at the end of this chapter, we discuss a number of ship manifests from Baltimore to the Deep South in the first sixty years of the nineteenth century.

Given the Angolan Supply Zone of the captives on the *Putnam*, it is most likely they were members of the Kobenda, the Congo and the Muscongo tribes. These groups lived near the Congo River, which dominated the region's geography, society and economy. In fact, the city of Cabinda was situated at the mouth of the Congo River. Those who lived along the Congo River were mostly fishermen at the time, and many slaves were either local or brought from the interior.

These captives probably spoke Kivili, Kiyyombe or Kiwoyo, which are all distinct dialects of the Bantu language. If this is true, then this may indicate that some of these slaves from the Angolan Supply Zone may have traveled across the continent from East Africa, where the Bantu people predominate to the West Coast.

The manifests of other Baltimore ships that traveled from Baltimore to the Deep South are also extant. Most of these crafts carried only a handful of slaves. Sometimes more than one slave dealer in Bal-

---

Court, May 29, 1839. James Moore Wayne (1790–1867) was the associate justice of the South Carolina Supreme Court for many years.

457 "A Report of Twenty-One Vessels Engaged in the Slave Trade," University of South Carolina, Summer 1839.

timore employed the same ship for the same purposes. One example of this is the brig *Temperance* owned by James Beard of Baltimore. The ship sailed on March 20, 1848, bound for New Orleans to a trader there named Stephen Watts Wikoff.[458]

In fact, Mr. Beard often served as the captain of his own ship in voyages from Baltimore to New Orleans in the 1840s. Many other ship owners in the nineteenth century also captained their own ships, as we shall see subsequently in this chapter.

James Beard of Baltimore owned the six slaves received by Mr. Wikoff. Their names and ages were Richard (25), Mary (19), Eliza (20), Maria (12), Ellen (10), and Henry, who was three months old.[459] Notorious slave trader, Austin Woolfolk, sent slaves to New Orleans on the same voyage. Specifically, he also sent slaves to Mr. Wikoff. Their names and ages were Philip (24), John (40), Sophy (23), and Sophy's pale black child named William.[460] Much more will be said about Austin Woolfolk (1797–1847), in Chapter Six of this study to follow.

Other slave ships that left Baltimore in the period were destined for other Deep South ports. David Anderson of Kentucky, for example, received five slaves from Baltimore on December 9, 1818, and four more from Mr. Woolfolk on the same voyage. Another example is the schooner *Missouri.* On March 1, 1819, Mr. Robert Hart sent three slaves to the "Alabama Territory." They were named Maria, Paul and John.[461] On the same voyage, Moses Little, also a Baltimore dealer, sent eleven slaves to Alabama: Jim, Joshua, George, Isaac, Joseph, Ned, Robert, Harriet, Rose, and Rose's children, Maureen and Armemento.[462]

Another ship traveling to the Alabama territory from Baltimore was the *Ere*. Baltimore trader John Gilmore sponsored the shipment. On March 1, 1819, Mr. Gilmore sent six slaves on the voyage in question, three men and three women. Their names were Charles Hare, Ra-

---

458 Manifest of the brig Temperance, March 20, 1848.
459 Ibid.
460 Ibid.
461 Manifest of schooner Missouri, March 1, 1819.
462 Ibid.

chel Hymes, Pheebe, Sam, Jacob and Charlotte.[463]

Henry Coalman, also of Baltimore, sent two slaves on the brig *Clio* on March 20, 1819. One of these was William Davis, a twenty-two-year-old, five foot six, "very black" slave, and the other slave was Emmeline, a fifteen-year-old, five foot one, and light black in color.[464] The latter may have been a Muslim slave.

John R. Myrick of Baltimore, another slave trader, sent eight slaves, four men and four women to a dealer in New Orleans. The ship *Commodore Patterson* was captained by a New Orleans skipper named P. C. Wedarstrandt. The names of the slaves were Harriet, Dick, Peter, William, Peggy, Jenny, Fanny and John.[465]

On very rare occasions, slave dealers would send several dozen slaves at a time in their shipment. Joseph S. Donovan, for example, sent ninety-three captives on the *John C. Calhoun* captained by John L. Lowell on October 24, 1850. The trip was from Baltimore to New Orleans, where they were delivered to a trader named J. M. Wilson. The *John C. Calhoun* was named after the South Carolina politician, who was also the sixteenth president of the United States.[466]

Other nineteenth-century merchant ships that left Baltimore for the Deep South with a cargo of slaves included the schooner *Ann*, the *Thomas Hunter*, and the *Wild Cat*. The first two of these were on the

463 Manifest for ship Ere, March 1, 1819. John Gilmore (1788–1846), the son of Thomas and Elizabeth Gilmore and husband of Ann Brumfield Gilmore, was an important businessman and slave dealer in nineteenth-century Baltimore.

464 Manifest for brig Clio, March 20, 1819.

465 Manifest of ship Commodore Patterson, March 19, 1819. Peter C. Wedarstrandt, who was born around 1796, sent a number of slaves to New Orleans between 1807 and 1860.

466 Manifest of John C. Calhoun, October 24, 1850. Joseph S. Donovan sold slaves in Baltimore from 1843 until his death in 1861. His slave-trading business remained in operation by his wife Caroline until 1863 when it was closed and the slaves there were liberated by the Union Army. For more on Donovan's business, see Ralph Clayton's Cash for Blood, (Baltimore: Heritage Books, 2002). For more on the Forks in the Road Slave Market in Mississippi, see Jim Barnett and H. Clark Burkett, "The Forks in the Road Slave Market at Natchez," Mississippi History Now, http://mshistorynow.mdah.state.ms.us.

Baltimore to New Orleans route, while the third was on the path from Baltimore to Natchez, Mississippi, one of the largest slave hubs in the Deep South, particularly at the famous Forks in the Road Slave Market.

Mississippi, at the time, had slave markets in Aberdeen, Crystal Springs, Vicksburg, Woodville and the city of Jackson. But by far, the largest slave market in the first sixty years of the nineteenth century was the Forks in the Road Market at the intersection of Liberty Road and Washington Road, about a mile east of the city of Natchez itself. The Forks in the Road site appears on maps of Natchez, Mississippi, as early as 1818. These earliest map illustrations of slave markets in the city are on Catherine Street. There are two "Negroe Markets" shown at the Forks in the Road site. They were among the largest markets of slaves in the United States for much of the nineteenth century. A number of the Baltimore slave traders also had offices in Natchez, Mississippi.

The rise of the slave markets in Mississippi was preceded by the invention of the steamboat in 1814, as well as the introduction of Mexican cotton into the US economy in the early 1820s. These facts helped to expand the plantation culture in Mississippi.

Mississippi cotton farmer, William Johnson, in a diary entry from May 14, 1841, gives us a sense of some of the business going on at Natchez. He tells us, "I rode out to the Forks in the Road Market to try and swop [sic] Stephen off for someone else, but I could not find one I liked." Similar deals were conducted at the slave markets in Natchez throughout the first sixty-five years of the nineteenth century.

Several prominent Natchez townhouses, complete with dozens of slaves and sometimes their own slave jails, were within sight of the Natchez slave markets. Three of these prominent houses in the city were the D'evereau House, the Linden family house, and the building known as "Monmouth House."

Northerner, Joseph Holt Ingraham, visited the Forks in the Road Markets, but he says the practice of slavery there was different than in other places he had been. He remarks, "Slaves at Forks in the Road Market were not sold at auction, nor all at once, but singly and in parties in proportion to the wishes of the buyers.[467] Indeed, some of the

467 Joseph Holt Ingraham, quoted in Jim Barnett, "The Forks in the

Maryland slave traders, like John Armfield, for example, set up offices in Natchez more easily to accommodate their business there.

During a week of December 1839, another ship, the schooner *Ann*, while it rested at Jackson's Wharf on Fells Point in Baltimore, was seized by government officials on the suspicion of being fitted and soon to be engaged in the African slave trade. By that point, the schooner had not yet made its maiden voyage.[468] Britain, by 1808, had ended their Atlantic slave trade, so the US government seized the *Ann*.

Ralph Clayton, in an article entitled "A Bitter Inner Harbor Legacy: The Slave Trade," published in the *City Diary*, from July 12, 2000, describes some of the other merchant ships from Baltimore that carried slaves. He relates:

> Ships with names like *Agent, Architect, Hyperion, General Pinckney, Intelligence, Kirkwood, Tippecanoe,* and *Victorine* made their runs from wharves along the Inner Harbor, as well as at Fells Point.[469]

Mr. Clayton adds this comment used as an epigram for this chapter:

> Greed made for strange bedfellows. Many of Baltimore's slave dealers shipped together on the same brigs, barks, ships, and schooners making their cyclical runs to New Orleans.[470]

Clayton goes on to give examples of traders sharing ships. He tells us:

Road Slave Market at Natchez," in Journal of Mississippi History, 63, (Fall, 2001), pp. 169–187. Ingraham (1809–1860) was a New England clergyman and abolitionist. He spent several years at sea, then worked as a teacher of languages in Mississippi. In the 1840s, Ingraham produced Arthur's Magazine. He became an Episcopal priest in 1852, after which he pursued abolitionist causes.

468 Manifest schooner Ann, December 17, 1839.

469 Ralph Clayton, "A Bitter Inner Harbor Legacy: The Slave Trade," in City Diary, July 12, 2000.

470 Ibid.

> In October of 1845, Campbell, Donovan, and Slatter shipped 117 souls aboard the *Kirkwood*, from the Frederick Street Dock. The *Tippecanoe* sailed from Chase's Wharf, in January of 1842, with 114 souls shipped by Purvis, Slatter, and others.[471]

Chase's Wharf was an 1840s-era warehouse located at 1401 Thames Street, in the heart of Fells Point, in Baltimore. Clayton gives this summation at the end of his article:

> For 45 years, thousands of families and individuals were sent south on their final passage. For most on board this meant a death that came when families and loved ones were separated and "Sold South"—a separation where few returned. It also signified almost certain separation from one another in New Orleans; large families were rarely sold to the same buyer.[472]

The profits for these trans-Atlantic voyages were immense. Ralph Clayton, in his essay "Baltimore's African Slave Connection," published in April of 2002, speaks about these profits. He tells us:

> In 1849, reports surfaced indicating that a Baltimore clipper ship had earned $400,000 from just eleven slave-trading voyages over a four-year period.[473]

At times, these brigs and clipper ships were owned by the slave traders themselves. In Virginia, for example, the firm of Franklin and Armfield of Alexandria, Virginia, owned two ships called the *Tribune* and the *Uncas* employed in the run to New Orleans.[474]

These ships were later sold to a notorious owner of a slave jail in Washington named William H. Williams. Franklin and Armfield owned

471 Ibid.

472 Ibid.

473 Ralph Clayton, "Baltimore's African Slave Connection," April 4, 2002.

474 Manifests for Tribune and Uncas, March to June 1847.

another ship, the *Isaac Franklin*, named after the partner of the Alexandrian firm of Franklin and Armfield. It eventually was sold to their former agent from Frederick, George Kephart.[475]

On April 20, 1826, slave trader Austin Woolfolk rowed several slaves, at the foot of Fells Point in Baltimore, out to the waiting schooner the *Decatur,* then at anchor. When the wind was right, the ship set sail with its human cargo bound for the slave market in New Orleans. There was a mutiny on the voyage. On May 2, the crew of the whaling ship the *Constitution*, bound for Nantucket, spotted the *Decatur*. Believing that the crew needed supplies, the captain of the *Constitution* pulled alongside the schooner and asked for permission to board.

The slaves of the *Decatur* ordered the remaining crew to allow entry. Armed with muskets and sidearms, the crew members from the *Constitution* restored order on the *Decatur*, and nineteen slaves were taken aboard the *Constitution*—eight women, four men and seven children. The remaining fourteen male slaves were left on board the *Decatur*, along with the ship's crew, at least those who were not thrown overboard earlier during the mutiny.

Three days later, on May 5, the brig *Rooke* approached the *Decatur* and took the remaining fourteen slaves aboard their ship. When the *Rooke* arrived in the port of New York a short time later, all fourteen slaves escaped into the city. Although great expense was made to recapture them, only one slave, a man named William Bowser, was apprehended. He was discovered in Westchester, New York, and returned to the *Decatur,* still at the New York port.[476]

475 Manifest of ship Isaac Franklin, September 28, 1838. For more on the mutiny on the Decatur, see Ralph Clayton's "Baltimore's Own Version of the Amistad: Slave Revolt," in Baltimore Journal, January 7, 1998.

476 Manifest of brig Rooke, May 5, 1826, in Niles Weekly Register, May 20, 1863, p. 202.

Mr. Bowser was put on trial for escaping in a New York court. Mr. Woolfolk attended the trial. During the proceedings, Bowser stood and stared at Woolfolk and then reportedly said that he forgave the slave trader for all the injuries he had brought upon him, and that he hoped someday to meet up with him in Heaven. Subsequently, on December 15, 1826, Mr. Bowser was executed for having murdered two members of the white crew named Galloway and Porter.[477]

In addition to ship manifests for voyages from Baltimore to New Orleans, there are also several extant from Baltimore to Savannah, Georgia. Austin Woolfolk, for example, on March 17, 1829, sent twenty-four slaves on a voyage of the brig *Aurora,* which was captained by George Adams.[478]

On October 18 and December 6 of 1828, Mr. Woolfolk sent slaves aboard the schooner *Sally.*[479] On October 2, 1828, to cite another example, Mr. Woolfolk shipped slaves to Savannah aboard the steamer *Cherokee*.[480]

A variety of other slave traders from Baltimore and their manifests of moving slaves to the Deep South market are also extant. Many of those are listed in the appendix to this chapter. This brings us to the thirteen major slave dealers in Baltimore in the mid-nineteenth century, the subject matter of the next, and central, section of this fifth chapter.

Baltimore Slave Dealers and Traders: 1800 to 1860

By the end of the 1820s, a number of slave dealers already were operating in Baltimore. Hezekiah Niles, the editor of the *Weekly Register*, in that same city and same year, remarks:

> Dealing in slaves has become a large business. Establishments have been made in several places in Maryland and Virginia at which slaves are sold like cattle at a state fair.[481]

---

477 William Bowser is discussed in Ralph Clayton's "Baltimore's Own Version of Amistad," Baltimore Chronicle, January 7, 1998.

478 Manifest of brig Aurora, March 17, 1829.

479 Manifest of schooner Sally, October 2, 1828.

480 Manifest of schooner Cherokee, October 2, 1828.

481 Hezekiah Niles, "Slave Dealing," in Weekly Register, June 26, 1828. Mr. Niles (1777–1839) was an American editor and publisher of his Baltimore-based Niles National Weekly Register.

By the year 1839, slave dealer Hope Slatter advertised his slave jail in the *Baltimore Sun*. He says that his slave jail "Features separate apartments for male and female slaves."[482] Slatter would continue to advertise in the *Sun* and other publications over the next several years in Baltimore and elsewhere, as we shall see later in this chapter.

The earliest evidence for slave traders in Baltimore comes from an April 1802 report of a Joseph Ennells and a Captain Frazer, who took slaves from Baltimore to Philadelphia.[483] In this very early period, slave dealers were called "Speculators" or "Interlopers" and many appear to have visited the city in the early years of the nineteenth century. By the year 1860, J. S. Buckingham (1786–1855), in his *American Historical Statistics*, volume one, chapter twenty-three, observes:

> There are two extensive slave dealers and several smaller ones in the city of Baltimore. The principal ones have amassed large fortunes in the traffic.[484]

Mr. Buckingham goes on to indicate that the two "extensive" traders are Austin Woolfolk and Hope Slatter. In fact, in the first sixty-five years of the nineteenth century, more than a dozen major slave traders operated in Baltimore. We will enumerate them here, and then discuss them one at a time in this section—the main section—of chapter five:

1. Austin Woolfolk (1796–1847)
2. Hope H. Slatter (1790–1853)
3. James F. Purvis (1760–1836)
4. Joseph S. Donovan (1801–1861)
5. Moody and Downs slave traders
6. James Bates at the Barnum City Hotel

482 Ibid.

483 Anonymous, "Hope Slatter," in In Light of History 1, no. 1, March 26 to April 3, 2016.

484 Joseph Ennells mentioned in Scott Shane's "The Secret History of City's Slave Trade," in The Baltimore Sun, June 20, 1999. Joseph Ennells and his partner, James Frazier, were bounty hunters from Philadelphia who made their money by capturing runaway slaves and returning them to their owners. See Daniel E. Meaders, Kidnappers in Philadelphia (Cherry Hill: Africana Homstead Legend Publishers, 2009).

7. B. M. and William Campbell
8. Wilson, Hines, and Fairbanks
9. George Kephart
10. William Harker
11. John Woods
12. John N. Denning
13. Jonathan M. Wilson (1797–1831)[485]

The first and most notorious of the Baltimore slave traders in the nineteenth century was Austin Woolfolk, whose reign in Baltimore lasted from 1818 until 1841, five years before his death. Woolfolk was born in Tennessee. He served in that state's militia during the War of 1812 and participated in the Battle of New Orleans. In the battle, Andrew Jackson, the only general who served in both the Revolutionary War and the War of 1812, won two major battles during this war. President Jackson also was the only American president who supervised slaves coffles in the US, as we have indicated earlier in this study.

The battle in which Woolfolk contributed occurred when the British headed toward Louisiana in late 1814. Jackson—anxious to atone for his Revolutionary War experience—won the battle with Woolfolk's help. It was at this battle that Woolfolk saw the fortunes to be made on the backs of African slaves—and that is precisely what he did.[486]

When Austin Woolfolk first arrived in Baltimore, he was only nineteen years old, but he was an entrepreneur with a gift for imagining a market long before it even existed. In the beginning, Woolfolk used the Baltimore City Jail to store his captives. As cotton became the crop of the Deep South, as well as the invention of the steamship in 1814, Woolfolk decided to build his own jail, and he did so in 1818. Later, Woolfolk's brothers and other relatives joined him in Baltimore to share in the profits. As we shall see, several members of the same

---

485 J. S. Buckingham, "Slave Traders in Baltimore," in American Historical Statistics (London, 1860). James Silk Buckingham (1786–1855) was a Cornish-born writer, journalist and traveler. It was said of him that he "fused a new light in Indian journalism in America." He published an autobiography in 1855 by Longmans, Brown, and Green in London.

486 See more on each of these figures in the analyses below.

family would often engage in the domestic slave trade in America in the nineteenth century. The Woolfolks were one such family.

Mr. Woolfolk set up relationships with traders elsewhere in Maryland, including Annapolis and the Eastern Shore, as well as Washington, DC and Alexandria, Virginia, as we shall see in Chapter Six. By 1821, Austin Woolfolk's Baltimore business included a whitewashed house and private jail located on Pratt Street at the intersection of what is today Martin Luther King Jr. Blvd. in Baltimore. In 1824, Woolfolk referred to himself as the "Justly Celebrated."[487]

Mr. Woolfolk's slave trading business was on the north side of Pratt Street, west of Cove Street, which is now Fremont Avenue in the city near what was then the Three Tuns Tavern. Frederick Douglass, in his famous Fourth of July speech, refers to Mr. Woolfolk's business as the "Head of Pratt Street."[488] Douglass is referring here to this site. The speech of Douglass titled "What to the Slave is the Fourth of July" was delivered on July 5, 1852.

In the speech, Douglass argues that for the disenfranchised slave population, the Fourth of July had no real significance, so black folk ought not to celebrate the festivities that go along with that day.

After Woolfolk set up in Baltimore, his uncle, John Woolfolk, established slave trading businesses and offices in New Orleans and Natchez, Mississippi. John ran the business, sold captives, acted as a bank, and remitted tens of thousands of dollars that sustained a supply chain of slaves.

The combination of newspaper advertisements, developments in financial matters, and an unusual corporate structure (for the day) gave the Woolfolks a competitive advantage, for they were in it before anyone else. Woolfolk was also in business with five of his brothers. They set up slave pens in a number of locations in Maryland, including Baltimore, as we have shown, and in the city of Easton on the Eastern Shore of Maryland.

Even early on, however, Woolfolk was not without his critics. An-

---

487 Austin Woolfolk served in The Battle of New Orleans, which was conducted on January 8 to the 18, 1815. It was called the "most one-sided battle of the War of 1812."

488 Mr. Woolfolk called himself this name, mostly in the 1820s and 30s, during the height of his slave-trading business.

ti-slavery Quakers arrived in town at Fells Point to inspect the ships owned by Mr. Woolfolk. He brushed aside the criticisms, however, and continued with his business model. In 1826, there was a mutiny on one of Woolfolk's ships called the *Decatur*, which was mentioned in the previous section of this chapter. The mutineers, as we indicated, threw the captain and three members of the crew overboard.[489]

Abolitionist Benjamin Lundy covered the *Decatur* story in his Baltimore newspaper *The Genius of Universal Emancipation*.[490] Another young abolitionist arrived in Baltimore to contest Woolfolk's business. His name was William Lloyd Garrison. Among other things, Garrison suggested that Woolfolk's business was the "Moral equivalent of Kidnapping."[491]

On January 9, 1827, while Mr. Lundy was investigating public records of Woolfolk's ships, Woolfolk and Lundy met on a Baltimore street corner. Woolfolk assaulted Mr. Lundy and by-standers pulled the strapping slave trader off the slight newspaperman.[492]

Later, Mr. Lundy wrote about the experience: "With a brutal ferocity that is perfectly in character with his business, he choked me until my breath was gone, and stamped me in the head and face, with the fury of a veritable demon."[493] Earlier, Lundy had said of Mr. Woolfolk, "He is a monster in human shape," among other things in the *Genius* in late 1826. Lundy had moved his family to Baltimore in October of

489 Frederick Douglass, quoted in Calvin Schermerhorn's The Business of Slavery and the Rise of American Capitalism (New Haven: Yale University Press, 2015). The Three Tuns Tavern was on the northeast corner of Pratt and Paca Streets in downtown Baltimore.

490 Niklas Frykman, Mutiny and Maritime Radicalism in the Age of Reason (Cambridge: Cambridge University Press, 2015). Dr. John Woolfolk (1824–1890) was the uncle of slave trader Austin Woolfolk.

491 Benjamin Lundy, The Genius of Universal Emancipation (London: Forgotten Books, 2016), pp. 1–24. Lundy (1789–1839) was an American Quaker and abolitionist from New Jersey. He published several anti-slavery newspapers and magazines and traveled widely. Lundy attempted to establish a colony outside the US for freed slaves but did not succeed in that endeavor.

492 Quoted in Amy Reynolds, "William Lloyd Garrison, Benjamin Lundy, and Libel," in Communication, Law, and Policy 6, no. 4 (2001).

493 Ibid.

1825. This enabled him to print the *Genius* on a weekly basis, as opposed to monthly.

The week after the assault, Woolfolk pleaded guilty to the assault charges, but the judge, one Nicholas Brice, agreed with Woolfolk's attorney that the slave trader had been provoked. Consequently, Woolfolk was ordered to pay a fine of one dollar.

The judge also urged Woolfolk to bring libel charges against Lundy, but a grand jury refused to indict him.[494] Between 1818 and 1846, Austin Woolfolk shipped nearly three thousand slaves from Baltimore to New Orleans, as well as to other cities in the Deep South, such as Savannah, Georgia; and Charleston, South Carolina, for example.

When Woolfolk rose to hear his sentence, many of those present were surprised that Judge Brice ordered the infamous slave trader to pay a fine of one dollar. After the trial, Woolfolk continued as one of the leading slave dealers, profiting by hundreds of thousands of dollars, well into the 1830s. Lundy, on the other hand, continued his abolitionist cause, managing from then on to steer clear of Mr. Woolfolk.

Eventually, Mr. Lundy (1789–1839), returned to New England where he continued to work for abolitionist issues. Later, he moved to Lowell, Illinois, where he again worked for abolition. He also died there.

One other aspect of Mr. Woolfolk's business is pointed out by Ralph Clayton in his essay "Baltimore's Own Version of the 'Armistad' Slave Revolt." Clayton informs us:

> Led by Woolfolk, the slave coffle made its way down Pratt Street to Philpot Street, and to the Wharf at the foot of Fells Point. There, they were placed in small boats and rowed out to the Schooner, *Decatur*, at anchor a short distance offshore. Later, when a good wind blew, the Ship set sail with its human cargo bound for the Market in New Orleans. It was the 20th of April 1826, and the course of the lives of everyone on board was about to change dramatically.[495]

494 Benjamin Lundy, The Life, Travels, and Opinions of Benjamin Lundy (Philadelphia: William Parrish, 1847), p. 29.
495 Ibid.

Austin Woolfolk then paraded his slaves in a coffle, from his place of business in Baltimore, near the present Inner Harbor, across Pratt Street East to ships waiting off the shore of Fells Point. Woolfolk's name first appeared in the Baltimore newspapers and other publications in the *Baltimore Directory* in 1819.

Austin Woolfolk's Georgia connection relative to Baltimore is first noted in the *Columbian Museum and Savannah Gazette* on April 24, 1819.[496] Thus, Austin Woolfolk had a slave-trading business in Baltimore, as well as connections in the states of Georgia and South Carolina, in the earliest years of the nineteenth century.

Mr. Woolfolk preferred to move his slave coffles in Baltimore in the middle of the night, chained together and on foot. Hope Slatter, and others, often employed carriages or omnibuses to move his slaves from his slave jail to packet ships at the Baltimore Harbor or at Fells Point. A typical example of Woolfolk's ships moving to the Deep South is the voyage of the *Helen E. Miller* that embarked on November 15, 1852, on its way to New Orleans, the largest slave-trading hub in the Deep South. Aboard that ship was twenty-year-old Martha Weems, who said her final goodbyes that day to her family in Baltimore. Weems was one of one hundred and fifteen slaves on that voyage whose final destination was the Louisiana city.[497]

Compared to later traders in Baltimore, Woolfolk's advertisements in the *Easton Gazette*, the *Centreville Times*, the *Cecil Republican*, the *Baltimore Gazette*, and the *Federal Gazette* in Washington, always spoke of seeking a "reasonable number of slaves." This is particularly true throughout the 1820s.

The reins of the slave trade in Baltimore passed from Mr. Woolfolk to a man named Hope H. Slatter, who was originally from Clinton, a small town about fifteen miles northeast of Macon, Georgia. Slatter became involved in the slave business in Baltimore around 1835. In February of that year, he took advertisements out in the *Baltimore Republican* and the *Commercial Adviser*, which show that

---

496 Shermerhorn, p. 222. Nicholas Brice (1777–1851) was born in Anne Arundel County, Maryland, and died in Baltimore. He was a Federal judge for many years in Maryland.

497 Quoted by Clayton in "Armistad."

Slatter wished to purchase "several seamstresses and small fancy girls for nurses."[498]

The term "Fancy Girl" was employed in Maryland and Virginia in the first half of the nineteenth century to denote a slave girl who had been forced into sex work to repay the expense of bringing her to the Chesapeake region. An African American teenager named Alice, for example, was purchased in Virginia in 1833 and later sold as a "fancy girl" in Mississippi for more than double her original purchase price.[499]

In November of 1833, Isaac Franklin, a Virginia slaver and partner in the firm Franklin & Armfield, wrote a letter to his agent, John Ballard in Virginia, regarding whether the former had any "Fancy Girls" among his captives. Franklin wrote, "We have no Fancy Girls on hand but your girl, Minerva and she is cautious."[500]

The slave in question was a woman named Minerva Robinson, who refused to participate in her sale as a "Fancy Girl" at that time.[501] John Ballard operated his slave-trading business from the lobby of the Exchange Hotel in Richmond on 14th and Franklin Streets. From the 1850s on, when the hotel was constructed, he ran that establishment, as well.

At any rate, in July through September of 1838, Hope Slatter ran a series of twenty-seven lengthy advertisements in the *Baltimore Sun* offering to pay cash for slaves. One typical ad of Mr. Slatter's looked like this:

> Cash For Negroes
>
> The Subscriber has built a large and extensive establishment and private jail for the keeping of Slaves. This new building located on Pratt Street, one door from Howard Street and opposite the Circus or Repository, is not surpassed by any establishment of its kind in the United

498 "Austin Woolfolk Family," in Columbian Museum and Savannah Gazette, November 15, 1852. The Columbia Museum of Art is in Columbia, South Carolina, at 1515 Main Street. The Savannah Gazette is the newsletter of the Savannah directory in that city.

499 Manifest of Helen E. Miller, November 15, 1852.

500 Hope Slatter, advertisement for slaves, The Baltimore Republican, February 15, 1835. The Baltimore Republican and Commercial Adviser was a newspaper published in the city from 1827 until 1883.

501 Ibid.

States. All rooms are above ground. Office in the basement story. N.B. I can always be found there, or a line left at the bar of the Owings Globe Inn, at the corner of Howard and Market Streets, will be attended to my absence. Having as a wish to accommodate my Southern friends and others in the Trade, I am determined to pay the highest prices with good and sufficient titles. Persons having such property to dispose of would do well to see me before they sell, as I am purchasing in the New Orleans Market.[502]

In the mid-nineteenth century, The Globe Inn and Hotel was located at Howard and Market Street in Baltimore. It originally was owned by Mr. J. R. Thomas, who sold the hotel to J. W. Owings. Thus, it became called the "Ownings Globe Inn" in Hope Slatter's time in Baltimore. Mr. Slatter also mentions the slave trade from the Chesapeake Bay region to what he refers to as the "Southern Market."

Mr. Slatter's reference that "All rooms are above ground" points out the fact that at his slave jail, captives were kept "above ground" as opposed to other Baltimore traders at the time who fitted their slave jails with dungeons often underground.

Mr. Slatter closes the above advertisement with a price list. He reveals:

Prices

Likely Fellows, aged 13 to 23…
$500 to $650

Women of the Same Age and Quality….
$300 to $500

The Best Field Hands…
$300 to $400[503]

502 Isaac Franklin to John Ballard, November 26, 1833. John P. Ballard's slave-trading firm in Richmond was on Franklin Street between 13th and 14th Streets. The Exchange Hotel was on Franklin Street, as well. The Gothic Revival building was built in 1841.

503 Ibid. Mr. Ballard bought Minerva Robinson for the sum of four hundred dollars. The Exchange Hotel, built in 1841, is a four-story Gothic

The establishment to which Mr. Slatter refers was a two-story, brick building with barred windows. In the rear of the building, at 244 W. Pratt Street, and along its western side was a bricked paved yard about forty feet wide and seventy-five feet long. The yard contained a few benches, a hydrant, and many wash tubs and rope clotheslines. The slaves spent their daylight hours in the courtyard.[504]

While the slaves waited to be purchased by new owners, they were not required to do much work. They spent their time playing cards and dancing and singing to the sounds of banjos, harmonicas and fiddles. Occasionally, passers-by would toss pennies into the yard.

On the west side of the yard was the auction block. Even today, on the east side of the building, the brick fireplace that was used for cooking and warmth can still be seen.[505] In Chapter Seven of this study, we shall say more about Mr. Slatter's auction block in Baltimore.

There are two extant descriptions of Mr. Slatter and his operation. One writer at the time says that Slatter was:

> A man of much intelligence and tact, of good address and public spirit, although because of his business he was a social outcast.[506]

Another chronicler of the slave trade era in Baltimore is a man named Daniel Drayton, an ardent abolitionist. In his "Personal Memoir," he speaks of encountering Mr. Slatter at the railway station in Washington, DC, on April 22, 1848. When Slatter was about to board the train with a coffle of Negroes on their way to Georgia, Drayton says about the dealer, "He stood on the platform chatting along with the chaplain of the senate, a Methodist brother, as an "old gray-haired villain."[507] Thus, Mr. Slatter appears to have had business connections in Savannah, Georgia, as well. This, of course, is also another example

Revival building designed by Isaiah Rogers.

504 Hope Slatter, "Cash for Negroes," The Baltimore Sun, September 21, 1838. The circus or repository was located at Pratt and Howard Streets in Baltimore.

505 Ibid.

506 John Stephens, Slatter as Administrator (London: Forsyth and Harris, 1858), pp. 1–23.

507 Ibid.

of moving slaves from the upper to the lower south, this time by rail, as well as the Methodist religious revivals at the beginning of the nineteenth century, during the Second Great Awakening.

Daniel Drayton (1802–1857) is also a significant figure because he orchestrated the bold escape of seventy-seven DC area slaves on the evening of April 18, 1848. The slaves quietly slipped away from their quarters in Washington, near Georgetown, and they walked through the unpaved and barely lit streets to the ship the *Pearl*, which was waiting in dock on the Potomac River. Winifred Conkling, in her recent book *Passenger on the Pearl*, catalogs the experiences of the escaped slaves on the *Pearl*. The book was published by Algonquin Young Books in 2015.

A few years earlier, on May 28, 1841, Mr. Slatter was visited by the poet John Greenleaf Whittier (1807–1892), who was a Quaker and an abolitionist. Joseph Sturge, an English Quaker, accompanied Mr. Whittier. The two visitors made an inspection in the interest of the anti-slavery movement. Mr. Sturge begins his account of Slatter's facilities this way:

> Perhaps my account may not be accurate in every particular, as I was interrupted before I had done conversing with him. Their tale was enough to harrow up every soul not absolutely petrified by participation in the "crimes of the blackest hue."[508]

The "Their" to whom Sturge refers are two slave girls from Frederick County, Maryland, being interviewed by the visitors. When Slatter found out what the visitors were doing, he stormed into the yard and said, "Slavery according to Christianity, and justified by the ablest divines in this country, in the North, as well as the South. I treat my niggers in the kindest manner. When they arrive, I give them the most pleasant homes, and everyone is furnished with a good bed, and a net to keep off the mosquitos. Why damn it, there is not a happier set of laborers on God's Earth than the niggers in the South."[509]

508 Ibid.

509 Daniel Drayton, "Personal Memoir on Hope Slatter," April 22, 1848. Drayton (1802–1857) was born in southern New Jersey near the Delaware Bay. He committed suicide in 1857 after ingesting a lethal dose of Laudanum, which he got from a local chemist.

Mr. Sturge concludes the encounter in his memoir this way:

> I retired with a firmer resolution than ever to wage a war of extermination against the nefarious and bloody system, and with a mind filled with abhorrence on account of such wickedness. If I had needed anything to impress indelibly upon my mind, a sense of the injustice of slavery, and to make the principles of abolition a part of my nature, the scenes I witnessed in this slave prison would have been sufficient.[510]

Here, Mr. Sturge displays the attitude of arrogance typically displayed by northern abolitionist of the day regarding the practice of slavery. One final aspect of Hope Slatter's involvement in the slave trade in Baltimore is that in his coffles from Fells Point to his slave jail on Pratt Street, he preferred to use the new "horse-drawn omnibuses" to move the slaves to his property and slave jail, while he usually followed on horseback.

Several photographs are extant of these omnibuses, including one of a two-horse drawn carriage that resembles a San Francisco trolley car with rubber wheels.[511]

In addition to the slave-trading of Austin Woolfolk and Hope Slatter, the most prominent Baltimore slave dealers in the nineteenth century were Bernard M. Campbell, his brother Walter, and Joseph S. Donovan. In the mid to late-1840s Donovan was calling himself a "Slave Merchant" in advertisements in the *Baltimore Sun*, like this one from July 23, 1847:

> Negroes Wanted
>
> The highest cash prices will be given for Negroes I wish to purchase. I wish to purchase a large lot of Negroes for Sugar and Cotton Planters. I also will give the largest prices for House Servants or Mechanics. Those having such for sale will find it to their interests to call at my

510 John Greenleaf Whittier, quoted in Stanton Tierman, "Whittier on Slatter," The Baltimore Sun, July 24, 1863. Joseph Sturge (1793–1859) was a Quaker, abolitionist and activist. He founded the British and Foreign Anti-Slavery Society in London.

511 Ibid.

> office, on Camden Street, in the rear of the Railroad Depot, and later in other states.[512]

Mr. Donovan points out that by the year 1847, the two main crops in the Deep South were cotton and sugar. Indeed, by the turn of the nineteenth century, sugar cane was being grown in Maryland, Virginia, North Carolina, South Carolina, Georgia and Louisiana, as well as the tobacco crop in the Chesapeake Bay region, with the predominant amount of sugar consumption in the Chesapeake from Louisiana and from Cuba.

Often slave traders in the mid-nineteenth century positioned their businesses so that they were adjacent to the local railroad station, as was the case here with Mr. Donovan's place of business. The term "Mechanic" referred to by Mr. Donovan in the above advertisement refers to any skilled laborer with a trade, like carpenters, coopers, brick makers, ship's captains, or even horse trainers, for examples.

In another advertisement in the same newspaper from April 26, 1851, Donovan enquires about:

> The undersigned continues at his old stand No. 13 Camden Street to pay the highest prices for Negroes by Railroad or Steamboat, will find it convenient to secures their Negroes, as my Jail is adjoining the Railroad Depot, and near the Steamboat Landings. Negroes received for safe keeping.[513]

Mr. Donovan alludes to the fact that in addition to maintaining a slave jail in Baltimore, he also takes on boarders who belonged to other traders. In fact, out of town traders would frequently come to Baltimore, stay in local hotels, and then board their slaves at Mr. Donovan's jail, or at other slave jails in the city.

It is also clear from the quotation above, Mr. Donovan employed the American railroads to move his slaves from Baltimore to the Deep South, as the ship manifests mentioned earlier in this chapter. Donavan also indicates that he moved slaves from the Upper South to the Deep

512 Joseph Sturge, quoted in Steven Deyle, Hope Slatter: An American Trader (Oxford: Oxford University Press, 2005), p. 77.

513 Ibid.

South by steamship from the Baltimore ports to Mississippi and Louisiana, as we shall see in the appendix to this chapter.

Some of the Baltimore hotels where these visiting slave traders stayed included Hotel Stafford on Mount Vernon Square and the Ownings Globe Inn at Baltimore and Howard Streets, mentioned earlier. The Sinner's Hotel, on the southwest corner of Albemarle and Water Streets in Baltimore, and at the Barnum's City Hotel, at Fayette and Calvert Streets, were also places where the out-of-town traders stayed.

Between November of 1843 and December of 1852, Joseph Donovan organized sixty-five shipments of slaves from Baltimore to New Orleans, including some listed in the previous section of this chapter. During that time, Donovan's voyages carried a total of 2,113 slaves, making his business one of the largest slave-trading firms in Baltimore, as well as in the state of Maryland.[514]

Colonel John Tilghman previously dealt with the southern slave market with his agent Spencer Grayson. On November 29, 1849, or so, the Queen Anne's County records claim that Col. Tilghman dealt a number of slaves to Mr. Donovan, including one "Harriet Turner, born around 1828, and died in 1865."[515]

Harriet Turner was one of sixty of Mr. Tilghman's captives who moved between his Poplar Grove Estate in Queen Anne's County and his farm in Talbot County.[516] Later, she would pen an autobiography called *Incidents in the Life of a Slave Girl* using her married name Harriet Jacobs.[517]

Mr. Donovan also did business with a man named John Bradshaw, who operated a hotel in Cambridge on the Eastern Shore of Maryland, or so Ralph Clayton tells us in his book *Cash For Blood: The Balti-*

514 Ibid.

515 Joseph S. Donovan, "Negroes Wanted," in The Baltimore Sun, July 23, 1847.

516 Ibid., April 26, 1851. Andrew McLaughlin married Frances Barnum. Andrew worked for Frances' father, David Barnum. When David died in 1844, McLaughlin took control of the Barnum Hotel.

517 Manifests of Joseph Donovan, quoted in Josephine F. Pacheco, The Pearl: A Failed Slave Ship on the Potomac (Chapel Hill: University of North Carolina Press, 2005), p. 121.

more to New Orleans Slave Trade.[518] Another Baltimore slave dealer who did business from a hotel was James Bates. He used a desk in the lobby of Barnum's City Hotel in the 1840s in Baltimore to perform his slave-trading duties.

Zenus Barnum and Andrew McLaughlin owned the Barnum's City Hotel in Baltimore at Fayette and Calvert Streets. They advertised in the *Baltimore Sun* in the spring of 1858. In the ad Barnum and McLaughlin say:

> Negroes For Sale
>
> Barnum's City Hotel
>
> Monument Square, Baltimore[519]

The pair goes on to say that the hotel is the most comfortable in the city, it has "reasonable prices," and both short and more lengthy stays can be arranged. At any rate, James Bates conducted his slave-trading business in the lobby of Barnum's Hotel.[520] Mr. Barnum also operated the circus in the city of Baltimore for many years, later called Barnum and Bailey Circus, beginning in April of 1871. One final extant record of Mr. Donovan's slave-trading firm involves him going to the home of a former slave named William H. Williams. Donovan arrived at the home in Washington, DC, on the mall and took away his family. Although Mr. Williams was indeed free, his family was still owned by a man in New Orleans who wanted them returned.[521]

---

518 "Harriet Turner," in Secretary of State Pardon Records, MSA S1108-2, November 3, 1849, p. 66. Col. John Tilghman (1785–1866) was the son of Judge James Tilghman of Centreville in Queen Anne's County, where he owned a tobacco farm. The Rev. Spencer Grayson (1734–1784) of Prince William County, Virginia, was a chaplain in the Revolutionary Army and a slave-trading agent for Col. Tilghman.

519 Ibid. The Poplar Grove Farm was a vast estate in Queen Anne's County, Maryland, held for over three hundred years by the Emory family.

520 Harriet Jacobs, Incidences in the Life of a Slave Girl (New York: CreateSpace, 2014). Jacobs (1813–1897) was born into slavery in North Carolina. At the age of eighteen, in 1841, she secretly boarded a boat bound for Philadelphia, New York, and then freedom. Later, she wrote her autobiography under her married name.

521 Ralph Clayton, Cash For Blood: The Baltimore to New Orleans Slave Trade (Berwyn Heights: Heritage Books, 2002), pp. 103–109 and 415.

Mr. Williams, a former slave himself, nevertheless became a slave dealer and the owner of the notorious "Yellow House," that we will discuss in the next chapter of this study. Mr. Williams also appears to have done business with some of the slave markets in Natchez, Mississippi.

The Baltimore slave-trading firm of the Campbell brothers, Bernard and Walter, was one of the most lucrative firms in that trade. The original location of their company was at 26 Conway Street, but they later moved to 242 West Pratt Street. The Campbells regularly advertised in the *Baltimore Sun*, like this ad from January 20, 1849:

> Negroes Wanted
>
> Persons with Slaves to sell will find us located at the extensive establishment formerly owned by Hope H. Slatter. We have purchased his entire possessions on Pratt Street, No. 244, at which place all who have slaves to sell will be sure to get the highest prices, when the Negroes are young and healthy.[522]

Before Mr. Slatter sold his slave jail to the Campbells, while still on Conway Street, the Campbells also advertised thusly:

> Slaves Wanted
>
> All persons who desire the largest kind of prices for Slaves they might wish to sell will be sure to receive it by calling at our Office at no. 26 Conway Street.[523]

In another advertisement from the *Baltimore Sun*, dated July 1, 1845, Mr. Campbell was selling slaves, rather than buying them. He informs us:

> For Sale
>
> A first-rate cook, washer, and ironer with her two female children. She is well qualified for her profession being a first rate pastry, beignet and bread maker A situation in the Country would be preferred. Her husband,

---

522 Bernard Campbell, "Negroes Wanted," in The Baltimore Sun, January 20, 1849.

523 Ibid.

a first-rate Coachman, can be purchased if desired.[524]

Again, Mr. Campbell seems to believe that the most valuable aspect of this slave for whom he advertises are the woman's skills, as well as those of her husband. The advertisement says nothing else about the woman, her husband, nor about her two daughters, other than they are more suited to the "Country life." He does not even give the names of his captives in the advertisement.

The Campbell brothers also served other roles in the slave-trading business of the nineteenth century. In the spring of 1862, for example, the District of Columbia Compensation Emancipation Act required that all slaves in the district must be given a numerical value, so that the owners could be compensated.

The commissioners, at that time, brought in from Baltimore, "The experienced dealer in slaves, B. M. Campbell."[525] Mr. Campbell was to provide "expert and independent opinions as to the values of slaves."

For example, on June 16, 1862, Mrs. Margaret Barber, a Washington slave owner, came to Mr. Campbell to have him evaluate the worth of her twenty-eight slaves. After examining Mrs. Barber's property, he valued the slaves only to be worth $9,331.30. The commission was told earlier by Mrs. Barber that her captives were worth $23,400.[526]

Mr. Campbell gave similar estimates usually in favor of the side of the commission, often evaluating at one third the estimates of slave owners, as in the above case.[527]

Another role that Bernard M. Campbell fulfilled was frequently being at the center of the machinations of several Maryland slaves who became prominent in Baltimore. One such slave was Daniel Hawkins, who was released from the Baltimore City Jail on July 25, 1851, and placed in Mr. Campbell's jail.

Later, Mr. Hawkins' name appears on one of the manifests of

---

524 Ibid., July 1, 1845.

525 District of Columbia Compensation Emancipation Act was signed into law on April 16, 1862, by President Abraham Lincoln. This act ended slavery in the city of Washington, and it required payment to slave owners upon the release of their slaves.

526 Margaret Catherine Barber's 1862 Compensation Petition #366.

527 Ibid.

Campbell's ships moving from Baltimore to New Orleans.[528] Earlier, we mentioned Harriet Turner, an author and slave of Col. Tilghman. Turner was another prominent slave of B. M. Campbell's purchased from Col. Tilghman.

For the most part, Bernard Campbell did business in Baltimore while his brother Walter conducted slave trading throughout Louisiana, although his main office was in New Orleans. From that spot, he did the buying and selling, like this bill of sale:

> Know all men by these present that I, W. C. Campbell of New Orleans, for the sum of seven hundred dollars, do bargain and sell to Mr. T. P. Leather, a Negro Girl, age sixteen, named Charlott Cooper. Said girl is fully guaranteed against all vices, maladies by the Law & is hereby declared a Slave for Life.[529]

Again, the emphasis in this advertisement is on the health of the young girl in question, as well as her ability for reproduction, and thus additional slaves for Mr. Campbell. Campbell also makes it clear that Charlott is a "Slave for Life," as opposed to a term of years of indenture.

The Baltimore firm of Moody and Downs was located at 37 South Street in Baltimore and owned by a man named Nathaniel Austin. He later moved a few doors up the street to 24 South Street. The Moody and Downs firm was first owned by Hope Slatter and later was sold to Nathaniel Austin.[530]

---

528 Anonymous, "Needles in a Haystack," in Landscapes of Slavery and Freedom. Two other documents are relevant to the life of Daniel Hawkins. The Maryland State Archives database, Legacy of Slavery in Maryland, lists a Daniel Hawkins as being admitted to the Baltimore City Jail on July 22, 1851. A few weeks later, still in July of 1851, a Daniel Hawkins is listed as residing in Lancaster County, Pennsylvania. Could it be that this is the same Daniel Hawkins who escaped the Baltimore jail and went north to Pennsylvania?

529 Bill of Sale, W. C. Campbell to T. P. Leather, May 15, 1848.

530 Moody & Downs, owned by Nathaniel Austin, had a slave market in Baltimore at No. 37 South Street. Ellynor Sebold, in her book Love Across the Ocean (Aden Basin, New York, 2016), p. 24, also mentions the slave-trading business of Mr. Austin.

The address of James Purvis's slave-trading business was at Sinner's Hotel on the southwest corner of Albermarle and Water Streets. The residence of Purvis was on Gallows Hill, between Eden and Asquith Streets, near the Missionary Church in East Baltimore. Purvis was the nephew of Isaac Franklin, one of the proprietors of the largest slave jail in Virginia—Franklin & Armfield.[531] This, of course, is another example of multiple members of the same family engaged in a slave-trading firm in the nineteenth century.

James Bates, a Baltimore slave dealer mentioned earlier, also did his business from the Barnum City Hotel.[532] In the Baltimore directories from 1856 and 1860, Mr. Bates advertised his two businesses at Number 1 President Street, near Pratt Street in Baltimore. In 1856, he claimed to be in business as an iron founder, "ready to fix any kind of machinery," while in 1860 directory, he informs us:

> We are at times purchasing slaves, and in paying the highest prices for the same.[533]

George Harker, another Baltimore slave trader, also advertised his business in the *Baltimore Sun*. In the edition from August 24, 1842, he tells us he has for sale:

> For Sale: A likely Negro Boy, about twenty years old, and has about fourteen years of service. He is a first-rate hand with horses and will be sold at a bargain, if immediate application be made to the Subscriber at Number two South Street, two doors below Baltimore Street.[534]

531 James Franklin Purvis was the nephew of Isaac Franklin. Clayton, in "Bitter Inner Harbor," suggests that Purvis's slave jail was on Harford Road in Baltimore.

532 "James Bates, 1 President Street," Baltimore Directory, 1856.

533 Ibid., 1860, "Gallow's Hill" was so named because executions took place there in Baltimore in the 1850s. A recent book by Tracey Matthew Melton called Hanging Henry Gambrill is about one of those executions that took place in April of 1859.

534 George Harker, "For Sale, a Likely Negro Boy," in The Baltimore Sun, August 24, 1842. Harker was also sometimes called "William" Harker. His slave-trading business was south of Baltimore Street on the west side of

Mr. Harker mentions the skills this young boy has with horses. In this regard, as we shall see later in this study, it is quite like the runaway slave advertisements in the Chesapeake Bay region that usually listed the skills a particular slave possessed. Mr. Harker's slave business was located on what today would be Number Five Calvert Street in Baltimore. He also had an office at Number forty-five Front Street in Dorchester County on the Eastern Shore of Maryland. His partner there was named Shivers, so the business was Harker and Shivers, Dealers in Slaves.[535]

A slave merchant named John Wood, who advertised himself as an auctioneer, had a female slave for sale in the *American & Commercial Daily Advertiser* from December 13, 1813. The slave is:

> A healthy negro Wench, seventeen years old, frequently came from the Country. Any person wishing to possess a valuable servant will do well to embrace the present opportunity.[536]

Again, Mr. Wood includes in his advertisement the fact that the woman being sold is quite adept at domestic chores. In another advertisement from the same newspaper, Mr. Wood simply advertised for his business on Commerce and Pratt Streets as a "Slave Dealer."[537]

John N. Denning (1813–1883), another Baltimore trader, in two separate editions of the *Baltimore Sun,* in 1848 and 1852, wishes to buy slaves. In the first advertisement from December 14, 1848, Denning says:

> Negroes Wanted: I will pay the highest prices in cash for any number of Negroes with good titles, slaves for life or for a term of years, in large or small families, or single negroes. I will also purchase Negroes restricted to remain in the State, if they sustain good character. Communications promptly attended to and liberal

---

Calvert Street in downtown Baltimore.

535 Charles Shivers and D. S. Harker's place of business was at 45 Arch Street, between Front and Second Streets.

536 John Wood, "A Healthy Negro Wench," in American and Commercial Daily Advertiser, December 13, 1813.

537 Ibid.

commissions paid by John N. Denning, at No. 104 Exeter Street, near the Methodist Episcopal Church.[538]

Mr. Denning points to the fact that sometimes slaves in Maryland were not always "slaves for life," but some were, in fact, slaves "for a term," similar to the indentured servants described much earlier in the colony/state, in this study.

Four years later, in 1852, also in the *Baltimore Sun*, Mr. Denning's advertisement begins this way: "Five Thousand Negroes Wanted." The remainder of the ad looks pretty much like the one from 1848, except it adds the words "I am always in the Market with Cash."[539] Mr. Denning worked in the slave trade in Baltimore from 1839 until 1855, often partnering with both Joseph Donovan and Hope H. Slatter.

For a time, Mr. Denning's slave-trading business, at least in Baltimore, was located at 18 South Frederick Street, just a few hundred feet from the present-day location of the Holocaust Memorial. Later, the business moved to Number 104 Exeter Street in Little Italy near the Methodist-Episcopal Church.

Mr. Denning also traded on the Eastern Shore of Maryland, as witnessed by a correspondence between the slave trader and Dr. John Whitbridge (1793–1878) concerning the purchase of an unknown female slave on the Eastern Shore.[540]

The surviving written records also indicate that Mr. Denning's wife, Ann Denning, ran a boarding house at 14 and 16 South Frederick Street. His son was a stone cutter there as well, according to the *Baltimore Directory* from 1850. The Denning family occupied much of South Frederick Street in the early nineteenth century.

Mr. Denning was sued in July of 1854 when Jane Dorman pur-

538 John N. Denning, "Negroes Wanted," The Baltimore Sun, December 14, 1848. Steven Deyle, in his book Carry me Back: The Domestic Slave Trade in America (Oxford: Oxford University Press, 2006), p. 133, reports that, "Denning offered to pay the highest prices for five thousand Negroes." The Baltimore American and Commercial Advertiser published in the city from 1830 until 1839. Also see: Maryland State Archives Document 3392.

539 Ibid.

540 John N. Denning, "Five Thousand Negroes Wanted," in The Baltimore Sun, December 2, 1852.

chased a twelve-year-old slave girl named Henrietta from him for three hundred and fifty dollars. Four years later, Ms. Dorman told the court that, "Since her purchase, Henrietta has become vicious and turbulent, frequently running away." She asked the court for her money back, or at least to allow her to sell Henrietta out of state. Ms. Dorman won her case, and she did just that.[541]

Another Baltimore slave trader, James Franklin Purvis, mentioned above, was born in South Carolina in 1760. He died in November of 1836. In the 1820s and 1830s, Purvis was in the slave-trading business in Baltimore. He came to Baltimore from Chesterfield County, South Carolina, sometime between 1818 and 1822. Purvis was associated with the firm of Franklin and Armfield, who we will discuss in Chapter Six.

Purvis, the nephew of John Armfield, mostly worked as an agent of Franklin and Armfield. He had offices in Baltimore as well as in Frederick, Maryland. Purvis' nephew, a man named Thomas Jones, acted as Franklin and Armfield's agent on the Eastern Shore at his office on Main Street in Easton. Purvis was in business with the Alexandrian firm of Franklin and Armfield as early as 1830. This is yet another example of multiple family members involved in the same slave-trading firm.

Indeed, the familial relations of Mr. Purvis point to another aspect of slave traders in the nineteenth century. Often it was the case, as we have seen, that multiple members of the same family took part in the "Family Business," brothers, cousins and nephews. This was true of Mr. Purvis, Mr. Woolfolk and other Baltimore slave dealers, as well.

On April 12, 1836, Alabama slave, James Williams, ran away from a farm there. Eventually, after many fits and starts, Williams was taken by his owner to Baltimore. On October 16, 1836, Williams was offered to James Franklin Purvis for the sum of seven hundred

---

541 Dr. John Whitbridge (1793–1878) written about by John Scharf, History of Baltimore County and City (Philadelphia: Louis Everts, 1881), p. 756. Dr. Whitbridge was born in Rhode Island but spent most of his life living on Charles Street in Baltimore. He is buried in Green Mount Cemetery there. See: Maryland State Archives, SC 5496-24297. A number of John Dennings letters pertaining to his slave trading are extant.

dollars. Purvis completed the sale and then locked Williams in his slave jail in Baltimore.

Later on, Williams wrote a very compelling autobiography entitled, *The Narrative of James Williams: An American Slave*, published in Boston in 1838 by Isaac Knapp.[542] His narrative includes a compelling description of his slave auction on the block, as we shall see in Chapter Seven.

Jonathan M. Wilson (1797–1831) operated his slave-trading firm in a number of locations. He also had multiple partners, particularly in Baltimore, including Hope Slatter and Joseph Donovan. In the 1820 Baltimore directory, Wilson is listed as a "Slave Dealer," along with his partner a man named Hindes. Thus, the business was known as Wilson & Hindes.

By the year 1860, a Jonathan M. Wilson is listed as a "Slave Dealer" in the *New Orleans Directory* in the third ward of that city, but clearly, it is not the Baltimore trader mentioned earlier. He could have been a relative.[543] This brings us to the end of our exposition of the thirteen slave traders in the *Baltimore Directory* in 1850.

The end of the slave jails in Baltimore came on July 24, 1863, a short time after the Battle of Gettysburg. On that date, Colonel William Birney of the Union Army, along with a Lieutenant Sykes and a Sergeant Southworth, proceeded with their troops to Slatter's jail, which by now had been bought by the Campbell brothers.

By an order from General Schenks, Birney enlisted the male negroes into the Union Army and released the female slaves. In his report after the incident, Birney writes:

> In this place, I had found twenty-six men, one boy, twenty-nine women, and three infants. Sixteen of the men were shackled together by couples at the ankles by heavy irons. I sent for a Blacksmith and had the

542 Baltimore Directory, 1850.

543 James Williams, Narrative of James Williams: An American Slave (Baton Rouge: LSU Press, 2013). Williams (b. 1805) was a driver or overseer for many years on a cotton plantation in Alabama. His was the first slave narrative published in the United States.

shackles and chains removed.[544]

From there, Birney proceeded to the slave jails of Wilson, Hines, and Fairbanks, as well as at Joseph Donovan's facility, where he executed similar evacuations. The era of the slave jail was over in Baltimore, but the effects of these facilities lingered for many years afterward.

Birney's foray in Baltimore came on the heels of President Abraham Lincoln issuing General Order 329 on October 3, 1863, which gave the war department authority to recruit colored troops into the Union Army. President Lincoln believed this strategy would be particularly successful in border states like Maryland, Missouri and Tennessee. Ironically, Congressman John W. Crisfield of Maryland (1806–1897), who was opposed to General Order 329, immediately found that five of his slaves had joined a colored troop just days later.[545]

Col. William Birney (1819–1907) was the son of James Birney, an ardent abolitionist. After liberating the slaves in Baltimore, and pursuant to President Lincoln's order, Col. Birney became the leader of the 22nd US Colored Troops. His regiment of black soldiers had shown "good discipline" and "had harmed no one."[546]

In addition to the slave traders mentioned above, there were also a number of "Traveling Traders," who regularly visited Baltimore to deal in slaves. George Kephart of Frederick County, Maryland, mentioned earlier, David Anderson of Kentucky, and Barthalomew Accinelly of Virginia, for example, came to town, gathered purchased slaves, and

544 New Orleans City Directory, 1860.

545 General William Birney, "Report on Recruiting of Negro Men into the Army," July 27, 1863. Birney (1819–1907) was a general in the Civil War era US Army. His father was James G. Birney and his brother David B. Birney, another Civil War general. General John P. C. Shenks (1826–1901) was also a member of the US House of Representatives from Indiana.

546 Congressman John Crisfield (1806–1897) was both a member of Congress and a slave owner. He was born near Galena in Kent County and served the first district from 1847 until 1849. The city of Crisfield, Maryland, is named after him. Jonathan M. Wilson (1797–1849) was one of Baltimore's first slave traders. He operated his business there beginning in 1820 and then later from 1839 until 1849 when he died.

shipped them on packet ships that regularly made the run from Baltimore to New Orleans.[547]

Men like these gentlemen would stay in local hotels while conducting their business with slave traders like Slatter, Donovan, and the Campbell brothers. They often placed the slaves they had purchased in Baltimore in the slave jails of Woolfolk, Purvis, and Hope Slatter, for example, until they were ready for the shipment of their captives.

Mr. Kephart's facility was on Buckeystown Pike in the Tuscarora area of Frederick County. Kephart's partner was a man named John C. Cook. The building, built around 1850, served as Kephart's home. It is now part of the Frederick County Historical Trust. The house is a two-story brick building. The large chicken house that was the original slave pen on the property now is used as a shed.[548]

In the years 1827 to 1830, a number of other minor Baltimore businesspeople shipped slaves to the Deep South. Among these include George Turpin using the ship *Independence* and its captain, Thomas Taylor, to move slaves South in 1827. Mr. Turpin also employed the ship the *Sally* for similar purposes the following year. Robert Goodwin sent slaves to New Orleans on the *Hannah Bartlett* with a Mr. Swift serving as captain in 1827.[549]

In 1829, John Chapman, another Baltimore slave trader, did business with traders in New Orleans. He employed the services of Captain Jebez Tyler and the ship the *Independence*. Mrs. Mary Bradford sent slaves south on the ship *Laura* with Henry Delano as the master, and a Baltimore woman, Eliza Coale, used the *Dekalb* and its captain, Henry Travers, to transport slaves to the southern market.[550]

Other minor slave traders in Baltimore mentioned above include Robert Hart, Moses Little, John Gilmore, Johns Hopkins, Henry

547 William Birney (1819–1907) was a professor, Union army general, and the son of a prominent southern abolitionist.

548 George Kephart (1795–1869) was born at Licksville in Frederick County and died in Leesburg, Virginia. He purchased the slave jail at 1315 Duke Street in Alexandria for the firm of Franklin and Armfield.

549 George Kephart House, on Buckeystown Pike, Tuscarara, Maryland. Frederick County Historical Trust.

550 Manifest of ship Hannah Bartlett, May 18, 1827.

Coalman, John W. Walker and John Myrick. Each of these seven men was slave trading as early as the second decade of the nineteenth century in Baltimore, where many of these ship manifests are extant.

Many of these minor slave dealers dealt with the larger traders in the city, as well. Each of the seven also appear in various ship manifests in the early nineteenth century, where slaves were shipped south. Indeed, an appendix of ship manifests from Baltimore to the Deep South appears at the end of this chapter.

Johns Hopkins, the founder of the famous hospital and university in Baltimore, for example, on the packet ship the *James Monroe* on March 4, 1819, sold a captive named John Kelly to a dealer in New Orleans. Mr. Kelly was "twenty-one years old, five feet eight, and very black."[551] John Middleton Myrick also sold slaves to New Orleans on the *Commodore Patterson* on March 20, 1819.[552]

Moses Little, who began life as a slave, became a slave trader in Baltimore. On March 2, 1819, Mr. Little shipped several slaves to New Orleans on the packet ship the *Missouri*.[553] John W. Walker of Baltimore also did business with the firm of William & James in New Orleans. Mr. Walker transported his captives on the *Clio* on March 22, 1819.[554]

Other nineteenth century slave traders also existed in Maryland. On the Eastern Shore, John Bradshaw conducted a slave-trading business in a hotel in the city of Cambridge and Thomas M. Jones had a slave business in the city of Easton that had various contacts with the Baltimore traders. Mr. Jones partnered with Fredericksburg, Virginia, slave trader Samuel Alsop. George Kephart, mentioned above as a traveling trader, also had a place of slave trading in the city of Frederick. More will be said about Mr. Alsop in Chapter Six of this study

551 Manifest of ship Dekalb, July 27, 1829. The schooner Wildcat was built in 1828 in Michigan. In October of 1829, it went missing off the coast of Cuba, killing the crew of thirty-one. Eliza Ann Coale (1799–1856) was born in England and later moved to Maryland, where she went into the businesses of slave trading and tobacco farming.

552 Manifest of ship James Monroe, March 4, 1819. George Turpin had a slave-trading business in Baltimore and a tobacco farm in Talbot County. After his death, his wife Sally continued the business in both locations.

553 Manifest of ship Commodore Patterson, March 20, 1819.

554 Manifest of ship Missouri, March 2, 1819.

to follow.

Mr. Kephart acted as the agent for Franklin and Armfield in 1846 when he bought the property that would later become Franklin and Armfield. Kephart's business became "The chief slave-dealing firm in Virginia, and perhaps anywhere along the border between Free States and Slave States."[555]

It is likely that the "Capehart" in Harriet Beecher Stowe's 1852 book *Uncle Tom's Cabin* was George Kephart, who was born near Frederick, Maryland, in 1788.[556] Finally, Jonathan M. Wilson, a Virginia native who did slave trading in Baltimore, did business there between 1839 and 1849. He had multiple business partners in those years, including Hope H. Slatter and Joseph N. Donovan.

By the year 1860, Mr. Wilson was living in New Orleans, where he was operating a store depot in the third ward of that city.[557] In the city of Annapolis, William Hooper was in the slave-trading business, and John Ware had established a similar firm in Port Tobacco, Maryland. John Bradshaw operated his slave trading on Main Street in the city of Cambridge, on the Eastern Shore, and Thomas Jones' slave pen was in Easton, also on the Eastern Shore.[558]

William Hooper (1848–1909) is significant because he was born a slave in North Carolina, became a slave trader in Annapolis, Maryland, and was the original president of the Huntsville Normal School, a school for indigent blacks. Hooper was a good and well-respected

555 Manifest of ship Clio, March 22, 1819. John Middleton Myrick (1716–1804) was one of the earliest slave traders in the Baltimore to New Orleans route. His son, John Middleton Myrick Jr., also took part in the business.

556 See note 543. John Bradshaw's slave-trading business in Cambridge is discussed in Ralph Clayton's Cash for Blood, on pp. 103–109 and 415.

557 Harriet Beecher Stowe, Uncle Tom's Cabin (New York: Dover Books, 2005). Thomas Walker (1758–1797) was a British slave trader. His son, John W. Walker, opened a slave-trading firm in Baltimore beginning in the late 1790s.

558 Some of Jonathan M. Wilson's letters survive in the Wilson Family Papers, 1841–1938, like one to his brother on December 8, 1848. Samuel Alsop was a Virginia physician and master builder, as well as being a slave trader. He built the Spotsylvania County Museum. His family's tobacco farm was called Oakley.

businessman who also was something of a philanthropist, way ahead of his time for a black man.[559]

John Ware had his slave-trading business on Main Street of Port Tobacco, the seat of Charles County in southern Maryland. Mr. Ware also had a slave pen at his establishment on Main Street. He remained in the slave-trading business throughout most of the 1840s and 1850s.[560]

This brings us to pieces of nineteenth-century art that depict slave dealers and slave jails in Baltimore, the subject matter of the next section of this fifth chapter. We move, then, to slave jails in art.

Baltimore Slave Traders and Slave Jails in Art: 1800 to 1863

Several pieces of art that depict various aspects of the material in this chapter are extant. We will discuss nine of those pieces. The first image is a mid-nineteenth-century photograph of one of the "Omnibuses" that carried Hope Slatter's slaves from Fells Point and wharves on the Inner Harbor to his slave jail at Pratt and Howard Streets in Baltimore, or vice-versa, from the slave jails to Baltimore ports. A grey and a bay pull the oblong-shaped car, looking like a San Francisco trolley car on rubber wheels.[561]

The second image is a photograph of the Baltimore Harbor taken in the 1850s. It shows a two-mast packet ship that carried slaves from Baltimore to New Orleans and other ports in the Deep South. The spot in the photograph today would be the site of the Inner Harbor Pratt Street Pavilion in Baltimore.[562]

The third description is another "Omnibus" that contained a number of slaves drawn by two large grey horses. The omnibus looks like a rather large stagecoach and contains slaves on the inside as well as the outside of the coach. The picture is owned by the Maryland

559 Thomas Jones' slave pen and slave-trading business was in the city of Easton, on the Eastern Shore of Maryland.

560 William Hooper (1848–1909) was a slave trader in the city of Annapolis, but he was born a slave in North Carolina.

561 John Ware's slave business in Port Tobacco is mentioned in Steven Deyle's Carry Me Back: The Domestic Slave Trade (Oxford: Oxford University Press, 2005), pp. 104–107.

562 Image of Hope Slatter's omnibuses. In Clayton's "Bitter Inner Harbor," Baltimore Sun, July 12, 2000.

Historical Society in Baltimore.[563] This image is a good representation of what many of the Baltimore slave ships looked like in the 1820s to 1850s.

An illustration of the slave ship the *Putnam* is the content of image four. The illustrator is anonymous, but it was completed sometime in the 1850s. As pointed out earlier, the *Putnam* was registered for a while in Baltimore, Philadelphia, Providence, Boston, New York City, and New Orleans, although built in Baltimore. By 1858, she was operating as an illegal slaver under the name the *Jefferson Davis,* the ship named after the president of the Confederacy.[564]

Image five is a painting entitled *Kabenda.* The artist is Francis Meynell (1891–1975), an English illustrator. It shows a view of the West African city of Cabinda, the place from which the *Putnam* purchased its slaves in Angola. The image is owned by the National Maritime Museum in London.[565] As we have seen in Chapter Three of this study, Kabenda was a slave port in Angola in West Africa along with the Ports of Luanda and Benguela.

B. M. Campbell's slave jail at 26 Conway Street in Baltimore is the content of image six. It shows the concrete enclosure of the underground jail there. Six or eight cells are on both walls. A large iron gate lies open to the enclosure. Later Campbell moved his enterprises to 242 West Pratt Street when he purchased Hope Slatter's slave jail.[566]

A seventh image description is a drawing of Pratt Street looking west in the early nineteenth century. On the right is the Baltimore Museum of Fine Arts. Horse-drawn wagons move down the street. On the lower left of the image, a trader is loading slaves into an omnibus. It is most likely Hope Slatter, for he employed these omnibuses to transport his captives from his slave jail to ports in the city, or vice-versa, as we

---

563 Photograph of Baltimore Harbor, 1850. It was taken by H. Clarke from Federal Hill. The image is owned by the City Life Museum in Baltimore. For more on John Ware's business in Port Tobacco, see the Alexandria Phenix Gazette, August 27, 1833, as well as Steven Deyle's Carry Me Back.

564 See Note 555.

565 www.staugustinelighthouse.org. Francis Meynell (1891-1975), the son of a journalist, was a British poet and printer.

566 Contemporary photograph of Baltimore slave trader marker.

have indicated earlier in this chapter.[567]

There is a sign on the south side of Pratt Street in contemporary Baltimore erected recently by the Maryland Historical Trust. The sign is entitled "Baltimore Slave Trader Marker." The sign commemorates the slave trading going on in Baltimore not far from the location of the sign. It also points out that the *Baltimore Directory*, from 1845 and 1850, put "Slave Traders" between "Silversmiths" and "Soap" in the mid-nineteenth century, and lists more than a dozen slave-trading firms, most of whom were discussed earlier in Chapter Five.[568]

The ninth and final description of this chapter is a copy of a manifest from the schooner *Wildcat* that carried slaves from the Chesapeake Bay region to New Orleans. On this manifest, the ship carried six slaves: Willy (20), Jack (25), Hector (20), Adam (20), and two women named Maria (20) and Mary (17). Similar manifests are extant for many voyages sponsored by Baltimore dealers, as indicated in the appendix to this chapter.

This brings us to the major conclusions we have made in this chapter, followed by the notes of the same. In Chapter Six, a companion chapter to Chapter Five, we explore the phenomena of slave traders and slave jails in Washington, DC, and the Commonwealth of Virginia.

Conclusions

We began this fifth chapter by making some very general comments on the phenomenon of slave merchant ships out of the Port of Baltimore from 1800 until 1865. As we have seen, many of these ships were actually built in Baltimore, such as the *Putnam*, for example. A number of these merchant ships conducted international as well as domestic trading in the period. Other ships simply traveled from Baltimore to New Orleans and other ports in the Deep South, like Natchez, Mississippi and New Orleans in the nineteenth century before 1865.

In the main section of this chapter, we described and discussed the

567 Baltimore directories, 1845 and 1850.

568 Manifest of schooner Wildcat, October 9, 1829. The Baltimore Museum of Fine Arts was the predecessor to the Baltimore Museum of Art. It was built in the 1870s and modeled after the Museum of Modern Art in New York City.

thirteen major slave dealers in Baltimore in the period, as we saw in the *Baltimore Directory* from 1850. We also indicated that many of these Baltimore slave traders also built their own slave jails or slave pens in the city. Among these major slave dealers in Baltimore, who also had slave jails, were Austin Woolfolk, Hope Slatter, Joseph Donovan, and Bernard and Walter Campbell.

We also enumerated a number of minor Baltimore slave traders who sent slaves to the southern markets. Among these minor Baltimore traders were John Chapman, Johns Hopkins, Robert Hart, Moses Little, George Turpin, John Middleton Myrick, and many other slave dealers.

In the central section of Chapter Five, we also introduced many other slave traders elsewhere in Maryland including Annapolis, Frederick, and at Easton and Cambridge on the Eastern Shore. Among these minor Maryland traders, as we indicated, were people like William Harker, George Kephart, John Wood, John Bradshaw, Thomas Jones and John D. Denning.

In the third section, we introduced nine different pieces of nineteenth-century art that depict the materials in this chapter. As we have seen, some of these show aspects of the Baltimore dealers' work, like the Omnibuses that Hope Slatter employed to move his slaves in Baltimore from Fells Point to his slave jail. Other of the nine images described show depictions of some of the slave ships that sailed from Baltimore, such as the *Putnam*, for example.

Another image depicts the city of Cabinda in Angola from which the Putnam secured slaves in West Africa. One of the nine pieces of art that accompanies this chapter is a contemporary sign that sits on the south side of Pratt Street in present-day Baltimore. And finally, one of the nine images shows the concrete underground slave jail of Bernard and Walter Campbell in a photograph from the 1840s.

This brings us to the notes of this fifth chapter, followed by a sixth chapter, in which we explore the phenomenon of slave dealers and slave jails in Washington, DC, and the Commonwealth of Virginia in the nineteenth century. After the notes, we have supplied an appendix of ship manifests, from Baltimore to the Deep South from 1800 until 1860.

Appendix: Manifests of Ships from Baltimore to the Deep South: 1800 to 1860

In this appendix we have listed the slave ships that traveled from Baltimore to the Deep South in the first sixty years of the nineteenth century. The first part of the appendix lists manifests of ships from 1800 to 1820; the second part, from 1821 until 1845, and the third part from 1846 until 1860. All tolled, we have listed the ship manifests of twenty-eight ships and their destinations. All of these voyages embarked from ports in Baltimore.

Part One: 1800 to 1820

Ship	Year	Destination
Missouri	1819	New Orleans
Ere	1819	Alabama Territory
Clio	1819	New Orleans
Commander Patterson	1819	New Orleans
James Monroe	1819	New Orleans

Part Two: 1821 to 1845

Ship	Year	Destination
Isaac Franklin	1826	New Orleans
Constitution	1826	New Orleans
Rooke	1826	New York
Independence	1827	New Orleans
Hannah Bartlett	1827	New Orleans
Sally	1828	Savannah
Cherokee	1828	Savannah
Laura	1829	New Orleans
Dekalb	1829	New Orleans
Aurora	1829	Savannah
Wildcat	1829	New Orleans
Isaac Franklin	1838	New Orleans
Ann	1839	New Orleans

Tippacanoe	1842	New Orleans
Putnan/Echo	1845	New Orleans
Kirkwood	1845	New Orleans

Part Three: 1846 to 1860

Ship	**Year**	**Destination**
Tribune	1847	New Orleans
Uncas	1847	New Orleans
Temperance	1848	New Orleans
Pearl	1848	Philadelphia
John C. Calhoun	1850	New Orleans
Thomas Hunter	1850	Natchez, Mississippi
Helen Miller	1852	New Orleans

Ralph Clayton, in his essay "A Bitter Inner Harbor Legacy: the Slave Trade," published in the *City Diary*, listed another six ships for which manifests are extant from Baltimore to New Orleans. These ships were the *Agent, Architect, Hyperion, General Pinckney, Intelligence*, and *Victorine.* This brings our total to thirty-four ships with their manifests that are extant from Baltimore to New Orleans. A similar appendix is also attached to Chapter Six. It lists ship manifests in Washington and Virginia ports to the Deep South from 1800 to 1860.

This brings us to Chapter Six, an analysis of slave traders and dealers in Washington, DC, and the Commonwealth of Virginia, in the first sixty-five years of the nineteenth century. It is to the District of Columbia and Virginia, then, to which we turn next.

Chapter Six: Slave Traders and Jails in Washington, D.C. and Virginia

It occurred to me that I must be in an underground apartment, and the damp, moldy odors of the place confirmed my suppositions.

—Solomon Northrop, *Twelve Years A Slave*

There was a general washing, and combing, and shaving, the pulling out of grey hairs, and the dying of the hair of those who were too grey to be plucked out without making them bald.

—John Brown, Virginia slave

If any of your slaves wish to purchase their freedom, make a Contract with them, accordingly if you know they have good in them, and give them some of the wealth that Allah has given you.

—The Holy Qur'an 24:33 (Author's translation)

Introduction

In this sixth chapter, we have five principal goals. First, to make some description of slave ships owned by slave traders in Washington, DC, and Virginia in the nineteenth century. We have supplied an appendix at the end of this chapter, which summarizes the manifests of slave ships from the District of Columbia and Virginia in the first sixty-five years of the nineteenth century.

The second goal of this chapter is to make some remarks about the phenomena of slave traders and slave jails in Washington, D. C., and the Commonwealth of Virginia, particularly from Richmond and Alexandria to the Deep South from 1800 until 1865.

In the third and main section of Chapter Six, we will describe and discuss forty or so major slave traders in these areas in that period. These slave dealers, for the most part, operated in the city of Washington, as well as in Alexandria and Richmond, two large cities in Virginia during that time. Other slave traders in Virginia, as we shall see in this chapter, existed in Petersburg, Christianburg, in the city of Luray, and in Warrenton in that commonwealth.

In the fourth aim of this chapter, we will introduce and discuss several prominent slaves who may be identified with the forty or so traders mentioned above. Among these slaves is Solomon Northrop, the focus of the book and movie called *Twelve Years a Slave*, directed by Steve McQueen and produced in 2013.[569] We also will explore other prominent Virginia slaves, including Anthony Burns, John Brown and Henry Clay Bruce.

In the final section of this chapter, we will enumerate and discuss several pieces of nineteenth-century American art that depict or illustrates the slave dealers and slave jails mentioned earlier in the chapter.

Following the conclusions and the notes, we also have supplied an appendix on slave ship manifests mentioned in the above analysis. Much like the appendix on ship manifests we have included at the close of Chapter Five on Baltimore slave ship manifests are extant in the District of Columbia and the State of Virginia, as well.

Before moving to the Washington and Virginia slave traders, however, we have to point out that like the Baltimore slave dealers in the cities of Virginia and in Washington, DC, sometimes owned their own ships in conducting their business. At times, the owners of these slave ships also functioned as their captains, as we shall see in the next section of this chapter, or they hired traditional skippers from the maritime industry, but others captained their own vessels.

We move, then, to slave trading ships in Washington and Virginia, the topic of the first section of this chapter.

Slave Ships in Washington and Virginia

The purpose of this section is to examine the phenomenon of slave ships owned by Washington, DC, and Virginia slave traders. In Alexandria, the firm of Franklin and Armfield, for example, had its own fleet of ships: the *Tribune, the Uncas*, and the *Isaac Franklin*.[570] The firm

569 Solomon Northrop, Twelve Years a Slave (Los Angeles: Graymalkin Media, 2014).

570 More will be said about Franklin and Armfield in Chapter Six.

also owned the *United States* and a fifth ship named the *Comet*.[571]

The *Tribune* was captained by a man named Smith, and the *Uncas* by Captain Bousch. These two crafts made monthly visits, carrying slaves from Alexandria to the Deep South. In a September 1834 document, we find this description of these two ships: "They are both vessels of the first class, commanded by experienced officers. These ships at all times will travel up the Mississippi River by steam."[572]

In this quotation, it speaks of slaves traveling by steamships up the Mississippi River in the first sixty-five years of the nineteenth century, particularly after the invention of the steamship in 1814. By the 1820s, slaves traveled on in-land coffles from the east to the Deep South. By the late 1830s, they moved by rail, as well, with the same destinations. Thus, by the 1840s, slaves in the Chesapeake Bay region moved by land coffles, by steamship, and by the new American railroads, as we shall see later in this chapter.

The brig *Comet*, also owned by Franklin and Armfield, sailed from Alexandria to New Orleans. One voyage in 1831, with 164 slaves aboard, struck some rocks in the Atlantic, and the ship had to be abandoned. The slaves were rescued and taken to Nassau, New Providence, where they were declared free by the colonial authorities.[573]

The *Enterprise*, a sixth ship, was another ship owned by Franklin and Armfield, which sailed between Alexandria and Charleston in the 1830s. On one voyage in 1835, the ship carried seventy-five slaves valued at $40,000. These captives belonged to a Washington/Virginia trader Joseph W. Neal.[574] More will be said about Mr. Neal later in this chapter.

Records indicate that in 1836, Franklin and Armfield sold the

571 Ibid.

572 New York Historical Society Manuscript Collection related to slavery.

573 Manifest of brig the Comet, December 6, 1831, Alexandria to New Orleans. New Providence is the most populated island of the Bahamas, containing about seventy percent of the total population. It also contains the national capital, Nassau. It was originally a Spanish colony but later was acquired by the British Empire.

574 Manifest of ship the Enterprise, February 11, 1835, Alexandria to Charleston.

Tribune and the *Uncas* to Washington, DC, slave dealer, William H. Williams, who also will be discussed later in this chapter. At least two other Virginia slave traders owned ships to transport their slaves south in the nineteenth century, after the collapse of the tobacco crop in the Chesapeake Bay region and the rise of the cotton and sugar crops in the Deep South, as well as the invention of the steamship in 1814 and the introduction of Mexican cotton in the United States in the 1820s. Their names were R. H. Banks and R. L. Marsh, both of whom operated out of Norfolk.[575] Nathan Simpson, one of the only Jewish slave traders in this study, also owned his own ship named the *Crown*. When these Virginia-based ships returned from the Deep South, they carried back sugar, molasses, whiskey, cotton and other staples.

At first, the firm of Franklin and Armfield employed whatever ships were available to them, such as the *Shenandoah* of Georgetown and the *Ariel* and the *James Monroe*, both registered in Norfolk. Often, in the early years of the partnership, Franklin and Armfield shared these ships with other traders. But by 1834, they had purchased the *Tribune,* the *Uncas*, the *Isaac Franklin*, and the *Comet,* all mentioned above. All four of these crafts were built in the shipyards of Baltimore. In fact, as we saw back in Chapter Five, a significant number of American slave ships that were built in Chesapeake Bay City and were involved in both the international and the domestic slave trades, were built from the mid-1820s to around 1860.

The *James Monroe*, to cite one example, set out from Alexandria to New Orleans, on August 3, 1826, carrying thirty-four slaves. This included twenty-seven men, six women and one infant. The *Shenandoah*, to mention a second example, began as a slave ship. It was built by A. Stephens & Sons, in Glasgow, Scotland, and captained by James Iredell

575 "Interstate Slave Traders by Water," Robie12gs@aol.com.

Waddell. It was christened the *Sea King*.

Later, the Confederate government purchased the ship in September of 1864 and changed the name to the *Shenandoah*. In that same year, it was scuttled and burned, so its slave life came to an end.

In the beginning, the ships of Franklin and Armfield made their voyages south once a month. Later, voyages occurred once every two weeks. A typical cargo from Alexandria included between a hundred and two hundred and fifty slaves, the average being around one hundred and eighty captives.

In the summer months, Franklin and Armfield conducted slave coffles overland to Mississippi that, on average, would take six to eight weeks. Often, Franklin and Armfield hired other Virginia or Maryland traders to accompany their coffles to the Deep South up until the Civil War.

Each of the ships of Franklin and Armfield was between one hundred and sixty and two hundred tons and carried between one hundred and fifty and two hundred slaves. Each brig had two holds, the after-hold had room for eighty women, and the main hold had room for one hundred male slaves. The slaves were laid on platforms, one of which was raised a few inches. The other platform was halfway up to the deck, similar to what we had seen back in Chapter Two, when we discussed the Middle Passage.

Somewhere around 95 percent of Franklin and Armfield's captives were transported on their ships. This allowed the firm to sell in the off-season, between October and May, increasing the company's revenue considerably. Franklin and Armfield grew to be one of the largest slave-trading firms in all of the South, but only 5 percent of all of Franklin and Armfield's slaves moved by land or rail.

By 1850, Franklin and Armfield controlled more than 50 percent of the coastal trade between the Potomac River ports and New Orleans. More will be said about Franklin and Armfield when we discuss slave traders in the Commonwealth of Virginia.

Among the Virginia slave ships was a brig named the *Planter*. It sailed bi-weekly from Petersburg to New Orleans. One voyage of the *Planter* was conducted by slave dealer Francis H. Hoyer in Norfolk, who shipped nine slaves on February 19, 1819. The names of those nine captives were Henry, Isaac, Peter, Mundavis, Randall, Sinah, Daniel, Leroy and Patty. Ten days earlier, on the same brig, Mr. Hoyer sent nine men and five female slaves from Norfolk to New Orleans.[576] Mr. Hoyer was one of the earliest slave dealers in Norfolk.

A variety of other ship manifests survive from the first half of the nineteenth century. As in Baltimore, slave dealers in Virginia often shared the use of slave ships. On February 18, 1819, John and Sam Corby, Thomas Martin, and James Reynolds shared a voyage of the ship *Planter* from Richmond to New Orleans.[577] Two weeks earlier, on February 4, 1819, the same gentlemen also shipped slaves from Richmond to New Orleans. Petersburg traders George Davis and N. Wilkinson also shared the use of the *Planter* to transport their slaves to New Orleans, to give another example.[578]

Another good example was the ship called the *Clotilde*. It was a two-masted schooner, eighty-six feet long. It appears to have been the last known ship to bring captives from Africa to the United States. Eventually, however, it too was burned and was scuttled in Mobile Bay, Alabama, in 1865 during the American Civil War.

At times, some of the Virginian owners of slave ships also served as their captains. This was particularly true in Norfolk, where W. T. Foster, R. H. Banks and R. L Marsh were masters of the ships they owned. This was also the case with Francis H. Hoyer of Norfolk on a voyage from Norfolk to New Orleans on February 19, 1819, where Hoyer was both the captain and the owner of the ship.[579] Thomas Pringle of Alexandria, Virginia, also captained the ship he owned on voyages to New Orleans.[580]

This was also true, as we saw in Chapter Five, that some of the Baltimore slave traders owned their own ships and sometimes cap-

576 Manifest of ship the Planter, February 19, 1819, Petersburg to New Orleans.

577 Ibid.

578 Ibid.

579 Francis H. Hoyer, in manifest from February 19, 1819, in Inward Slave Manifests for the Port of New Orleans, 1818–1820.

580 Thomas Pringle (1759–1834) was a Scottish writer, poet and abolitionist. He also was engaged in the slave trade. Pringle was also instrumental in the publication of Mary Prince's (1785–1833) biography called *The History of Mary Prince* published in 1831.

tained them. This brings us to slave traders in Washington, DC, in the nineteenth century, the topic of the next section.

Slave Dealers in Washington: 1800 to 1865

In the nineteenth century, there is extant evidence for three major slave dealers and several minor ones in Washington, DC. We will enumerate them here and then speak about them one at a time:

John Beattie, O Street
William H. Williams, on the Mall, 8th and B Streets
Simpson & Neil, Robey's Tavern, Independence, btw 7th & 8th Streets
Joseph W. Neal and Company. Slave Pen at Potomac Park
John Gadsby Decatur House, Lafayette Square
George McCandless Tavern, Miller Tavern, 13th and F. Streets
Edward Burrows, Lloyd Tavern., 7th and Pa. Avenue, Potomac Park
Nathan Simpson
Nathan Balford Forest, Union Tavern, 201 Massachusetts Avenue
Robey and Neil

There is some evidence that the earliest slave trader in Washington was a man named John Beattie (1738–1818), whose primary business was on O Street in the District of Columbia. Beattie also had other locations along Wisconsin Avenue in Georgetown. It appears Mr. Beattie's O Street business opened in 1760.

Another trader, named Edward Burrows, was working as a slave trader in Washington by the year 1794.[581] Beattie and Burrows were among the earliest slave traders in the Chesapeake Bay region.

There is also extant evidence of slave pens in what is now Potomac Park. One at the Decatur House, fronting what is now Lafayette Square, and one at McCandless Tavern in Georgetown. The tavern was located at the southwest corner of Wisconsin Avenue near M Street.[582]

581 John Beattie, discussed in Robert Benedetto, Historical Dictionary of Washington (Lanham: Scarecrow Press, 2003), p. 194. Edward Burrows is discussed on that same page, as well.

582 George McCandless, discussed in Peter McCandless, *Slavery, Disease, and Suffering in the Southern Low Country* (Cambridge: Cambridge University Press, 2011), p. 70.

McCandless Tavern was owned by George McCandless, whose business was at the corner of High and Bridge Streets in Georgetown. McCandless agent, John J. Sailor, took an advertisement out in the *Virginia Gazette* in which he says, "Cash for Slaves, Apply at McCandless Tavern, Georgetown."[583]

Decatur House, constructed in 1818 to honor naval hero and commodore Stephen Decatur (1779–1830), was the residence for the Decatur family after that date. In 1821, slave quarters were built adjoining the house. In 1836, Susan Decatur sold the property to hotel magnate John Gadsby for the sum of twelve thousand dollars. Gadsby also owned the nearby National Hotel, whose staff included many enslaved persons in the 1830s.

Mr. Gadsby used the Decatur House site as a slave jail from 1836 until the year of his death in 1844. The property was then sold many times until finally, in April of 1862, slavery was abolished in the District of Columbia. Albert Boschke's 1857 survey map of Washington still shows the property as having the function of slave trading at that time.[584]

Another Washington slave pen sat at the southwest corner of 7th Street and Pennsylvania Avenue NW, where the National Archives is now located. The establishment was known as Lloyd's Tavern. The place has been memorialized by the note of the sale of a young girl named Margaret. She was seized from her master after he had trouble keeping up with his rent. Later, she wrote an autobiography.[585]

An American slave memorial is now located along the waterfront of West Potomac Park, where slave trading took place in the early nine-

583 John J. Sailor, "Cash for Slaves," in The Virginia Gazette, October 23, 1824. The same advertisement appeared on the same day in the National Intelligencer. The National Hotel was founded by John Gadsby (1766–1844) in 1827 on Pennsylvania Avenue and Sixth Street in Washington. In early 1857, there was a mysterious disease prevalent at the hotel. Four hundred people became sick, and three dozen people died of the disease.

584 Albert Boschke, Survey Map of Washington (Washington, 1857), p. 34. Boschke was a German-born civil engineer who served as a draftsman on the "US Coast Survey." Realizing there was no modern map of the District of Columbia, he made one in 1857 and published it at the same time.

585 Discussed in Scott Christianson, With Liberty for Some (Boston: Northeast University Press, 2000), p. 152.

teenth century. The memorial is parallel to the river and is in the form of a timeline, which features the history of slavery in Washington.[586]

In 1819, when Miller's Tavern at 13th and F Streets caught fire, a bystander named William Gardiner refused to participate in the bucket brigade, loudly condemning the place as a slave prison. It is not clear whether Mr. Gardiner was correct or not about Miller's Tavern, but it may well have been an eighth business in Washington, DC, in the slave-trading business there. Josephine Pacheco, in her book the *Pearl*, suggests that Miller's Tavern is the same location where Jesse Torrey found a female slave imprisoned in a garret on F Street, who was waiting to be sold south.[587] Later, this same captive attempted suicide by jumping to her death from the third floor of a slave jail, as we shall see later in this chapter.

By far, the three most significant slave traders in Washington were those of Messrs. Williams, Robey and Neal. Mr. Williams' slave jail, called the Yellow House, was on what today would be the Mall in Washington. The building was a three-story house, with slaves initally kept in the basement. Traders removed them to a yard outside on auction day.

The property of Mr. Williams had bars on the windows and twelve-foot walls surrounding the property. Mr. Williams also had ferocious dogs that patrolled the compound. One of the most interesting aspects of Mr. Williams' slave business is that he and his wife were both slaves long before he became a slave trader.

Mr. Williams' slave jail was a three-story brick building, covered with plaster and then painted bright yellow, so it might more easily be identified. By 1836, Williams' business was booming, so much so that he was able to purchase two of Franklin and Armfield's ships mentioned earlier, the *Tribune* and the *Uncas*. Mr. Williams also was involved in a number of court proceedings over the years.

586 Josephine Pacheco, The Pearl (Chapel Hill: University of North Carolina Press, 2005), p. 34.

587 Slave Memorial, West Potomac Park, Washington, DC. The site was chosen because it is within short walking distance to the Lincoln Memorial, as well as the Martin Luther King, Jr. Memorial. Jesse Torrey (1787–1834) was born in New Lebanon, New York. He was the son of a Revolutionary War hero and abolitionist. A number of his letters survive, including one to Thomas Jefferson dated August 15, 1815, about the question of abolition.

For example, Mr. Williams, who, as indicated earlier, started out a slave himself, sued a Mr. Duvall to prevent him from selling Williams' wife and child. After being freed from Mr. Duvall, Williams went into the slave business himself. That was after working eight years for Duvall in order to purchase his wife and son.[588] Later, Mr. Williams was accused of importing slaves who were criminals into the state of Virginia.

Apparently, Williams purchased twenty-four slaves who were convicted and sentenced to death for felony offenses, which included arson, rape, murder, poisoning and insurrection. Williams was convicted of the charges and he was fined five hundred dollars, which he promptly paid.

The site of Mr. Williams' complex today would be on Independence Avenue, just east of Ninth Street, or 8th and B Streets, in the district. This central location of a slave jail in the district captured the attention of abolitionists. Ironically the Museum of African Art now stands just a block from the site of Mr. Robey's tavern and slave pen, which was also on the Mall on the present site of the Federal Aviation Administration, also on Independence, between 7th and 9th. From April 1833 until October 1834, E. S. Abdy, a Fellow of Jesus College Cambridge in England, visited Mr. Robey's establishment several times.

Abdy left this account in his book *Journal of a Residence and Tour in the United States of North America, From April 1833, until October of 1834*. Edward Strutt Abdy (1791–1846) was an English academic who was notable for his writings on racism. In his book, he tells us this about Robey and his jail:

> One day I went to see the "Slave Pens" —a wretched hovel, "right against" the Capitol, from which it is a distance of about half a mile, with no house intervening. The outside alone is accessible to the eye of a visitor; what passes within being reserved for the exclusive observations of the owner, a man named Robey and his unfortunate victims. It is surrounded by a wooden paling fourteen or fifteen feet in height, with posts outside

588 Ibid.

> to prevent escape, and separated from the building by a space too narrow to admit the free circulation of air. At a small window above, which was unglazed and exposed alike to the heat of Summer and the cold in Winter. So, trying to the constitution, two or three sable faces appeared, looking out wistfully to while away the time and to catch a refreshing breeze; the weather became extremely hot. In this wretched hovel of all colors, except white—the only guilty one---both sexes and all ages, are confined, exposed indiscriminately to all the contamination which may be expected in such society and under such seclusion.[589]

Mr. Abdy points out that Robey's slave jail was near the Capitol, it has fourteen foot walls surrounding it, that the captives must have trouble receiving a proper amount of air, and they may be subject to the "contagion" or "contamination" that often occurs when people are put in such close quarters.

Edward Abdy continues his analysis at Robey's slave jail in Washington:

> The inmates of the Gaol [Jail], of this class, I mean, are even worse treated; some of them, if my informants are to be believed, having been actually frozen to death, during the inclement winters which often prevail in this Country. While I was in the City, Robey had possession of a woman, whose term of slavery was limited to six years. It was expected that she will be sold before her expiration of the period, and sent away some distance, where the assertion of her claim would subject her to ill-usage. Cases of this kind are very common.[590]

589 William H. Williams' slave jail was located between Seventh and Eighth Streets, just south of the Smithsonian. The facility was sometimes called "Williams' Private Jail."

590 E. S. Abdy, Journal of a Residence and Tour in the United States of North America, From April of 1833 until October of 1834 (Stroughton: Books on Demand, 2013). Edward Strutt Abdy (1791–1846) was an English legal scholar. He was educated at Jesus College, Cambridge. He never mar-

Mr. Abdy mentions a few important points about slavery in Washington in the nineteenth century before the Civil War. First, not all captives there were slaves. In fact, the woman described above appears to have been an indentured servant, for she had a strict limit to her enslavement. Second, it is crucial that she is sold before the terms of her indentured contract have been fulfilled, if any profit is to be made by Williams in her regard. And finally, when the woman is sold, it will probably occur when she is sold to a trader in the Deep South.

Robey, like the other Washington slave dealers, regularly advertised for the acquisition of slaves, such as in this ad from 1842:

> Negroes Wanted
>
> Persons wishing to dispose of Negroes from ten to twenty-five years of age, both sexes, can obtain cash for them, by applying to the subscriber, two doors East of the Union Tavern Stage Office, Bridge Street, in Georgetown. N.B. A smart girl, 11 to 13 years of age, would be desirable.[591]

The Union Tavern, located at 201 Massachusetts Avenue in northeast Washington, DC, is still a tavern and pub. It has been in business there since the early 1840s. Robey tells us he wishes to acquire both male and female slaves from the ages of ten to twenty-five.

The *Washington Spectator,* from December 4, 1830, speaks of a "drove consisting of male and female slaves chained in couples, and starting from Mr. Robey's Tavern, on foot."[592] Today there is a small mall on the original site of Robey's Tavern. The tavern and slave pen, like its neighbor, the Yellow House, had a large holding pen for slaves until they were ready for auction. Brought in from surrounding areas, as well as the Baltimore and Annapolis ports, the slaves were subjected to brutal conditions before their sale, often in dungeons built in their

---

ried. Late in life, he took up hydrotherapy.

591 Ibid.

592 W. Robey, "Negroes Wanted," in The Washington Spectator, December 4, 1830. The Washington Spectator is a left-leaning, political periodical, founded by Tristam Coffin in 1974. It is published monthly.

slave pens.

Jesse Torrey, abolitionist and Philadelphia physician in 1817, wrote *A Portraiture of Domestic Slavery in the United States.*[593] In this work, Dr. Torrey relates the story of a suicide attempt at Robey's Tavern of a woman about to be shipped off to Georgia. She was so distraught, Torrey reports, about the prospect of being separated from her family, she threw herself from a third-story window of Robey's Tavern. She survived the fall with multiple injuries but was not separated from her family.[594]

The 1827 *Washington City Directory* lists Robey's Tavern as being on the east side of Ninth Street between D and E Streets. Although Joseph W. Neal had offices at Seventh Street and Pennsylvania Avenue, he also conducted his slave business at Robey's Tavern.

Indeed, much of the slave trading that went on at Robey's Tavern in the nineteenth century was conducted by the firm of Simpson and Neal. Simpson was Nathan Simpson mentioned above. Mr. Neal was Joseph W. Neal who, along with his partner, took out the following advertisement in the *Washington Globe* of November 13, 1834:

> Cash for Negroes
>
> We will at all times pay higher prices in cash for likely young Negroes, of both sexes, either in families or otherwise, than any other purchasers who are now or may come later into the market. All communication will meet attention. We can at all times be found at W. Robey's Tavern, at the corner of Seventh and Maryland Avenue, in Washington City.
>
> —Simpson and Neal[595]

In this advertisement, Mr. Neal suggests he gives the highest pric-

593 Ibid.

594 Jesse Torrey, A Portraiture of Domestic Slavery in the United States (London: Forgotten Books, 2015). Torrey (1787–1834) was a Philadelphia physician and businessman. He was also a good friend of Thomas Jefferson. Many letters between the two are extant.

595 Ibid. The Washington Globe is a weekly Sunday newspaper founded in 1901.

es in Washington for slaves. He answers all inquiries about his slave business promptly, and he may be found at Robey's Tavern in the city where he conducts his trade.

Nathan Simpson and Joseph Neal were partners in a slave-trading business in the 1830s. There are extant records that they engaged the US merchant ship the *Enterprise* in moving slaves for their business at that time. Nathan Simpson also owned a slave ship called the *Crown*, as we indicated earlier. Simpson is also important because he was a Jewish slave trader. Dutch Jews brought slaves to the island of Curacao in the eighteenth century, up to 15,000 of them. Nathan Simpson's partner was a man named Isaac Levy, who owned a number of other slave ships in addition to the *Crown*. Among these ships were the *Charlotte*, the *Caravio,* the *Nassau* and the *Four Sisters*.

A number of other Jewish slave traders can be seen in the New World in the early nineteenth century. Moses Lindo, a Jew born in London in 1712, established an indigo and slave business in South Carolina with concerns doing business with London.[596] Isaac Monsanto, a Dutch Jew, established a slave-trading firm in New Orleans in 1756, to cite two examples. Asa Levy, whose business was on Locust Alley between Exchange Place and Franklin in Richmond, was also a Jewish slave trader.

A final slave trader, who did business in the District of Columbia, was Nathan Bedford Forrest (1821–1877). He advertised in the *Washington Globe* in 1853 for his desire to procure:

> 500 Negroes Wanted
>
> We will pay the highest prices for good Negroes. We also have a good lot of Virginia Negroes for Sale.[597] Mr.

596 Joseph W. Neal, "Cash for Negroes," in Washington Globe, November 13, 1834. Also see: James M. Goode (ed.), The Soul of Washington, D.C.: Historical Selections (Washington: Smithsonian Books, 2015), particularly the piece entitled "Two Items Regarding Slavery."

597 Moses Lindo (1712–1774) began his slave trading business in Charleston in the 1750s. Lindo was born in Germany and began his slave business by bringing African indentured servants to America. Nathan Bedford Forrest (1821–1877) was a lieutenant general of the Confederate Army during the American Civil War. He was known as being a "self-educated,

> Forrest wishes to purchase five hundred Negroes. He gives the highest prices, and he has available a number of Virginia Slaves for sale. The U. S. Army Military History Institute owns an image of Mr. Forrest in his Army uniform. The image number is: 497491. He stands before his business in the photograph, wearing his Army uniform.

This brings us to an analysis of Slave Dealers operating in the Commonwealth of Virginia in the nineteenth century, the topic of the next section.

Slave Traders and Slave Jails in Virginia: Nineteenth Century

In the Commonwealth of Virginia in the nineteenth century, the major centers for slave trade were in Richmond, Alexandria, Warrenton, Norfolk, Luray and Petersburg. In each of these cities, a significant amount of slave trading went on from 1800 to 1865. Altogether, the city of Richmond had nearly twenty major traders in that period. We will list seventeen Richmond slave traders here, and then discuss them one at a time:

1. Bacon Tait
2. Robert Lumpkin
3. R. H. Dickerson
4. Rice C. Ballard
5. Lancaster Denby and Company
6. John and Samuel Corby & Company
7. David Kirby
8. Luther Libby
9. E. W. Blackburn
10. Edward Eacho
11. Goodwin and Templeton
12. Thomas Taliaferro
13. Pulliam & Davis
14. Silas Omohundro

---

brutish, and innovative soldier." He also bought and sold slaves in Washington in the 1850s and 1860s.

15. Miller's Tavern
16. Abingdon Trading Center
17. Richard R. Beasley and Robert R. Jones

In addition to these seventeen businesses being slave traders in the nineteenth century, a number of them also owned slave jails at their establishments. Among those traders with jails were Lumpkin, Goodwin and Templeton, Blackburn, and Bacon Tait. The most significant of these is the establishment of Robert Lumpkin. Lumpkin's jail in Richmond was known as "The Devil's Half-Acre."[598] The establishment was three blocks from the present capitol in Richmond. Lumpkin's firm was in business from the early 1830s until the middle of the Civil War, around 1862.

Lumpkin was a prominent slave trader who bought and sold black human beings throughout the south. He turned Lumpkin's jail into the largest holding facility of slaves in the Upper South for well over twenty years. The site had earlier been owned by Bacon Tait, who practiced slave trading from 1830 on. In November of 1844, Lumpkin purchased three lots in Richmond for six thousand dollars.[599]

Robert Lumpkin was known as having a flair for cruelty. Those who ran away or tried to escape his compound were beaten publicly or still worse, tortured. Inside the jail was a whipping post, at which slaves were flogged unmercifully. Lumpkin also kept slaves at four other lots on Wall Street, now 15th Street, in Richmond. The area was collectively known as "Lumpkin's Alley."[600]

The property known as "Lumpkin's Jail" was four separate buildings: Lumpkin's residence, a guest house for visiting traders, a kitchen and bar, and a slave pen. The two-story slave pen was forty feet long.

598 Robert Lumpkin's jail was three blocks from the Capital House in Richmond, Virginia. The business began there in 1831. Bacon Tait was a white slave trader married to a free black woman in Richmond. Hank Trent has recently published a biography of Tait with LSU Press in 2017.

599 "Detail of Plan of the City of Richmond Drawn From the Actual Survey by Micajah Bates, 1835," in Preliminary History of Lumpkin's Jail Property.

600 "Lumpkin's Alley" was so named because Lumpkin's jail was adjacent to the alley in question. A number of slave traders in Richmond operated near that alley.

On the ground floor was the main jail, which typically held slaves who were about to be sold south. The jail held slaves for a short time until auctioned off, to plantation owners, or other traders, often in the streets of Richmond.

Lumpkin's jail was situated along Shockoe Creek and featured barred windows, high fences and chained gates. The yard of the jail more resembled a chicken coop than a collection of human beings. Because of the crowded conditions at Lumpkin's jail, inhabitants often died of disease, like cholera or dysentery, or starvation, if not from the beatings and the torture.

Many of those who survived the Middle Passage were taken off slave ships in Richmond and placed in Lumpkin's jail, which was a slave market that sat on the canal near the railroad tracks. This is where slaves were groomed, fed and dressed up to be sold at auction on the river. Once purchased, they were placed on a slave ship or a train headed to the Deep South or took part in a land coffle traveling from the Chesapeake Bay region to the Deep South, particularly to places such as Savannah, Charleston, Natchez, Mississippi, and New Orleans, Louisiana.

Robert Lumpkin eventually impregnated one of his slaves, a woman named Mary. She later became Lumpkin's wife. They had five children, two of whom were sent to finishing school in the North.[601]

During the Civil War, Robert Lumpkin sent Mary and their children to Pennsylvania so they would not be sold back into slavery. When Lumpkin died in 1866, he left all his land and property to Mary, who was by then legally allowed to possess them.

A year earlier, in April of 1865, the Union Army had captured Richmond, and all the slaves at Lumpkin's jail were emancipated, much like what we saw with Col. Birney's liberation of the slaves in Baltimore's slave jails, in Chapter Five of this study.

Finally, in 1867, Mary Lumpkin sold the property and land to Nathaniel Colver, a Baptist minister, looking for a place to establish a seminary in Richmond. The Colver Institute began as a black seminary,

601 Michael Paul Williams, "Mary Lumpkin," in Richmond Times-Dispatch, February 23, 2005. The Rev. Nathaniel Colver (1794–1870) was a US Baptist clergyman and preacher noted for his sermon.

but later it became the Union Theological Seminary. Thus, the land and property went from being the "Devil's Half-Acre" to "God's Half-Acre" in a matter of forty years.[602]

There is some evidence that Mary Lumpkin had at least some contact with the unfortunate slaves of her husband. There is a report that, on one occasion, she smuggled a hymnal into Lumpkin's jail for a man who later would become an escaped slave of her husband named Anthony Burns, or so an article in the *Smithsonian* asserts.[603] Later, Burns became a prominent Virginia slave, as we shall see later in this chapter.

Like the other Virginia traders, Robert Lumpkin regularly advertised for his business, as well as for runaway slaves who had escaped his firm. In the *Richmond Examiner*, for example, Lumpkin offered a five-hundred-dollar reward for the return of a slave named Lewis, who is "About twenty-four years old and five foot ten or eleven inches, and of a very black complexion."[604]

In another advertisement from the *Richmond Dispatch* dated January 11, 1865, Robert Lumpkin wishes the return of a slave named John Muse. He is, "Thirty years old with a dark complexion, a high forehead with a small knot. I will give a reward of one thousand dollars if delivered to Lumpkin's jail."[605]

From 1808, when the British outlawed the international slave trade until the end of the Civil War, an estimated three hundred thousand slaves were sold in Lumpkin's jail. Lumpkin was known as a "Bully Trader," for his harsh treatment of his slaves. He sold men, women and children who became slaves in the cotton and sugar fields of the Deep South, and where slavery was still legal.

Recently, archeological work has begun at the former site of Lumpkin's jail and business. Archeologists have dug fourteen feet into the earth before discovering the foundation wall of the jail. Numerous artifacts have been recovered, including clothes, shoes, toys and books.

---

602 Ibid.

603 Ibid.

604 Robert Lumpkin, "$100 Reward," in Richmond Examiner, March 15, 1853.

605 Robert Lumpkin, "Wanted: Return of Slave John Muse," in Richmond Times-Dispatch, January 11, 1865.

They have not, however, found any whipping rings, iron bars or chains typically associated with finds related to slaves.[606]

A number of first-person narratives of experiencing Lumpkin's jail are extant. One visiting abolitionist from Syracuse, New York, wrote about visiting the courtyard connected to Lumpkin's jail. He writes, "I entered an open courtyard. Against one of the posts sat a good-natured fat man, with his chair tipped back. It was Mr. Lumpkin. He greeted me courteously and showed me his jail."[607]

The visitor continued his description:

> He thenes on to describe his Jail, at least the outside. On one side of the open Court was a large tank for washing and lavatory. Opposite was a long, two-story brick house, the lower part fitted for men and the second story for women. The place was a kind of Hotel or boardinghouse for Negro Traders and their slaves.[608]

The anonymous New York visitor of Lumpkin's jail suggests that the facility sometimes was used by Lumpkin as a boarding house where slaves could be kept for a short time while visiting that area of Richmond.

The design of Lumpkin's jail was much like what we have seen in some of the slave castles and forts in Africa, back in Chapter Three, where there were separate facilities for men and women. We also see in this advertisement that Mr. Lumpkin is now conducting his slave auctions in a hotel, a precursor to patterns in Washington and the Chesapeake Bay region in general later in the nineteenth century, as we shall see in Chapter Seven.

In addition to these major slave traders in Richmond in the nine-

---

606 Matthew R. Laird, "The Archeological Significance of the Lumpkin's Jail Site," in Richmond Times-Dispatch, September 19, 2015.

607 Joseph Henry, "On Visiting Lumpkin's Jail," in the New York Observer, May 17, 1853. Also see: Alfred L. Brophy, "University, Court, and Slave: Pro-Slavery Academic Thought and Society and Jurisprudence, 1831–1861," in Industrialization and Society in the Old South (New York: Oxford University Press, 2016).

608 Ibid. One interesting feature of Lumpkin's Boarding House is that the male and female slaves were kept on the same floor, separated by a wall, an unusual situation at the time.

teenth century, there were also a significant number of auctioneers who also dealt in the slave business. Among these were E. B. Cook at 70 Main Street, Dabney and Chuthern, and Otis Dunlop on Main Street between 14th and 15th Streets, and Edward D. Eacho on 14th Street near the Exchange Hotel was also an auctioneer of slaves.[609]

Other minor nineteenth-century slave traders in Richmond, Virginia, include Fleming Tucker on the northwest corner of Clay and 18th Street, John Owenhiser on Wall Street and Locust, William Martin on the west side of 17th Street between Broad and Marshall, and Moses Elias Levy's business at Exchange Place and Franklin, again mentioned earlier. Mr. Levy's business is one of the only Jewish slave traders in the Chesapeake Bay region during the nineteenth century, as we pointed out earlier in this chapter.

Three of the largest slave dealers in Virginia were in Alexandria. The Price and Burch Company at 1315 Duke Street began by Charles M. Price and James Burch continued in the slave business from the mid-1830s until the Civil War. The firm of Franklin and Armfield was, perhaps, the largest and most prominent of all the slave-trading establishments. Joseph Bruin and Company in Fairfax County was another significant slave trader in the middle of the nineteenth century.[610]

Joseph Bruin's slave jail was a two-story brick building from which Mr. Bruin conducted his slave-trading business in Alexandria. The technical name of the establishment was "Bruin and Hill." Most of their business was to transport slaves from slave markets in the Chesapeake region to ports in the Deep South. At the beginning of the Amer-

609 Elizabeth Kambourian, "Slave Traders in Richmond," in Richmond Times-Dispatch, February 24, 2014. Moses Elias Levy (1782–1854) was a Jewish American businessman who was born in Morocco and died in Virginia. In the 1830s and 1840s, he was in the slave-trading business. Charles M. Price (1839–1910) was a slave trader in Alexandria just before the Civil War.

610 Joseph Bruin & Company, later called Bruin & Hill, was at 1707 Duke Street in Alexandria. In 1858, Charles M. Price and John Cook purchased the Franklin and Armfield property in Alexandria. A short time later, Cook left the partnership, whereupon he was replaced by Mr. Birch. Then, the firm was known as Price & Birch, Dealers in Slaves.

ican Civil War, Joseph Bruin was captured by the Union Army and imprisoned in Washington, DC. US Marshalls confiscated his business, including the slave jail, and used it as the Fairfax County Court House until the end of the Civil War.[611]

All that remains today of Mr. Bruin's business is the two-story structure that housed the slaves. Joseph Bruin's living quarters, the kitchen and bar, as well as the wash house/visitor house, no longer are extant. At the end of this chapter, there is a description of an image of Mr. Bruin's slave business just after the Civil War. The firm of Franklin and Armfield, however, had more tentacles stretching out in the slave business than any other firm, as we shall see next.

Franklin and Armfield, located at 1315 Duke Street in Alexandria, was built beginning in 1810 as a residence, but later housed the offices of the largest slave-trading firm in the antebellum South. The firm started in 1828 with the partnership of Isaac Franklin and John Armfield. The site was designated as a national historic landmark in 1978.

The property at Franklin and Armfield now houses the Freedom House Museum and is owned by the Northern Virginia Urban League.[612] The Freedom House puts on exhibits concerning the history of slave trading, as well as the lives of some of the slaves who were kept there in the nineteenth century.[613]

Isaac Franklin (1789–1846) was born on a plantation in Sumner County, Tennessee. At the age of twenty-one, he went into business with his older brothers, James and John. His job was to transport slaves by flatboat down the Mississippi River to New Orleans. Many of these slaves had traveled by slave coffles inland from Maryland and Virginia to Nashville, Tennessee Natchez, Mississippi, and other cities in the

---

611 Quoted in "The Archeology of the Bruin Slave Jail," Columbia Equity Trust, 1776 I Street NW, Suite 500, Washington, DC. By 1847, Joseph Bruin had the largest slave-trading firm in Alexandria and one of the largest in Virginia, as well as the Upper South.

612 Freedom House Museum, Northern Virginia Urban League. A marker now is placed in front of the building that tells us, "Isaac Franklin and John Armfield leased this brick building with access to wharves and docks in 1828, as a Holding Pen for enslaved people…Slave Traders operated the property until 1861."

613 Ibid.

Deep South.

Isaac Franklin is a fine example of two aspects of nineteenth-century slave trading. First, like many slave dealers during that time, it was a family business. Several members of the Franklin family took part in the business. Secondly, he was a good example of moving slaves by steamship in the early decades of the nineteenth century, beginning with the development of the steamship in 1814.

In 1828, Isaac Franklin formed a partnership with John Armfield. Armfield was Franklin's nephew by marriage. From their offices in these cities, Franklin and Armfield sold their slaves to southern planters. In addition to doing business in New Orleans, the firm also engaged with firms in Saint Francisville and Vidalia, Louisiana, where they had both offices and slave jails.[614]

Like the other Virginia slave traders, Franklin and Armfield heavily advertised their slave business. One advertisement from the *Alexandria Phenix Gazette* on May 17, 1828, for example, tells us this about their business:

> Cash In Market
>
> The Subscribers, having leased for a term of years the largest three-story brick house on Duke Street, in the town of Alexandria formerly occupied by General Young. We wish to purchase one hundred and fifty likely Negroes of both sexes between the ages of eight and twenty-five. Persons who wish to sell would do well to give us a call, as we are determined to give more than any other purchasers that are in Market, or that may hereafter come into Market. Any letters addressed to the Subscribers through the Post Office at Alexandria, will be promptly attended to. For information, enquire at the above described address, as we at all times can be found there.[615]

614 Quoted in Columbia Equity, p. 22.

615 Franklin and Armfield, Alexandria Phenix Gazette, May 17, 1828. General Andrew Jackson Young (1814–1889) was a Confederate War hero and southern patriot of the Georgia Calvary. The Alexandria Phenix Gazette was a daily newspaper, except Sundays, published from 1825 until 1833, by

Franklin and Armfield intend to give top dollar for slaves, now as well as in the future, their three-story firm is the largest townhouse in Alexandria, and they may be reached at a post office box in Alexandria. This firm was the largest in the city, as well as in the state of Virginia for most of the nineteenth century.

The "General Young" referred to in the quote above is General Andrew Jackson Young (1814–1889), head of the eleventh Georgia Calvary and defender of the city of Athens, Georgia, during the American Civil War. The building on Duke Street was originally built as the residence of General Young and his family.

For a number of years, from 1828 until 1846, the Duke Street property was leased by Franklin and Armfield. In 1846, George Kephart, discussed in Chapter Five, and acting as an agent of Franklin and Armfield, purchased the property for that firm.[616] Twelve years later, in 1858, it was sold to a third trading firm, Price, Burch and Company, discussed earlier in this chapter. A description of the firm can be seen at the end of this chapter.

The building on Duke Street was originally constructed as a residence for General Andrew Young, but it passed into the hands of slave traders from 1828 until 1861. The complex then served as a Civil War prison for Union Army deserters from 1861 until 1865. In 1863, the location on Duke Street also provided the first home of the Shiloh Baptist Church.

The slave pens of Franklin and Armfield were finally destroyed in the 1870s. After the war, the house was the home of Alexandria Hospital from 1878 until 1885. The building was converted into apartments and renovated as office space in 1984.[617]

The Franklin and Armfield offices were in an L-shape, Adamesque style, with three stories colored gray painted brick. Although the building has undergone considerable renovations, the original pine flooring, open well, and three flight iron staircase, are all original. The

---

Mr. S. Snowden and W. F. Thorton.

616 Geoge Kephart is discussed at length in Chapter Five. The Confederate 11th Georgia Calvary was organized in the city of Athens in November of 1864.

617 Quoted in Columbia Equity, p. 164. The Shiloh Baptist Church was the first Baptist church to be established in northern Virginia in 1863.

east wall of the ground level once separated the male quarters from the female space, as did most of the slave jails in Virginia and the district at that time.

At the height of the business of Franklin and Armfield, in the 1830s, the company sold between one thousand and twelve hundred captives per year. This made it one of the key players in the interstate slave trade that transported captives from ports in the Upper South, like Baltimore, Annapolis, Washington, Alexandria, Norfolk, and Richmond, to markets further south in Charleston, Savannah, Mobile in Alabama, and to Natchez, Mississippi, and New Orleans in Louisiana.

In 1858, Franklin and Armfield sold the slave jail on Duke Street to Charles M. Price and John Cook, who remained in the same business. The pair still owned the establishment when Union troops entered the business on May 24, 1861. They found the slave jail empty except for one male slave chained to a wall in the basement. This was much like Colonel Birney's liberation of the Baltimore slave jails discussed back in Chapter Five.

Around the same time, John Cook placed a slave named Lucy Couch in a slave jail in Baltimore, where she remained for the next sixteen months. She was finally liberated, as well, by General Birney when the Union Army entered the establishment.[618]

The Rev. Joshua Leavitt of New York visited the establishment of Franklin and Armfield in January of 1834. Leavitt had been told that Armfield "bore the character of a gentleman of fair character for integrity and openness in his dealings, and one who was ever-ready to afford any facilities for redressing whatever abuses might grow out of the nature of his business."[619]

Another abolitionist, a man named George Drinker, who was an Alexandrian Quaker, confirmed the positive view of Armfield, and add-

618 Lucy Couch (1767–1849) was born in Connecticut, married Samuel Root, and had nine children.

619 Joshua Leavitt, quoted in "Alexandria to New Orleans: The Human Tragedy of the Interstate Slave Trade," Part II, www.connectionnewspapers.com. Leavitt (1794–1873) is buried in the Green-Wood Cemetery in Brooklyn, New York. Leavitt (1731–1802) was an early New England Congregationalist preacher. He was born in Connecticut and served as pastor throughout churches all over New England. He was also a staunch abolitionist.

ed that he was very careful to avoid buying free blacks, and often "went to much trouble and expense… to keep his business free from everything that would contravene the law."[620]

The following year, in 1835, a Boston abolitionist named Professor E. A. Andrews (1787–1858), also described visiting Franklin and Armfield's establishment. Andrews reported that Armfield's reputation was so good that when many slaves were faced with the prospect of being sold south, they inquired if they could be "sold to Mr. Armfield."[621]

The tentacles of the business of Franklin and Armfield extended very far. One advertisement taken out by them in the *Washington Globe*, from November 25, 1833, for example, shows the firm's many agents elsewhere in the Chesapeake Bay region. The advertisement announces:

> Cash in Market
>
> We will pay cash for any number of likely Negroes, of both sexes from 12 to 50 years of age, Field Hands, also Mechanics of every description.[622]

The ad is signed by the following:

> R. C. Ballard & Co., Richmond. J. M. Saunders & Co., Warrenton
>
> George Kephart, Fredericktown
>
> James F. Purvis, Baltimore
>
> William Hopper, Annapolis. Grimm, Fredericksburg, Virginia
>
> Thomas M. Jones, Easton, Eastern

620 Ibid. George Drinker, born in 1760, was an Alexandrian Quaker and Virginia abolitionist.

621 Ethan Allen Andrews quoted in Alexandria to New Orleans. Andrews (1787–1858) was an American lexographer and editor of books. He was the author of Slavery and the Domestic Slave Trade, published in Boston in 1836, as well as Latin-English and Latin-German lexicons.

622 Franklin and Armfield, "Cash in Market," in The Washington Globe, November 25, 1833.

Shore of Maryland[623]

This advertisement, of course, reveals just how widespread the Franklin and Armfield firm was in the Chesapeake Bay region. It extended to Richmond, Warrenton, and Fredericksburg in Virginia, as well as Baltimore, Annapolis, Frederick, and in Easton and Cambridge on the Eastern Shore of Maryland, as well as other offices in the Deep South.

Mr. Bacon Tait, another Richmond slave dealer, had his place of business at 15th and Carey Streets. Like most of the other Richmond traders, Mr. Tait regularly advertised in the 1830s and 1840s. Mr. Tait's name is listed in an 1844 slave manifest for a ship in New Orleans, along with two other traders named Luther Libby and Thomas Bouder.[624] More is said about Virginia ship manifests in the appendix to this chapter. Bacon Tait was also a prominent Richmond city councilman up until the Civil War.

R. H. Dickenson moved his slave-trading firm to the Bell Tavern in Richmond on January 2, 1841.[625] Thomas Taliaferro had his slave dealing business in Richmond at the City Hotel, later to be known as the Saint Charles Hotel.[626] In the early 1840s, the area in Richmond bounded by Broad Street to the North, Cary Street on the South, 14th Street on the West, and 17th Street in the East, was filled with businesses in the slave trade.

Dickinson also points out that traders only sold their merchandise

---

623 Ibid. Steven Deyle, in his Carry Me Back, discusses all these slave traders.

624 Ibid.

625 Bacon Tait operated his slave-trading business on the southeast corner of Cary and 15th Streets in Richmond. The property was originally employed as a slave jail by Lewis L. Collier. The Saint Charles Hotel was a three-story brick building in Richmond on North Second Street. It was built in 1781 and had an iron balcony on the second floor.

626 R. H. Dickenson (1811–1873), like many early slave traders of the nineteenth century, began his business in a tavern called the Bell Tavern, where he moved on January 2, 1841. Richard Henry Dickerson was the son of William W. Dickerson, a wealthy planter in Caroline County, Virginia. The Charles Hotel in Richmond, as well as the Exchange Hotel, the Ballard Hotel, and the Bell Tavern, are the main places that slave traders stayed when they were trading in Richmond.

if the price was right. He told one auctioneer, for example, "Offer Richard [a slave] for sale in your public auction at your place of business, if they are selling tolerably well… but if they are not, then confine him in Gaol [Jail] until the prices rise.[627]

Richard Henry Dickinson (1811–1873) began selling slaves in Virginia around 1840. At the time, he sold other goods as well. By the mid-1840s, however, he was entirely in the slave-trading business. Throughout his career, Dickinson partnered with several other traders, including Nathaniel and Charles Hill. Even as late as March of 1865, Dickinson & Hill were still advertising in the Richmond newspapers, and the *Virginia Gazette*, in the buying and selling of captives.[628]

Around the same time, the Confederate government placed a hundred percent tax on slaves owned by Virginia traders. As a result, Dickinson & Hill took the following advertisement out in various Virginia newspapers. "In consequence of increased taxes of one hundred percent, we hereby give notice that our charges and commissions will be ten percent."[629] This is significantly lower than their earlier fees.

Rice C. Ballard (1800–1860) was also in the slave-trading business in Richmond. At first, he was partners with Franklin and Armfield, but he left the business around the year 1830 to pursue other endeavors. From 1830 until his death in 1860, Ballard's major business was buying up plantation lands in the Deep South particularly in Mississippi and Kentucky.[630]

Rice Carter Ballard began working in Richmond for Franklin and Armfield in the late 1820s. By the early 1840s, Ballard had settled down on one of the plantations he owned in the Mississippi Valley. Ballard and his wife Louise had three children. The University of North Carolina owns a collection of Ballard's letters and papers (Collection number 04850).

Samuel Alsop (1776–1859) of Fredericksburg, Virginia, men-

627 Ibid.

628 Dickenson & Hill, "Slaves Wanted," in The Virginia Gazette, March 21, 1865.

629 Ibid.

630 Rice Ballard (1800–1860) at the age of thirty went into the slave-trading business in Richmond. In the final five years of his life, he bought up plantation lands in the Deep South.

tioned earlier in Chapter Five, agreed to escort a slave coffle to Mississippi for Franklin and Armfield, but the weather in Alexandria held up the departure. Mr. Alsop used the event to return a forty-two-year-old slave whom Alsop found "not suitable to me" to Rice C. Ballard of Richmond discussed earlier.[631] Mr. Alsop's partner in his slave-trading business on King Street in Fredericksburg was John A. Alford, so the firm was called "Alsop and Alford, Dealers in Slaves."

Mr. Alford was co-owner of the 150-ton ship the *Agent*, which sailed from Alexandria to New Orleans in the fall of 1819. Mr. Alford relied on Hector McLean & Company to sell his slaves in New Orleans. Alford made a dozen trips on the Alexandria to Louisiana route, in the fall months of 1819 alone, and many more journeys in the 1820s and 1830s.

Samuel Alsop (1776–1859) also was an architect and builder. He built the Alsop family home known as Fairview in Spotsylvania County, Virginia, in 1837. Alsop also built houses for several other family members, all in the Federalist style. His slave business was located in Fredericksburg, as we indicated in the above analysis.

Silas Omohundro (1807–1864), another prominent member of the Richmond City Business Council in the 1850s and 1860s, was in the slave business at that time. Earlier, he had worked for Franklin and Armfield in the 1830s, but by the mid-1840s, he was in business for himself. Omohundro married one of his slaves whom he manumitted along with his children in his will in 1864. Omohundro is important for no other reason than he kept very careful and meticulous records.

Silas Omohundro also owned a boardinghouse right next to his slave jail. When the dealers in Richmond planned an auction, visiting traders would stay there, or at the many hotels nearby, such as the Saint Charles, the Exchange, the Ballard, the City Hotel or the Bell Tavern, much like what we have seen in Baltimore in Chapter Five.[632]

631 Samuel Alsop (1776–1859) mentioned in Elizabeth Kambourian, "Slave Traders in Richmond," in Richmond Times-Dispatch. Alsop was born in Spotsylvania County, Virginia. His family estate, called Fairview, was the largest private home in the county in the nineteenth century. The manor house was built in 1837. In 1850, Alsop owned more than one hundred slaves. See: Virginia Department of Historical Resources, document 088-0012.

632 Ibid.

Peter Pulliam had his Richmond slave business on the west side of Locust Alley, between Main and Franklin, in the city. Later, he had a partner named Betts, so the firm was then called Pulliam & Betts. Mr. Pulliam also conducted slave auctions in Richmond on the site of the Odd Fellows Hall on Franklin Street.

Another Richmond slave trader, Charles T. Wortham, owned a warehouse and dock on 15th Street in Richmond between Main and Cary Streets. Charles Wortham utilized the space as a slave jail in the mid-nineteenth century. The dock there allowed him to auction captives directly from his place of business. Mr. Wortham's brother, William, acted as "General Agent" and "Collector" for the Richmond firm. The Wortham brothers is another example of multiple family members involved in the same slave-trading firm, particularly in the Richmond and the Alexandria areas.

The firm of Beasley & Jones, and then Beasley, Jones, & Wood, was another large slave-trading firm in Richmond. The business was located at 800 East Broad Street. Account ledgers from the years 1835 until 1851 are extant. They show the names of slaves sold, as well as business conducted with other traders, including, for example, a sale to another Richmond firm, Lancaster Denby & Company, from January 1, 1835.

One way to see the growth of firms in the slave trade in Richmond is to look at the *Richmond Directories* between 1845 and 1865. In 1845, only nine businesses were associated with the trade. By the year of the 1852 *Richmond Directory,* that number had increased to twenty-eight firms listed as "Slave Traders." By the *Directory* of 1860, that number had dwindled to eighteen, and by 1865 to zero.[633]

Indeed, the economics of slave trading in Richmond was staggering. In 1856, the Richmond *Enquirer* suggested that the revenue of the Dickenson & Hill firm to be two million dollars, and a year later, to have been three and a half million. In 1852, Richmond began collecting a tax on slave jails in the city. In 1860, the Virginia General Assembly proclaimed that all slave traders in the state, and particularly in Richmond, had to have a license to do so.

---

633 "Slave Traders," Richmond City Directory, 1845, 1850,1860, and 1865.

The white and slave populations of Richmond in the first sixty years of the nineteenth century also reveal some of these facts listed above. In 1800, Richmond had a population of 5,737, with 2,293 slaves and 607 free blacks. By 1840, the city's population had grown four-fold to 20,000 people, with 7,500 slaves and 2,400 free blacks. Twenty-five years later, all black people in Virginia were free.

The Abingdon Trading Center in Washington County, Virginia, acted as a hub for slave trading in that county. Between 1810 and 1860, the center, using river, canal and overland routes, a significant number of slaves were processed and moved from that hub in southwest Virginia to Washington County, Virginia, which includes the cities of Bristol, Emory and Abingdon. The center acted as a slavery focal point for Danville, Norfolk and Alexandria, often being the agent for points west from those spots.[634]

In Baltimore, as we have seen in Chapter Five, the slave trade in Richmond came to an end during the American Civil War in February of 1865. A year earlier, Virginia passed into law a new constitution for the state that also prohibited slavery. Similarly, the District of Columbia prohibited the practice of slavery on April 16, 1862, when President Lincoln signed an act abolishing slavery in the district.

Besides those in Richmond and Alexandria, other Virginia slave dealers in the nineteenth century existed elsewhere in the Commonwealth. In Warrenton, for example, the business of Jordan M. Saunders, and his partner, David Burford, was also in the Virginia slave trade. For the most part, Saunders' firm acted as an agent for Franklin and Armfield. Indeed, Mr. Saunders lived in New Orleans from 1829 until 1831, doing their business there, as well as that of James F. Purvis in Natchez, Mississippi.[635] In that regard, Mr. Saunders led many overland coffles from Warrenton to Natchez before the Civil War, mostly for the Franklin and Armfield firm.

634 The Abingdon Trading Center was a slave-trading firm from 1800 to 1860, just before the beginning of the Civil War.

635 Jordan M. Saunders, who died in 1886, was born in Alabama and moved to Warrenton, Virginia, where he went into the slave-trading business. He was never married, but some of his letters have survived. For example, one to David Burford of Smith County, Tennessee, his slave-trading partner, in which Saunders discusses national politics.

In 1831, Saunders moved to Warrenton, Virginia, where he again operated as an agent of Franklin and Armfield. The 1840 census of Fauquier County lists Jordan M. Saunders as a white, single male, between the ages of forty and forty-nine "who owns seven slaves."[636]

At least five other significant Virginia slave dealers operated in Richmond. George W. Apperson, and his business on the west side of Birch Alley conducted business in the slave trade there. Apperson also had a slave jail at the same location.[637] Lee and Bowman, a firm on Franklin Street between Mayo and 15th Streets, also operated a slave jail.[638]

Peck and Lay Company, on Main Street and 19th Street just opposite the Union Hotel, also sold slaves at auction in the nineteenth century.[639] William Wyatt was a clerk for the J. J. Dornin Company on Main Street between 15th and 17th Streets. Wyatt and Dornin were also sometimes agents of Bacon Tait.[640] A man named Solomon Myers, on the corner of Cary and 15th Streets, also operated as an agent of Mr. Tait.[641] Mr. Myers, along with Solomon Davis, Samuel Reese and Mr. Levy discussed earlier, were all Jewish slave traders in Richmond, Virginia.

One of the most interesting of the minor Richmond traders was Dr. Peterfield Trent, who lived and did business on the southeast corner of Marshall and Seventh Streets in Richmond. Trent advertised himself as being in the business of "Negro Broker and Sales."[642] Trent was trained as a surgeon and operated in that capacity throughout his adult life. His son, William Peterfield Trent (1862–1939), was an English professor at Columbia University in New York City.

David M. Pulliam and Hector Davis, on the west side of Wall Street near Franklin Street in Richmond, advertised themselves as "Pulliam and Davis: Auctioneers & Commission Merchants."[643] This

636 1840 Virginia census of Fauquier County.

637 George Apperson's business was also on Birch Alley.

638 Mentioned in Kambourian. The Union Hotel was built in 1817 in Richmond by Dr. John Adams. It later became an Army hospital.

639 Ibid.

640 Ibid.

641 Ibid.

642 Ibid.

643 Ibid. Hector Davis (1816–1863) was the son of John S. Davis of Goochland County, Virginia. His slave-trading business in Richmond was

firm was one of the largest in Virginia at the time. William Martin, Edward Matthews, Charles McMurray, William Murphy and Dabney Price, all advertised themselves as "Negro Traders" in the pages of the *Virginia Gazette*.[644]

Pulliam & Davis tell us they sold other goods, like Produce besides slaves; they also sold other Plantations goods, like Slave clothing, tools, and Farm Equipment, and that their Office is to be found on Wall Street, in the City of Richmond.

Pulliam & Davis advertised regularly in the pages of the *Richmond Times-Dispatch*, like this 1852 ad:

> Pulliam & Davis will attend to the selling of Plantation accessories, the selling of Produce, and to the acquiring of Negroes at their Wall Street Office, just opposite The City Hotel in Richmond.[645]

Pulliam & Davis were sued by one of their slaves on September 16, 1854. A man named George Aler alleged that Mr. Pulliam had mistreated him. The case *Pulliam v. Aler* went all the way to the US Supreme Court, where in January of 1859, the court found in favor of Mr. Aler. The slave received damages from the Pulliam & Davis firm.

John Toler, John B. Davis, S. Grady, R. Faundron, W. Abrahams, and Robert Alvis, all of Richmond, Virginia, also advertised themselves as slave traders.[646] William Gouldin, whose business was on the west side of Governor and 13th Streets in Richmond, called himself a "General Agent and Collector."[647] William Dupree, at Mayo Street near

---

on the west side of Wall Street near Franklin Street.

644 Ibid.

645 Pulliam & Davis, Richmond Times-Dispatch, February 6, 1852. The Peter Pulliam & Hector Davis (1816–1863) business was on the west side of Wall Street near Franklin. Hector Davis was the son of John S. Davis, also a slave trader in Richmond. When Hector Davis died in 1863, he had a huge estate, including $14,000 worth of slaves. Besides Hector Davis, Pulliam sometimes did business as Pulliam & Company. At other times, he had another partner in Richmond named Betts, and thus the business was Pulliam & Betts.

646 Mentioned in Kambourian.

647 Ibid.

Franklin, called his firm "Negro Traders."[648]

Asher Levy, whose business was on Locust Alley between Exchange Place and Franklin Street, and who we introduced earlier in this chapter, also advertised as a "Negro Trader."[649] Alexander Nott, on the southwest corner of Main Street and 15th Streets, referred to his business "Alexander Nott and Company" as "Auctioneer and Commission Merchants."[650]

And another slave jail in Richmond was simply referred to as "The Cage." It was located at the northwest corner of 17th and Main Streets in Richmond.[651] Although the owner of this facility is not known, it may well have been one of the major slave traders of Richmond, like Bacon Tait, Pulliam & Davis, or Robert Lumpkin.

Charles T. Wortham, on 15th Street between Main and Cary, referred to his business as "Forwarding and Commission Merchant & Auctioneer."[652] Alexander Smith, at the corner of 8th and Broad Streets, called himself a "Negro Trader."[653] The firm Smith and Edmondson used the same identification for their business in Richmond.[654] The Smith family, Alexander and William James Smith, is another example of multiple family members working together in the slave trade. Between 1844 and 1854, the latter made countless trips from Richmond to Charleston, South Carolina, buying and selling slaves. In fact, his account books for those years are extant.

James M. Taylor and Son, at the corner of Bank and 11th Street in Richmond, called his business "Slave Trader."[655] Leonard T. Slater, whose firm was on the east side of 17th Street between Broad and Marshall, simply advertised his business as "Trader."[656] Fleming Tucker did the same in the capital city of Virginia. Tucker's firm was on the

648 Ibid.
649 Ibid.
650 Ibid.
651 Ibid.
652 Ibid.
653 Ibid.
654 Ibid. Leonard Slatter was the brother of Hope Slatter.
655 Ibid.
656 Ibid.

northwest corner of Clay and 18th Streets.[657] Samuel Reese also referred to his business as "Slave Trader." His firm was located on the east side of 17th Street between Broad and Grace Streets.[658]

Other nineteenth-century slave dealers in Virginia could be found in Norfolk, Petersburg and Warrenton. In the former, R. H. Banks and R. L. Marsh both owned slave jails connected to their businesses.[659] A number of ship manifests of Messers Banks and Marsh are extant, as we shall see in the appendix to this chapter.

In Petersburg, Mr. George Davis was the most prominent nineteenth-century slave dealer in the city.[660] The Petersburg Hustings Court House at 1 Courthouse Avenue was used to auction off slaves in the 1840s and 1850s.[661] Later, slave auctions will move again in Virginia, this time to the establishments of the major traders in the city. More will be said about slave auctions in the Chesapeake region in the nineteenth century, as well as slave auction blocks, in Chapter Seven of this study.

And another significant slave trader in Petersburg was the "Thomas Branch and Sons," a firm located at 37 River Street.[662] J. M. Saunders & Company had a slave-trading business in Warrenton, Virginia, as we indicated earlier. This firm also had offices in Baltimore, Rockville and Frederick in the middle of the nineteenth century.[663]

Another Virginia slave-trading firm in the nineteenth century was the partnership of Richard R. Beasley and William H. Wood, or Beasley and Wood, also located in Petersburg. Between 1834 and 1845, the firm conducted slave coffles from Petersburg to Natchez and Port Gibson, Mississippi, where the slaves would be placed on ships and sent further south. Richard Beasley's office was in Norfolk, while his partner, Mr.

657 Ibid.

658 Ibid.

659 Ibid.

660 Ibid.

661 Ibid.

662 In addition to being in the slave-trading business, Thomas Branch & Sons were also bankers. See: Howard Bodenhorn, "Private Banking in Antebellum Virginia: Thomas Branch & Sons," in The Business Historical Review 71, no. 4 (1997), pp. 513–542.

663 See Note 631.

Wood, did the firm's trading in Natchez, Mississippi. Mr. Wood also was in the slave-trading business in Luray, Virginia. His partner there was a man named D. T. Jones. Their firm was on Main Street and called Wood & Jones, Traders in Slaves.

The earliest overland slave trader in Virginia was John Butterworth, who began his slave coffles traveling to what would become the Forks in the Road Market in Natchez, Mississippi. The earliest trips to Mississippi, for which there is historical evidence, was on April 6, 1818. This trip began in Petersburg and took six to eight weeks to reach Natchez, where the coffle slaves were sold.[664] Mr. Butterworth also hired out the labor of his slaves along the coffle route to farmers and town people, who also fed the captives along the way.

Finally, there also were a number of slave auctioneers in Richmond in the first sixty-five years of the nineteenth century. Many of these auctioneers conducted the sales of many of the slave traders mentioned in this chapter. Four of the most important auctioneers in the city were J. J. Dornin at Cary and 15th Streets, James E. Goddin at 11th and Bank Streets, James Nott Shine at Main and 15th Streets, and N. M. Lee and Company at Franklin and Mayo Streets.[665]

This brings us to several prominent Virginia slaves, who at times, resided in a number of the Virginia facilities mentioned above, the topic of the next section of this chapter.

Prominent Virginia Slaves from Slave Jails: 1800 to 1862

In many of the slave facilities mentioned above, a number of prominent Virginia slaves can be identified. In 1854 at Lumpkin's jail, for example, a man named Anthony Burns escaped the Commonwealth of Virginia only to be found in the city of Boston. After a trial, Burns was returned to Virginia under the provisions of the Fugitive Slave Law of 1851. The US Congress passed this statute in September of 1850 as part of a compromise that year between southern slave owners and northern free soilers.

The act required, in part, that all escaped slaves in the north must

664 Petersburg to Natchez, Franklin and Armfield, April 6, 1818.

665 Again, Kambourian mentions all these businesses in the article mentioned earlier.

be returned to their masters, and that the citizens of the north must cooperate and comply to the provisions of this new law. This caused a violent riot that broke out in Boston, as abolitionists protested the decision to return Mr. Burns to his home state.[666]

When Burns was returned to Richmond, he was taken to Lumpkin's jail for four months, an ordeal that was later described in the March 17, 1855, issue of the *Anti-Slavery Bugle*. That publication relates:

> He was taken to Richmond, where he was kept in a little Pen in the Trader's Jail for four months, with irons on his wrists and ankles, so tight that they wore the flesh through to the bone, and during the month of August, they gave him a half a pail full of water every two days.[667]

Charles Stevens wrote a biography of Anthony Burns entitled *Anthony Burns: A History*.[668] Stevens says this about the conditions in which the slave was kept:

> The place of his confinement was a room only six or eight feet square, in the upper story of the Jail, which was only accessible through a trap-door. He was allowed neither a bed nor air. Fetters also prevented him

---

666 The Fugitive Slave Act of 1850 was passed on September 18, 1850, as part of a compromise between southern slave owners and the abolitionist north. It required, in part, that all captured escaped slaves, no matter where they are apprehended, must be returned to their owners, even southern ones.

667 "Anthony Burns," in Encyclopedia of Virginia, http://bit.ly/2sFW-4wl. Burns (1834–1866) was a slave owned by Charles Suttle of Alexandria. He had many activities he was allowed, not afforded to other slaves. He was free, for example, to hire out his labor. He also supervised at least four other slaves for Mr. Suttle. After escaping Suttle's Farm, Mr. Burns boarded a ship in Richmond bound for Boston, where he became a preacher. He was later caught, tried, and taken back to Virginia. The Anti-Slavery Bugle was an abolitionist newspaper founded in New Lisbon, Ohio, in 1845. The Ohio American Anti-Slavery Society published the paper. It ceased publication in 1861.

668 Charles Stevens, Anthony Burns: A History (New York: Create Space, 2012).

> from removing his clothing by day or night, and no one came to help him; the indecency resulting from such a condition is too revolting for a description, or even a thought.[669]

Mary Lumpkin took pity on Burns after his return. She gave him pen and paper by which he secretly sent letters to friends in the north, pleading for help.[670] Publications from all over the US reported Burns' escape. The *Richmond Examiner*, however, considered Anthony Burns to be a runaway and argued that his return was morally justified. It was nothing more than the stealing of property. Wherever the case was discussed, it either strengthened the abolitionist's spirit or the south's commitment to the institution of slavery.[671]

A second and perhaps the most notable of slaves residing in the District of Columbia and the Commonwealth of Virginia facilities outlined above was Solomon Northrop. He was the author of *Twelve Years a Slave*, written in 1853.[672] Northrop, a free man, was kidnapped in Washington, DC, held in a slave jail for a while, and then sold into slavery. Upon arriving at the slave jail, Northrop speaks of a passage used for an epigram for this chapter. He writes:

> It occurred to me that I must be in an underground apartment, and the damp, moldy odors of the place confirmed my suppositions. The noise above continued for at least an hour when, at last, I heard footsteps approaching from without. A key rattled in the lock, and a strong iron door swung back upon its hinges, admitting a flood of light. Two men entered and stood before me. One of them was a large powerful man, forty years of age, perhaps, with dark, chestnut colored hair, slightly interspersed with grey. His face was full, his complexion flush. His features were grossly coarse and expressive

669 Ibid.

670 Williams, "Mary Lumpkin."

671 "Anthony Burns," The Richmond Examiner, March 20, 1855.

672 Solomon Northrop, Twelve Years a Slave (Los Angeles: Graymalkin Media, 2014).

> of nothing but cruelty and cunning.[673]

Mr. Northrop continues his description:

> He was about five feet ten inches high, of full habit and without prejudice. I must be allowed to say that he was a man whose whole appearance was sinister and repugnant. His name was James H. Birch, as I learned afterwards, a well-known Slave Dealer in Washington.[674]

James H. Burch was born in Henrico County, Virginia, in 1836. He went into the slave business before the Civil War and partnered with Theophilus Freeman. Freeman handled the partnership's business in New Orleans. In fact, Freeman was the slave trader who sold Solomon Northrop in that city. Freeman was married to a woman who had previously been his slave. She was a molatto woman named Sarah Conner. In the film version of *Twelve Years a Slave*, Theophilus Freeman's part is played by Paul Giamatti.[675] James Burch's major place of business was in Washington, and that is where Mr. Burch encountered Solomon Northrop.

The slave trader to whom Solomon Northrop refers to in the above quote, of course, is James H. Burch, rather than Birch. He was the brutal Washington slave dealer who first kept Mr. Northrop in bondage. Later, *Twelve Years a Slave*, became a best-selling book and a movie depicting the slave's life by the same name.[676]

Another prominent Virginia slave who spent some time at Lumpkin's jail was Henry Clay Bruce (1836–1902). When Bruce was a boy, he was taken for auction to Lumpkin's jail and sold at auction to a North Carolina planter. Later, in 1895, Bruce wrote an autobiography entitled *Twenty-Nine Years a Slave, Twenty-Nine Years a Free Man*.[677] This text was published in York, Pennsylvania, by Amstadt &

673 Ibid.

674 Ibid.

675 Twelve Years a Slave is a 2013 film directed by Steve McQueen. The screenplay was written by John Ridley.

676 See note 668.

677 Henry Clay Bruce, Twenty-Nine Years a Slave, Twenty-Nine Years a Free Man (York: Amstadt & Sons, 1895). Bruce (1836–1902) was the

Sons.[678]

A final prominent Virginia slave was a man named John Brown who was traded from Virginia to Georgia, to New Orleans. Later, he also penned an autobiography. Before being sold the first time, he describes the conditions before his sale. In a passage employed as an epigram for this chapter, he tells us:

> There was a general washing, and combing, and shaving, the pulling out of grey hairs, and the dying of the hair of those who were too grey to be plucked without making them bald.[679]

This behavior is similar to how slave ship owners prepared their slaves at the end of the Middle Passage voyages to America. They were bathed, their hair cut, and their bodies treated with a mixture of ash and oil to give them a bright and healthy appearance, as we have seen earlier in Chapter Two where we discussed the preparations for sale of Middle Passage slaves before arriving in the New World.

Smith goes on to point out that they were given new suits of clothing and new shoes, and then they were dressed for sale.[680] Smith goes on to suggest that the slaves for sale were classified as "Extra," "Second Rate," and "Ordinary." These were terms that applied to men as well as women. Children, on the other hand, Smith points out, were priced as to their height.[681]

This brings us to a number of pieces of art, mostly from the nineteenth century, that depict much of the material outlined in this chapter. It is to art, then, that we next turn, followed by the conclusions and the

---

brother of the first black United States senator, Blanche K. Bruce. They were born to slave parents. Their master was named Lemuel Bruce. One thing that was different about the Bruce brothers is that, even early on, both could read and write.

678 Ibid.

679 John Brown (1810–1876) autobiography was originally published in London by W. M. Watts in 1855, http://bit.ly/2qWYMNG. More recently, Dennis B. Fredin's Bound for the North Star was published by Houghton-Mifflin Harcourt in 2000. Mr. Fredin discussed Brown at length.

680 Ibid.

681 Ibid.

notes to this chapter.

Washington, DC, and Virginia Slave Dealers and Jails in Art: 1800 to 1865

In this final section of this chapter, we shall describe and discuss several pieces of art that have depicted many of the slave traders and slave jails we have seen above in Washington and the Commonwealth of Virginia. The first image entitled *Scene in the Slave Pen in Washington* is an illustration of Solomon Northrop's *Twelve Years a Slave.*[682]

The image shows a slave prostrate on the floor of a slave pen. Two white men stand above the slave, beating him with a long cat-of-nine tails. The slave appears to be secured to a wall behind the men with a thick chain.[683]

Image two, from Corey's *History of Richmond Theological Seminary*, shows an early illustrated version of Lumpkin's slave jail. The image shows a two-story, wood structure with a wood shingle roof, surrounded by a three-rail fence. The structure, of course, would later become the slave jail and other buildings of Robert Lumpkin's property, complete with slave jail, slave yard, and whipping posts.[684] And still later, the property became the Union Theological Seminary in Richmond.

Images three and four were produced by British painter Eyre Crowe, who in 1853 visited Richmond, Virginia, working as the secretary to British novelist W. M. Thackery, who was on a lecture tour. While on tour, Crowe spotted a slave auction in progress in the city on Wall Street. His sketches nearly caused him to be removed from the auction house, for the Virginian planters thought he was an abolitionist, when in fact he was sketching the proceedings before him unfolding.[685]

682 Scene of a slave pen in Washington, illustration in Nortrhrop's Twelve Years a Slave. See Note 668.
683 Charles H. Cory, illustration of Lumpkin's slave jail in History of Richmond Theological Seminary (Bibliobazaar, 2009), sappingattention.blogspot.com.
684 Ibid.
685 Eyre Crowe, Thackery's Hunts and Homes (London, 1897). Crowe (1864–1925) was a British diplomat and English painter of historical and genre scenes. He was a student of William Darley and later of Paul Delaro-

Mr. Crowe also witnessed slaves being taken to a railroad depot to be shipped further south. Two paintings from his sketches that day were later entitled *After the Sale: Slaves Going South From Richmond* and *Slaves Waiting for Sale*.[686] These paintings were exhibited in London in 1854 and 1861, respectively. These paintings played an important role in spreading anti-slavery sentiments in both America and the British Isles.[687]

An illustration entitled *Franklin and Armfield: Dealers in Slaves* appeared in George W. Featherstone's *Excursions Through the Slave States*, which was published in two volumes in London in 1844. The image shows four white slave traders on a hill under a tree in nineteenth-century America. Each of the four carry long rifles. They all gaze below at a valley full of slaves apparently being prepared for sale.[688]

A mid-nineteenth-century image of the Price, Birch & Company at 1315 Duke Street in Alexandria, shows the front of the establishment. The sign above the ground floor reads, "Price, Birch and Company: Dealers in Slaves." In front of the building on the street are three black men dressed in Union Army uniforms. One carries a long rifle with bayonet. A fourth soldier stands in the doorway of the property, looking forlornly.[689]

Another illustration of Robey's Tavern on F Street in Washington DC, shows a young woman perched in a third-floor window ready to throw herself down in destruction. This is an illustration of a true story, in which the woman jumped and survived her injuries. She survived the fall with multiple injuries, but she was no longer separated from her family, as she had feared. This illustration comes from the 1817 book

---

che, while in Paris. William Makepeace Thackery (1811–1863) was a British novelist, known principally for Vanity Fair.

686 Ibid.

687 Ibid.

688 Illustration of Franklin and Armfield in George Featherstone's Excursions Through the Slave State (London, 1844). George William Featherstone (1811–1864) was a British traveler and writer.

689 Photograph of Price, Burch & Company, Library of Congress, Prints and Photographs. Jesse Torrey (1787–1834) was a Philadelphia physician and abolitionist. Many of his letters to Madison and Jefferson, for example, are extant. Micajah Bates (1797–1861), from Hanover County, Virginia, was an artist and cartographer.

A Portraiture of Domestic Slavery, written by Philadelphian physician and abolitionist Jesse Torrey.[690] Mr. Torrey describes the woman's leap, and its aftermath, in some detail.

Image number eight is a detail of an actual city plan of Richmond drawn from an actual survey conducted by Micajah Bates in 1835. The image includes lots 62 to 64, owned by Lumpkin, on the shores of the Old Shockoe Creek in Richmond.[691]

Image number nine is an advertisement from the *Richmond Times-Dispatch*, from an issue in 1857, for the firm of Pulliam & Davis. The same ad appeared as a page in the *Richmond City Directory* from 1852. The advertisement reads:

> Pulliam & David
>
> Auctioneers and Commission
>
> Merchants
>
> Richmond, Virginia[692]

Finally, an advertisement taken out in the *Virginia Gazette* by Richmond dealer Thomas Taylor dated February 17, 1812, informs us:

> Slaves: Will Be Sold
>
> Before the Door of the Eagle Tavern
>
> At Twelve Noon, On The Twenty-

---

690 Jesse Torrey, "Robey's Tavern," in A Portraiture of Domestic Slavery (Philadelphia, 1817). For a good treatment of Robey's Tavern, see Lincoln's Citadel: Washington During the Civil War by Kenneth J. Winkle (New York: Norton, 2013), particularly Chapter Two entitled, "At War with Washington: The Abolitionists." Also see Francis X. Clines, "The Closing of the Circle," in New York Times, January 19, 2009. Clines says that Robey's Tavern was on the spot where the US Department of Education now is. He also speaks of Robey's slave coffles marching through the streets of Washington. He says, "A group consisting of males and females chained in couples."

691 Illustration in Laird.

692 Richmond City Directory, 1852. Thomas Taylor was a Richmond slave trader. A number of his letters survive, including one to John C. Rutherford from December 12, 1853.

Fourth

In 1812, Mr. Taylor's announcement in the *Virginia Gazette* is another example of slave auctions in Virginia moving away from the county courthouse and town squares and toward the notion of being held in private pubs, taverns and hotels.[693] More will be said about this phenomenon of slave auctions in hotels and taverns in Chapter Seven.

By the 1830s, as we shall see, that transformation was complete. By then, slave auctions in Richmond occurred at the establishments of the major slave traders there, and they no longer were conducted at taverns and hotels. More will be said about the history of slave auctions in the Chesapeake Bay region in Chapter Seven, to follow.

After the conclusions and the notes to this chapter, we have included an appendix on slave ship manifests on ships traveling to the Deep South from the District of Columbia and cities in Virginia, such as Alexandria, Richmond and Norfolk, in the first sixty years of the nineteenth century. This brings us to a summary of the major conclusions in this chapter, followed by the notes of the same. This will be followed by an exploration of the phenomena of slave auctions and slave blocks in the Chesapeake region, from 1800 to 1865, the subject matter of Chapter Seven.

Conclusions

We began this sixth chapter by making some brief comments on slave ships owned and operated by Washington, DC, and Virginia slave traders. The major goal of this chapter was to make some remarks about the phenomena of slave dealers and slave jails and pens in Washington, DC, and the Commonwealth of Virginia, in the first sixty-five years of the nineteenth century.

In the third section of this chapter, we described and discussed the six major slave traders at work in the period in Washington, including William H. Williams' Yellow House, Robey's Tavern, and Joseph Neal's trading company in the district. We also introduced and discussed eleven other minor slave traders operating in Washington during the nineteenth century up until the Civil War.

In the fourth section, we explored a variety of slave dealers and

693 Virginia Gazette, February 17, 1812.

slave jails in the Commonwealth of Virginia in the first sixty-five years of the nineteenth century. We began the section by looking at seventeen major slave dealers in Richmond, as well as a variety of minor dealers in that same city. This was combined in this chapter with a discussion of slave dealers who existed in Alexandria, Norfolk, Warrenton and Petersburg in Virginia from 1800 to 1863. As we discovered, there were more significant slave traders in Richmond than in the remainder of other locations in the state combined.

That material was followed by a section devoted to a number of prominent Washington and Virginian slaves who had some relations with the slave dealers and slave jails outlined in the earlier sections of this chapter.

Among these prominent slaves, as we have seen, were Anthony Burns, John Brown, Henry Clay Bruce, and Solomon Northrop, who wrote *Twelve Years a Slave* in the 1850s and is the subject matter of a recent 2013 film directed by Steve McQueen by that same name.

This section on prominent slaves was followed by an analysis of ten separate pieces of art that illustrate some of the aspects of slave dealers and slave jails, presented earlier in this chapter. Some of those illustrations, as we have seen, were completed by a British painter, but most were made by Americans in the nineteenth century, and one is a city plan.

Next in Chapter Seven will be an analysis of the phenomena of slave auctions and slave auction blocks in the first sixty-five years of the nineteenth century.

Appendix: Slave Ship Manifests District of Columbia and Virginia: 1800 to 1865. Ship Year Origin Owner Destination

Ship	Year	Origin	Owner	Destination
Tribune	1819	Alexandria	Franklin and Armfield	New Orleans
Uncas	1819	Alexandria/Washington	Franklin and Armfield	New Orleans
Isaac Franklin	1819	Alexandria/Washington	Franklin and Armfield	New Orleans
United States	1819	Alexandria	Franklin and Armfield	New Orleans
Pearl	183?	Washington?		Philadelphia
Comet	1846	Alexandria	Geo. Kephart	New Orleans
Enterprise	1825	Alexandria	Franklin and Armfield	Charleston
Shenandoah	1859	Washington	Conf. Navy	New Orleans
Ariel		Norfolk	F. Hoyer	New Orleans
James Madison	1846	Norfolk	F. Hoyer	New Orleans
Planter	1843	Petersburg/Richmond	F. Hoyer	New Orleans
Enterprise	1842	Washington	U. S. Navy	New Orleans
Crown	1845	Washington	N. Simpson	New Orleans
Charlott	1850	Washington	Isaac Levy	New Orleans
Caracao	1850	Washington	Isaac Levy	New Orleans
Nassau	1852	Washington	Isaac Levy	New Orleans
Four Sisters	1853	Washington	Isaac Levy	New Orleans

In this appendix, we listed seventeen ships and their manifests. These ships were owned by seven different men in the nineteenth century. These men had businesses in Alexandria, Washington, Norfolk, Richmond, and Petersburg. The voyages listed here extend from 1819 until 1853. This brings us to Chapter Seven of this study, an exploration of slave auctions and auction blocks in the Chesapeake Bay region, from 1800 to 1865, the subject matter of the next chapter. It is to slave auctions in the Chesapeake region, then, to which we turn next.

Chapter Seven: Slave Auctions and Slave Auction Blocks in Early Virginia

Washington and Maryland

They have a Slave Auction every month at the Court House, and then they sell you and get one every month at the same place.

—Fountain Hughes, Virginia slave

After the men and women are sold, the children are put on the stand. I was the first to be put up. On my appearance, several voices cried, "How old is that little Nigger?" On hearing this expression, I burst into tears.

—Henry Watson, *The Narrative of Henry Watson*

Islam does not prohibit Slavery but retains it for two reasons The first reason is War, whether it is a Civil war or a Foreign War, in which the captive is either killed or enslaved, provided it is not a war between Muslims…The second reason is the sexual propagation of slaves which would generate more slaves for their owner.

—Abdul-Latif Mushtahari, *Thoughts on Hadith*

Introduction

Many of those slaves who survived the Middle Passage were brought to the Chesapeake Bay region and then to market for auction, in ports, courthouses and hotels, and later in major slave traders' businesses. Sometimes they were sold to the highest bidder, and at other times they were purchased at a fixed price or a price determined beforehand between buyer and seller.

Once sold, the slaves were under the complete control of their masters. In the early history of the Chesapeake colonies, slaves worked in the cultivation of tobacco. Later, they assisted in growing other crops, particularly when slave traders in the Chesapeake Bay region began selling slaves south to help on cotton fields, and later in the growing of sugar cane.

The production of cotton in the United States began in Florida in 1556. By 1607, the Jamestown colony in Virginia attempted to produce cotton, with no success. By the eighteenth century, cotton began to be cultivated throughout the south, so much so that between 1830, when 750,00 bales of cotton were produced there, to 1850 when more than three million bales of cotton were produced in the Deep South.

The attempt of sugar cane production in the United States also began in the Jamestown colony in 1619, again with very little success. After 1700, the two major producers of sugar were Cuba and Louisiana. In fact, by 1750, more than eighty percent of sugar consumed in the American colonies came from those two locations.

In the meantime, in the Chesapeake Bay region, tobacco crop production began to wane in the 1660s, principally because of price stability and quality control issues. With the reduced production of tobacco, there was also a concomitant need for labor in the growing of that crop. Thus, farmers in the Chesapeake Bay region began selling their African slaves in the Deep South.

In this chapter, we have the following goals. First, to introduce the phenomenon of slave auctions in the District of Columbia, Virginia and Maryland in the nineteenth century. Second, to describe and discuss several first-person narratives of slave auctions in the Chesapeake Bay region, some by slaves and some by outside white visitors. In this chapter, we will examine the stories of ten slaves and three of these white abolitionist visitors.

For the third goal in this chapter, we will examine and discuss several wooden and stone auction blocks and platforms that have survived the period of slavery in Virginia, Maryland and the District of Columbia. We will explore in the following pages of this chapter more than a dozen separate Auction blocks or stones in Virginia, Maryland, and the District of Columbia, many that still exist.

Finally, we shall discuss a number of nineteenth-century pieces of art, which illustrate or depict slave auctions in Virginia, Maryland and the District of Columbia from 1800 until 1865.

The History of Slave Auctions in the Chesapeake Bay Region: 1800 to 1863

Debra Meyers, in her book *Order and Civility in the Early Modern Chesapeake*, suggests that white planters in the Chesapeake Bay region categorized slaves at slave auctions into "four rather broad categories." They are the "Genteel Servant," the "House Wench," the "Skilled Slave," and the "Herculean Slave."

This first category of slaves, the Genteel Servant, is a "meek, Sambo type," respectful and obedient. The House Wench refers to the best of "Domestic Servants," who are also the most likely to abscond from their masters. The Skilled Slave refers to those captives who have acquired the most important skills necessary in a farm environment, including carpentry, becoming a wheel-wright, as well as horsemanship and animal husbandry, for example.

Finally, the Herculean Slave is "strong, obedient, and powerful." They are capable of performing extraordinary physical feats. This fourth category of slave became crucial in maintaining the operation of a tobacco farm before the nineteenth century in the Chesapeake Bay region.

Dr. Meyers continues her analysis:

> This broad categorization also provided the planters with a lens through which to analyze how race, class, and gender intersected to shape the planter's conception of himself, his slaves, and the world in which he lived.[694]

Indeed, a copious amount of extant material is available concerning the conducting of slave auctions in Washington, Virginia and Maryland from the early seventeenth century on. It is best to see the development of the history of those auctions to have occurred in three distinct stages. Those stages may be summarized this way:

> Phase One: 1660s to 1720s. The Court House and Public Spaces Period.
>
> Phase Two: 1720 to 1820. Transition

694 Debra Meyers, ed., Order and Civility in the Early Modern Chesapeake (Lanham: Lexington Books, 2014), p. 177.

Period: Court Houses to Jails, Hotels and Taverns.

Phase Three: 1821 to 1865. Major Slave Traders Period.

In the first phase mentioned above, slave auctions in the Chesapeake Bay region mostly occurred in county courthouses, and other public spaces, like town squares and central town market places. There is evidence that slave auctions happened in Denton, Maryland, early on, for example, on the steps of the Caroline County Courthouse not far from the main slave market. In the early seventeenth century in Leonardtown, Maryland, in southern Maryland, officials also sold slaves at the county courthouse very early on, as well.

This phenomenon was also true in Cambridge, the county seat of Dorchester County at the city of Easton's courthouse built as the county seat of Talbot County in 1709. It was also true at Chestertown, whose courthouse was the seat of Kent County built in 1697. Centreville, whose courthouse was built in 1710, was the county seat for Queen Anne's County on the Eastern Shore of Maryland. Slaves were auctioned there from early on, as well.

Slave auctions also took place in Hagerstown at the then public square, as well as the first courthouse of Prince George's County. Dorchester County, Maryland, also conducted their earliest slave auctions at their county courthouse, as did Frederick County in their earliest history.

There is also sufficient evidence of slave pens and jails—and thus slave auctions—in Saint Mary's City, Oxford, Annapolis, Baltimore County, and Worchester County in Maryland. And in all these locations, slave auctions originally were conducted at the county courthouse, or other public places, such as town squares and major town market places. This phenomenon was true in Washington, DC, as well, as we shall see later in this chapter. Often these slave auctions were conducted, at least early on in the Chesapeake Bay region, by county sheriffs and their deputies.

The same first phase was true in Virginia counties, as well. On Onancock Island, for example, the seat of Accomack County, slave auctions were held at the county courthouse by sheriff deputies from

1699 until 1775. In the Virginia counties in the Blue Ridge Mountains, slave auctions were also handled by local sheriffs. Addtionally, this phenomenon was true in larger cities in Virginia, like Charlottesville and Petersburg, to cite two other examples.

The city of Christianburg, Virginia, also conducted slave auctions on a square wooden box, as we shall see later in this chapter. It is enough now, however, to point out that in phase one, slave auctions in Virginia and Maryland were usually conducted in county courthouses or other public spaces, including town squares and central town markets.

The original Page County, Virginia, courthouse in Luray, to cite another Virginia example, regularly held slave auctions on the steps of the courthouse in the city's earliest history. Evidence suggests as early as 1725, slave buying and selling were going on there.[695] The earliest slave auction in the Jamestown colony was conducted in 1638 on the newly constructed town square. In that first auction, twenty-three slaves were sold. It was also maintained at the time that "Baptism does not alter the status of a slave" in the Virginia colony as it had elsewhere in the New World.[696]

The unit of the slave trade at that time in Virginia was one "peca"or one male slave in peak condition. One peca was worth two female slaves and one baby. In Abingdon, Virginia, whose first courthouse was built in the 1790s, also conducted their earliest slave auctions at the courthouse.

In Shenandoah County, Virginia, slave auctions were conducted early on at the county courthouse, as well, as early as 1810. In fact, they were still being conducted there on March 29, 1858, so Shenandoah County appears to have skipped the second and third phases of our history outlined above. Bethany Veney, a prominent Virginia slave, was sold at the courthouse. Later, she published her autobiography entitled *The Narrative of Bethany Veney: A Slave Woman* in Boston in 1889 by George H. Ellis.[697]

695 Anonymous, "Celebrate Luray's Bicentennial," http://bit.ly/2Njd7fc.

696 Wesley Craven, White, Red, and Black: Seventeenth Century Virginia (Charlottesville: University of Virginia Press, 1961), p. 31.

697 Bethany Veney, The Narrative of Bethany Veney: A Slave Woman (Boston: George H. Ellis, 1889). Veney (1815–1916) was born a slave in Lu-

The Historic Fairfax County Courthouse, built in 1742 at a site called Spring Field, was also the place for slave auctions in the county's early history. Indeed, auctions were held at the front door of the courthouse as early as 1745.

The original courthouse of Albemarle County was built after the county seat moved from Scott's Ferry to Charlottesville. Indeed, the courthouse was the first public building in the county, erected in 1762. Local elections, as well as slave auctions, were conducted there, beginning in 1763. In May of 1781, the Virginia General Assembly authorized that the Charlottesville Courthouse was to be used as the temporary state capitol building when British troops had attacked Richmond at that time.

The Historic Fairfax County Courthouse at 4000 Chain Bridge Road was built in 1800. Early on, slave auctions for the county took place there. In fact, the courthouse changed hands several times from Union to Confederate control. Indeed, the first officer casualty of the Civil War, John Quincy Marr, took place there on the grounds of the courthouse. From the 1830s on, slave auctions were conducted by the major slave traders of the county, and they ceased in the early 1860s. The Petersburg Hustings Courthouse, at One Courthouse Avenue, was also used to auction slaves in its earliest history.

The city of New Market, Virginia, established in 1794 and incorporated in 1796, built its first courthouse in 1795. At the time, New Market was the Shenandoah county seat, and slave auctions took place there at the General District Court. This original make-shift structure was replaced in 1810, as we have outlined in the earlier analysis.

William Dunally, in his book *African-American Family in Slavery and Emancipation*, sums up this first phase about which we have been speaking. He writes, "slaves were auctioned by sheriff's deputies on auction blocks erected in courthouse squares. This was true in Abingdon, Roanoke, Bristol, and New Market, up until the Civil War."[698]

The current Washington County Courthouse in Abingdon was

---

ray, Virginia, and published her autobiography in 1889. She was nearly one hundred and two years old when she died.

698 William Dunally, African-Americans in Slavery and Emancipation. Quoted in "The Making of African-American Identity," National Humanities Center, Vol. I, 1500–1865.

built in 1830 and renovated in the 1860s. The old courthouse in Roanoke, which was designed by H. H. Huggins and completed in the Classical Revival style, was built in 1909. It replaced an earlier courthouse from the 1820s. The Bristol County Courthouse, designed by Architect Frank Irving Cooper in that city, was first completed in 1826 and renovated in 1894 and 1904. Slaves were sold in all of these county courthouses prior to the Civil War.

Fountain Hughes, an early Virginia slave, also describes the first phase of this slave auction history in the Chesapeake region. In an epigram for this chapter, he writes:

> They have a slave auction every month at the courthouse, and then they sell you and get one hundred, two hundred, five hundred dollars. They pretty much does this same thing every month at the same place.[699]

Vaughn Scribner, in his essay "The Commodification of Slaves in Tidewater Virginia," speaks of this first phase, as well, in relationship to early Williamsburg:

> Despite Williamsburg's distance from the coast and its relatively paltry population, court days were set aside in April, October, June and December for slave auctions at the courthouse that drew colonists to these auctions and to the courthouse.[700]

In Warrenton, Virginia, fifty miles south of the District of Columbia, at the courthouse of that city, Fauquier County conducted their early slave auctions on the steps of the courthouse. Later in this chapter, we also shall see that there is extant in Warrenton the base of a stone auction block there.[701]

In addition to slave auctions occurring at county courthouses in this

699 Interview with Fountain Hughes, June 11, 1949. Interviewed by Herman Norwood in Baltimore, North Carolina Digital Services.

700 Vaughn Scribner, Debra Meyer, ed., "The Commodification of Slaves in Tidewater Virginia," in Order and Civility in Early Modern Chesapeake (Lanham: Lexington Books, 2014), p. 27.

701 Kate Brenner, Images of America: Warrenton (Glenside: Arcadia Books, 2014).

first phase, sometimes they were conducted in other public buildings, establishments, and other public places, including town squares and town market places. Some of the earliest slave auctions in Baltimore, for example, were conducted in the Baltimore fish market. The market sold a variety of goods in the early history of the city, including slaves. The fish market opened in 1787. The site is now Port Discovery at 35 Market Place near the Pratt Street Pavilion of the Inner Harbor, but in its earliest history, the business of buying and selling slaves went on there.

Other public spaces were sometimes employed for slave auctions in Baltimore. Another example is Lexington Market, in the early nineteenth century, also auctioned slaves. This market opened in 1782. The first building on the site was erected in 1803. Slaves were auctioned there from the very beginning of the structure.

A third possibility of public spaces where slave auctions sometimes were conducted in the colonial period are the many town squares, where various kinds of public business were conducted in many colonial towns. The town square was a place to congregate, hold public meetings, and sometimes to conduct other activities. There is a good bit of evidence that in some smaller towns, slave auctions were conducted on the town square, often in front of the courthouse.

Slave auctions were held throughout the state of Virginia, from early on, at town squares. This was true at Williamsburg's Merchants Square, at the court square in Charlottesville, by Nathaniel Crawley at the town square of Indian Field in York County, and in the mid-1700s at the market square in Petersburg, where slaves were sold at public auction.[702]

The Petersburg Hustings Courthouse at One Courthouse Avenue was employed to auction slaves shortly after the 1793 construction of the courthouse. The original building was just south of the current courthouse that began construction in 1837 and completed in 1839. By the building of the new courthouse, slave auctions there were now carried out by the major slave traders of the county, such as Richard R. Beasley and William H. Wood, introduced earlier in Chapter Six.

In phase two of the above scheme, slave auctions in the Chesa-

702 Petersburg Markey Square, discussed in James A. Bailey, Old Petersburg (Brookfield: Donning Books, 1976), p. 13.

peake Bay region began to move out of courthouses and public spaces and taken over by county jails, where usually a keeper and his family resided. We also start to see, during this transitional period, the phenomenon of slave-trading businesses independent of any county authority and the idea of conducting slave auctions in hotels and taverns.

The Clover Hill Tavern in Appomattox County, Virginia, for example, began to take over the job of conducting slave auctions bequeathed to them by the county's courthouse.[703] When Thomas Bluett first encounters Job Diallo, who was introduced in Chapter One, to cite another example, it was at a tavern in Delaware that doubled as the county jail. Job had escaped from a farm in Maryland and fled to the Delaware Bay.

The Eagle Tavern in Richmond is another tavern where slaves were sold in the early nineteenth century. Richmond trader Thomas Taylor sold captives there as early as February 17, 1812, when he tells us that "Slaves will be sold before the door of the Eagle Tavern at twelve noon, on the twenty-fourth" of that year (*Virginia Gazette*, February 17, 1812). Another broadside for the sale of eleven slaves was to take place eight days later, on February 24, 1812. These sales foreshadowed Richmond's rise as a major hub of the domestic slave trade.

The Eagle Tavern was built in Richmond in 1787 on the south side of Main Street between 12th and 13th Streets. At the time, the Exchange Hotel and many other establishments had slave jails and showrooms where slave auctions took place in the first sixty-five years of the nineteenth century.

Mr. W. Robey's tavern in Washington, DC, took on a similar task around the same time. At other places, like Wicomico County on the Eastern Shore of Maryland, the conducting of slave auctions was performed by a jail keeper who resided at the county jail. The jail keeper often lived downstairs with his family, while jailed slaves were in cells

703 "Clover Hill Tavern," discussed in Burke Davis, The Civil War: Strange and Fascinating Facts (San Antonio: Wings Books, 1960). The Clover Hill Tavern, including its guesthouse and slave quarters, are now structures within the Appomattox County Courthouse, which is now a national historical park.

on the second floor. This building had the same set-up until 1942.

The John Byrd Tavern in Salisbury, the seat of Wicomico County, was the site of slave auctions in the mid-nineteenth century. There was also a slave jail there. The building was razed in 1878 to make way for the new county courthouse, built in that year, on the east side of Division Street. Salisbury began in the second period of our history with Byrd's tavern and then proceeded to the first phase, with the new courthouse in 1848.

The John Byrd Tavern was built around 1805. For the next sixty years or so, it acted as a community center, where elections, slave buying and selling, and town business were conducted. There were slave pens in the basement and at the rear of the building throughout most of the nineteenth century.

Another example of slave auctions in this second phase is the business that went on in the 1830s and 1840s at the St. Louis Hotel's Bath Saloon. There Joseph Le Carpentier, a local auctioneer and under court order from the First Judicial District of the State of Louisiana, conducted regular slave auctions. He also held similar auctions at the Saint Louis Hotel in New Orleans. One example was on March 24, 1840, where he sold twenty-nine slaves in the lobby of the hotel.[704]

Another example of this second phase and the move of slave auctions to hotels and taverns is a slave jail that existed in Rockville, Maryland, on the northwest corner of West Jefferson and South Washington Streets called the Hungerford Tavern. It was named after its owner, Charles Hungerford, and located on the main road midway between Georgetown and the county seat in Frederick. The tavern itself was twenty by twenty feet, two rooms, a bar and a kitchen. Beginning around 1744, Hungerford also rented a connected house with three rooms in a twenty-two by twenty-two-foot space.

Earlier in Montgomery County, slave auctions were held on the steps of the county courthouse. By the 1720s, however, they took place at the Hungerford Tavern, a building built early in the eighteenth century. For a while, the tavern also served as the Montgomery County Courthouse, complete with a jail that sometimes housed slaves waiting

704 Linda Duyer, A New History of Early Salisbury (Salisbury: Lulu Books, 2014), p. 101.

to be sold.

The jail at the Hungerford Tavern housed people serving short-term sentences, or those awaiting trial or execution. Often runaway slaves were held in the jail until their owners reclaimed them. Slaves not claimed were sold to slave traders such as Hope Slatter and Austin Woolfolk, or they were used to pay off debts owed by their purchasers. Earlier, we spoke of the Eagle Tavern in Richmond, where slave auctions often took place in the 1850s.

Two other examples of the second phase are in Page County, Virginia, and Fredericksburg. In the former, in the city of Luray, at the corner of Main and Court Streets, the city conducted slave auctions in front of the Laurance Hotel, where we shall see later in this chapter, there is still a stone auction block that earlier had been employed for that purpose. Since these auctions took place in front of the hotel, this is another good example of the second phase in the above history.

Similarly, in the 1850s, slave auctions occurred "in front of the Planter's Hotel," in downtown Fredericksburg, or so an advertisement stated in the *Fredericksburg News* from December of 1857 and March of 1858. More will be said about this site, as well, when we turn to the section in this chapter on auction blocks and stones.

At the close of this second phase, at the very end of the eighteenth century, we begin to see several new phenomena regarding slave auctions in the Chesapeake Bay region. First, some slave ship captains began selling their human cargo while the slaves were still on board or at port. Secondly, captains sold slaves at private wharves. For example, Hector Davis, introduced in Chapter Six and a partner in the firm of Pulliam & Davis, published an advertisement in the *Richmond Business Directory* that said:

> We will sell Negroes, both publicly and privately, as we pledge our best effort to obtain the highest prices.[705]

In the 1852 *City Directory* of Richmond, Pulliam & Davis tells us:

---

705 Joseph LeCarpentier was part of a prominent New Orleans family throughout most of the nineteenth century. The Fredericksburg News began publication in 1788. Other than 1862 to 1865, it was continuously published until the 1920s.

> Pulliam & Davis
>
> Auctioneers and Commission
>
> Merchants, in Richmond, Virginia
>
> Continue to offer their services in the Buying And Selling of Negroes, At our offices on Wall Street, opposite the City Hotel.[706]

The City Hotel, located on East Main Street near Broad Street in downtown Richmond, faced Wall Street. Pulliam & Davis were among the major slave traders in Richmond in the first sixty-five years of the nineteenth century. They called themselves "Auctioneers and Commission Merchants" at that time in the *Richmond City Directory* of 1850.

A third, and perhaps most important development at the end of the second phase of The History of Slave Auctions in the Chesapeake Region, is that we begin to see the early development of large-scale slave traders in the area. By the opening of the nineteenth century, some of the major slave dealers in Washington, Maryland and the Commonwealth of Virginia held slave auctions at their own establishments, or even in the city streets of Richmond.

Mr. Davis' advertisement, from the close of the eighteenth century, suggests the captive he has for sale may be purchased publicly or privately. By the beginning of the nineteenth century, we see the arrival of large, big-scale slave dealers and slave traders in both states and in the District of Columbia. Replacing the city jail, taverns and hotels, we now see companies arising like Franklin and Armfield of Alexandria that kept and sold slaves in their own facilities. By the 1820s, the transformation of slave auctions in Washington, Virginia and Maryland now had fully moved from public to private jails and along with them slave auctions, as well.

By the mid-nineteenth century, over four dozen slave traders were working in Richmond, a dozen in Alexandria, and more than a dozen in Baltimore, as we have seen earlier in Chapters Five and Six. This brings us to several first-person narratives of slave auctions, the subject matter of the next section of this chapter.

---

706 Hector Davis, "We Will Sell Negros," Richmond Business Directory, May 29, 1852.

First-Person Narratives of Slave Auctions

In this section, we shall explore a number of first-person slave auctions in Maryland and Virginia, primarily in the nineteenth century. Henry Watson was born enslaved in Virginia, and at the age of eight, was sent to Richmond to be sold at auction. In his book, *The Narrative of Henry Watson: A Fugitive Slave*, he begins to describe the experience of a slave auction:

> At last, everything was ready, and the traffic in human flesh began. I will attempt to give as accurate an account of the language and the ceremony of a slave auction as I possibly can. "Gentlemen, here is a likely boy; how much? He is sold for no fault; The owner wants money. His age is forty. Three hundred dollars is all that I am offered for him. Please to examine him; he is warranted sound. Boy, pull off your shirt, roll up your pants, for we want to see if you have been whipped." If they discover any scars, they will not buy, saying that the nigger is a bad one. The Auctioneer seeing this he cries, "Three hundred dollars, gentlemen, three hundred Dollars, is that all I am offered? His Master has informed me that he is an honest boy and belongs to the same Church as he does." This turns the tide frequently, and the bids go up fast; and he is knocked off for a good sum.[707]

Here Henry Watson, a slave, imitates the auctioneer, making sure he tells the slave to take off his shirt to see if he has been whipped and has scars to prove it. He also mentions that the slave in question attends church with his master, a sure way to increase the size of the bids. Mr. Watson continues his analysis in this passage used as an epigram for this chapter:

> After the men and women are sold, the children are put on the stand. I was the first put up. On my appearance, several voices cried, "How old is that little nigger?" On hearing this expression, I again burst into

707 Richmond City Directory, 1852.

> tears and wept so that I have no distinct recollection of his answer. I was at length knocked down to a man whose name was Denton, a slave trader, then purchasing slaves for the Southern Market. His first name I have forgotten.[708]

The Mr. Denton to whom Henry Watson refers is most likely Vachell Denton, whose father, also Vachell Denton (1700–1754), established a large plantation in Somerset County, Maryland, on the state's Eastern Shore. Watson then turns to a description of the buyers. He informs us:

> Each of the traders have private jails, which are for the purpose of keeping slaves in, and they are generally kept by some confidential slave. Denton had one of these jails to which I was conducted by his trusty slave; on entering, I found a great many slaves there, waiting to be sent off as soon as their numbers increase. These jails are enclosed by a wall about sixteen feet high, and the yard is for slaves to exercise in and consists of but one room, in which all sexes and ages are huddled together in a mass. I stayed in this jail but two days when the number was completed, and we were called out to form a line. Horses and wagons were in readiness to carry our provisions and tents so that we might camp out at night. Before we had proceeded far, Mr. Denton gave orders for us to stop for the purpose of handcuffing some of the men, which, he said in a loud voice, "had the Devil in them." The men belonging to this drove were all married and all left their wives and children behind; he, judging from their tears that they were unwilling to go, had them made secure. We start-

---

708 Henry Watson, The Narrative of Henry Watson: A Fugitive Slave (Brecksville, OH: Leopold Books, 2015), p. 11. Henry Watson (b. 1813) was born into slavery near Fredericksburg, Virginia. After escaping, Watson met abolitionist William Lloyd Garrison to whom he recounted his life in slavery and escape.

> ed again on our journey. Mr. Denton took up the lead in his sulky, and the driver, a Mr. Thornton, brought up the rear.[709]

Mr. Watson also points out that many of the slave traders have their own slave jails, and that Mr. Denton, the master of Watson's auction, had one as well. Henry Watson points out that quite often, trusted slaves performed some of the functions of a slave auction, including as auctioneer. He describes the interior and exterior of a slave jail, and he tells us that men were handcuffed, particularly when they acted unruly, while female slaves were not. He also tells us that because many of the men were married, several refused to go on the coffle.

Earlier, it was suggested that the Mr. Denton to whom Henry Watson refers is most likely Vachell Denton, the dealer who sold Job Diallo in Chapter One to Mr. Tolsey on Kent Island. Mr. Denton also conducted his slave-trading business throughout the Upper and Lower South, even employing slave coffles in the 1820s from Annapolis and Baltimore to Natchez, Mississippi, and New Orleans, Louisiana.

From Mr. Watson's analysis, it should be clear that he was in a coffle on his way to the Deep South. He says as much in the opening of his next paragraph. Watson relates:

> I will not weary my readers with the particulars of our march to Tennessee, where we stopped several days for the purpose of arranging our clothes. While stopping, the men were hired out to pick cotton. While in Tennessee, we lost four of our number who died from exposure on the road. After a lapse of three weeks, we started again on our journey, and in about four weeks we arrived in Natchez, Mississippi. We were taken to a slave pen which Mr. Denton had previously hired for us; we had our irons taken off and our clothes changed, for Mr. Denton was expecting visitors to ex-

709 Ibid., p. 12. For more on Vachell Denton, see the Somerset County Judicial Records, 1723–1725, vol. 839, p. 93b; and vol. 842, August 1730, p. 7b.

> amine his flock.[710]

During the march south on the coffle, which often took up to eight weeks, slaves were sometimes hired out to work for farmers along the way. Mr. Denton, the master, hired out a slave jail to be used upon the arrival of the slave coffle in Mississippi before being sold at auction.

Later in the narrative, we find out that Mr. Watson was purchased from the block by an Alexander McNeill, a partner in the firm McNeill & Fiske. Mr. McNeill tells Watson that he wants a boy to suit himself. Watson describes the relationship this way:

> He took a great fancy to me, and after some discussion about the price agreed to at last the master took me to his store. He told me my duty for the future would be to wait upon him—"to jump when I was spoken to, to run when I was sent on errands, and if I did not mind my Ps and Qs, I should be flogged like all Hell."[711]

The Mr. McNeill to whom Watson refers was Alexander McNeill, a partner of McNeill & Fiske Company, who were traders of slaves. O'Neill also owned a plantation on which Henry Watson was forced to work as a farmhand after he refused to identify the slave who had stolen a pig from the farm. Altogether, O'Neill kept Watson for five years, until he was given to James O'Neill, Alexander's brother.

In his autobiography, Watson describes Alexander McNeill this way, "He had a dark complexion, sharp grey eyes, a peaked nose, and compressed lips. Indeed, he was a very bad- looking man." Watson thought James McNeill, on the other hand, was a much more lenient and compassionate master.

Henry Bibb (1815–1854), born into slavery in Kentucky and eventually sold in New Orleans, describes his experience at a slave auction this way:

> When we arrived at the city of Vicksburg, he [the trad-

710 Ibid., pp. 12–13.

711 Ibid., p. 17. Vachell Denton was the man who sold Job Diallo to Mr.Tolsey of Kent Island. He was the grandson of Thomas and Letitia Vachell Denton, for whom the town of Denton, Maryland, is known. Their son, Henry, Vachell's father, was a judge on the Eastern Shore of Maryland.

> er] intended to sell a portion of his slaves there and stopped for three weeks trying to sell them. But he met with very poor success. We then had to pass through an examination or inspection by a city officer, whose business it was to inspect slave property that was brought to the market for sale. He examined our backs to see if we had been much scarred by the lash. He looked at our limbs to see whether we were inferior. As it is hard to tell the age of a slave, they look into their mouths at their teeth and prick up the skin on the backs of their hands. But the most rigorous examinations of slaves by those slave inspectors was on their mental capacity. If they are found to be intelligent, then this is the most objectionable. In fact, it undermines the whole fabric of his chattelhood.[712]

Henry Bibb mentions a number of features we have seen before—that coffles in America sometimes stopped for two or three weeks while the white master hired out his laborers, that the slaves went through a city inspector to make sure the product was of the proper quality, that the slaves' backs should be checked for previous whippings, that the slaves' teeth would be examined by potential buyers along the way, and finally, that the inspectors should check for signs of intelligence, a sure sign a slave would be objectionable, or unruly.

In his *Narrative of the Life and Adventures of Henry Bibb,* he describes the process of running away and the phenomenon of his beatings, even if he was not a runaway slave. Mr. Bibb describes a paddle which is "made of a piece of hickory timber, about an inch thick, three inches wide and about eighteen inches long" if any slave gets out of line at an auction, if you will forgive the pun.[713]

---

712 Ibid. The quote also appears in Jack L. Schermerhorn, The Business of Slavery (New Haven: Yale University Press, 2015), p. 30. Alexander McNeill was also the owner of noted slave Henry Watson.

713 Henry Bibb, Narrative of the Life of Henry Bibb (New York: Create Space, 2016), p. 36. Bibb (1815–1854) escaped slavery in Kentucky and fled to Canada, where he began an abolitionist newspaper called The Voice of the Fugitive.

A third first-person narrative of a slave auction comes from Maryland slave Josiah Henson. He was born enslaved in Maryland and sold at the age of seven when his owner died, along with his mother and siblings. In his autobiography, *Truth Stranger Than Fiction,* Henson sketches out a description of the slave auctions of his day. Mr. Henson informs us:

> Common as are the slave auctions in the southern states, and naturally as a slave may look forward to the time when he will be placed on the block, still the full misery of the event—of the scenes that precede and succeed it—is never understood until the actual experience comes. The first sad announcement that the sale is to be, the knowledge that all ties to the past have been severed, the frantic terror at the idea of being sent "down South."[714]

Three points may be made regarding Mr. Henson's remark on slave auctions in the Deep South in the nineteenth century. First, he suggests that slaves looked forward to the day they were to be sold. It is not clear if this was actually true as a general rule. Second, along with the sale, would come the surety of separation from family and friends. And finally, terror would certainly come after the auction.

Henson goes on to describe the biddings on his siblings, who were auctioned first. Then his mother was next on the block. She was purchased by Mr. Isaac Riley of Montgomery County. Then it was Henson's turn:

> My mother half distracted with the thought of parting forever from all her children, pushed through the crowd while the bidding for me was going on, to a spot where Mr. Riley was standing. She fell to his feet and clutched his knees, entreating him in tones that only a mother could do. But the man not only turned a deaf ear to her, but he completely disengaged himself from her with violent blows and kicks as to reduce her to the

714 Josiah Henson, Truth Stranger Than Fiction: The Life of Josiah Henson (New York: Dover Books, 2010), pp. 12–13. Henson (1789–1883) was born into slavery in Charles County, Maryland. He escaped to Upper Ontario, Canada, in 1830, and founded a labor camp and school there.

> necessity of creeping out of his reach, while mingling the groan of bodily suffering with the sob of a broken heart. As she crawled away from the brutal man, I heard her sob, "Oh Lord Jesus, how long, how long will I suffer this way?"[715]

Mr. Henson speaks of how distraught and anxious the slaves are and how insensitive the buyer, Mr. Riley, is to the needs and desires of another. Another Virginia Slave, William J. Anderson, in his autobiography called *The Life and Narrative of William J. Anderson*, also describes the process of his being "sold South" in 1827. In this portion of his narrative, he tells us:

> In due time we arrived safely in the slave pen at Natchez, Mississippi, and here we joined another large crowd of slaves which was already stationed at that place. Here scenes were witnessed which are too wicked to mention. The slaves are made to wash and shave. Their heads were combed and their best clothes were put on; and when called out to be examined, they are to stand in a row—the women and men apart—then they are picked out and taken into a room and examined. A large, rough slaveholder takes a poor female slave into a room, makes her strip, then feel and examine as if she were a pig, or a hen, or some other merchandise. Oh, how can a poor slave husband or father stand and see his wife, daughters and sons, thus treated?[716]

Mr. Anderson points out that the slave jail at Natchez, Mississippi—at the famous Forks in the Road Site—had already been constructed by 1827, that other slaves were there upon his arrival, that certain "female" slaves were taken for "private" examination, and that the hus-

715 Ibid. Isaac Riley (1774–1850) and his brother George, bought five hundred acres in what today would be Bethesda, Maryland. The farm was at 11420 Old Georgetown Road, Rockville. The "Riley House: Josiah Henson's Site," is a pamphlet completed by John Milner and Associates, 5250 Cherokee Avenue, Alexandria, Virginia.

716 Ibid., p. 14. Mr. Isaac Riley was the owner of Josiah Henson.

bands and fathers of these women were indignant at this process.

William Wells Brown, in the 1849 narrative called, *The Narrative of William W. Brown: A Fugitive Slave*, also describes the process of being "sold South." Brown describes the activity on a steamship full of slaves travelling down the Mississippi. He relates:

> There was on the boat a large room on the lower deck, in which the slaves were kept, men and women promiscuously—all chained, two and two, and a strict watch kept that they did not get loose; for cases have occurred in which slaves have gotten off their chains, and made their escapes at landing places while the boats were taking in wood; and with all our care we lost one woman who had been taken from her husband and children, and having no desire to live without them, in the agony of her soul jumped overboard and drowned herself. She was not chained.[717]

William Wells Brown tells us that slaves were kept indiscriminately with males and females together, that some captives were able to get loose from their shackles, and that many of the slaves contemplated or even committed suicide, such as the woman in Brown's narrative.

Mr. Brown goes on to describe the slave auction that transpired when the ship arrived in New Orleans. He describes the slave pens in which the captives were held until their sale, as well as what he calls the "Coffle House Auction Rooms," which were kept by a man named Isaac M. McCoy, who sold them at public auction in a coffee house in a tavern.

Thus, Mr. Brown is part of the second phase of slave auctions outlined in the above analysis. Brown ends his narrative, or at least this section of it, by speaking of slaves being placed "on the box" and given to "the highest bidder."[718] The box in question was a wooden,

717 William J. Anderson, The Life and Narrative of William J. Anderson (New York: Create Space, 2014), p. 49. Anderson was born into slavery in Hanover County, Virginia. His autobiography was published in Chicago by the Daily Tribune in 1857.

718 William Wells Brown, The Narrative of William W. Brown (New York: Create Space, 2015), p. 23. Brown (1814–1884) was born into slavery

eighteen-inch square structure, about a foot high. The box was stored in the tavern when it was not being used for auctions.

Mr. McCoy's son, Isaac M. McCoy, Jr. (1829–1855), was a Virginian auctioneer. There are extant ship manifests that show the elder Mr. McCoy sending slaves south, including one from January 1, 1808, when he shipped a twenty-seven-year-old slave named Abraham Brown to New Orleans. Later in the century, there is evidence that Mr. McCoy, the son, had an office in that Louisiana city. More is said about Virginia ship manifests in the appendix at the end of Chapter Six. The McCoy family was another example of multiple family members engaging in the same slave-trading firm prior to the Civil War.

Another first-person narrative of a slave beating and a slave auction can be seen in Maryland slave Thomas Johnson. His 1909 autobiography *Twenty Years a Slave* tells us, "Hardly a day passes without someone of my long-oppressed people being led to the whipping post, or even to auction when many are sold off to Georgia, or to some other far off southern state."[719] In the same account, Johnson speaks of the mean-spiritedness of the slave buyers and the surliness of the slave sellers.[720]

Another first-person narrative of a slave auction is that of Virginia-born woman Bethany Veney (1813–1916), introduced earlier in this study. She wrote an autobiography in 1889 called *Aunt Betty's Story*. In that narrative, she tells us:

> When we arrived in Richmond, we again were shut up in jail, all around which was a high fence, so high that no communication with the outside world was possible. I say we, for there was a young slave girl whom McCoy

in Kentucky. He eventually became a noted abolitionist, playwright, novelist and historian. The Elder Isaac M. McCoy (1784–1846), born in Uniontown, Pennsylvania, was a Baptist missionary, ordained in 1804, and thus was part of the First Great Awakening. Later, McCoy was an auctioneer in New Orleans.

719 Ibid., pp. 24–25.

720 Thomas Johnson, Twenty Years a Slave (New York: Amazon Digital Services, 2010), p. 29. Thomas Lee Johnson was born on Rock Raymond Drive in Stafford, Virginia, in 1836. He went on to be a Baptist minister and abolitionist, and thus he also was involved in the First Great Religious Awakening. His autobiography was published in 1909.

> had taken to the Richmond market. The next day, as the hour for the auction drew near, Jailer O'Neille came to us with a man, whom he told to take us along to the dressmaker and to charge her to "fix us up fine." The dressmaker was a most disagreeable woman, whose business it was to array such poor creatures as we in the gaudiest and most striking attire conceivable that, when placed upon the auction stand, we should attract the attention of all present, if not in one way, why then in another. She put a white muslin apron on me and a large cape, with great pink bows on each shoulder, and a similar rig also on Eliza. Thus equipped, we were led through a crowd of men and boys to the place of sale, which was a large, open space on a prominent square, under cover.[721]

Veney's sale is part of the first phase of The History of Slave Auctions outlined earlier since the auction was in a public place. It is also clear that Veney's purchase involved two of the men discussed above—Isaac McCoy and Alexander O'Neill. Mr. O'Neill was the sheriff and county jailer for Henrico County, Virginia, for many years in the nineteenth century. Later, Mr. O'Neill became a major slave trader in Richmond, as well, much like his father before him.

Veney goes on to speak of an old slave woman who wanted to give her advice about the sale. Veney writes:

> I have been told by an old Negro woman certain tricks that I could resort to, when placed upon the stand, that would be likely to hinder my sale; and when the doctor who was employed to examine the slaves on such occasions, told me to let him see my tongue, he found it coated and feverish, and turning from me with a shiver of disgust, said he was obliged to admit that at the moment I was in a bilious condition. One after another of the crowd felt my limbs, and asked me all manner of questions, to which I replied in the ugliest manner I

721 Ibid.

> dared; and when the auctioneer raised his hammer and cried, "How much do I hear for this woman?" The bids were so low I was ordered down from the stand, and Eliza was called up in my place. Poor thing, there were many eager bids for her, for, such as she, the demands of slavery were insatiable.[722]

Clearly, one piece of advice the old woman gave Ms. Veney was to feign disease or injury, so that she might not be sold. One of the most compelling first-person narratives of a Chesapeake Bay region slave auction comes from Virginia-born Solomon Northrop and his autobiography *Twelve Years a Slave*, published in 1841, discussed in Chapter Six. Northrop begins his description of a slave auction this way:

> The very amiable pious-hearted Mr. Theophilus Freeman, partner or consignee James H. Burch, and keeper of the slave pen in New Orleans, was out among his animals in the early morning. With an occasional kick of the older men and women, and many a sharp crack of the whip about the ears of the younger slaves, it was not long before they were all astir, and wide awake. Mr. Theophilus Freeman bustled about in a very industrious manner, getting his property ready for the sales room, intending that day, no doubt, to do a rousing business.[723]

Theophilus Freeman was Burch's New Orleans partner. His office and slave jail were on Charles Avenue, just opposite the Charles Hotel. By all accounts, Freeman was a greedy, ruthless, immoral slave trader. He was also the man who gave Solomon Northrop the new name "Platt."[724]

---

722 Bethany Veney, Aunt Betty's Story (Harrisonburg: Garrison Press, 1998), p. 18.

723 Ibid., pp. 20–21.

724 Northrop Solomon, Twelve Years a Slave (Los Angeles: Graymalkin Media, 2012), p. 44. It is estimated that between 1804 and 1862, Theophilus Freeman sold 135,000 people into slavery. Many of his auctions took place at the St. Charles Hotel at the corner of Gravier and Common

Northrop's description above is part of the third phase of our History of Slave Auctions in the Chesapeake Bay region. Northrop goes on to describe being fed in the afternoon and then is ordered to dance. The following day, potential buyers came to look at Freeman's "New Lot." He says they felt the hands of the slaves and asked to see the slave's teeth.

Sometimes a man or woman was taken to a private room and inspected more carefully. These private sessions were sometimes occasions for sexual molestation between potential buyers and slaves. One old gentleman bought Northrop, along with another young slave named Randall, who cried when separated from his people.[725]

The planter who purchased Randall was from Baton Rouge. With his new purchases, he was ready to depart. "Don't cry, Mama. I will be a good boy. Don't cry," said Randall, looking back as they passed through the door. Then Northrop adds:

> What has become of the lad, only God knows. It was a mournful scene, indeed. I would have cried myself if I had dared.[726]

Other first-person narratives of slave auctions were penned by Hester Jane Carr, Rachel Findley of Powhatan County, Dennis Holt of Campbell County, and Willis M. Carter.[727] Another first-person narrative of a slave auction comes from a slave named Julius Lester, who authored a book entitled *To be a Slave*.[728] He relates the horror of being sold on the block. He writes:

> I don't know how old I was when I found myself standing on the top of a high stump, with a lot of white folks walking

---

Streets in New Orleans. An old registry of the hotel that is still extant, has a forged signature of Abraham Lincoln. The hotel is now called The Hilton New Orleans Saint Charles Hotel.

725 Ibid., p. 45.

726 Ibid.

727 Ibid., p. 47.

728 Dennis Holt is significant for his petition to Judge Hunter Marshall of Campbell County, Virginia, that asked to be declared "Free" after the death of his master, Andrew Holt.

around and looking at the scared little boy that was me.[729]

Mr. Lester mentions being sold while he stands on a stump around which several white folks have gathered. He also states how frightened he was in this environment of slave trading in early Virginia. In this case, the slave auction was conducted on a tree stump, as opposed to the wooden boxes or slave stones in other Chesapeake Bay locations, as we shall see later in this chapter.

Hester Jane Carr (1816–1834) was born in Accomack County, Virginia. In her autobiography, she tells us, "The auction took place on a raised platform, with the auctioneer in the center of the structure and slaves brought one at a time up on the platform. An audience, mostly tobacco planters, surrounded the platform." In Ms. Carr's analysis, a wooden platform is used in her auction. It is raised, so all can see, and it is surrounded by white tobacco farmers.

William McGlascoe Carter (1852–1902) was born in Albemarle County, Virginia. He received a formal education at the Wayland Seminary in Washington, DC. He went on to become a teacher, newspaper editor and political activist. His motto was said to be "Justice For All." He is important for our purposes because he also describes a Virginia slave auction he attended at age ten.

Mr. Carter's first-person description tells us the auction took place in Alexandria, Virginia, in front of a slave jail. It may well have been the firm of Franklin and Armfield, but we have not been able to establish that fact. The ten-year-old boy speaks of a wooden box on which the auctioneer stood and a second box on which the slaves were brought one at a time. Mr. Carter gives this analysis in his autobiography, "I stood on a box of wood. The box was surrounded by white folks who all bid for me in increments of twenty-five dollars."[730]

Mr. Carter's description of his auction tells us there were two wooden boxes, one for the auctioneer, and one on which the slaves would stand. Again, the audience consisted of white, tobacco farmers in northern Virginia, and finally, the bids were given in increments of

729 Julius Lester, To Be a Slave (New York: Dial Press, 1969), p. 29. His novel is a non-fiction children's book.

730 This manuscript is owned by the Library of Virginia, Accession number: 51546.

twenty-five dollars.

B.A. Botkin, another slave, describes being placed on the block. He tells us:

> They stood me up on a block of wood, and a man began to bid me. I felt mad. You see, I was young then, too young to know any better. I don't know what they sold me for, but the man who bought me made me open my mouth to look at my teeth. They turned all of us this way and that and sell us like turning and selling a horse.[731]

Mr. Botkin speaks of many of the elements of a slave auction we have seen before—such as standing on a wooden box, the opening of one's mouth so his teeth could be examined, and the turning this way and that like selling a horse—but he is also very prescient that he was far too young to really understand what was transpiring, nor how to interpret the experience.

A third abolitionist traveler from the north visited Richmond in 1855 and left this description of a slave auction in progress:

> About a dozen gentlemen crowded to the spot, while the poor fellow was stripping himself, and as soon as he stood on the box, bare from top to toe, a most rigorous scrutiny of his person was instituted. The clear black skin, front and back, was viewed all over for scars, sores and diseases, and there was not any part of his body left unexamined.[732]

This anonymous, northern abolitionist speaks of the auctioned slave standing on a wooden box. He is examined for scars, front and back, and there was no part of the slave's body that was left unexamined.

Swedish writer, Fredrika Bremer visited at least three different slave auctions on her trip to America in 1854. She speaks of these auc-

731 Lester, p. 29.

732 B. A. Botkin, A Treasury of Southern Folklore (New York: Random House, 1988), p. 131. Benjamin A. Botkin (1901–1975) was a Harvard educated scholar who spent most of his adult life as a high school English teacher in Boston.

tions in an essay called "Impressions in America." She tells us about one of the auction houses she visited, "I saw nothing especially repulsive, except the whole thing."[733] Bremer adds:

> I cannot help but feel astonishment that such a thing and such a scene are possible in a community that calls itself "Christian."[734]

Ms. Bremer found the auction process to be "repulsive," from beginning to end, and she finds that such goings-on could be conducted by people who call themselves Christian. Indeed, in this she finds "astonishment."

Finally, an abolitionist account, or perhaps a commentary on it, can be seen in an ironic 1829 poster paid for by the Abolitionist Society of America. The poster proclaims, in part:

> Advertisement for a slave auction in 1829, along with other commodities that underlines the dehumanizing nature of slavery and of slave auctions.[735]

In this description, as well as those discussed earlier, they seem to concentrate on ten different elements. First, the auctions frequently were conducted in public places, then in taverns and hotels, and then finally on the properties of the major slave dealers. Thus, we are in the second or third phases of the history of slave auctions outlined earlier. Secondly, after being kept in a slave jail for a short time, the slaves were washed, combed and dressed up in their fanciest clothes. This is similary to what we saw at the end of Middle Passage voyages, where slaves would be bathed and cleaned up to present them in the best conditions.

Thirdly, before the sale, the captives were prodded, pushed and examined minutely to detect imperfections. Fourth, they were often oiled with a mixture of oil and ash to give their bodies a luster. Fifth, they were sometimes taken to "private rooms" where they were more

733 Fredrika Bremer, "Impressions of America," in New Sketches of Everyday Life (Stockholm, 1858), p. 19.

734 Ibid. Bremer (1801–1865), in addition to being a Swedish writer and scholar, was also a very early European feminist and social critic.

735 Fredric Bancroft, Slave Trading in the Old South (New York: Ungar, 1931), p. 284.

thoroughly examined, and perhaps sexually assaulted. Sixth, any rowdy or unruly slave was punished with the whip and more. Seventh, the slaves were sold one at a time. Eighth, the sale took place using a wooden box, a stone auction block or a raised wooden platform, so it was easier for all to see.

Ninth, the slave went to the highest bidder, or at a set price established beforehand. And finally, the slaves had usually been previously certified before the sale, so that the seller may take a *Caveat emptor* attitude about the sale.

To this point, most of the first-person descriptions of slave auctions were written by slaves who usually took part in the auction. There are also other extant first-person narratives of slave auctions from the viewpoint of white abolitionists. Already, we introduced the narrative of Fredrika Bremer, a Swedish writer in the nineteenth century, who found the auction process to be repugnant. We will now look at two more of these white abolitionist narratives.

First, Joseph Ingraham, the author of *Southwest by a Yankee*, published in 1835, tells us this about a slave auction he had seen:

> A line of Negroes... extended in a semi-circle around the right side of the yard. There were in all about forty. Each was dressed in the usual uniform of slaves, when the market, consisting of a fashionably shaped, black-fur hat, roundabout and trousers, of course corduroy velvet, precisely such is worn by Irish laborers, when they first come over the water, good vests, strong shoes, and white cotton shirts, completed their equipment. This dress they lay aside until after they are sold, or wear out as soon as may be; for the negro dislikes to retain the indication of having recently been in the market. With their hats in their hands, which hung down their sides, they stood perfectly still, and in close order, while some gentlemen were passing from one to another examining for the purpose of buying.[736]

---

736 Abolitionist poster, Abolitionist Society of America, 1829, in Our Quaker Friends of Ye Olden Times (Lynchburgh: J. P. Bell Co., 1905), p. 36.

Another abolitionist's account of a slave auction comes from British writer G. H. Andrews writing for the *London Illustrated News*. He gives this account of viewing a slave auction in Richmond in 1861. He speaks of meeting a freed black man who worked in a bar. He entered into conversation with him. Andrews continues the story:

> On the bar counter in front of us were some slops of wine and beer and crumbs of biscuits. A number of flies were feeding upon them when I asked him if the slaves were contended with their lot. He instantly turned a tumbler glass down upon the counter and a few of the flies which were now imprisoned under it. There was fire in his eye, and his whole body was agitated as he pointed with his finger to the glass in which the captured flies were buzzing. "Why," said he, "don't those flies continue to eat and drink as before? There is plenty there for them, enough to last them a week, but they will neither eat nor drink, for they have lost their liberty, and without that, nothing else is of value."[737]

Mr. Andrew's conversation with a presumably former slave highlights the flies' desire for food but also points out that their desire for freedom trumps any other need. The black man is clearly making an analogy of the flies to the slaves. Basic needs are of great importance, but freedom is far more important than any other commodity.

Finally, Frances Ellen Watkins Harper (1825–1911), African American abolitionist and suffragist, poet and writer, completed a poem she called, "The Slave Auction." The opening stanza of that poem tells us this:

> The Sale began—young girls were there
> too,
>
> Defenseless in their wretchedness

737 Joseph Holt Ingraham, Southwest by a Yankee (New York, 1835), p. 194. Ingraham was born in Portland, Maine, in 1809. He was an Episcopal minister and abolitionist. His most important work is The Throne of David published by Roberts Brothers in Boston in 1868. George Henry Andrews (1821–1885) was an American newspaper editor and politician from New York.

Whose stifled sobs of deep despair
Revealed their Anguish and Distress.[738]

Ms. Harper's poem goes on for another five stanzas, ending with this one:

You will not know how desolate
Are bosoms rudely forced to part.
And how a dull and heavy weight,
Will press life-drops from the heart.[739]

All five stanzas of Harper's poem are filled with tenderness and poignancy that can be seen in the opening and closing.

In all, we have given the first-person narratives of sixteen people, thirteen slaves and three white abolitionist visitors, one from Sweden, one Briton, and one American. This brings us to the next section of this seventh chapter, a description and discussion of several extant auctions stumps, stones blocks and wooden boxes and platforms from the Chesapeake Bay region mostly from the nineteenth century.

Extant Auction Blocks in Washington, Virginia and Maryland

In the District of Columbia and the states of Virginia and Maryland, there are a number of nineteenth-century auction blocks that still exist in those areas. We will speak of eleven of them in this section. Six are in Virginia, three in Maryland, and two in Washington. The first of the latter was an auction block made of wood owned and used by Sheriff C. M. Castleman during the Civil War. Mr. Castleman, at that time, set up his wooden auction block "in front of the courthouse door."[740]

738 Frances Harper, "The Slave Auction," in American Poetry: The Nineteenth Century (New York: Library of America, 1996), p. 117. Frances Ellen Watkins Harper (1825–1911) was an abolitionist and women's rights advocate in the second half of the nineteenth century.

739 Ibid.

740 G. H. Andrews, "Slave Auction in Richmond," in London Illustrated News, April 27, 1861. George Henry Andrews (1821–1885) was an American newspaper editor and abolitionist. He served in the New York State Senate from 1864 to 1867.

In a March 4, 1861, advertisement, the sheriff explains, "Being Court Day, I will sell at Public Auction, in front of the Court House Door, the following Free Negroes…"[741] One at a time, Sheriff Castleman sold these free negroes after they stepped individually one after the other upon the wooden box. This procedure, of course, runs counter to the history of slave auctions in the Chesapeake Bay region. The sheriff, in the mid-nineteenth century, conducted his auction at the site that earlier, in Maryland and Virginia, slave auctions were usually conducted—at county courthouses.

In Washington, when William H. Williams and others were conducting slave auctions at their own slave jails, Sheriff Castleman also sold free negroes in auctions in the city on his wooden auction block at the city courthouse.[742] The other extant Washington auction slave box was located at Decatur House at 1610 H Street, Northwest. There was also a slave pen located in the same place, as we have indicated in Chapter Six. Like at many other nineteenth-century locations, the wooden box at Decatur House was used for the auctioning of slaves and free blacks in the nineteenth century.[743]

In an article in the *Washington Post* on March 5, 1996, writer Mary Ann French describes the use of this auction block at Decatur House on Lafayette Square in Washington. The box and the facilities there were owned by Englishman John Gadsby, who sold slaves on the northwest corner of the square in the mid-nineteenth century.[744] Mr. Gadsby (1766–1844) also owned the National Hotel at the corner of Pennsylvania Avenue and Sixth Street.

Gadsby's facility at Decatur House is one of the only surviving urban slave quarters. These days the house is employed as an educa-

741 Sheriff C. M. Castleman, "Slaves for Sale," in Virginia Gazette, January 21, 1961. Castleman was sheriff of Washington, DC, in the late 1850s until the end of the Civil War. For more on him, see the Alexandrian Gazette, vol. 61, no. 286, November 1860.

742 Ibid.

743 More is said about William H. Williams and his Yellow House slave jail in Chapter Six of this study.

744 Decatur House at 1610 H Street at the southwest corner of Jackson Place and H Street near the White House now serves as the National Center for White House History.

tional space by the National Trust for Historic Preservation of the city of Washington.[745]

Mr. Gadsby's slave business was one of the earliest firms in the city. It appears as though his slave jail was constructed sometime in the early 1820s, and the Englishman continued in that business until his death in 1844. At that point, his son took over the business and continued until the end of the Civil War.[746] The same wooden box was employed to conduct the slave auctions at the Gadsby's jail, both in the courtyard of the building, as well as behind the house.

John Gadsby (1766–1844) was an English tavern keeper in Alexandria, Baltimore, and Washington, DC. He came to the US in 1796 when he bought the Union Tavern in Alexandria from John Wise. A short time later, he purchased the National Hotel in Washington at Pennsylvania Avenue and Sixth Street. This was followed by Gadsby buying the Indian Queen Hotel in Baltimore at the corner of Hanover and Baltimore Streets.

These purchases were followed by the buying of the Franklin Hotel in Washington, DC. Mr. Gadsby retired to Decatur House in 1831 at the age of seventy. The auction block at The Decatur House was employed at Gadsby's slave jail there.[747]

The Virginia auction stones are located in Luray, Warrenton, Campbell, Christianburg and Fredericksburg. The Maryland auction blocks may be found in Sharpsburg, Hagerstown, Upper Marlboro, Prince George's County and at the Sotterley Plantation in southern Maryland.

The auction block in Luray, Virginia, is on Main and Court Streets near the Chamber of Commerce Building. The block is made of native

---

745 Mary Ann French, "Auction Block at Decatur House," in The Washington Post, March 5, 1996. John Gadsby (1766–1844) was a wealthy British businessman who owned several hotels in Alexandria, Washington, and Baltimore, such as the Union Tavern, the National Hotel, and the Indian Queen Hotel in Baltimore. The National Trust for Historic Preservation is a privately funded, non-profit organization, based in Washington, DC, founded in 1949.

746 Ibid.

747 "John Gadsby," in David M. P. Freund, Biographical Supplement and Index (Washington, 1997), p. 134.

sandstone and is about five feet high with a seventeen-inch square platform. A page from the *Page News and Courier* from August 31, 1961, describes the purpose of the stone:

> This native sandstone block... which stood at the corner of Main and Court Streets at the Chamber of Commerce Building...was used as a perch for slaves about to be sold at auction... The stone is said to be one of the few still in existence.[748]

Not surprisingly, this slave auction stone in Luray is just a stone's throw from the railroad station on South Broad Street. A marker at the site states that the stone is a "symbol of a dark past of man's inhumanity toward his fellow man."[749] The inscription adds, "It is also a symbol of how far we have come in learning to respect its victims and in resolving to go forward into the future with mutual respect and understanding."[750]

In a column from the *Page News and Courier*, Jacob Seekford (1857–1939) wrote perhaps the most poignant account of slavery in Page County, Virginia, in the mid-nineteenth century. He informs us:

> In 1856, when the southern slave buyers would come into this country and would buy slaves and take them to the South in large droves of colored men and women. In 1856, just in front of the house of the door where "Skeet" Good lives in Marksville, was the place where they sold slaves..." whether an ancient slave Block or a carriage/horse "step-down stone," the thought remains that this block is a historic symbol to Page Coun-

748 Decatur House was built by Stephen Decatur in 1808. John Gadsby bought the house in 1836, at which time they added a two-story structure to the back of the house for slave quarters. The building remains one of the few urban slave facilities in America. The Indian Queen Hotel in Baltimore was owned by John Gadsby, as well.

749 Anonymous, "Auction Block of Luray," in The Page News and Courier, August 31, 1961. The Page News Courier was the result of the merger of The Page News, established in 1881, and The Page Valley Courier, which began in 1867. The Page News and Courier began publication in 1911.

750 Ibid.

ty's past.[751]

The stone in question is now part of Inn Lawn Park in Page County. It consists of a two-foot square base of cement topped by a two-foot-tall block of local sandstone. Not far from this spot at 116 South Court Street in Luray sits the original Page County Courthouse, where slave auctions often occurred throughout the county's early history.

Contemporary scholar Kevin Levin writes about the Luray stone. He believes the best evidence that the block was used for slave auctions comes from a man named Lynnwood Berry, who was born in Virginia between 1889 and 1895. Mr. Berry confirms that an old Luray slave told him that the stone was used as a slave auction block.[752]

The site of this Page County stone at Inn Lawn Park has served many functions over the years. At one point, it was the location of the Laurance Hotel. In fact, the stone appears in a photograph of the hotel from a 1920s series of postcards related to the stone and building at the corner of Main and Court Streets. But whether the stone is a slave auction block or a carriage step-down stone is not entirely clear.

Mr. Levin also tells us about a certain house in Luray used as a slave-holding pen.[753] The house in question was known as the Smoot Building named after the mayor of Luray, Henry J. Smoots (1828–1900), who owned the house in the mid-nineteenth century. The house still stands on the northwest corner of West Main and North Court Streets.

Scholar Kevin Levin also speaks of another auction stone. He says, "I am also aware of another stone in Page County, Virginia, that may have served as an auction block. The origin of that stone, however,

751 Ibid. Jacob Richard Seekford (1857–1939) was a magistrate for many years in Luray, Virginia. The Luray Times-Dispatch, from July 2, 1909, reports that he was acquitted of "Betrayal" at that time in the city.

752 Jacob Seekford, "Luray Auction Block," in The Page News and Courier, May 17, 1933. Inn Lawn Park in Luray, Virginia, is at 103 Zerkel Street.

753 Lynnwood Berry, quoted in Kevin Levin, "My Fredericksburg Battlefield," www.cwmemory.com. The Laurance Hotel still exists in Luray, Virginia, at 2 South Court Street. It was established in 1883 there.

is in question."[754]

Ironically, this second stone in Page County was sold several years ago at an auction, and it is believed that it originated either from the auction site at Marksville, Virginia, or from another county in the valley.[755]

Kevin Levin thinks the best argument for the Fredericksburg block being employed as an auction block are two advertisements taken out in the *Fredericksburg News* in December of 1857 and March of 1858, informing the public that "Servants" and "Valuable Slaves" will be sold "in front of the Planter's Hotel."[756] This is the site, of course, of the same corner where the alleged auction block still stands. William H. Fitzhugh conducted these two auctions calling himself the "Acting Executor." The J. B. Timberlake and Company was identified in the advertisement as "Auctioneers."[757] John B. Timberlake (1849–1927) is the auctioneer in question. He is also famous for another reason—US patent # 822,981 issued on January 25, 1904. Mr. Timberlake invented the wire coat hanger.[758]

The remains of a slave auction block in Warrenton, Virginia, fifty miles south of Washington, DC, is an L-shaped stone, about eighteen inches on the two sides. This appears to be half of the original base of the stone, which most likely had another structure on top of the base, on which slaves stood for auction.[759] The block is near the 1779 "Gaol House," or "Jail House," which is now a museum. It is also close to the home of General William Fitzhugh Payne leader of

754 Ibid.

755 Ibid. Henry J. Smoots (1828–1900) was born in Shenandoah, Virginia, and eventually moved to Luray, where he became mayor. Marksville is an unincorporated town in Page County, Virginia.

756 Ibid.

757 Kevin Levin, "Fredericksburg Slave Block," in Fredericksburg News, December 18, 1857, and March 21, 1858.

758 Advertisement for John B. Timberlake and Company. Timberlake (1777–1828) was an auctioneer and sometime slave trader. A biography of him was published in Boston by Houghton-Mifflin in 2006.

759 Ibid.

the famous Black Horse Cavalry. William Dunaway speaks of the Warrenton slave block in his *The African-American Family in Slavery and Emancipation.*[760]

There is also an auction block on the Green Hill Plantation off Route 728 near Campbell, Virginia. It consists of an eighteen-inch square block resting on four square stone posts about two feet high and was most likely used at slave auctions. It looks like a table with four stone legs on which the slaves stood.

Next to the auction block is another small stone about eighteen inches square on which the auctioneer stood. The slave auction block in Fredericksburg, Virginia, is located on the corner of Charles and Williams Streets. In that spot, the item looks more like a stump than a stone.[761] This stone was not far from where George Washington's mother, Mary Ball Washington, lived.

The earliest account of the stone block in question comes in S. J. Quinn's *History of the City of Fredericksburg*, initally published in 1908 and re-distributed by the Cornell University Press in 2009. Mr. Quinn assents to the auction block theory. In fact, in his history, he tells us:

> There is probably no relic in Fredericksburg that calls forth more vividly the days of slavery than does this stone block.[762]

Although Mr. Quinn ascribes to the auction block theory, the block in question has been the subject of some controversy. Since 1924, the stone's purpose has been called into question. Some believe it was a block for the mounting of horses, which makes sense given the location for it was in front of Planter's Hotel in downtown Fredericksburg. At any

760 Slave auction block in Warrenton. William Henry Fitzhugh Payne (1830–1904) from Facquier County, Virginia, was a general in the Confederate Army.

761 William Dunaway, The African-American Family in Slavery and Emancipation (Cambridge, Cambridge University Press, 2003), p. 37.

762 Green Hill Plantation near Campbell, Virginia. A photograph of the slave auction block from 1960 is included in the National Humanities Center resource toolbox in the article entitled "The Making of African-American Identity," 1500 to 1865, Volume 1.

rate, the block was officially recognized as a historic landmark by the Fredericksburg City Council in 1984. Evidence for the stone being an auction block in an 1857 newspaper advertisement that announces that slaves will be auctioned at The Planter's Hotel. The advertisement was placed in the *Daily Star* by a local auctioneer named N. B. Kinsley.[763]

Another advertisement from the *Fredericksburg News* in the December 22, 1757, edition, two months after Mr. Kinsley's ad, also announces a slave auction "in front of the Planter's Hotel."[764] A Virginia slave named Albert Crutchfield contended that he was sold from the block when he was fifteen years old.[765] Indeed, he appears in a postcard circa 1920 standing behind the slave block. His obituary also reported that he "distinctly" remembered being sold on that block.[766] The postcard shows Crutchfield standing atop the block.[767] Another postcard from the same series shows him standing next to the stone. He is dressed smartly in a 1920s suit, his hat in his left hand, and a cane in the right.[768] On the back of this postcard is written:

> In the days before the Civil War, this block was used for the sale and annual hire of slaves. Albert Crutchfield, shown in the picture, was sold from the block in 1859, at which time he was a boy of about fifteen years old.[769]

Many critics have raised doubts about the utility and purpose of the stone block in downtown Fredericksburg, arguing that it was not used to sell slaves, but rather to mount or dismount from horses and carriages. At any rate, the stone in question remains at the spot. More

---

763 S. J. Quinn, History of the City of Fredericksburg (Ithaca: Cornell University Press, 2009), p. 168. The Planter's Hotel, which was built in 1855 by R. T. Knox and Brother, is now the Knoxanna Apartments.

764 Planter's Hotel. These ads appear in "Fredericksburg Remembered," http://bit.ly/36uKYca.

765 Ibid. Albert Crutchfield (1850–1931) was the son of Mammy Judy Crutchfield of Spotsylvania County, Virginia. Albert was born into slavery there and was owned by the Oliver family.

766 Ibid.

767 Ibid.

768 Ibid.

769 Ibid.

recently, in September of 2017, the citizens of Fredericksburg held a public forum on what should be done with the slave block. In an article for the *Associated Press* dated September 24, 2017, author Dennis Foley attended the forum.

Mr. Foley states that the city council offered two options about which the town's citizens could comment. "Keep the block in place with additional information and protections, or move the block to a museum." Foley tells us that one hundred people came to the forum at the James Monroe High School, "about a quarter of them spoke." In June of 2019, the Fredericksburg City Council voted six to one to move and relocate the slave auction block to a nearby Fredericksburg Area Museum.

There is a wooden box in Christianburg used in the mid-nineteenth century to conduct slave auctions there. When not being employed, it was kept at the sheriff's office or in a closet at the Montgomery County Courthouse at 55 East Main Street.

The final auction block in Virginia is in Blacksburg. It has four columns or legs that prop up an eighteen by eighteen-inch square slab that sits upon the legs, so it looks like a table. It exists on Main Street near the courthouse, the site of slave auctions in the late eighteenth and early nineteenth centuries. Thus, it is part of the first phase of our auction history in the Chesapeake Bay region outlined earlier in this chapter.[770] Sylvia Cannon, a freed Virginia slave, speaks of how this block was employed in Blacksburg. She writes:

> I see'em sell plenty of colored folks away in dem days, cause that's the way White Folks made heeps of money.

770 Ibid.

> Course, they never know how much a slave would sell for. They just stand them up on the block, about three feet high, and the Speculator bids him off just like they was horses. Them who was bid off never say nothing. I don't know who bought my brothers, George and Early. I have seen some slaves sold twice before I was sold; and I see slaves when they are travelling like hogs to Darlington. Some of them be women folk, looking like they weren't going to get down, they were so heavy. The Slave Auctioneer spoke of his business as though he were selling hogs.[771]

Sylvia Cannon speaks of the sadness that enveloped the environment of the Virginia slave auctions in the 1850s. She also employs the popular metaphor at the time that "Slaves were sold like hogs." She even suggests that at times, some slaves were sold more than once before an auction was complete, or even before it began in some cases.

There is also some evidence of a surviving wooden auction block in Lynchburg, Virginia. It was employed in front of a tavern there before the Civil War. In 1853, Lewis Miller, in his *Sketchbooks*, has left an illustration of seven slaves dancing and singing around this auction block. One slave plays a fiddle, another a banjo, and a third a percussion instrument, while four other slaves, all dressed in white, sing and dance around the block.[772] Another image of Miller's is discussed at the close of this chapter.

A similar block existed in the town of Christianburg and was made of wood, as we have pointed out in the above analysis. The Blacksburg auction block was also a wooden box used in the years up to the Civil War in that city.

In regard to Maryland extant auction blocks in Sharpsburg, Mary-

---

771 Sylvia Cannon was a South Carolina slave, interviewed for the Federal Writer's Project in Florence, South Carolina. At the time, she was eighty-five years old. "Hogs to Darlington" is a reference to Boss Hogs Smokehouse in Darlington, South Carolina.

772 Lewis Miller, Sketchbooks. Miller (1796–1882) completed a number of watercolors sketches of slave life. The Encyclopedia of Virginia contains an article on the artist.

land, at the corner of Main and Sharp Streets in Washington County, there is an old block and upper stone. It stands a few hundred feet from the site of the Antietam National Cemetery, as well as the battle there. The Sharpsburg block has an inscription that reads:

> From 1800 until 1865, this Stone was used as a slave block. It has been a famous landmark at this original location over 150 years.[773]

There is also a slave auction block in Hagerstown near the old jail on Jonathan Street. In the nineteenth century, it is likely that the jail often housed runaway slaves, who were auctioned off with the use of the stone located in front of the jail.[774] The original jail of Washington County was a log cabin located at 26 and 28 Franklin Street in Hagerstown. In 1818, the state legislature authorized the building of a new jail on Jonathan Street.

The budget authorized by the legislature for the new jail in that year was $12,000.[775] After construction of the new jail, slave auctions took place there on a wooden box in front of the entrance.

There is a slave block on the lawn of an old hotel on Main Street in Upper Marlboro of Prince George's County. The hotel was originally the home of John Rogers (1723–1789), an American lawyer and judge of Upper Marlboro. He was also a Maryland delegate to the Continental Congress in 1775 and 1776.[776] The Upper Marlboro Block was likely the site of the late eighteenth and early nineteenth-century slave auctions. In this sense, the activities of this site are best to be seen as part of the second phase of the history of slave auctions in the Chesapeake Bay region, outlined in an earlier section of this chapter.

There is also extant a stone slave block at the Sotterley Plantation

773 Sharpsburg slave block, Sharpsburg, Maryland.

774 Old jail on Jonathan Street, Hagerstown, Maryland.

775 John Rogers (1723–1789) built a house at this spot and later the Old Hotel was built in its place. Rogers was an American attorney and judge from Upper Marlboro, where the Old Hotel could be found. Rogers was also a delegate to the Continental Congress from Maryland.

776 James Bowles in 1699 bought the land on which the Sotterley Plantation was to be built. He built a four-room house there in 1703. Later, it was expanded to become a plantation estate, complete with auction block.

in Hollywood, Maryland, in Saint Mary's County. The block was used for slave auctions occurring in southern Maryland from the 1840s on, until the close of the American Civil War. Indeed, after slave auctions in St. Mary's City were no longer conducted at the courthouse there, they were moved to this plantation, where southern Maryland traders presided over the auctions. The auction block is not far from the famous slave cabin on the grounds of the plantation.[777]

Finally, there was also a slave auction block in the slave yard of Hope H. Slatter's slave jail in Baltimore. It was on the west side of the yard against the east wall of the building. In that spot today stands a brick fireplace once used for cooking and warmth. Mr. Slatter's establishment was demolished sometime in the 1870s. A gasoline station now sits at the site. The location of the Slatter slave yard is now a parking lot.[778]

In addition to these slave auction blocks in Maryland, Virginia, and the District of Columbia, there are also several other blocks still extant in the Deep South. In an 1855 brochure for a slave auction, for example, by the slave-trading firm of J. A. Beard & May is extant and digitalized by the University of Pennsylvania Library.[779] The brochure includes a picture of the slave block employed in the slave auctions conducted there.

This auction in question was one of the largest slave sales in North America in the nineteenth century. It took place over two days, March 13 and 14, 1855. In total, 178 captives were sold—men, women and children. The site of the auction was the Banks Arcade in New Orleans.

Tim Talbot in his essay, "Lexington Kentucky Cheapside Slave Auction Block," writes about the wooden block used in the Cheapside slave auctions there.[780] William Henry Brooke's (1772–1860) portrait

777 Washington County Historical Society, "Historical Chronology," https://washcohistory.org, pp. 1–2.

778 "Hope Slatter," quoted in Stanton Tierman, "Baltimore's Old Slave Markets," in The Baltimore Sun, n.d. Also see, Heather A. Williams, Help Me to Find My People (Chapel Hill: UNC Press, 2012), p. 221.

779 Brochure, J. A. Beard & May Company, published May 1855.

780 Tim Talbott, "Lexington Kentucky Cheapside Slave Auction Block," https://explorekyhistory.ky.gov.

of a New Orleans slave auction in the French Quarter, shows the auction block located in the middle of the rotunda. The image, a twelve by twenty-inch painting, is owned by the Historic New Orleans Rotunda Collection.

This brings us to a number of pieces of nineteenth-century American and British art depicting the activities of the Chesapeake Bay region slave auctions, the topic for the next section of this chapter.

Chesapeake Slave Auctions in Art: 1800 to 1865

A variety of historical and contemporary pieces of art that are extant depict the phenomenon of slave auctions in the nineteenth century. One illustration of a slave auction, completed by David Claypoole Johnston (1798–1865) and owned by the Princeton University Art Museum, shows two young slave men sitting on stools while they wait for the auction to proceed. Standing above them is a young slave woman, one child in arms, another clutching her waist at her side.[781]

Toward the rear of the scene stands a white planter dressed in a suit with a top hat. A door stands between this planter and a second man who is leaning against the wall, his arms crossed at his chest. On the door between these two men is a sign announcing the auction, which is about to take place.[782] Mr. Clay was a Philadelphia-born cartoonist, printmaker, and artist in Boston.

A second image of a Chesapeake Bay region slave auction is entitled *Slave Auction in Christianburg, Virginia*. The 1850s illustration comes from Lewis Miller's *Sketches 1853–1867*.[783] It shows a male auctioneer standing on a square wooden box. In his right hand is a baton or a whip. A male slave dressed all in white stands before the box. To the right is a group of Chesapeake Bay planters wearing top hats and

---

781 David Claypoole Johnston, Slave Auction, Princeton University Art Museum. Johnston (1799–1865) was born in Philadelphia and became a noted cartoonist, printmaker and author in Boston. He died in Dorchester, Massachusetts.

782 Ibid.

783 Lewis Miller, Slave Auction in Christianburg, Virginia, in Sketchbooks, 1853–1867. Miller (1796–1882) was a Pennsylvania Dutch folk artist noted for his watercolors of historical and everyday events. See Note 772.

bidding on the slave.[784]

An illustration from the *Illustrated London News* dated February 15, 1861, features a white auctioneer who stands on the second step of four steps leading to a wooden auction platform. The man wears an expensive suit and fancy hat. He holds a baton in his right hand. Above the auctioneer on the platform stands a slave family—husband, wife, and baby held by the wife. Another slave sits on the first step. The platform is surrounded by Virginia planters, all looking up at the wares. The caption of the illustration reads:

> Virginia's most valuable export in years prior to the Civil War may have been slaves and tobacco.[785]

A fourth illustration of a nineteenth-century slave auction was produced by Theodore R. Davis on July 13, 1861, entitled *A Slave Auction in the South*. In the illustration, a white auctioneer stands on a wooden auction platform. He is grasping a roll of paper in his right hand and is in the process of selling a family—husband, wife, and small infant. Behind the scene are dozens of slaves, one being examined by a white planter.[786] Mr. Davis (1840–1894) was a Boston-born correspondent and illustrator for *Harper's Weekly*.

LeFevre J. Cranstone's *Slave Auction, Virginia* is a multi-colored image of an auction in the Chesapeake Bay region. The painting features a white slave dealer on a slave platform that is ascended by three wooden steps on the left. The dealer/auctioneer is dressed in black and wears a white hat. To the trader's right, also on the platform, is a black woman in a summer dress and white apron. One bidder sits in a chair with a newspaper in his lap. Two dozen others, some slaves and some planters, are assembled around the slave platform.[787]

784 Anonymous, "Virginia's Most Valuable Export," Illustrated London News, February 15, 1861.

785 Ibid.

786 Theodore R. Davis, "A Slave Auction in the South," in On the Plains and Across the Plains (New York: Create Space, 2012), p. 111. Davis (1840–1894) was born in Boston and became a correspondent and illustrator for Harper's Weekly. Most of his paintings are of significant military and political events.

787 LeFevre J. Cranstone, "Slave Auction, Virginia," in Views of

Cranstone's painting is reminiscent of the work of Englishman Eyre Crowe, particularly his painting *Slaves Going South After Being Sold at Richmond* and *The Sale of Slaves at Richmond, Virginia* completed in 1853 discussed at the end of Chapter Six.

Mr. Cranstone's painting was last sold at Sotheby's in London in 1990. Prior to that time, the painting was in private hands. In 1991, the Virginia Historical Society bought the painting, using funds provided by Mr. and Mrs. Robert Jeffress, the director of the society.[788] And this is where the painting is now located.

The other artistic renditions and depictions of slave auctions in this chapter are photographs of some of the auctions blocks and stones discussed in this chapter. One photo is of the plaque that accompanies the Luray, Virginia, stone block discussed in a previous section of this chapter.[789]

Another photograph is of the auction block in Fredericksburg, Virginia, which stood outside the Planter's Hotel in the nineteenth century. There is also an image of the block showing an African American man dressed in a 1920s dark suit and flat cap standing atop the stone.[790]

An illustration of a Maryland slave auction dated 1849 is attached to a publication of Henry Bibb's *Narrative of the Life and Adventures of Henry Bibb: An American Slave*. This text is owned by the University of North Carolina Library. In the illustration, a white auctioneer stands on a round table in the middle of the scene. He holds a gavel above his head in his left hand, and a young black baby is in his right hand. To the left is a planter with a whip standing over a group of four slaves. In the center in front of the round table is a young female slave on her knees imploring another planter who is standing. All around the

---

Antebellum America (Wheeling: Ogleby Institute, 1984), p. 49. Cranstone (1822–1893) was a British landscape painter who also wrote verse. He traveled to America in 1859, where he completed several landscapes of the American countryside.

788 Eyre Crowe, "Slaves Going South," Virginia Historical Society. Crowe (1824–1910) was born in London and was a member of the Social Realism School of painting there. His first exhibit at the Royal Academy of Arts was in 1846, his final show there in 1908.

789 Photograph of Luray auction block, in Seekford.

790 Photo of auction block in Fredericksburg. In Quinn, p. 131, see Note 763.

table are other planters and several slaves, some of whom are in chains. On the wall of the slave auction room, to the right, is an announcement of the "Slave Sale."[791]

A depiction from the *Richmond News* shows a Virginia planter examining a young black slave dressed in a white shirt, khaki pants and black shoes. The planter is dressed in the style of a southern gentleman. He appears to be examining the left eye of the young woman. Behind the two are several other planters and an auctioneer, who sits at a table reading a newspaper. There is no date on the image, and the artist is unknown.[792]

An image from Montgomery County, Virginia, from May 12, 1852, owned by the Abby Aldrich Rockefeller Folk Art Museum in Williamsburg, shows a woman with a baby sitting on the left of the image. A white trader/auctioneer stands on the wood auction block, a whip in his right hand. A male slave stands before the box, clad in white, and handcuffed in the front. Three planters to the right are haggling over the price of the slave. The caption of the image reads:

> Miss Fillis and child, with Bill being sold at a Publick Auction, on May 12th.

A twelve by twenty-inch painting of a slave auction was created by James Cranstone LeFevre (1820–1893) while visiting Richmond in the late 1850s. The British painter displayed the character of the auction scene just before the American Civil War.

This brings us to the major conclusions made in this seventh chapter. In the eighth and ninth chapters to follow, we will return to the phenomena of Muslim runaway slaves in Virginia (Chapter 8), followed by Muslim runaway slaves in Maryland (Chapter 9).

Conclusions

We began this seventh chapter by introducing a developmental history of slave auctions in the Chesapeake Bay region. There we have indicated that slave auctions in the area can be seen as having three sep-

791 Photo accompanying Henry Bibb's autobiography, see Note 713.

792 Ibid. Owned by University of North Carolina Library. Anonymous, "Southern Auction," in Richmond News, May 20, 1853. Anonymous, Auction Block, Aldrich Rockefeller Folk Art Museum, Williamsburg, Virginia. This image of Miss Fillis and Bill was also one of Lewis Miller's pieces.

arate stages. In the first of these, slave auctions in Virginia, the District of Columbia, and Maryland mostly were conducted at county courthouses throughout early Maryland, the City of Washington and in Virginia, or at other public spaces, such as central town squares, or market places, beginning in the earliest period of the colonies.

In the second phase, as indicated, the job of slave auctions in the Chesapeake region passed to county jails, as well as private hotels and taverns where slave dealers often were now conducting their business. In the third phase, as shown, slave auctions in Virginia and Maryland now were mostly conducted on the properties of the major slave traders in cities like Baltimore, Alexandria, Annapolis, Washington, DC, and Richmond.

In the second section of this chapter, we introduced and discussed sixteen separate slave narratives of slave auctions in the Chesapeake Bay region. Thirteen of these narratives are written by Maryland and Virginian slaves, while three were first-person narratives of white abolitionist visitors, one American, one Swedish, and one British.

From these first-person narratives of slave auctions in Maryland and Virginia, we suggested that they consisted of ten different elements. These can be summarized this way:

1. Slave auctions were often conducted at county courthouses and other public spaces in the earliest portions of the colonies, followed by county jails, hotels and pubs, and then on the properties of major slave dealers from 1820 to 1865.
2. Slaves usually were kept in slave jails for a short time before their sale.
3. The captives were prodded, poked and examined for even the most minute imperfections.
4. They were washed, combed and oiled with a mixture of oil and ash to give them a sheen before auctioning.
5. They were sometimes taken to private rooms where they were more thoroughly examined, and perhaps sexually assaulted.
6. Any rowdy or unruly slaves were punished on the spot by their dealers.

7. The slaves were sold individually, one at a time.
8. Slave auctions took place on a stone or wooden auction block or auction platform built for that purpose.
9. Slaves went to the highest bidder or sometimes at a fixed priced established beforehand.
10. And finally, the slaves had been previously certified, so the buyers may have recourse in regard to sales that were misleading. In that regard, illnesses and disabilities possessed by the captives were declared before the sale. They did this so the owners could claim a *caveat emptor* status in regard to the sale.

In the third section, we described and discussed eleven extant slave auction stones and blocks. As we have seen, five of these are in Virginia, four are in Maryland, and two in the District of Columbia. Also, some of these stones and blocks are involved in controversy concerning their original intended purpose.

In the final section, we introduced twelve separate pieces of art depicting slave auctions in the Chesapeake region in the nineteenth and twentieth centuries. Four are illustrations, two are nineteenth-century paintings, and several are photographs of the auction blocks discussed earlier.

In Chapters Eight and Nine to follow, we shall return to the phenomenon of Muslim runaway alaves in Virginia (Chapter Eight), as well as Muslim runaway slaves in Maryland (Chapter Nine). In this sense, this study has done a full circle, in that where the study began it now comes to an end, as well. We move now to Chapter Eight on Virginian Muslim runaway slaves.

Chapter Eight: Muslim Runaway Slaves in Virginia

The cultural distance between African and African American culture was even wider than we imagined. Beginning at the point of initial enslavement and transport from Africa, through the dreaded Middle Passage and on to the United States most of the slave's past had been obliterated.

—W. E. B. DuBois, *Essays*

In traditional religion there are no creeds to be recited; instead the creeds are written in the heart of the individual. There are no sacred Scriptures. Religion in African society is not written on paper, but in the hearts of believers.

—John S. Mbiti, *African Religion and Philosophy*

Oh, you believers, let your slaves and those of you who have not yet come to puberty, ask leave of you three times before they come into your presence.

—The Holy Qur'an 24:58 (Author's translation)

Introduction

As in its Chesapeake Bay partner, Maryland, the Colony/State of Virginia experienced a persistent problem for Virginia landowners of runaway slaves and servants fairly early on in their history from the middle of the seventeenth century on. These servants and slaves may have fled from abusive masters simply to take a break from hard labor or to search for family members, who absconded from their masters' farms.

Other slaves or white indentured servants were lured away by neighboring landowners attempting to steal their labor or by freed blacks or sympathetic white people, often abolitionists, who tried to help them.

Allan D. Austin, in his *African Muslims in Antebellum America,* speaks of the kind of information available on the lives of early American Muslims when he writes:

> ...Much evidence of the Muslim presence has survived. Lists of slaves include Muslim names. Some family and church documents, including birth and death notices of slaves, add an occasional informative note; runaway advertisements provide useful descriptive information; and some slaves became worthy of notice in print for a variety of reasons.[793]

Allan Austin, as well as many other contemporary scholars, write of the value of runaway slave advertisements in general, and more specifically, in the colonies and states of the Chesapeake Bay region in the seventeenth, eighteenth and nineteenth centuries. He also points out that many prominent Muslim slaves in America became "worthy of notice" and thus are known for some acclaim. Several of these notable Muslim slaves were introduced in the first chapter of this Study.

Early Virginia court records also reveal that both whites and blacks ran away from their masters, sometimes together, but the punishment of white servants was considerably more severe than that of black slaves. As early as 1643, in the Virginia colony, the General Assembly passed several laws that established penalties for runaway slaves and servants.

This 1643 law was promulgated on March 2, 1643, by the Virginia colonial government responding to the problem of runaway indentured servants in the colony. The statute began: "Whereas there are divers loitering runnaways in the Collony who very often absent themselves from their Masters..." A number of other laws followed in the Commonwealth of Virginia in regard to the same phenomenon.

These laws regulated movement, identified chronic offenders, and sometimes were branded with an "R" standing for "Runaway," or they often had their haircut very short to be identified as chronic offenders.

In September of 1663, Virginia lawmakers were concerned about the "unlawful meeting of slaves and servants." The burgesses directed the landowners to "take especiall care that their servants and slaves do not depart from their houses on Sundayes or any other day without

---

793 Allan D. Austin, African Muslims in Antebellum America (London: Routledge, 1984), p. 5.

lycence from them."[794]

One reason this comment mentions "Sunday" is because the master and his family well may be away at church on that day, so slaves may more easily escape on Sunday. This is also a primary reason why slave owners began to take their captives along with them to worship services in Virginia.

This 1663 bill foreshadowed a 1680 Virginia law aimed at preventing "Negroe insurrections."[795] This law begins by noting, "The frequent meeting of considerable numbers of Negroe slaves under the pretense of feasts and burials."[796] The planters apparently believed that if slaves were allowed to meet, they would be more likely to hatch a plot, to run away, or even to rise up in rebellion, even at burials and funerals.

A few years later, in 1676, Nathaniel Bacon led an armed rebellion against the rule of Governor William Berkeley. This was the first major rebellion to occur in the American colonies. After the Bacon Rebellion in 1680, the Virginia burgesses passed the law outlawing negro insurrections. Bacon (1647–1676) was the English-born Virginia colonist who instigated what came to be called "Bacon's Rebellion" of 1676, which collapsed when Bacon himself died of dysentery that same year.

In more modern times in Virginia, similar legal provisions likely began to be enacted after the Nat Turner Rebellion in Virginia in 1831 that came after the South Carolina slave rebellion led by Denmark Vesey in 1822. After these events, white slave owners often grew alarmed at the fast-growing influence of Baptist slave preachers, beginning in the early 1800s, in the First Great Awakening.

Denmark Vesey (1767–1822) was a literate, skilled carpenter and leader of a slave rebellion in Charleston, South Carolina, that began in June of 1822. Nat Turner (1800–1831) was an enslaved

794 The primary sources we have consulted for this chapter include Latham A. Windley, ed., Runaway Slave Advertisements (Westport: Greenwood Press, 1983), four volumes; "Unknown No Longer: A Database of Virginia Slave Names," an on-line database created by the Virginia Historical Society; and the "African-American Families Database On-Line," produced by the Central Virginia History Researchers, Virginia Act XVIII, September 1663.

795 Virginia Law for the Prevention of Insurrections, 1680.

796 Ibid.

African American who led a rebellion of slaves and freed blacks in Southampton County, Virginia. The rebellion began on August 21, 1831. Both of these rebellions may have been an impetus for these new Virginia laws.

In fact, several places in early Virginia, public funerals for slaves were prohibited, especially at night when runaways would be more difficult to detect. Already in 1687, for example, the laws of Northern Neck, Virginia, prohibited public funerals for slaves because their owners feared that the captives might have hatched plots at those occasions.[797]

In many places in Virginia, night funerals were forbidden for similar purposes. This is significant for our concerns because in many West African societies in the seventeenth and eighteenth centuries, funerals were conducted at night.

One extant illustration by Italian Giovanni Cavezzi is of a nighttime funeral in West Central Africa shows ten male dancers moving clockwise around the deceased on a pillowed bier.[798] Clearly, this West African funeral was conducted at night, and missionary Cavezzi was able to sketch the scene. This funeral was likely in the Angolan Supply Zone, for Father Cavezzi spent a significant amount of time there in the seventeenth century.

Similar provisions were enacted in communities in the Tidewater region of Virginia. There, slaves were forced to conduct funerals and burials in the daytime, so that slaves could not easily escape if held at night. A number of other counties, particularly in the seventeenth and eighteenth centuries in Virginia, also prohibited night funerals and oth-

---

797 Denmark Vesey (1767–1822) was a literate, skilled carpenter and leader among African Americans in Charleston, South Carolina. In June of 1822, he was accused of being the ringleader of a rebellion, was convicted, and then executed. Northern Neck is the northern-most of three peninsulas on the western shore of the Chesapeake Bay in the Commonwealth of Virginia.

798 Donald P. Irish, ed., Ethnic Variation in Dying, Death, and Grief (London: Routledge, 2014), p. 55. Image of a West-Central African funeral by Fortunato da Alamendini, after a watercolor by Giovanni Cavezzi (1621–1678). Cavezzi was an Italian Capuchian who spent many years in Africa.

er religious ceremonies.

While it may have been the West African custom of conducting night funerals and burials, it also served practical purposes for the Virginia landowners. West African funerals at the time included a long procession in which people would pass by the grave, shouting, chanting and singing favorite hymns and songs. Thus, these masters could see if any of their slaves were missing during these processions. In a publication on ethnography of the National Park Service, one of the early slave funerals is described this way:

> They cry, and bawl and howl around the grave and roll in the dirt, and make many expressions of the most frantic grief... sometimes the noise that they make may be heard from as far away as one or two miles.[799]

At any rate, night funerals were the practice in Senegal, Gambia, Angola, portions of Nigeria, and many other places in West Africa in the seventeenth, eighteenth and nineteenth centuries. This may be why slaves in early Virginia were sometimes prone to conduct their funerals and burials at night, away from the planter and his farm.

The fact that many early Virginia slaves were Igbo and Yoruban also lends credence to the desire for night funerals in early Virginia. Funerals of both of these tribes, including the Ibibio, were mostly conducted at night in the seventeenth and eighteenth centuries in West Africa.

Blacks in seventeenth-century Virginia often insisted that funerals be conducted at night, perhaps their West African origins at work. Burials were made so that heads faced west, the same direction of the sun, as in many West African cultures in the eighteenth century, or Islam in general, as well, from very early on.

In March of 1643, the problem of fugitive slaves still vexed Virginia landowners. During a session of the Virginia General Assembly, the burgesses responded to what they called, "The divers loitering of

799 Quoted in "African-American Heritage and Ethnology," the National Park Service, the Park Ethnology Program. Giovanni Cavazzi da Montecuccola (1621–1678) was an Italian Capucian missionary and illustrator, noted for his illustrations of seventeenth-century life in Africa, particularly in Angola.

runaways in the Collony who very often absent themselves from their master's service."[800]

The actions of these slaves and servants cost their owners time, sometimes two or three months, before they were recovered. Their masters would be at great charge in recovering them, not to mention the loss of labor that the runaway slave had not done while away.

By October of 1669, the burgesses of the colony admitted that these early laws have "hitherto in greate parte proved to be inefectuall."[801]

Runaway slaves in Virginia mostly fled to Maryland, but sometimes as far north as New York and New England. Indeed, a slave named Anthony Burns ran away from a farm in Stafford County, Virginia, and he was later arrested on May 24, 1854, in Boston under the provisions of the Fugitive Slave Act of 1850, discussed previously in Chapter One.[802] Before that time, nothing was on the books about disciplining or punishing slaves in the Virginia colony/state.

By 1680, the Virginia General Assembly restricted the ability of slaves to meet at gatherings, and specifically at funerals. It also became legal at that time for a white planter, or his agent, to kill an escaped slave who resisted capture.

In 1705, again in Virginia, a comprehensive law allowed planters to discipline their slaves to the point of maiming and even killing them. Now, in 1705, Robert King Carter, for example, sought permission from the burgesses to dismember his runaways.[803]

Mr. Carter, who was one of the wealthiest Virginia planters and thus was called "King" Carter (1662–1732), owned a large estate in Lancaster County, Virginia. He served as the Speaker of the House of Burgesses from 1696 until 1698, and as the treasurer of the colony from 1699 until 1705.

In that same year, he asked the burgesses for permission to "chop

800 Virginia Fugitive Slave Law, March 1643.

801 Ibid.

802 Virginia Runaway Slave and Servant Law, October 1669.

803 Anthony Burns was discussed earlier under prominent Virginia slaves in the opening chapter of this study. Burns was born into slavery in Virginia, escaped, and later was found in the city of Boston. After being recaptured, he was returned to his Virginia owner.

off the toes" of "two incorrigible negroes" named Bambarra Harry and Dinah, who may well have been Moslems. Although this punishment seems gruesome, it must have been effective, for in 1725 Carter again asked permission to dismember two more slaves, whose names were Will and Bailey, in a similar manner.[804]

In one of his letters, Mr. Carter wrote to one of his property managers and expressed his desire that a certain slave woman be kept at home, "now that she has tasted the hardships of the woods."[805] About another slave, a man named Ballazore, another Muslim name, Carter observes that "He is incorrigible and nothing less than dismembering will reclaim him."[806] Carter adds:

> I would have you outlaw him and get a Court Order for taking off his toes. I have cured many a negroe of running away by this means.[807]

This new Virginia law of 1705 called for a reward of a thousand pounds of tobacco to anyone who apprehended a fugitive slave. This was to be repaid by the escaped slave through his or her additional work when they return. This, the act's authors believed, would discourage runaways "when they know soe many spies are upon them."[808]

This comment most likely refers to the air of freed blacks and white abolitionists who formed their first organization in Virginia in the early years of the eighteenth century and were aggressively looking to aid Virginia runaway slaves at that time.

A year later, in 1706, the burgesses revised the law when the reward was deemed to be too steep for the colony's coffers. Thus, at

---

804 Virginia Act Concerning Servants and Slaves, 1705. Robert "King" Carter (1663–1732) of Lancaster County, Virginia, was president of the Governor's Council in colonial Virginia and one of the wealthiest men in early Virginia.

805 Henry Winecek, An Imperfect God (New York: Farrar, Straus, and Giroux, 2003), pp. 46–48. Winecek, born in 1952, is an American journalist, historian and editor. He writes about architecturally significant projects related to slavery.

806 Ibid.

807 Ibid.

808 Ibid.

that time, the reward for the recovery of a Virginia runaway slave was reduced to two hundred pounds of tobacco, down from the original provision of a thousand pounds.[809]

Beginning in the year 1736, landowners in Virginia started to advertise in the new *Virginia Gazette* for their absconded slaves. Indeed, in the colonial period alone, the *Gazette* featured more than four thousand runaway advertisements from 1736 until 1783. These advertisements affirmed a strong desire on the part of the slaves to escape to freedom. They increased exponentially in the 1740s and 1750s and ceased being published in 1865 at the end of the Civil War when the thirteenth amendment freed the slaves.

In this chapter, we have the following aims. First, to give a general description of the reality of runaway slaves in the colony and state of Virginia in its earliest history. Secondly, to explore and analyze what we know of the phenomenon of suspected Moslem runaway slaves in Virginia. Thirdly, we will describe and analyze a number of pieces of art depicting Virginia runaway slaves in the seventeenth century to the nineteenth century. This will be followed, as have the other chapters of this study, by an analysis of the major conclusions made in this chapter, as well as the notes of this eighth chapter.

Runaway Slaves in Virginia

All tolled, we have examined 3,257 runaway slave advertisements in Virginia. This figure is nearly double the number of runaway advertisements examined in Maryland, as we shall see in the next chapter. These advertisements come from twenty-four different Virginia and national newspapers and other publications, with the predominant number from the *Virginia Gazette* beginning in 1736.

This is the same number of newspapers examined in Maryland. We also consulted *The Virginia Herald*, *The National Intelligencer*, *Harper's Weekly*, *The Virginia Argus*, *The Winchester Evening Star*, *The Richmond Inquirer*, *The Virginia Almanack*, *The Virginia Publick Occurrences*, *The Richmond Whig and Public Advertiser*, as well as fourteen other smaller, local Virginia papers.

These runaway slave advertisements, as found in these twen-

809 Ibid.

ty-four Virginia newspapers, sought the return of slaves from the age of ten to the age of sixty. Most of these fugitives were young, single men in their twenties. The average age was twenty-seven, the same age as the suspected Maryland Muslim runaway slaves in the next chapter. Male Virginia absconders, like those in Maryland, outnumber women four or five to one, as we shall see in Chapter Nine to follow.

The earliest Virginia advertisements come from the seventeenth century, beginning with a 1649 ad in the *Publick Occurrences* for a man named Sambo. Ending with the most recent of these Virginia runaways during the Civil War, in the early 1860s, with a one named Tom Binford in February 1864, and another named Jibril, the Arabic name for the Angel Gabriel, in Henrico County, around the same time.[810]

Several pieces of information, like the Maryland runaway advertisements, are provided in the Virginia newspapers. The ads usually include a slave's name, gender, age, shade of the bond person's skin, date of escape, where he may be headed, any unusual physical characteristics, any illness or disease they may have had, and the skills possessed by the particular slave.

Most of the Virginia runaway slave advertisements mention the clothing the runaway was wearing when fleeing, as well as other clothing of their owners, particularly that of their mistress, they may have taken with them.

Frequently, these Virginia advertisements mention items that were stolen from the master, including articles of clothing, firearms, horses, money, and any number of boats taken in the escape. The female runaways most often absconded with other slaves, and with clothing owned by their mistresses, with money, or both. The male slaves were more likely to leave with firearms, horses, money, or boats belonging to their masters.

Sometimes the advertisements mention biographical material about a slave, "He is a Mandingo," "He is from the Eboe Country" or "He comes from Guiney." A significant number of the Virginia ads mention the style of the slave's hair. "His fur is long on top and short on the sides," "He wears his wool bushy" or "She wears her hair piled

810 Virginia law to reduce reward for recovered runaway slave, November 27, 1706.

up on the top of her head." Of the 3,300 Virginia runaway slave ads we examined, 360 of them mention the hair of the captives, about the same percentage as in the Maryland runaway advertisements we shall see in Chapter Nine of this study, to follow.

Often these Virginia advertisements mention some personal characteristics of the runaway. "He gets along well with others," "She sometimes has a mean streak" or "He is usually complaisant." These comments almost always pertain to how well the slave gets along with other people, particularly with their masters and sometimes with animals like dogs and horses. They might say, for example, "He is quite artfull with horses" or "Horsemanship is his greatest skill."

The overwhelming number of Virginia runaway slaves abscond in the spring and summer months. Very few of these Virginia slaves escaped in the wintertime, nor in autumn. The majority of them escaped from April to October.

These nearly 3,300 Virginia runaway ads came from twenty-four different counties in Virginia. More than half of them are from Accomack, Orange, Chesterfield, Fairfax, Mecklenburg, Albemarle and Henrico Counties. The average reward offered for the Virginia runaway slaves was twenty shillings before the Revolutionary War, to a high of $378.00 by the Civil War.

The reward offered by the landowners was frequently related to the specific skills of the runaway. The more skills a slave possessed, the more is offered for his or her return. These are what we referred to earlier in this study as "Skilled Slaves."

One interesting aspect of the Virginia runaway ads is that the bounty for recovering a fugitive slave was larger if recovered outside the colony. The reward for Jefferson's slave, Sandy, for example, was forty shillings inside Albemarle County, four pounds if taken in the colony and ten pounds if discovered outside the colony.[811]

Of these 3,300 advertisements, more than 80 percent are for men and boys. Only one in five of the runaways are female. Very few of the Chesapeake runaways were over the age of forty, both male and female. The female ads in Virginia often mention a woman's marital status, but rarely for the men.

811 Ibid.

A significant number of the early Virginian advertisements for runaway slaves mention the tribal scars possessed by the captives. "He has some tribal marks and is missing some front teeth," "He has a horizontal scar completely across his forehead" or "He has three vertical scars beneath both eyes."

As we shall see in the next section of this chapter, fourteen of the fifty-one suspected Virginia Muslim runaway slaves had tribal scars received back in Africa that may be identified simply by the clans or tribes from which they came back in Africa.

Sometimes the Virginia runaway ads mention other permanent scars or imperfections that a slave may have. Often these are related to a slave's gait or his speech. In January of 1835, Eliza S. Perkins, for example, describes a fugitive slave in the *Richmond Whig and Advertiser*. She tells us about her slave Billy:

> He is about twenty years old, stands six feet high, and is a skinny boy with a dark complexion. He speaks with a slight stammer and has a scar near the corner of his right eye from a horse's kick that barely missed blinding him.[812]

Mrs. Perkins "demands" that Billy be returned to her son in Richmond, or at least be committed to the jail there. She even speculates where Billy may be. "He may be lurking around 'Rocketts' in Richmond, or possibly he has gone to the city of Petersburg."[813]

Rocketts was an outdoor market on the outskirts of Petersburg at the time. The scar near the corner of his right eye implies that Billy was from the Wolof Tribe of the Senegambian Supply Zone and most likely knew Arabic. If this was true, then Mrs. Perkins was wrong about the source of the scar in the corner of her slave's right eye. It is more likely that Billy had the scar when he came from Africa.

The vast number of Virginia advertisements describe the slave's skills, "He knows a little of carpentry and the Cooper's business, and he took away some tools with him" and "He is very good working with wood."[814] Thomas Jefferson's "Sandy" "was a left-handed shoemaker

812 See Appendix A of Chapter Ten.

813 Virginia Gazette, September 14, 1769.

814 Richmond Whig and Advertiser, January 19, 1835.

and something of a horse jockey."[815] Later, in the same advertisement from September 24, 1769, Jefferson also tells us about Sandy:

> He is greatly addicted to drink, and when drunk is insolent and disorderly, in his conversation he swears much and his behavior is artful and knavish. He took with him a white horse, much scarred with traces, of which it is expected he will endeavor to dispose.[816]

Jefferson's Sandy stealing a horse is consistent with the fact that when slaves stole horses, it was almost always by men. Female slaves rarely absconded with horses in Virginia. Women slaves in the commonwealth were more likely to steal items of clothing owned by their mistress, or they absconded with money that belonged to their owners.

The possessors of some skills were more likely to run away than others. One category of skilled slave that had a real chance of succeeding at an escape was watermen. The rivers, creeks and inlets of the Chesapeake Bay region made their skills particularly valuable. Africans employed as skippers, sailors and boatmen greatly increased after the mid-eighteenth century, as well.

Slaves who worked on their master's boats or were hired out to ships' captains were accustomed to being away from home and from direct supervision for long periods. This gave these sailors a kind of freedom not possessed by the average field hand. Sailors, ferrymen, boat builders, and other mariners appear in a significant number of the runaway slave ads in both Virginia and Maryland, as well as the District of Columbia. The role of the mariner in the early colonies was a crucial one, and it often was the job from which early Virginia servants and slaves absconded.

Cambridge, for example, ran away in early 1768, assisted his master, John Holladay, the customs inspector on the Rappahannock River at Fredericksburg, Virginia.[817] It was much easier for boatmen in early Virginia to escape their masters than any other occupation, in both Virginia and Maryland, for they often absconded when the master was

815 Ibid.

816 Ibid.

817 Ibid.

away from the boat.

A ferryman named Cuff, for another good example, was owned by Humberston Skipwith, and who ran away from his Elm Hill estate on April 26, 1753. Skipwith says of Cuff:

> He worked as a ferryman for me. He is a low, chunky fellow, very black and unusually polite. He may pass as a free man using another man's papers. $20.00 reward, in state and $40.00, out of state.[818]

The Elm Hill Estate is near Bakersville, Virginia, in Mecklenburg County. The plantation house, built in 1800, is noted for its massive stone chimneys. The property also originally had two smokehouses to cure meats to feed both the owner's family and the slaves.

Among some West African tribes, the name "Cuff" or "Cuffee" was often given for boys born on Friday. The name "Mingo" in West African is often given to male babies born on Sunday, from the Spanish and Portuguese "Domingo," which means Sunday. The name "Sambo" in many West African societies, such as Senegal and Gambia, as well as the Ivory Coast and Ghana, was reserved for the "Second Son."

The name Sambo is actually a derivative of Samba, which is usually a male name in West Africa. In America, of course, the name Sambo became a derogatory term to signify the laziness, lethargy and stupidity of a slave, but back in Africa, it was not seen that way.

At least five of our suspected Virginia Muslim runaway slaves are identified with the Dismal Swamp and the Moslem communities of Maroons who lived there. We already have described one of the five, a man named Osman, in the first chapter of this study, under the section on prominent Virginian Muslim slaves.

As we have seen in Chapter One, Captain Osman was the highest-ranking African American officer in the Union Army before the American Civil War. He may well have been a leader of the Maroons in the Dismal Swamp, as well, in the mid-nineteenth century.

A second Muslim slave identified with the Dismal Swamp community was a man named Jean Saint Malo, who was a leader of the Maroon community in the swamp. Malo died on June 19, 1784. He

818 See Note 805.

was a leader of the Maroons several decades before Captain Osman.[819] Osman may well have come from Portuguese East Africa or Angola, for he had a Portuguese name, as did Saint Malo.

The third Moslem runaway associated with the Dismal Swamp was an unnamed slave of James Buchanan, for he advertised in the *Virginia Gazette* on December 13, 1770. About this anonymous slave and his two companions, Mr. Buchanan tells us:

> Three negroes imported from Africa on the ship, *Yanimarew.* One is five foot six, twenty-eight years old, with a very dark complexion. He cannot yet speak English to be understood. He may be lurking near the Swamp.[820]

The *Yarimarew,* a British ship, brought slaves from Africa to Bermuda and then on to the Chesapeake Bay region in the 1770s. The auction in question was conducted on September 6, 1770, and included two hundred and forty slaves. The British captain of the *Yarimarew* was Thomas Atkinson. He worked for the Virginia slave-trading firm of Carter and Trent of Albemarle County. More is said about Virginia ship manifests in the appendix attached to Chapter Six, as well as a similar appendix at the end of this study.

In fact, Thomas Jefferson over the years did some business with the Carter and Trent firm. Charles Carter, the son of William Carter, exchanged several letters with Thomas Jefferson. In October of 1783, the president bought three horses from Carter. In subsequent exchanges in 1789, and then again in 1794, Jefferson bought slaves from the firm. The "Trent" of this firm is John L. Trent. The "Carter" is Charles Carter mentioned earlier.

President George Washington purchased a slave named Henry

---

819 Ibid. John Holliday was a Virginia pioneer and ship captain. He was the first man to build a log cabin in the colony at Hamon Creek.

820 Virginia Gazette, April 21, 1768. Humbertson Skipwith (1791–1863) owned a tobacco farm and a ferry service in the 1750s. His son, Fulwar Skipwith (1836–1900), inherited the farm, but the ferry business went out of business. The Rappahannock River, which flows through Fredericksburg, is a two-hundred-mile-long river in eastern Virginia. It flows from the Blue Ridge Mountains in the west to the Piermont Region and the Chesapeake Bay. George Washington often attended church in Fredericksburg.

Washington in 1763. He was purchased specifically to work on a project organized by the president whose purpose was primarily to drain the Dismal Swamp.[821] Henry was African born and came from Eboe Land. "Eboe Land," of course, is "Igbo Land," one of the largest tribes in the Niger Valley Supply Zone, or the Bight of Benin Supply Zone, as outlined in Chapter Two. Henry may very well have been a member of the Islamic Faith, as many people were at the time in the North Niger Valley Supply Zone.

The fourth Muslim slave identified with the Dismal Swamp of Virginia and North Carolina was a man named Mingo Pocosin, who, for a while close to the Civil War, was also the leader of the Dismal Swamp Maroons. Many of these slaves associated with the Dismal Swamp also were identified with black magic and supernatural activity, like Grace Sherwood (1660–1740), who was charged with bewitching a neighbor's crop.

Grace Sherwood was tried twice, in 1698, and again in 1706. She was found guilty the second time and released after serving eight years in prison in 1714 in Prince Anne County, Virginia. She was also known as the "Witch of Pungo," a tribe in the Windward Coast Supply Zone, where there were a significant number of Muslims in the eighteenth century.[822]

Finally, in September of 1863, a Union soldier only identified as "G" wrote to his college mentor at Oberlin, Ohio. G's job was to interview Maroons in the swamp. He interviewed a man named Ibrahim, or Abraham Lester, and his wife, Larinda, on Cranny Island, near Norfolk. The two told G that they were born in Africa, where they were married. They had a Muslim wedding and had lived in the swamp for three years, perhaps as part of a Muslim Maroon community there.[823]

821 Ibid., April 26, 1753. The Skipworth Family Papers reside at the College of William and Mary Library. The Elm Hill Estate is located in Bakersville, Mecklenburg County, Virginia. The house was built around 1800. It was placed on the National Registry of Historical Places, in 1979.

822 Ibid., December 13, 1770. The Great Dismal Swamp Maroons were freed and escaped slaves, some of whom were Muslims, who resided in the marshlands of the Great Dismal Swamp. More has been said about the Dismal Swamp throughout this study.

823 Ibid., April 27, 1763. John Carter and John L. Trent were in the

Indeed, paintings of the Maroons in the Dismal Swamp by David Edward Cronin, completed in 1888, like *Fugitive Slaves in the Dismal Swamp*, show black Maroon men wearing what appears to be African Muslim headdress.[824]

Other skilled slaves who were valued include domestic servants who lived cheek by jowl in intimacy with their masters. These domestic servants comprised the highest percentage of skilled runaways, and the advertisements for them frequently suggest "they could pass for free."

Many of the domestic runaways were women. A slave named Nanny, for example, the property of the recently deceased John Thompson of Albemarle County, took the opportunity presented by her master's death and so absconded in the summer of 1766.[825] Nanny's master also indicated that she had a scar "on her left hand," suggesting she may have been a member of the Igbo Tribe of the Northern Niger Valley Supply Zone, or the Wolof Tribe of the Senegambian Zone. Both of these tribes had a significant number of Muslims by the early eighteenth century, and both marked the left hands of their women.

Another painting of the Dismal Swamp was by a Virginia artist Thomas Moran in 1862. The painting is entitled *Slave Hunt in the Great Dismal Swamp* and is 86.4 by 111.8 cms. This artwork is discussed at the end of this eighth chapter.

Suspected runaways in Virginia who wished to pass as free persons needed a paper testimony from a white adult to validate the claim. In July of 1773, Thomas Hill was captured on the Isle of Wight in Virginia under suspicion of being a runaway, though he claimed to be free. Jailer John Taylor announced that if Hill were free, "It would be

---

slave-trading business in Albemarle County at the turn of the nineteenth century. Henry Washington (1740–1801) was a one-time slave of George Washington. Later, he joined Governor Lord Dunmore's Ethiopian Regiment of freed blacks.

824 Grace Sherwood (1660–1740), farmer, healer and mid-wife, was accused by her neighbor that she had transformed herself into a cat, destroyed the neighbor's crops, and killed some of his livestock. Sherwood is the last known person to be convicted of witchcraft in Virginia. Thomas Atkinson (1735–1800) was a warrant officer in the Royal Navy. Later, he commanded ships for the Royal Africa Company.

825 Ibid.

proper for a Friend of his to make the claim appear true."[826] He meant, of course, a white friend.

The Isle of Wight County, Virginia, is named after the Isle of Wight in the English Channel. In Virginia, the county is in the Virginia Beach-Norfolk area of the state. The county has two incorporated towns, Smithfield and Windsor. The original courthouse was built in 1800 in Smithfield, where slave auctions took place from the beginning.

The courthouse in Smithfield, Virginia, was replaced in 1850. By then, slave auctions were being conducted at the Smithfield Inn. This, of course, is consistent with the first two phases of the History of Slave Auctions discussed in Chapter Seven of this study, where slave auctions in Virginia moved from county courthouses to taverns and inns in the very early nineteenth century.

One of the strongest sources for achieving egalitarian status among Virginians of all colors was the Great Awakening. Evangelical religion provided some support for some standing against the landed gentry. Prior to the revolution, the Great Awakening preachers had challenged the landed elite and the New Light Baptist and Methodist preachers, often laypersons and people without the education of the established Anglican clergy.

Religion in this First Great Awakening eschewed ritual and ceremony in favor of personal religious experience. It made Christianity an intensely personal religion and fostered a deep sense of spiritual conviction and redemption and encouraged introspection and a new standard of personal morality. It also valued being "born again," as was Nicodemus' narrative in the Gospel of John.

Unlike the Second Great Awakening, which occurred around 1800

826 Soldier G, Union Soldier, Cranny Island, near Norfolk. Cranny, or Craney Island is a land mass in the city of Portsmouth in the South Hampton Roads region of eastern Virginia. Prince Anne County is an independent entity of the independent city of Virginia Beach. The Pungo Tribe of Angola, also called the Pungo Ndongo, was an African tribe begun by its leader Pungo Andongo who died in 1626 during an epidemic. Today, there is a rural community in the southern part of the city of Virginia Beach known as Pungo. It is likely the founders of that community most likely were from the Angolan Supply Zone and Muslim.

and reached out to the unchurched, the First Great Awakening focused on people who already were church members. One way that the First Great Awakening had a profound effect on the black population is that it was the impetus for many African Americans to turn to the Baptist faith from the mid-eighteenth century on.

The Great Awakening, or the New Light Religion as it was called, emphasized the spiritual equality of blacks and whites. This seemed to provide a measure of freedom for Virginia's slaves. In 1772, the House of Burgesses Committee on Religion, chaired by the provincial treasurer, Robert Carter Nicholas, who himself was plagued by runaway slaves on his farm in Hanover County, drafted a bill prohibiting slaves from attending Baptist worship meetings, without the permission of their masters.

The same proposed bill would also outlaw night meetings of these sects.[827] Robert Carter Nicholas (1728–1780), the son of Dr. George Nicholas and Elizabeth Carter Burwell of Williamsburg, was one of the leading conservative patriots in Virginia and served as a member of the House of Burgesses, in the mid to late eighteenth century, as well as a number of other political offices in that state.

Another planter, Landon Carter (1710–1778), attributed the restiveness of Virginia slaves to the effects of Baptist preachers. Carter wrote, "I believe it is from these inculcated doctrine of those rascals."[828] Landon Carter was best known for his observations on Virginia life leading up to the revolution in his book *The Diary of Colonel Landon Carter.*[829] The persistent complaint about negro Baptists in the eighteenth century tells us much about the deep and sometimes ecstatic religious experiences of the slaves, which were in sharp contrast to the calm and staid Anglican worshippers of the white planters. Apparently, the ecstatic religious experiences of the slave Baptists worried their white farm owners. They were concerned the New light Religion

827 David Edward Cronin, Fugitive Slaves in the Dismal Swamp, 1888. Cronin (1839–1925), also known as Seth Eyland, was an American painter, illustrator and journalist.

828 Virginia Gazette, June 24, 1766. Also see J. Brent Morris, "Life in the Swamp," New York Times, October 19, 2013.

829 Ibid., July 8, 1773. John Taylor was the sheriff on the Isle of Wight in the 1770s. Thomas Moran, Slave Hunt in the Dismal Swamp.

would be an impetus for slave rebellions in Virginia.

Accusations also went the other way as well. The Rev. Thomas Turpin (1708–1790), a prominent white Virginia Baptist minister, who also worked along the Georgia coast, complained bitterly that slaves under his charge often secretly organized Roman Catholic societies, sometimes conducting their own services.[830] The Rev. Turpin's complaint was part of a larger anti-Catholicism movement in the Virginia and Georgia colonies, going all the way back to 1642 when Virginia enacted a statute prohibiting Roman Catholic settlers in the colony. Five years later, a similar ban was enacted in the Massachusetts Bay Colony.

Virginia and Georgia planters did not respond positively to this practice. As a result, many runaway slaves of the Deep South, in the seventeenth and eighteenth centuries, sought asylum among the Spanish in Florida where Catholics predominated. The insistence shown by these escaped Catholic slaves mirrored that shown by the successive waves of runaway slaves in the seventeenth and eighteenth centuries.

Thomas Turpin was a prominent figure in the First Great Awakening. He also was Thomas Jefferson's uncle by marriage. A few letters between the two are extant. Turpin was very concerned that Catholic slaves from elsewhere were causing havoc in the colony of Virginia. In two of his correspondence to Mr. Jefferson, Mr. Turpin complained about the growing Baptist faith throughout Virginia.

Landon Carter, mentioned above, also quotes from an anonymous letter called, "An Address to the Anabaptists Imprisoned in Caroline County, August 8, 1771." The article accused the Baptists of breaking up families and the causing of slaves to desert their masters.[831] In sever-

830 Virginia Law to Forbade Baptist Practice by Slaves (March 26, 1772). The bill was prompted when the sheriff of Culpepper County was ordered by the city council to arrest a slave who was a Baptist. Thomas Moran, Slave Hunt in the Great Dismal Swamp, 1862, oil on canvas, Philbrook Museum of Art, Tulsa, Oklahoma. Thomas Moran (1837–1926) was an American engraver, etcher, illustrator and printmaker of the Hudson Valley School.

831 Landon Carter (1710–1778) discussed in "Runaway Revolution in 18th Century Virginia," www.slaverebellion.org. Carter was, perhaps, the most prolific Virginia writer of his generation. He also served in the House of Burgesses from 1752 until 1768.

al of the Virginia runaway advertisements, the Evangelical movement that swept through Virginia, beginning in the 1750s, is prominently mentioned. Hannah, for example, a slave owned by Stephen Dence, "pretends much to the religion the negroes of late have practiced," a sure reference to the Great Awakening in the commonwealth, and to the black southern Baptists.[832]

The First Great Awakening accelerated the acculturation of enslaved Africans in Virginia, particularly to Baptist Christianity. The Baptist revival began in the 1720s, followed a few decades later by the Methodists. With religious conversion also came education for the enslaved, at least instruction for reading the Bible. By 1771, itinerant African American Baptist preachers were conducting services, sometimes secretly, around Williamsburg and other urban areas, such as Richmond, Alexandria, Blacksburg, Petersburg, and Abingdon, to name a few.

Aside from the few names of Virginia runaways described as fond of preaching or the singing of hymns, many of these Baptist preachers remained anonymous. The few names in the historical record were men of uncommon accomplishments in the organizing of Baptist churches, the establishment of church schools and mutual aid societies that began to spring up in the south in the late eighteenth century.

Baptist churches in the second half of the eighteenth century in Virginia were organized into regional associations. By the year 1810, they existed as follows:

Accomack	Meherrin
Albermarle	Middle District
Appomatox	New River
Culpepper	Portsmouth
Dover	Red Stone
Gochin	Roanoke

832 Landon Carter, The Diary of Landon Carter, also known as Living Awake (New York: Create Space, 2013). Robert Carter Nicholas (1728–1780), Virginia attorney and political figure, served in the US Senate. The Smithfield Inn still stands at 112 Main Street, Smithfield, Virginia. Slave auctions took place there in the beginning of the nineteenth century.

Greenbrier Strawberry

Holston Union

Ketochin[833]

Many of these preachers were born into slavery in Virginia. Nearly all of them were Baptists, at least until the mid-eighteenth century. One representative example is George Liele, born in 1737. He was the first African American ordained in the Baptist Church and preached to both whites and blacks on the indigo and rice plantations along the Savannah River in Georgia. He was freed during the Revolutionary War by the will of his owner, a man named Joshua Sharpe.

Mr. Liele was forced to flee America with the British to Jamaica to escape re- enslavement. Before he departed, he baptized a number of African American converts who would continue to work as missionaries in Virginia and Georgia, and beyond.[834] Many of his followers went on to open their own Baptist churches and congregations.

One of these baptisms mentions a woman named Hagar who accompanied a man named Andrew. The baptisms were described this way:

> Our brother Andrew was one of the black hearers of George Liele. Prior to his departure for Jamaica, he came up the Tybee River and baptized our brother Andrew, with a wench named Hagar, both belonging to Jonathan Bryan, Esq. These were the last performances of our brother George Liele in this quarter. About eight or nine months after his departure, Andrew began to exhort his black hearers, with a few whites mixed in.[835]

The figure of Hagar, or *Hajar* in Arabic, is the concubine of Ibrahim (Abraham), and the mother of Ismail, or Ishmael. She and her son, in the Islamic tradition, are the progenitors of the Muslim faith,

833 Thomas Turpin (1708–1790) married Mary Jefferson on April 5, 1732. They had eleven children.

834 Landon Carter, "An Address to the Anabaptists Imprisoned in Caroline County," August 8, 1771.

835 Virginia Gazette, March 26, 1767.

as expressed in Al-Qur'an in the following verses: 2:136, 3:84, 4:163, 6:84–86, 21:85, and 38:48.

Jonathan Bryan, the attorney who owned Andrew, tells us that his preacher-slave preached to both black slaves and white people. This appears to have been true of many of the black slaves who were made Baptist preachers by George Liele and others in the eighteenth century.

George Liele also baptized David George and Jesse Galphin, two Virginia runaways. These two men formed the nucleus of slaves who were organized by a white preacher as the Silver Bluff Baptist Church between 1773 and 1775. Later, David George would flee with the British to Nova Scotia, where he established a second Baptist church in that province, on his own.[836] This indicates that not all of Liele's Baptist preachers were black in the eighteenth century.

The abolitionist movement in Britain also affected slaves in Virginia. Indeed, in the years leading up to the American Revolution, several Virginia runaways based their claims to freedom on events that occurred in Britain. Some even going so far as to sue in court for their liberty on these grounds.

Aaron, the slave of Henry Randolph of Chesterfield County, for example, sued in general court under the name Aaron Griffin. Even after the case was decided against the slave, the first thing he did when he returned to Mr. Randolph's farm was to run away.[837]

Indeed, a significant number of Virginia slaves began to sue their owners in court, many because they claimed their indentured period has lapsed, and so now they were free. These court cases were not always decided on the side of the masters. Those who could establish their status as an indentured servant usually won their case. Indentured servants first took their masters to court in Virginia in the late eighteenth century.

The outbreak of the Revolutionary War also offered opportunities

836 John W. Davis, "George Liele and Andrew Bryan, Pioneer Negro Baptists," in Journal of Negro History 3, no. 2, (1918), pp. 119–127. Davis (1873–1955) was an American politician, diplomat, attorney, and writer. He served in the U.S. House of Representatives from 1911 to 1913.

837 Beth Barton Schweiger, The Gospel Working: Progress and Pulpit in Nineteenth-Century Virginia (New York: Oxford University Press, 2000), pp. 29–30.

for slaves to escape bondage by enlisting on either side of the conflict. Benjamin Harwood, the son of a white man, escaped his master near Williamsburg and lit out for the west. Other Virginia slaves actively fought for the British. Bands of runaway slaves joined Tory marauders that operated in the Lower Tidewater and the Eastern Shore of Virginia.

In fact, the Colonial Army and Militia were troubled by desertions throughout the early years of the war, especially during the summer of 1776. There were a great number of runaway advertisements for these deserters in the pages of the *Virginia Gazette*, as well as other Virginia publications. In July of 1776, for example, a deserter James Vaughn stole a horse and ran off from his regiment and encamped on Gwynns Island.[838]

This is consistent, of course, with the phenomenon that only men slaves absconded with their masters' horses. Gwynns Island is in the northeast part of Mathews County, Virginia, just south of the mouth of the Piankatank River, where it empties into the Chesapeake Bay.

The British Army also offered incentives for those who would come over to the "British cause." One of those incentives, of course, was a promise of freedom for slaves. In 1781, for example, the HMS *Savage* blockaded the Chesapeake Bay near Washington's Mount Vernon estate. Several of George Washington's slaves escaped on the British Sloop-of-War, including Sambo Anderson, Washington's slave discussed in the section on prominent Virginia slaves in the first chapter of this study.

With a more favorable environment after the revolution, more and more black slaves sought their independence. Many slaves after the war, were reluctant to return to bondage. Nevertheless, the number of Virginia runaway slave advertisements increased dramatically after the war and continued to increase up until the Civil War period, when slavery was abolished in the Virginia commonwealth.

Virginia planters found runaway slaves to be far more manageable than runaway servants. Because their condition eventually came

838 Davis., p. 121. The Silver Bluff Baptist Church, founded in 1750, was the first black Baptist church in Aiken County, South Carolina. The city of Aiken, as well as Aiken County, South Carolina, was named after William Aiken, the president of the South Carolina Railroad. The county is twenty miles northeast of Augusta.

to be defined by their color, slaves were more easily identified and thus captured. For this reason, the law no longer found it necessary to threaten with branding or to enjoin offenders to keep their hair cropped very short. Slaves were also less likely to find allies outside their masters' properties.

Although these Virginia runaway slave advertisements provide a wealth of information, it is imperative to remember that all the information about the runaways came from the perspective of their owners, the planters and farm owners of the slaves. Nothing in these advertisements suggest the point of view of the captives, or runaways, in question, nor where they thought they were going, nor why.

If and when these runaway slaves were found, every town and city in the south had jails in which they could hold slaves until their owners or their agents could arrive to redeem or reclaim their property. Some of these were county jails, while others were the jails and prisons built by the major slave traders in Alexandria and Richmond, for example. Much has been said about these slave jails in Chapters Five and Six of this study.

Servants and slaves ran away from their Virginia masters for many reasons. Some fled physical or emotional abuse. Some did it to take a break from hard labor. Some left to search for absent family members. During the summer of 1640, for example, a servant boy named Thomas Wood died, and a subsequent investigation revealed that he had been beaten repeatedly by his owner Peter Walker and Walker's hired hand, Samuel Lucas.

As a result, Wood ran away several times, but each time he was caught and returned to Walker's farm, whereupon Wood would only escape again.[839] The evidence presented at trial suggests that both Walker and Mr. Lucas treated their slaves in the harshest of manners, and may

839 Ibid., p. 127. The Randolph Family were Virginia tobacco farmers beginning with Henry Randolph (1688–1726). The Henry Randolph mentioned here is Henry Randolph III (1721–1771) of Chesterfield County. The Tybee River in Georgia is on the coast near Tybee Island. Jonathan Bryan (1708–1788) was born in South Carolina and owned a farm in Chatam County there. The Tybee River connects the Savannah River to the Atlantic Ocean. Chatham County was founded in 1777 on the Atlantic coast in southeast Georgia. The city of Savannah is in Chatham County.

have beaten Wood to near death.

Witnesses at the inquest suggested that Wood's treatment was typical for a boy of his age. The court agreed with Walker's claim that his servant had died of disease. His corpse, the court ruled, appeared just as "anie man might be dyeing of the Scurvey beinge much swelled."[840]

Late in 1654, slave John Casor fled the service of Anthony Johnson, discussed in the opening chapter of this study, and went instead to work for Johnson's neighbor, a man named Robert Parker. Once away from Johnson, Casor claimed that his former master had beat him continually and held him as a slave when he was, in fact, an indentured servant. On March 8, 1655, the Northampton County Court ruled in favor of Johnson, who himself was a freed African slave, and most likely was a Portuguese Muslim man from Mozambique.

It is significant that at the time the race of Johnson did not matter as much as the fact that he was a taxpayer and a law-abiding landowner. The court ruled that Parker "most unjustly kept" Casor and ordered the slave to return to the Johnson farm. In fact, Parker was also to pay Johnson's court costs.[841] Anthony Johnson, a.k.a., Antonio, from the Angolan Supply Zone, of course, was introduced and discussed back in Chapter One.

One other factor that may have greatly affected the number of Virginia runaway slaves is what has come to be called the "Bacon's Rebellion" of 1676. In that year, Nathaniel Bacon led a slave rebellion against the colonial government. His followers included a large number of dissatisfied servants and slaves, both black and white. The rebellion was an impetus for many runaway servants and slaves. It lasted for eighteen months, ending in early 1677.[842]

One effect that the Bacon Rebellion had on servitude in Virginia is

---

840 Ibid.

841 Henry Randolph V. Aaron Griffin. This case is discussed in Historical Scene Investigations. Also see Virginia Gazette, April 28, 1768. Robert Skipworth in the July 10, 1778, Virginia Gazette advertised for the return of "Pompey," alias Benjamin Harwood. He was fifteen years old and ran away with a sorrel horse.

842 Ibid., July 8, 1776. The Silver Bluff Baptist Church was originally founded in 1750 on Beach Island, South Carolina, by African American freed slaves.

that it marked the decline of white indentured servants in the colony, as well as the transition to the slave labor culture. Before then, the problem of runaway servants in the Maryland and Virginia colonies had been a problem going all the way back to the mid-seventeenth century.

By 1736, when the *Virginia Gazette* began its publication, there were nearly as many runaway servant advertisements as there were of slaves. These ads provided similar materials that the slave ads did: name, country of origin, physical characteristics, particular skills, and information about their personalities. There were so many runaway servants ads that the Virginia legislature, in March of 1643, passed a law forbidding the absconding of servants, but many did not heed the statute. In October of 1669, another law affirming the 1643 Virginia law was passed.

The runaway Virginia servant advertisements frequently mention that servants absconded with the same items belonging to their masters, as the runaway slave ads did. Women servants stole money and the mistress's clothing, while male servants absconded with horses, boats, firearms and cash belonging to their owners.

A typical runaway servant advertisement of the colony/state of Virginia looked like this:

> Ran away from the Subscriber, living in Benedict, on the 2nd of February last, an Irish Servant Man named Patrick Smith. About five foot four inches high and pretty thick set. He had on when he went away a Black Everlasting Waistcoat and a white jacket with metal buttons. Whoever shall secure said Patrick Smith or convey him to said Subscriber, shall receive Ten Shillings reward besides what the Law allows.[843]

This typical runaway Virginia servant advertisement gives the servant's name, clothing, place of origin, place of his absconding, physical characteristics, and the reward to be paid out for his recovery, in British

843 The case is discussed in an article called "Runaway Slaves and Servants in Colonial Virginia," published in the Encyclopedia of Virginia. James Vaughn, born in 1740, was a native of South Carolina. Later, he was a slave in Prince George, Virginia, where he worked as a shoemaker.

currency. It does not indicate Mr. Smith's age, though the runaway servant ads usually do. Thus, the advertisements for servants, as we can see, are significantly like those of runaway slave advertisements in Virginia.

The Virginia law "For the Prevention of Insurrections," pertained to servants, as much as to slaves. The Virginia Act Concerning Slaves and Servants, passed in 1705, also speaks as much about runaway servants as it does runaway slaves in the commonwealth. Nevertheless, not long after the Bacon Rebellion, the number of white indentured servants began to decline, while the number of enslaved Africans greatly began to increase. At the same time, Virginia began to pass legislation that instituted much more rigid distinctions between white and non-white, free and slave.

As the tobacco crops in the Chesapeake Bay region began to wane in the early eighteenth century, the number of white European indentured servants began to decrease, as well. At the same time, the number of African slaves began to increase. With a surplus of slaves after the beginning of the nineteenth century, the major Chesapeake slave traders began shipping captives south to the Deep South, as we have shown earlier in this study.

One interesting fact about the Bacon Rebellion is that the English-born Nathaniel Bacon (1647–1676) was a member of the "Governor's Council," and was one of the wealthiest men in the colony, but died of fever during his own rebellion.[844] Nonetheless, he fought vociferously for the civil rights of slaves.

Among the Virginia counties that had or harbored our suspected Muslim runaway slaves were: Fairfax, Henrico, Albemarle, Chesterfield, Page, Orange, Prince William, Lancaster, Accomack, Amelia, Appomattox, Lee, Rappahannock, Campbell, Culpepper, Fauquier, York, Westmoreland, Franklin, Roanoke, Frederick, Montgomery, Charles City, Northampton, the Isle of Wight, Mathews, and Arlington.

844 Ibid. John Casor of Northampton County on March 8, 1755, became the first man of African descent in the British thirteen colonies to be declared a slave. For more on the Thomas Wood case, see Tom Costa, "Runaway Slaves and Servants in Colonial Virginia," Encyclopedia Virginia. The HMS Savage was a sixteen-gun sloop of the Seagull Class of the British Royal Navy. The ship was launched in July of 1805 and served during the Napoleanic Wars.

This brings us to an analysis of fifty-one suspected Muslim runaway slaves in early Virginia, the topic of the next, and central section of this eighth chapter.

Suspected Muslim Slaves in Early Virginia

Among the 3,300 advertisements for Virginia runaway slaves, we have discovered fifty-one fugitives who are suspected of being Muslims. Forty-one of these are men, and ten are women. Of the fifty-one, fourteen have tribal scars that may help us to identify the runaways. Thirty-eight of the fifty-one have Islamic or Arabic names. These fugitive ads come from twenty-five different counties in the state mentioned above, and they may be found, as we indicated earlier, in twenty-four different local and national newspapers and publications in the colony/state.

Of the suspected Virginia Muslim runaways, three were from the seventeenth century, six from the first fifty years of the eighteenth century, thirty-one from the second half of the eighteenth century, and eleven from the nineteenth century. Thus, the heaviest period of runaway slaves in Virginia was in the second half of the eighteenth century.

The earliest Virginia Muslim advertisement is from 1649, a slave named Mingo. The most recent Muslim runaway was Jibril, or Gabriel, who ran away from the farm of Mosby Sheppard at Meadows Farm in Henrico County on July 2, 1864. Among these suspected Virginia Moslem runaways, there are ten Sambo, six Mingo, two Hagar, two Job or Ayyub, two Fatima, two Ali, two George or *Jorge*, and two Jem or Jemima.

As in our analysis of the Maryland materials, five different variables have been employed to identify these early Virginia Muslim slaves. The first of these is that they were born in Africa and now speak very little English. The second variable is the many tribal scars that can help to identify the runaways. We have identified fourteen runaway slaves in Virginia that may be identified solely by their clan, tribal or country marks back in Africa.

Geographical and biographical hints supplied by the masters of these fugitives is a third variable. They may say, "He is from the Guiney Country," "He is of the Mandingo Tribe," "He claims to be from the Ibo Country," or "He claims to be a Byte Negro." This latter slave is an indication that he was from the Bight of Benin Supply Zone of West Africa discussed in Chapter Two of this study.

The ability to speak or understand languages other than English is a fourth variable. Arabic predominated in the Senegambian Zone in the eighteenth and nineteenth centuries. Dutch was the language of the Sierra Leone Zone and some of the Windward Coast, and French was spoken in the Gold and Windward Coasts, as well as Abreda in the Senegambian Supply Zone.

And finally, Moslem and Arabic names also aid in identifying some of these fugitives as Muslim runaways. These languages, as outlined in the runaway slave advertisements, include French, Dutch, Portuguese, and Arabic, as we mentioned above. In our analysis, we only maintain that a particular slave is a member of the Islamic faith if he or she seems to possess at least three of the five variables listed above.

Several of the suspected Muslim slaves may be identified by their tribal marks. One negro man, for example, from Gambia named Jack is described this way:

> Jack, six feet high, very Black with a scar over his right eyebrow and three small strokes on either side of his face that look like this "I".[845]

This slave, Jack, was owned by Margaret Arbuthnott who advertised for his return in the *Virginia Gazette*, on October 10, 1745. The ad for Jack also indicates he was "imported from Gambia." The tribal marks suggest Jack was either a Mandinka (40 percent of the population) or a Fula (20 percent of Gambian population). Both the Mandinka and the Fula tribes were/are 90 percent Muslim in Gambia.[846] The three parallel, vertical marks beneath each eye suggest Jack was a Mandinka.

Another slave named Sambo, whose return was advertised by Purdie and Dixon, in the *Virginia Gazette* on November 2, 1769. Sambo was "Born in Africa and accompanied by Aaron, and he was branded

---

845 Ibid.

846 Nathaniel Bacon (1647–1676). His rebellion still remains one of the most controversial events in early Virginia history. Dr. John Mosby Sheppard (1817–1877) was one of the seven generations of Sheppards that lived at Meadows Farm, Henrico County, Virginia.

on both cheeks."[847] The tribal marks suggest he was from Senegal, most likely a Wolof or a member of the Fula, or Fulbe Tribe. More than 90 percent of both of these tribes were Moslems, as well, at the time, by the late eighteenth century.

Another Sambo, who came to this country in June of 1768, is also described as a "Mandingo." His owners, Gibson and Granberry, advertised for his return in the *Virginia Gazette* on June 26, 1768. Sambo's owners tell us this about the slave:

> A Negroe fellow of the Mandinka Tribe. Five foot six and appears to be about twenty-five years old. He entered the Country on June 23, 1768 and ran away three days later. He cannot speak English very sufficiently.[848]

If this Sambo was indeed a Mandinka, then it is likely that he was from Gambia, where 40 percent of the population is from that tribe. Richard Booker, in the *Virginia Gazette*, sought the return of his slave, Bonaud, on December 24, 1772. Booker relates, "He speaks French and he came from a place by the same name, in Ibo Country. He is small in stature and pitted with the smallpox.[849]

It is likely that Bonaud is related to French explorer Pierre Bonnard who established a camp at Albreda on the north bank of the Gambia River. If this is true, then this slave is from the Senegambian Supply Zone, as well, and thus was probably a Muslim, and most likely spoke Arabic.

One final runaway slave in Virginia named Sambo was owned by Gabriel Jones near Richmond. This Sambo, who appears in the June 16, 1775, edition of the *Virginia Gazette*, is described as "being five foot

---

847 Ibid.

848 Ibid.

849 Virginia Gazette, October 10, 1745.

six, of a dark complexion, with country marks on his face."[850] The face marks described by Mr. Jones suggest Sambo was most likely from Senegal or Gambia, either a Wolof, a Mandinka or Fulbe, and thus also knew Arabic.

Another Muslim slave from the same supply zone is a negro named Stephen. His owner, Aaron Trueheart, advertised in the *Virginia Gazette* on May 15, 1746. Trueheart describes his runaway this way:

> A negro man named Stephen. A brisk, sensible lad, about sixteen years of age. He is very artful and cunning. He has several scars on his face. He went away on a grey horse.[851]

Mr. Trueheart also provides a drawing of the three parallel, horizontal strokes beneath both eyes. This suggests Stephen was either a Wolof, a Mandinka or a Fula of the Senegambian Zone, and thus most likely spoke Arabic, the language in that area by that time. Again, the stolen horse of Mr. Trueheart is consistent with the fact that the female slaves rarely absconded with horses in Virginia in the eighteenth and nineteenth centuries.

George Robertson, on September 12, 1771, advertised for the return of his slave, Step, in the *Virginia Gazette*. Mr. Robertson's advertisement reveals this about Step:

> He is about six feet high, has a number of tribal scars, and is missing some front teeth. He is supposed to be about twenty years old, he cannot speak good English, since he has only been in the Country a short time.[852]

Robertson tells us in a separate runaway slave advertisement that Step spoke the "language of the Mohametans," and was "from the land of Gambia," two sure-fire signs that he was a Muslim captive. Again, the nature of the tribal scars indicates he was probably a member of

850 Ibid., February 14, 1772.

851 Ibid., November 2, 1769. Alexander Purdie (1743–1779) and John Dixon (1729–1829) were partners in a slave-trading firm from 1766 until 1775. Mosby Sheppard (1775–1831) was from Henrico County, Virginia. His home, Meadow Farm, is now a living history museum site.

852 Ibid., June 26, 1768.

the Yoruba Tribe from Nigeria who also branded their warriors on both cheeks, and thus from the Niger Valley Supply Zone, or possibly the Bight of Benin Zone, as outlined in Chapter Two.

Step also may be a member of the Fulbe or Fula Tribe of Gambia, and associated with the French Fort at Albreda, on the Gambia River, where they spoke both Arabic and French in the seventeenth and eighteenth centuries. If this were true, then Mr. Robertson's Step was a member of the Islamic faith.

A female slave named Jem, or Jemima, ran away from Gilchrest and Taylor on August 12, 1773. Her owners tell us this about Jem:

> From the West Indies. Twenty-seven years old, five foot eight. A tattoo on her right hand. She may be headed toward North Carolina.[853]

At five foot eight inches, Gilchrest & Taylor's slave Jem was the tallest of the Virginia female runaway slaves. A number of African tribes give tattoos to the right hand of their women. Among these are the "Sabella" mark, given to the female members of the "26s" gang in South Africa; the Zulu Tribe, also of South Africa, a Bantu people, also feature right-handed tattoos on their women. In Tunisia, and through much of North Africa, women wear right-handed marks made from henna. It is unlikely that Jem could be identified with any of these groups because none of them are West African, from which most slaves came to the Americas.

The Zezedi in Iraq have been tattooing the left hand for centuries. There is also some evidence that the Kurds, as early as the second millennium, placed tattoos on the left hands of females. More recently, Islamic areas of Albania, the Vlach people, for example, also mark

853 Ibid., December 24, 1772. Robin Law, in her essay, "Ouidah: A Pre-Colonial Urban Center in Coastal West-Africa," argues that Bonaud was from Ouidah, in David Anderson and Richard Rathbone (eds.), Africa's Urban Past (New York: Oxford University Press, 2000), p. 88. Col. Richard Booker (1707–1760) and his brother, Marshall Booker, were tobacco farmers in Chesterfield County, Virginia. Purdie & Dixon Printers was begun by Alexander Purdie (1743–1779) and his partner, John Dixon. Later, in 1774, Dixon formed a separate partnership with William Hunter, the firm becoming Dixon & Hunter.

the right hands and wrists of their women. At any rate, it is likely that Jem had an Islamic background, so her geography remains unknown, but most likely, she was a Wolof who tattooed the right hands of their women.[854]

What to make of the right-handed tattoo on the hand of Taylor and Gilchrest's slave Jem is not entirely clear. But the evidence certainly suggests it may have had an Islamic origin, possibly from the East African Zone in Mozambique or Madagascar, both of whom have right-handed tattoos going back centuries.

Both the Makonde and the Dinembo Tribes gave their women right-handed tattoos in the eighteenth century. It may be, then, that Jem was from the East African Supply Zone and associated with Arab slave traders from Oman or possibly from Yemen. If this were true, then Jem would be from the East African Supply Zone discussed in Chapter Two and may have traveled by way of a land coffle from East Africa to West Africa.

Two other possibilities are that Jem was a member of the Fulani or Fulbe Tribe of the Senegambian Supply Zone. The Fulani scarred both the right hand and the right eye of their warriors, and occasionally their wives, as well. At any rate, there are several possibilities, then, for the origins of this slave named Jem, and the Senegambian Supply Zone seems most likely her origin, and, if true, spoke Arabic and was most likely a Muslim. The Wolof Warriors of the eighteenth century also were marked on the right hand, as were their women. This seems the best guess for Gilchrest & Taylor's Jem.

S. E. Dillard, on February 19, 1864, advertised for his runaway slave, Tom Binford. Dilliard, who lived near Richmond, tells us about his fugitive slave:

> He ran away near Richmond. He is thirty years old, and has a scar across his forehead. He was originally brought to Charles City County and desires to make his way back there.[855]

854 Ibid., June 16, 1775. Gabriel Jones (1724–1806) was a Welsh lawyer and tobacco farmer. The Mississippi House Journal of 1768 speaks of the partnership between Gibson and Granberry.

855 Ibid., May 15, 1746. Aaron Trueheart (1699–1767) was a tobacco

Most likely, Mr. Dillard's slave Tom Binford had relatives or friends in Charles City County, which is east of Richmond and west of Jamestown. The southern border of the county is the James River. The eastern border is the Chickahominy River.

Many African tribes tattoo the forehead, including the Dinka Tribe of South Sudan; the Magnit and Surma Tribes of Ethiopia; and the Fulani Tribe, who often mark a horizontal line across the entire forehead. It is quite likely that Tom Binford was a Fulani Muslim. The Fulani are called the "Red Men of Nigeria," because the one parallel, horizontal line is made from henna with red ink. The Fulani are one of the largest tribes of the Niger River Valley Supply Zone, along with the Yoruba, Igbo, Hausa and Ijaw. He also could be from the Bight of Benin.

Another female slave named Bewdley is described as having "Guiney marks on her forehead." Bewdley was a common female name in the Sierra Leone Supply Zone in the eighteenth century. Again, it is likely that Bewdley is both a Muslim and a member of the Fulani Tribe from Nigeria, or the Sierra Leone Supply Zone, as indicated earlier.[856] Another Sambo was a runaway slave of Thomas Williams. Mr. Williams advertised for Sambo in the *Virginia Gazette* from January 25, 1815. Williams reveals about Sambo:

> He is twenty-five years old, about five feet ten high. He has a scar under his right eye and another on his right hand. He was born in Africa.[857]

The scars under the right eye and on the right hand are both signs of a Fulani warrior, particularly at the end of the eighteenth century, and thus knew Arabic. Similarly, an escaped slave named Bacchus, who was owned by John Austin Finnie, ran away around September 30, 1773, according to that edition of the *Virginia Gazette*. Mr. Finnie relates about his slave:

---

grower in Hanover County, Virginia.

856 Ibid., September 12, 1771. The Zazedi are ethnic Kurds, an indigenous religion to northern Mesopotamia, but they are not a Zoroastrian religion. John Gabriel Jones (1724–1806) was a Welsh American attorney and farmer. He also served in the Virginia House of Delegates.

857 Ibid., August 12, 1773.

> He is about nineteen years old and speaks broken English. He is tattooed on his right hand. He was born in Africa and came here recently.[858]

Bacchus' name points to another trend among Virginia planters in the late eighteenth century—a tendency to name slaves after classical or mythological figures. This trend can be detected beginning around 1750 and continuing to about 1820.

The marks on the right hand of Bacchus again are a dead giveaway of the Nigerian Fulani Tribe or the Wolof Tribe of the Senegambian Supply Zone. Benjamin Harrison in the January 14, 1775, edition of the *Virginia Gazette*, wishes the return of his slave, Nick. Harrison says about this slave:

> By trade a wheelwright. He is twenty-five years old, about five foot five and has a tribal scar over one eye. He is born in Africa and is a Mulatto man.[859]

The tribal markings suggest Nick may well have been a member of the Yoruba Tribe in Nigeria, who also tattooed their warriors over the right eye. This would make him come from the Niger Valley Supply Zone or the Bight of Benin Zone. Beginning in the seventeenth century, a large number of Yoruban slaves were brought to America, and particularly to the Commonwealth of Virginia, with Tribal scars above their right eye.

Indeed, there were a significant number of both Yoruban and Igbo slaves who arrived in Virginia, beginning early on. In fact, one can still see the Yoruban influences in many parts of the Commonwealth of Virginia. A group called Lingualine, for example, provides language translation services for Yoruban speakers. The Alliance of Yoruba, a group established in Washington, DC, also provide similar services. A "Yoruban Depot" in Lorton, Virginia, offers a number of Yoruban products for sale, including: *Orisi*, African angel statues; *Shango*, images of the God of Thunder; and *Ifi* products, a Yoruban word that means

858 Ibid., February 19, 1864. Also see: Geneaological Abstracts in 18th Century Virginia Newspapers, p. 443.

859 Ibid., January 25, 1815. John Taylor and George Gilchrist were slave traders in Glenn Allen, Virginia, Henrico County.

"spiritual path."

Even the religion department of the University of Virginia, in Charlottesville, offers a course called Religion 4100 "Yoruban Religion."[860] These facts are confirmation that members of the Igbo and Yoruba Tribes have settled from its very earliest history of the Commonwealth of Virginia.

A runaway Virginia slave named George was the property of Thomas Wilson of Chesterfield County. A request for George's recovery was advertised in the January 14, 1773, edition of the *Virginia Gazette*. Wilson describes George as being "African-born, Five foot eight, with Country marks on his face."[861] The country marks that Wilson includes in an illustration suggest he was a Yoruban from the Niger Valley Supply Zone or the Bight of Benin Zone.

In terms of runaway slaves with probable Muslim names, we can point to several. In the October 20, 1791, edition of the *Virginia Gazette*, Richard Hildrith wishes for the recovery of his two female slaves. Their names are "Hagar, age 56 and Dinah, age 33." They most likely are mother and daughter.[862] The fact that both mother and daughter had Muslim names adds to the possibility that the family was Islamic back in Africa.

Another Virginia slave named Hagar was Hagar Jumper, who was the absconded slave of Stephen Davis on August 14, 1800. Davis described her as "A dark brown, Mulatto woman, with short bushy hair. She claims to be descended from the Indians," and thus may have been a Mustee.[863]

---

860 Ibid.

861 Ibid., September 30, 1773. John Austin Finnie bought six and a half acres of land in Prince George's County, Virginia, and became a tobacco farmer. Sallie E. Dilliard's (1801–1871) family farm was in Virginia Beach, Virginia, where her family is still in business there. She was the wife of William Osburn Dillard.

862 Ibid., January 14, 1775. The Dinka people inhabit the Bahr el Ghazel region of the Nile River Basin. The Magnit are a nomadic people of Kenya. The Surma exist in South Sudan and southwestern Ethiopia. In order of percentage of the population in Sierra Leone Zone, the major ethnic peoples are the Temne, Mende, Limba, Fula, Mandinka and Krio. Among these, the Fula and the Mandinga used one horizontal tribal scar across the forehead.

863 Ibid., January 14, 1773.

Two slaves at George Washington's Mount Vernon estate were named Fatima and Little Fatima. They were most likely mother and daughter. Fatima, of course, was the name of the Prophet Muhammad's favorite daughter.[864] Again, the fact that both mother and daughter had Muslim names suggest they were practitioners of Islam back in Africa and maybe even in America.

A runaway slave owned by Elizabeth L. Carter of Prince William County, Virginia, was named Musa, the Arabic name for Moses. Mrs. Carter says of her Musa:

> He ran away on June 10, 1838. He is thirty-five to forty years old, born in Africa, and he has a scar that goes completely across his forehead.[865]

From Mrs. Carter's description, Musa was likely African born and from the Senegambia Supply Zone and thus knew Arabic. He may well have been a member of the Fulani or Fulbe tribe. Mrs. Carter's advertisement for Musa appeared in the *National Intelligencer* from the June 10, 1838, issue of that paper. This makes Musa one of the most recent suspected Muslim runaway slaves in Virginia.

Another likely Muslim runaway was Jibril, the Arabic name for Gabriel. He was owned by Mosby Sheppard of Meadows Farm in Henrico County. Mr. Sheppard's advertisement for Jibril can be found in the July 2, 1864, issue of *Harpers Weekly*.[866] In the Islamic faith, the Angel *Jibril* is the most important of the *Mala'ika*, or Angels, for he was the figure that brought the revelations of the Holy Qur'an to the Prophet, or *Nabi*, Muhammad.

---

864 University of Virginia Course Catalogue, 2014–2015. John Austin Finnie owned a tobacco farm in Amelia County, Virginia.

865 Ibid., October 20, 1791. Hosea Richard Hildreth (1761–1835) was a tobacco farmer in Henrico County, Virginia, and a teacher of mathematics, as well as a Congregationalist minister. He was also the father of Richard Hildreth (1807–1865), historian, journalist and novelist.

866 Ibid., August 14, 1800. Mary V. Thompson has worked at Mount Vernon in various capacities since 1980. She is currently, since 2008, a research historian. Elizabeth Landon Carter (1765–1852) grew tobacco in Westmorland County. Lorton is a town in Fairfax County, Virginia. About 20,000 people reside there.

Two other Virginia runaways with Muslim names are Ephraim and Obidiah. The former was owned by Marshall Jett of Farrowsville near Markham, Virginia, on Route 688. Mr. Jett took out an advertisement in the *National Intelligencer* on May 30, 1837. He describes Ephraim as being "twenty-five years old with a scar over his right eye."[867]

The tribal mark of Mr. Jett's Ephraim suggests that he was a Fulani from the Senegambian Supply Zone, and therefore spoke Arabic, the language of the day in Senegambia, or he may have come from the northern part of the Niger Valley Supply Zone, among the Yorubans.

Obidiah, also called Diah, was the slave of John Wise of Accomack County. Obidiah absconded, according to the *Virginia Gazette*, around November 29, 1864, during the American Civil War.[868] The name Obidiah, in both Hebrew and Arabic, means a "Servant of God." Another Mingo, who was owned by Jacob Walker, was "a fifteen-year-old boy with a yellow complexion."

Mr. Walker took out his advertisement for Mingo in the *Virginia Gazette* from September 5, 1755.[869] This Mingo could have come from the Portuguese word *Domingo*, which means Sunday. He thus would have originated in the Angolan Supply Zone, or possibly from the East African Zone, in Mozambique or Madagascar, where both areas had a significant number of Muslims in the mid-eighteenth century. If this latter theory is true, then it is likely that this Mingo traveled by way of a land coffle from East Africa to Angola in West Africa. If this were true, he might well have been a Muslim, as well, for he traveled in an Arab coffle much like Matteus de Sousa and Antonio discussed in Chapter One.

At least four other Cuffee and four other Mingo are among the Virginia runaway slaves. In addition, there is one Quash who ran away from the farm of William Neffen, according to the *Virginia Gazette*,

867 Mary V. Thompson, "Islam at Mount Vernon," Digital Encyclopedia. In addition to having a tobacco farm on the Isle of Wight, Thomas Wilson also resided in the 2100 block of Warren Street in Petersburg, Virginia. The major ethnic group and language in the Republic of Biafra is the Igbo, followed by the Efik, Ijaw and Ibibio.

868 Ibid.

869 National Intelligencer, June 10, 1838. Also see Harpers Weekly, July 2, 1864. Hagar Jumper appears in an 1800 Census in Petersburg, Virginia.

on December 19, 1736.[870] The reward offered by Neffen for Quash's recovery was ten shillings. Quash, or Quashee, is a Muslim name given to boys born on Sunday in certain areas of the Niger Valley Supply Zone, or the Bight of Benin Zone. The female equivalent is the name Quasheba. Both names were fairly commonly used in these areas of Africa in the late eighteenth century. These names were employed regularly in the Niger Valley Supply Zone in the eighteenth century.

The other four runaway slaves in Virginia named Mingo also were featured in the pages of the *Virginia Gazette*. Miles Selkin's Mingo absconded on January 5, 1782. He was a "Forty years old, black fellow, African born."[871] The Mingo of Thomas Willis ran away on February 7, 1751.[872] Matthew Phripp's escaped slave named Mingo, who was thirty-five years old, absconded on May 12, 1774.[873]

The runaway slave named Mingo, who was owned by Jacob Walker in the mid-eighteenth century, is described as "African-born, about fifteen years old, with a yellow complexion." The *Virginia Gazette* from September 5, 1755, says that Mr. Walker offered a "pistole" for the return of capture on his Mingo.[874]

Another runaway slave named Mingo, who was owned by Arthur Allen, escaped from his two-thousand-acre estate on March 3, 1673. This Mingo was one of the earliest recorded suspected Virginia Muslim runaway slaves.[875] Another possible early Virginia runaway of the Islamic faith is James Stone's Mingo, who escaped from his farm in Chesterfield County in 1649. This seventeenth-century date makes Mr.

870 Ibid., November 29, 1864.

871 Virginia Gazette, November 28, 1864. Elizabeth L. Carter (1818–1900) owned a tobacco farm in Prince William County, Virginia.

872 Ibid., September 5, 1755. George Jacob Walker (1725–1779) was a tobacco farmer in Henrico County, Virginia. Harper's Weekly was an American journal of civilization and American political thought published by the Harper Brothers from 1857 until 1916.

873 Ibid., December 19, 1736. Marshall Jett owned a tobacco farm in Farrowsville in Fauquier County, Virginia.

874 Ibid., May 30, 1771. Major John Sargent Wise (1846–1913) was a Confederate Civil War hero and later tobacco farmer in Accomack County, Virginia.

875 Ibid., March 22, 1772.

Stone's runaway Mingo one of the earliest suspected Muslim runaway slaves in Virginia. Mingo's running away is recorded in Deed Book XI and dated 1679 to 1691.[876] Another female escaped Virginia slave is a woman named Ali. Her owner, John Thomas, tells us about her, in the January 21, 1790, edition of the *Virginia Gazette:*

> She is eighteen years old, African-born and not very black. She ran away on January 21, 1790.[877]

Job, or Ayyuba, was a Virginia runaway with a Muslim name. He escaped the farm of Grace Williams on May 13, 1785. Job was "about five feet seven and a yellow Mulatto."[878] Ayyub Diallo, discussed in Chapter One, is the other Muslim slave named Job in this study. Two other suspected Virginia Muslim runaways named Sambo were owned by Alex Marshall and William Hunter of Orange County.

Mr. Hunter's Sambo was "Born in Africa, thirty years old and has a small visage." The May 16, 1745, advertisement for the return of Mr. Hunter's Sambo offered a twenty shillings reward for the slave.[879] This is consistent with the rewards for the recovery of runaway slaves in very early Virginia, which were still expressed in British currency. It was only by 1800 that the rewards for absconded slaves were given in American money.

Alex Marshall, the Virginian owner of the other Sambo, advertised for his recovery in the *Virginia Gazette* from November 4, 1763. Mr. Marshall tells us, "He is about five foot seven, pretends to be a doctor, and has large buckles on his shoes."[880] Another Virginia runaway slave named Quash was owned by William Nelson who advertised for the slave in the December 10, 1736, edition of the *Virginia Gazette*. Mr. Nelson, who offered ten shillings reward, observes about Quash:

> He speaks good English and French. He has very small

---

876 Ibid., October 13, 1796.

877 Ibid., September 8, 1801. Miles Selkin's tobacco farm was near Williamsburg, Virginia, in the late eighteenth century.

878 Ibid., January 5, 1782.

879 Ibid., February 7, 1751.

880 Ibid., May 12, 1774.

eyes and has lost the big toe of his right foot.[881]

The speaking of French implies he was from the Gold or Windward Coast, or possibly from the French Community at Albreda, on the Gambia River. One final way of identifying Muslim slaves in early Virginia is the many slave holdings sketched out in legal documents from the period. On the farm of Joshua Reed at the end of the eighteenth century, for example, he outlined the number of slaves he owned. Among these slaves was one family with the last name of Aba, a word that means "Father" in Arabic, Hebrew, and other Semitic languages, like Aramaic and Syriac.

What is significant about the Aba family is that all eleven members have Muslim names. The mother and father were Bedley and Sambo Aba. They also had nine children, four sons and five daughters. The names of the boys were Peter, Tom, Ishaq or Isaac, Yaqub or Jacob. The names of the Aba daughters were Jenny or Jemmy, Agga, Rose, Lucy, and Esther.[882]

The Aba family was sold to Henry Featherstone, Jr. of Chesterfield County sometime in the 1770s. Featherstone began manumitting the Aba family members starting with Bedley and Sambo in 1788 and 1789, and then the nine children between 1790 and 1808 ending with Esther. Needless to say, it is probably no coincidence that all the members of the Aba family had Muslim names. It certainly implies that they were members of the Islamic faith. Mr. Featherstone's father, Henry Charles Featherstone (1681–1759), came to Virginia from England and became a tobacco farmer in Chesterfield County there.

Similarly, the papers of the estate of John Davis of Surry County lists a slave named Mingo who was manumitted on June 22, 1792.[883] The property known as Moss Neck in Caroline County included a slave named Cuffee in a list from 1776.[884] Moss Neck Manor of Caroline County, Virginia, was an Italian villa built in the mid-nineteenth century. A slave owned by William Gooch, in Norfolk County, named Mingo

881 Ibid., September 5, 1755.

882 Ibid., March 3, 1673.

883 Ibid., May 13, 1785. Henry Featherstone's (1743–1827) farm was in Chesterfield County, Virginia. Although born in Virginia, Featherstone died in Smith County, Tennessee.

884 Ibid., May 16, 1745.

was arrested for breaking and entering in 1748.[885]

The farm of Mr. Edward Digges, in a 1758 summary of his holdings, lists a slave named Quash.[886] And another slave known as Quash is listed on the property called "Locust Grove" in Middlesex County during the Civil War in 1865.[887]

Countless other Virginia farms list similar holdings that often include slaves who clearly appeared to be members of the Islamic faith. In the next and final section of this eighth chapter, we shall introduce and discuss several pieces of art that depict and embody the suspected runaway slaves in Virginia in the seventeenth to nineteenth centuries.[888]

Virginia Runaway Slaves in Art

A number of nineteenth-century pieces of art, and even earlier, depict Virginia runaway slaves. A painting by William Sidney Mount called *The Power of Music* shows an escaped slave with hat in hand, staying out of sight, outside a Virginia barn. He listens to music played by three white planters inside the barn, one on fiddle, one with harmonica, and one singing along.[889] The second image of a Virginia runaway slave shows the determined slave rearing back on the reins of a large white horse, presumably owned by his master. The escaped slave is dressed in blue Confederate Army trousers, a bright red shirt, and a fancy red and black striped hat, again presumably stolen from his master. It is an evocative painting, the movement of which is as much about the slave as the horse.[890]

Winslow Homer completed a painting entitled *Contraband.* It is

885 Ibid., November 4, 1763.

886 Ibid., December 10, 1736.

887 Discussed in Christopher Thomlins, "The Speech of a Slave," www.americanbar.org. Christopher L. Tomlins teaches at the law school of the University of California at Berkeley. He mostly writes on the history and the law of slavery. Surry County was formed in 1656, from a portion of James City County, just south of the James River. It is one of the earliest incorporated counties of Virginia.

888 Ibid.

889 Virginia Gazette, June 22, 1792.

890 Moss Neck Manor of Caroline County, Virginia, was built in 1856. The manor was ten miles from the site of the Battle of Fredericksburg. During the American Civil War, the manor was used as the winter headquarters of the Confederate Army of Northern Virginia.

a watercolor made in 1875. In the image, a Union soldier dressed in a Zouave uniform offers a runaway slave boy some water from his Army-issue canteen. Both the boy and the man have looks of serenity on the faces.[891]

The fourth depiction of Virginia runaway slaves is entitled *The Fort Monroe Three*. The artist of the pencil sketch is unknown. In the depiction, three runaway Virginia slaves stand before General Benjamin Butler of the Union Army. It is clear that the three have escaped from their master. The general sits at a table, along with his secretary, recording the scene. The general is in the process of making inquiries of the three.[892]

Benjamin Butler (1818–1893) was a controversial and self-aggrandizing and colorful politician and military leader. He was also a state senator from Massachusetts, as well as a delegate to the Democratic National Convention in 1860.[893]

Finally, a painting on loan from the Harvard University Hutchins Center at the Philbrook Museum in Tulsa, Oklahoma, shows a slave family making a desperate dash to freedom in the Dismal Swamp of Virginia. The husband holds a club in his right hand and a knife in the left. Behind him are his wife and the small infant she clutches.[894] The

891 Virginia Gazette, May 21, 1748. William Gooch (1681–1757) was born in England, served as Lieutenant Governor of Virginia and proposed important legislation about regulations for tobacco inspection. "Locust Grove" is also known as the "Goodwin Farm." It is an historic property in Rapidin, Virginia. Middlesex County, Virginia, is on the Middle Peninsula of the Commonwealth of Virginia. Settlers first came there in 1640.

892 Estate of Mr. Edward Digges, Summary of Holdings, mentions a slave named Quash. This was the third Edward Digges. The first was an English barrister (1620–1675). His grandson is the Edward Digges discussed here. Mr. Digges also was one of Virginia's earliest settlers.

893 William Sidney Mount (1807–1868), American painter, best known for his genre work. He was born on Long Island and painted in New York City for many years.

894 Locust Grove Estate, Middlesex County, is a villa in the Italianate style designed in 1850 for artist and inventor Samuel F. B. Morse by architect Alexander Jackson Davis. Fifty years later, the mansion was expanded for its new owners, William and Martha Young. Alexander Jackson Davis (1803–1892) was a Dutch Reform painter of picturesque buildings in myriad

figures in this painting, of course, may have been members of the Islamic Maroon Community in the Dismal Swamp.

This brings us to the major conclusions we have made in this eighth chapter, followed by the chapter's notes, and then Chapter Nine, an analysis of suspected Muslim runaway slaves in Maryland.

Conclusions

The major purpose of this chapter has been to explore the phenomena of runaway slaves in the colony/state of Virginia, in general, and more specifically of runaway captives suspected of having been Muslims. We began this chapter with an analysis of some general observations about runaway slaves in Virginia. In this opening section of the chapter, we examined a series of successive laws passed by the Virginia burgesses to regulate the phenomenon of escaped slaves. These laws culminated in 1705 when the lawmakers gave permission to chop off the toes of incorrigible slaves.[895]

Altogether, we have examined 3,300 Virginia runaway slave advertisements. These were found in twenty-four different newspapers and other publications in colonial Virginia. These ads come from Virginia landowners in twenty-four separate counties of the colony/state. More than 50 percent of these 3,300 advertisements come from five Virginia counties—Accomack, Orange, Chesterfield, Mecklenburg and Henrico.[896]

In the remainder of this chapter, we have examined what we know of fifty-one suspected Virginia Muslim runaways. About those, we may make the following conclusions. Forty-one of the fifty-one were men,

styles. He was one of the great American antebellum architects. Samuel F. B. Morse (1791–1872), of course, was an American painter and inventor of the single-wire telegraph.

895 William Sidney Mount (1807–1868), The Power of Music, The Cleveland Museum of Art. Mount was an American painter known for his genre paintings, though he did paint some landscapes, as well. Winslow Homer (1836–1910) was an American landscape painter and printmaker. He was particularly known for his paintings of marine subjects.

896 Discussed in Jessica Dallow, "Antebellum Sports Illustrated," in Nineteenth Century Art Worldwide 12, no. 2 (2013). Painting by Winslow Homer, Contraband, 1875.

most of them in their twenties. Ten were women. The average age of these Muslim runaways is twenty-seven. They range from ten to sixty years of age. The height of these escaped Muslim slaves ranged from five feet two to six feet three, with the average at five foot seven. Five of the forty-one male slaves were over six feet tall. The tallest female slave of the ten women was five feet eight.[897] The tallest Virginia runaway slave was six foot three.

Forty-four of the suspected Muslim runaways were found in the *Virginia Gazette*. Seven of the fifty-one were discovered in a variety of other Virginia newspapers or national publications. Of the fifty-one Muslim slaves, ten of them, or 22 percent, mention specific skills related to the slaves. Four of the fifty-one were from the seventeenth century, thirty-seven from the eighteenth century, and ten from the nineteenth century.[898] The range of the Muslim escapees goes from 1649 until 1864.[899]

Forty-three of the fifty-one suspected Muslim runaways can be identified in terms of when they absconded. One was in the seventeenth century, five in the first half of the eighteenth century, twenty-eight in the second half of the eighteenth century, and six in the nineteenth century. Thirty-three of the fifty-one, or two thirds, had Islamic names. The origins of fourteen of these Virginia slaves may be identified by their tribal scars. Of the fifty-one, twenty-two or 45 percent are described as having stolen something from their masters: clothing, guns, horses, money and boats.

Six of the fifty-one suspected runaway Muslims were associated

---

897 Ibid.

898 Anonymous, The Fort Monroe Three. The artist may have been Alfred R. Wauld, who painted the picture of Jefferson Davis in 1865, when he also was imprisoned at Fort Monroe in Hampton, Virginia. Wauld (1821–1891) was a British-born American illustrator, mostly for Harper's Weekly. Also see Note 19. Benjamin Butler (1818–1893) was a Virginia politician and military figure during the Civil War.

899 Thomas Moran, Slave Hunt, Dismal Swamp, Virginia, 1862, 86.4 cm. by 111.8 cm. Moran (1837–1926) was born in Bolton, United Kingdom. He was a member of the Hudson River School of painting. Also: see the discussion earlier in Chapter Eight, as well as the chapter on Maryland Muslim runaways on the five variables outlined there.

one way or another with the Dismal Swamp of Southern Virginia and northern North Carolina. Of the fifty-one suspected Muslim captives, the African origins of thirty can be identified, or 62 percent. Of the fifty-one, thirteen were from Senegal and Gambia, ten from the Niger River Valley, one from the East African Supply Zone, one from the Gold Coast Zone, one from the North African Supply Zone, and five from the Windward Coast Supply Zone.

Several of the African tribes of the suspected Muslim runaway slaves also can be identified. They include the Yoruba, the Igbo, the Pungo, the Mandinka Tribe, the Wolof, The Fula or Fulani, and the Bantu people. Of the fifty-one suspected Muslims, thirteen or 28 percent, the tribal origins may be identified.

In identifying the fifty-one suspected Muslim slaves, we have relied on five variables. These may be summarized this way:

1. African born and little English, and speak Arabic or other languages.
2. Tribal marks and scars
3. Biographical information from the owner
4. Other historical information
5. Arabic and Islamic names[900]

In our analysis, we have suggested that if any individual runaway meets at least three of the five variables, then that individual was most likely a Moslem. In some cases, only meeting two of the characteristics seems sufficient. In very rare examples, a few suspected Muslims meet all five variables, and in some cases, the tribal scars, or Islamic names alone appears to be sufficient.

At any rate, we will turn our attention to Chapter Nine, an examination of suspected Muslim runaway slaves in Maryland. This will be followed by a final and conclusive chapter in which we explore and discuss the “Highlights” of this study of Muslim slaves in the Chesapeake.

---

900 Ibid.

Chapter Nine: Muslim Runaway Slaves in Early Maryland

> Advertisements for runaway slaves contain unique and substantial information on the ethical and cultural traits of individual slaves and are an underutilized source of data on American Slavery.
>
> —Michael Gomez, "Muslims in Early America"

> A number of runaway notices mention that the fugitives had no clothes on but a rag around the waist. Such slaves were generally Africans who had just arrived and still wore a piece of cloth handed down to them when they disembarked.
>
> —Sylviane A. Diouf, *Servants of Allah*

> True righteousness is one who believes in Allah, the Last Days, the Angels, the Book, and the Prophets; and he who gives wealth, in spite of a love for it, to relatives, orphans, the needy, the traveler, those who ask for help, and for freeing of slaves, and those who established prayer for them and gives them Zakat.
>
> —The Holy Qur'an 2:177 (Author's translation)

Introduction

Another source for discussions of Muslim slaves in the early Maryland colony/state, as in Virginia during the seventeenth to nineteenth centuries, are runaway slave advertisements. We will begin this chapter with an analysis of the phenomenon of Maryland runaway slaves in general, and Muslim runaway slaves in particular, during the period from colonial Maryland to the end of the Civil War. An anonymous article from the *Encyclopedia of African-American Culture* speaks of the value of runaway slave advertisements. The article tells us:

> Advertisements placed in hundreds of newspapers across America provide material for the study of runaway slaves. Thousands of slave owners across the south used the press to advertise for their absconded property. Runaway notices appeared in Virginia newspapers very early and continued up to the Civil War. More than any other source, these advertisements provide a vivid description of who the slaves were. The advertisements included the absconder's name, gender, age, height, weight, attire, and possible destination, along with a description of the runaway's personality, offers of reward, and other information that owners believed would lead them to the return of their property.[901]

Robert Hall, writing for the *Maryland Historical Magazine* in 1989, also describes the value of runaway slave advertisements. Dr. Hall observes:

> The historical value of newspaper advertisements for runaway slaves has been recognized for a long time. Beginning not later than 1916, with a relatively unadorned compilation in the first volume of Carter G. Woodson's *Journal of Negro History* ("Eighteenth Century Slaves as Advertised by Their Masters") these records of individual and group resistance to bondage has been known and occasionally utilized in reconstructing American social history.[902]

In the above quotation, Dr. Hall refers to Carter G. Woodson

---

901 Anonymous, "Runaway Slaves in the United States," Encyclopedia of African-American Culture (Thomas Gale, 2006).

902 Robert L. Hall, "Slave Resistance in Baltimore City and County, 1747–1790," in Maryland Historical Magazine 84, no. 1, pp. 305–306. Hall (1927–2012) was an American anthropologist who specialized in ethnohistory and ethnic studies. Carter G. Woodson (1875–1950) was an African American author, journalist and founder of the Association for the Study of African American Life and History.

(1875–1950), an African- American historian, author and journalist. Woodson was also the founder of the Association for the Study of African American Life and History. Dr. Hall also implies that several other scholars of runaway slave advertisements have done work in the field leading up to the present era.

Other scholars, like Michael A. Gomez, also point to the value of runaway slave ads. Gomez tells us this in this observation used as an epigram from in his "Muslims in Early America":

> Advertisements for runaway slaves contain unique and substantial information on ethnic and cultural traits of individual slaves and are an underutilized source of data on American Slavery.[903]

Professor Gomez goes on to tell us, "With regard to Muslims in early America, these advertisements occasionally provide names that are clearly Muslim but rarely identified as such. Names such as Bullaly, Mustapha, Sambo, Bocarry, and Mamado."[904] Gomez also implies that "Bullaly" is a corruption of the Muslim name Bilali, that "Bubacar" comes from Abu Bakr, and the name "Mamado" originally came from the West African Mamadu.[905]

All of these names appear among the Maryland runaway slave advertisements, mostly in the eighteenth and nineteenth centuries in the colony/state of Maryland, as well as in the Georgia and the South Carolina colonies/states.

Professor Gomez goes on to provide an analysis of the name "Sambo," that he says means "Second Son," among the Fulbe Tribe, an ethnicity spread throughout the West African Savannah.[906] Gomez then gives several examples of American slaves with these names, mostly in Georgia and South Carolina, but many can also be found in the Chesapeake Bay region, as we shall see in this chapter.

---

903 Michael A. Gomez, "Muslims in Early America," in The Journal of Southern History 60, no. 4 (November 1994). Gomez teaches history at New York University in New York City.

904 Ibid., p. 685.

905 Ibid.

906 Ibid.

These names may also be seen in Maryland and Virginia runaway slave advertisements, as well. At any rate, we have established in this analysis the significance and the importance of runaway slave advertisements in Maryland.

The purposes of this chapter are to explore the following goals. First, to give an introduction to the genre of runaway slave advertisements in Maryland from the colonial times to the Civil War period. As we shall see, this literary genre began in Maryland in the mid-seventeenth century and went all the way up to the American Civil War period, much like what we have seen in Virginia in the previous chapter.

Secondly, we wish to examine what we shall argue are fifty-five Maryland runaway slaves advertisements that most likely pertained to Muslim captives. Thirdly, we will also, at the end of this chapter, make some observations about ten pieces of runaway slave art that have been made by historical and contemporary artists in the colony/state in that period. We move, then, to an introduction to runaway slaves in Maryland, the subject matter of the first section of this Chapter Nine.

Runaway Slave Advertisements in Maryland

As we have seen in Chapter Eight of this study, runaway slave advertisements were notices taken out in local, state and regional, and even national newspapers, in which absconded slaves might be recovered, if a substantial enough reward was offered by their white owners.

A variety of newspapers in colonial Maryland published advertisements for runaway slaves. Among these publications are the following: the *National Intelligencer* in Washington, DC, the *Baltimore Sun*, *The Maryland Planter's Advocate*, the *Maryland Gazette*, the *Kent News*, the *Maryland Journal*, the *Baltimore Adviser*, the *Cambridge Herald*, the *Cambridge Chronicle*, The *Cecil Democrat*, the *Chestertown Telegraph*, the *Cumberland Civilian*, the *Worcester Banner*, the *Port Tobacco Times*, the *Montgomery County Sentinel*, the *Harford Democrat*, The *Hagerstown Torchlight*, the *Frederick Herald*, the *Elkton Press*, the *Eastern Gazette*, the *Annapolis Gazette*, the *Maryland Journal*, the *City Gazette and Advertiser*, and the *Baltimore Telegraph*.

For the most part, these runaway advertisements in Maryland

were mostly taken out by their masters, or their master's agents. The earliest ads for runaway slaves in Maryland come from the 1680s, with the majority of the advertisements in the last fifty years of the eighteenth century to the end of the Civil War.

From the twenty-four publications listed above, we have examined nearly 2,000 runaway slave advertisements in Maryland, only about half of what we examined in the Virginia ads. In addition to the information listed above, the following observations can be made about these Maryland runaway advertisements.

The runaways slaves in Maryland are predominantly male, about 85 percent are boys and men under the age of thirty-five, much like what we have seen in Virginia. Indeed, very few of the runaway slaves in Maryland were forty years old or older, both male and female, and only five who were forty-five or older.

Many of these slaves are described as having markings or tribal marks on their skin—holes in their ears; scars on their cheeks and foreheads; tribal marks on their breasts, hands, or backs; and other ritual markings they may have received in Africa. Again, much like what we have seen in the Virginia runaway advertisements. There were fifteen runaway slaves in Virginia with tribal marks that could be identified and a dozen more in Maryland.

The advertisements usually distinguish whether a slave was born in Africa, America, or the Caribbean. In this regard, the level of English the slave knew was generally recorded in the advertisement, as well as any other languages they might have known. These languages may be of some use in determining if a captive was a Muslim, for we know which areas of Africa spoke languages associated with Muslims in the seventeenth to nineteenth centuries.

Often mentioned in the ads was a description of a slave's personality. He is cunning, complaisant, impudent, sour, bold, artful, smooth-tongued, surly, sensible, talkative, shy, well-spoken, lusty or well-set. Many of the Maryland slaves were described as "being much cut" on their backs, due to "often whippings," an indication that they may have been uncooperative or unruly.

Some of the Maryland absconders ran away in groups of three to five, including men and women, and sometimes with white indentured servants, as well, although the punishment for white servants was generally harsher than for black slaves, sometimes considerably more harsh.

This judgment can be seen in C. Ashley Ellefson's "The Private Punishment of Servants and Slaves in 18th Century Maryland," (Maryland State Archives, vol. 819).[907] In fact, runaway servant advertisements in Maryland began in the 1660s and continued until the 1720s, often alongside those of runaway slaves. From the beginning of the Maryland colony, white European runaway indentured servants were given far more severe punishments for misbehavior than were black African slaves.

Several of the Maryland Muslim runaway advertisements mention that a runaway has "Indian blood" or is familiar with Indian ways of life. One ad even proclaims, "He speaks Indian well."[908] A few runaway ads say an individual is a "Mustee," a term used to designate the offspring of a black slave and a Native American individual.

A significant number of advertisements in Maryland mention the slaves having brass, pewter or even silver buckles on their shoes, which must have been a rare commodity. Many of the slaves could also read and write, again an unusual state among slaves of the south.

Indeed, as we shall see later in this chapter, a significant number of Muslim runaway slaves were literate, particularly the prominent ones such as Job Diallo, Kunta Kinte and Yarrow Mamout, mentioned in the opening chapter, as well as in an appendix in Chapter Ten.

Many of the advertisements for suspected Maryland runaways suggest that a captive may "appear to be free," is "almost white," "could easily write himself a pass" or "could easily pass as a Free Negro." In fact, the fear of freed blacks, particularly in urban areas like Baltimore, Annapolis or Frederick, is evident in many of the advertisements. Many of the ads speak of runaways being harbored by some white folks or by freed black people, in these areas.

Many of the escaped slaves in Maryland are believed by their owners to have changed their names so they could not be identified by their former African names. One advertisement says, "The Negro's name is Jupiter, but it is thought that he most likely calls himself by his

907 C. Ashley Ellefson, "The Private Punishment of Servants and Slaves in 18th Century Maryland," Maryland State Archives, vol. 819.
908 Maryland Gazette, June 8, 1776.

African name, Mueyon or Omtee."[909]

In other cases, a slave changed his name completely, so he could not be identified. Frederick Douglass, for example, contemplated what to call himself after escaping from slavery in Maryland. He says in his autobiography:

> The name given to me by my mother was Frederick Augustus Washington Bailey. I, however, had dispensed with the two middle names long before I left Maryland, so that I was generally known as Frederick Bailey. I started from Baltimore; I found it necessary again to change my name... I gave Mr. Johnson, Mr. Nathan Johnson of New Bedford, the privilege of choosing me a name, but told him he must not take from me the name Frederick, for I must hold on to it as a sense of identity.[910]

Thus, Frederick Douglass changed his name when he escaped from slavery in Maryland, but he did give the right to rename himself to New Bedford abolitionist Nathan Johnson (1784–1871).

It was Mr. Johnson that suggested the name Douglass. It was the name of a knight in Walter Scott's novel, *The Lady of the Lake,* so Mr. Johnson thought the name Douglass to be entirely appropriate, for Frederick was a kind of soldier of the abolitionists, and thus the analogy was quite appropriate.[911]

Physical characteristics about a slave's gait, speech patterns or body type also are common in the Maryland runaway slave advertisements. "He is a short, thick fellow, who limps with his right knee, and one of his buttocks is smaller than the other," "He is bow-legged and

---

909 Ibid., February 19, 1756.

910 Frederick Douglass, Narrative of the Life of Frederick Douglass (New York: Create Space, 2016), p 134. Douglass (1818–1895) was, of course, an African American social reformer, activist, orator, writer and statesman. After escaping slavery from Talbot County, Maryland, he joined the American Abolitionist Movement. Nathan Johnson (1784–1871) was a preeminent abolitionist in New Bedford, Massachusetts. His home at 21 Seventh Street is now a national historical landmark.

911 Ibid.

walks with a limp," "He speaks with a stammer" or "His right leg is stiff so he walks with a limp." Often the shade of blackness is recorded in the advertisements. "He is a very dark negro," "She is a Mulatto" or "Her color is closer to yellow than black."

It is important to reiterate that in runaway slave advertisements, we only have the perspective of the masters. We rarely get the point of view of the slaves for why they ran away, nor where they believed they were going, nor what they might have done when they got there.

One aspect of physical description that has been neglected by scholars who write about runaway slaves in colonial Maryland to the Civil War period is the various styles and lengths of their hair. One exception to this rule is an essay written by Shane White and Graham White of the University of Sydney in Australia. The essay is entitled "Slave Hair and African-American Culture in the Eighteenth and Nineteenth Centuries."[912] White and White introduce their essay this way:

> Typically, eighteenth century advertisements for runaway slaves supplied information about the miscreant's name, age, skin color, likely destination, and clothing. They also frequently describe the escape slave's hair.[913]

White and White go on in their analysis to tell us:

> What is striking about such descriptions is the great variety of hair styles they depict. We learn from them, to cite a few examples, that some slaves wore their hair long and bushy on top and that others cut it short, or combed and parted it neatly, or shaved it at the back or the front, or trimmed it in a roll. The African's hair may be closely cropped on the crown but left long elsewhere; or it could be tied behind in a queue, frizzed,

912 Walter Scott, The Lady of the Lake (London: Thomas Y. Crowell, 1892). Walter Scott (1771–1832) was a Scottish historical novelist, playwright and poet.

913 Shane White and Graham White, "Slave Hair and African American Culture in the 18th and 19th Centuries," in The Journal of Southern History 61, no. 1 (1995), pp. 45–76.

> combed high from the forehead, plaited, curled on each side of the face, filleted, cut in the form of a circle on the crown, knotted on top of the head, or worn long and bushy so that it is below the ears.[914]

Among the 2,000 Maryland runaway slave advertisements we have examined, over 300 of them mention the slave's hairstyle, about the same percentage we saw back in Virginia. As we have indicated, this data on hairstyles has been underutilized by scholars, either historical or contemporary writers. More work has to be done on this data and its implications of African American and slavery history in the Chesapeake Bay region and beyond.

Very few of the Maryland runaways left their masters in the winter months. Indeed, as Robert Hall observes:

> Not unexpectedly, one detects seasonal variation in the frequency of the runaways, with bulges during the Spring and Summer months and a noticeable decline during the late Autumn and Winter.[915]

In many of the Maryland runaway advertisements, their owners indicated where they believe the slaves were headed. If a slave had family or friends elsewhere in the colony or state, it is often indicated. Sometimes it simply says, "He went North" or "He was supposed to be headed toward Wilmington, where he has a wife with Charles Croxall."

Any distinctive occupational skills or other competencies also usually are noted. "He is a fine blacksmith," "He is a good Cooper" or "He is a good rider and gentle with horses." At times, an advertisement mentions a slave's musical or singing abilities. "He is quite good on the fiddle," "He beats on the drum pretty well," "He plays the Banjo," "He plays well the mouth organ" (harmonica) or "She has a beautiful singing voice."

One final aspect of this general analysis of Maryland runaway slaves is the value of the reward offered for the slave's return. We have examined nearly 2,000 Maryland runaway advertisements in the twen-

914 Ibid., p. 35.

915 Ibid., pp. 36–37.

ty-four publications mentioned above. These ads can be divided into three periods:

I. 1688 until 1799, 675 total ads, early Colonial period
II. 1801 to 1849, 860 total ads, first half of the nineteenth century
III. 1850 to 1864, 460 total ads, second half of the nineteenth century to the Civil War.

In the first period mentioned above, the average reward for an escaped Maryland slave was still determined in British currency. Thus, the average reward offered in the period was twenty-five shillings, much like what we saw back in Virginia in Chapter Eight.

By the year 1800, and the second period, the average reward offered in Maryland had jumped to \$178. In the third period between 1850 to 1864, the year slavery was abolished by the Maryland constitution, the average bounty for recovering a Maryland runaway slave had risen to \$278. This figure is significantly lower than what we saw in Virginia in the same period, of \$380. The payoffs or rewards recovered—in the county, colony or outside the colony—are progressively larger in Maryland, similar to the Virginia advertisements.[916]

This \$278 figure is considerably less than other states at the time, a full one hundred dollars less than Virginia, for example. Fogel and Engerman, in their Probate Appraisal Data-Set (ICPSR, 1974), suggest these figures for other states between 1820 and 1850 in the third period outlined above:

Virginia………..… \$380.00

North Carolina….\$425.00

South Carolina….\$430.00

Georgia………..\$475.00

Mississippi……...\$550.00

Louisiana……….\$560.00 [917]

916 Hall, p. 308.

917 Robert William Fogel and Stanley L. Engerman, "The Probate Appraisal Data-Set," (ICPSR, 1974). Also see their Time on the Cross: The

Conor Lennon, of the University of Pittsburgh's Economics Department, in his recent on-line essay, "Slave Escapes, Prices, and the Fugitive Slave Act," suggests that these figures of Fogel and Engerman are based on their "distance from the Mason-Dixon Line.[918] Using this variable, Maryland is the closest state and Louisiana the farthest away. In the same article, Lennon sketches out the growth in runaway slave prices in Richmond, Charleston, mid-Georgia and New Orleans.

He concludes that the mid-Georgia region grew the fastest and the Richmond area the slowest.[919] Richmond, of course, is closest to the Mason-Dixon Line, while Georgia and New Orleans are the most distant. Thus, the patterns of assigning rewards for runaway slaves are quite different in the various states in the nineteenth century.

These 2,000 advertisements for runaway slaves in Maryland examined here offered rewards ranging from no reward (only four of the total) to a high of $3,000 for three slaves together, or $1,000 apiece. The earliest advertisement for a Maryland runaway slave was in the *Kent News*, from 1688. The latest of the Maryland ads were during the Civil War in the early 1860s.

Of the three periods of runaway slave advertisements in Maryland, by far the middle period, from 1800 to 1849, had more runaways than the other two. This is different from what we saw in Virginia, where the second half of the eighteenth century had the predominant number of the runaway slave advertisements in the commonwealth.

Several Maryland scholars have done much work on runaway slave advertisements in Maryland. Perhaps the most significant of these are the team of Julie Dematteis and Louis S. Diggs, Sr., who compiled a collection of runaway slave ads in Baltimore County from 1842 to 1863.[920] This is the period when the slave traders of Baltimore, discussed in Chapter Five of this study, were at their peak. Much of the material in the next section of this chapter is garnered from the work

---

Economics of American Negro Slavery (New York: W. W. Norton, 1974).

918 Ibid.

919 Conor Lennon, "Slave Escapes, Prices, and the Fugitive Slave Act," Department of Economics, University of Pittsburgh.

920 Ibid.

of this pair.

Frank Cassell is another Maryland scholar who worked on Maryland runaway slaves. He has collected seven hundred runaway slave advertisements from the War of 1812 period.[921] The "University Libraries Guides" on slavery in Maryland also compiled a number of databases regarding Maryland runaway slaves. Among these databases are the following:

- Black abolitionist papers from 1830 until 1865
- Runaway slave ads in the *Baltimore Sun* (1837–1986)
- African American newspapers in Maryland (1827–1998)[922]

Another primary source for Maryland runaway slave advertisements are genealogical materials. The "Genealogy Decoded" website, for example, features four thousand runaway advertisements from 1685 until 1712.[923] The site called "Family Search," also has a heading called 'U.S. Runaway Slave Advertisements," produced by the National Institute.[924]

The Enoch Pratt Free Library in Baltimore also has a collection of what it calls "Slaves and Free Americans," which include reports and runaway advertisements from Hagerstown and Cumberland, Maryland, newspapers from 1790 until 1864. From these last seven sources alone, there are nearly eight thousand runaway slave advertisements in Maryland, Virginia and the District of Columbia.

This brings us to an analysis of the fifty-five suspected Muslim runaway slaves in Maryland, the second and central section of this ninth chapter.

Maryland Muslim Runaway Slaves

921 Julie De Matteis and Louis S. Diggs, Sr., "Runaway Slave Ads in Baltimore County," www.afrigenesis.com. De Matteis is a librarian at the Catonsville Public Library in Baltimore County, Maryland. Louis S. Diggs, Sr. is an African American writer and historian who specializes in African American history in Baltimore County, Maryland.

922 Frank Cassell, "Runaway Slave Ads from the War of 1812," quoted in Brett Jaspers, How More Than 700 Maryland Slaves Escaped During the War of 1812, WYPR radio broadcast. Also https://www.wypr.org.

923 Universities Library Guides of Slavery, Maryland. Databases.

924 Geneology Decoded, www.linkedin.com.

Among the nearly two thousand, Maryland runaway slave advertisements, there are fifty-five suspected to be Muslim runaways. Two of these ads are from the seventeenth century, forty-one from the eighteenth century, and twelve from the nineteenth century. The youngest of the fifty-five was ten years old, and the oldest was sixty, with only five over forty years of age. The average age for the Maryland Muslim runaways was twenty-seven years and five months, about the same as in Virginia.

The advertisements for the fifty-five suspected Muslim runaways came in only eight of the Maryland newspapers discussed earlier. These are the *Maryland Gazette*, the *Baltimore Sun,* the *National Intelligencer*, the *Annapolis Gazette*, the *City Gazette and Advertiser,* the *Baltimore Telegraph*, the *Denton News* and the *Baltimore Advertiser*. Of the fifty-five suspected Muslim runaways, more than half were in the *Maryland Gazette*, which began its publication in 1761.

The heights of the suspected Muslim runaways range from four foot three, a slave named Elinor, to a man named Pero, who was six foot six.[925] The average height of the fifty-five suspected Muslim slaves was five foot eight, the same figure in Virginia. Of the fifty-five possible Muslims, two-thirds or forty were men, and fifteen were females. Of the forty males, five were six feet or taller, while none of the women were over five foot eight. Again, these figures are similar to what we saw in Virginia, where the tallest female was five foot eight and the tallest male at six foot three.

Five different variables were considered in determining if a particular slave was a Muslim. The first of these was whether the slave was known to be African born and spoke little English. If they were American born, then it is quite likely they were not Muslims. The second variable is whether a slave speaks a language other than English. At least four of the suspected Muslims spoke Arabic, and as many as ten; fourteen spoke French; four knew or spoke Dutch, and one spoke German.

The third variable considered to determine if a Maryland runaway slave was a Muslim is biographical materials from the owners of the

925 Ibid.

runaways about their origins. They may say, "He is from the Guiney Country," "He is an Eboe," "He is a Bite Negro" or "He is a Gold Coast Negroe."

The fourth variable to decide if a particular slave was Islamic are the many tribal marks with which some slaves came from Africa. About a dozen of the fifty-five runaway Muslims can be identified simply from their tribal scars. Most of these, as we shall see, come from the Senegambian, the Niger Valley, and the Sierra Leone Supply Zones, much like what we saw in Virginia. In Maryland, we also discovered one German-speaking slave from Namibia who may be identified by the Wolof Tribe marking on her right hand, so she originally came from the Senegambian Supply Zone and may have spoken Arabic as well as German.

The fifth and final variable we have consulted in determining Moslem runaway slaves in Maryland is Islamic or Arabic names of the Maryland runaway slaves. Of the fifty-five, forty-five had Muslim or Arabic names, and many of these were employed multiple times.

Of the Maryland counties from which these suspected Muslim runaway slaves escaped thirty-three of the fifty-five are known. The thirty-three suspected Muslim slaves came from eleven different Maryland counties. These are Baltimore, Prince George's, Anne Arundel, Montgomery, Saint Mary's, Saint Anne's, Charles, Cecil, Worcester, Calvert, and Talbot.

The suspected Maryland Muslim runaway slaves had eleven Arabic or Muslim names for which there are multiples. There are ten Sambo; eight Hagar; eight Mingo; two Wali; two Cuffee; three Musa; two Ali; two Ayyub, or Job; two Esther; two Charles; and two Jem. Thirty-three of the fifty-five can be identified in terms of their origins in Africa. Four were from the Senegambia Supply Zone; five from Guinea, or the Sierra Leone Zone; ten from the Niger Valley Zone; ten from the Windward and Gold Coasts Supply Zones; and one was most likely from Namibia, in Southwest Africa, or the South African Supply Zone, but originally from the Senegambian Zone.

These figures are comparable to what we have seen in Virginia. Other Muslim names, besides those listed above, among the fifty-five are Maryam, Ishaq, Yusuf, Ismail, Musa, Cudjoe, Dinah and Sarah.

Many societies in West Africa give their children names according to the day of the week when a baby is born. Cudjoe for Monday, Quaco for Wednesday, Quamin on Saturday, Cuffee on Friday and Mingo on Sunday, from the Spanish and Portuguese word "Domingo" for Sunday. In many places in West Africa, the name Sambo was often used in the seventeenth to the nineteenth centuries to stand for the "Second Son" in a family. This is particularly true in the Senegambian Supply Zone among the Fulbe people, as Gomez established earlier in this chapter, as well as in other West African peoples at that time.

In regard to languages other than English, a report in the *Maryland Gazette* from August 12, 1784, a Cecil County planter named Thomas May, advertised for:

> A Negron named George. He is about 40 or 45 years old, five foot seven or eight, slender body and thin visage, not very black, plausible and complaisant, can speak pretty good English, a little French, and a few words of High Dutch. He has been to the West Indies and to Canada.[926]

The French and the Dutch imply that Mr. May's slave George was from the Sierra Leone Supply Zone or Dutch Guinea. A slave named Sue, a forty-five-year-old woman brought from South Carolina to Halifax, Virginia, and then to Baltimore, "was born in Africa, but her owner, Samuel Worthington says she talks something of the Guiney

926 Quoted in Vincent Harding, "American Runaway, American Freedom," in There is a River (New York: Harvest Books, 1993), pp. 324–345. Harding (1931–2014) was a Harlem-born social activist and scholar. He specialized in American religion and its relation to society.

dialect. She can also read a little English." The Dutch suggested the Sierra Leone Supply Zone, or the Windward Coast Zone, where there were a significant number of Muslims after the mid-eighteenth century. It may have been the case that both George and Sue, mentioned above, first were brought to the British Caribbean and then to North America.

In others, such as Seth, who ran away from Patrick Brannan's Baltimore County Free School in 1757, and Peter, who ran away from the Bush River Furnace in Baltimore County in 1762, both spoke French. This may imply the Gold Coast Zone, the Windward Coast, or possibly the Albreda French Community or Fort Saint Joseph in Senegambia.[927]

Sarah was a slave owned by Isaiah Smith of Talbot County. According to the *Maryland Gazette* of January 27, 1778, she "speaks Dutch and comes from the Guiney Country," or most likely the Sierra Leone Supply Zone, or the Windward Coast Zone.[928] Another slave named Musa was also "from the coast of Guiney." "He speaks French, but very little English."[929] The name "Musa," of course, is the Arabic equivalent of Moses. Musa remains one of the most popular male names among those of the Islamic Faith. Mr. Smith's slave Musa apparently refused to change his name to Moses.

The *Maryland Gazette* of September 20, 1793, tells us of Charles Thomas, "who is 26 or 27 years old, and speaks French."[930] The French suggested Sarah and Charles may have been from the Windward Coast, or possibly the Gold Coast Supply Zone, or Fort Albreda or Fort Saint Joseph in the Senegambian Supply Zone.

A brother and sister, Nanny and Cudjoe, were born in Ghana in

927 Maryland Gazette, August 12, 1784. Thomas May, who died in 1792, was a Cecil County tobacco farmer. He was also associated with the Elk Forge in Elkton, Maryland. A number of May's letters survive, including one to Levi Hollingsworth dated July 25, 1774, in the Hollingsworth Family Papers, 1748–1847.

928 Ibid., April 30, 1762. The Bush River Furnace became the Harford Furnace when William Pennell acquired the site in 1861. It is now a national historic district. It consists of five standing structures at James Run on the Bush River.

929 Ibid., January 27, 1778. Isaiah Smith, born in 1745, was a tobacco farmer in Talbot County, Maryland, on the Eastern Shore.

930 Ibid., September 20, 1793.

1686 and 1688. She was sometimes called "Queen Nanny," and they both spoke fluent French.[931] They were most likely Muslims from the Gold Coast. Another slave named George, also owned by Thomas May of Cecil County, "speaks French and a little Dutch," which may imply the Sierra Leone Zone.

Mr. May advertised for George in the August 14, 1784, edition of the *Maryland Gazette*.[932] The French and Dutch together suggested the Sierra Leone Supply Zone. Both Nanny and her brother had a "tribal scar on their right hands," an indication they were members of the Krobo Tribe of the Gold Coast Supply Zone, who could well have been Muslims among the Wolof Tribe of the Senegambian Supply Zone.

A planter at the head of the South River, David Owens' slave, Joe is described by Mr. Owens this way:

> He is five feet eight or there abouts, born in the Guiney Country. He speaks French but very little English. He has a long band across his entire brow.[933]

The French indicated he might have been from the Gold Coast or the Windward Coast Supply Zones. It is rare in the Chesapeake region where it is male slaves who have absconded with money. The tribal scar, one horizontal line across the forehead, also suggests the Gold Coast, particularly members of the Krobo Tribe in Northern Ghana, and thus the Gold Coast Supply Zone. Many of the Krobo Tribe were Muslims by the year 1750.

A slave owned by John Thompson in Talbot County advertised in the *Maryland Gazette* for a slave named "Sobett, a French negro woman. Mr. Thompson tells us in the *Denton News* from May 18, 1709:

> She is twenty-three years old, with marks above both breasts. She is very short, about four foot five. She speaks French. $30.00 reward.[934]

931 Southern Maryland Advertiser, February 2, 1863.

932 Ibid.

933 Maryland Gazette, August 14, 1784.

934 Ibid., January 12, 1862. Also see Maryland Historical Society Magazine 25, no. 4 (1930), for more on David Owens.

Again, the French suggested the Gold Coast, but the tribal marks more indicate the Pungo people of the Windward Coast or the Angolan Supply Zone. Many colonies of the Pungo Tribe converted to the Islamic faith by the close of the eighteenth century, particularly in Ghana, Angola and the Ivory Coast. Sorbett is the second shortest suspected Muslim slave in this study, at four feet five inches tall.

J. H. Stevens of Baltimore County and Thomas Stone of Charles County owned two other slaves who spoke French. Mr. Stevens' runaway was named Will. The planter sought him in the January 5, 1799, edition of the *Maryland Gazette*.[935]

Thomas Stone's Jack spoke French and thus was likely from the Gold or Windward Coasts. Mr. Stone, in his January 4, 1798, advertisement in the *Maryland Gazette*, offered $40.00 for his return.[936] By the very late eighteenth century, runaway slave advertisement rewards now were given in American currency.

David Harris of Upper Marlboro had a runaway slave named Tower. Mr. Harris tells us about his slave:

> He is five foot three or four. He took lots of cash with him. He is nineteen years old and speaks French. He may be headed to Philadelphia.[937]

Male runaway slaves in the Chesapeake Bay region rarely absconded with cash stolen from their masters. Almost always, in both Virginia and Maryland, money taken by runaway slaves was taken by female captives, usually domestic servants or house slaves.

The French suggested either the Gold Coast or the Windward Coast as to Tower's origin in Africa. Three other Maryland runaway slaves who spoke French were Lewis, Musa and Charles Thomas. The latter was owned by Mr. Stephen Spencer of Baltimore County. Mr.

935 Denton News, May 18, 1709. The Krobo Tribe in north and east Ghana is part of the Ga-Dangme ethno-linguistic group.

936 Maryland Gazette, January 5, 1799. Thomas Stone (1743–1787) was an American planter and attorney. He also was one of the signers of the Declaration of Independence. John H. Stevens (1820–1890) was a Baltimore County farmer for most of the nineteenth century.

937 Ibid., January 4, 1798.

Spencer, in the September 20, 1793, *Maryland Gazette* wishes for the return of his slave who is "26 or 27, about five feet ten, speaks French, and was born in Africa."[938]

Mr. Spencer also indicateed that his runaway slave had "three vertical strokes beneath both eyes," an indication of the Igbo Tribe of the Niger Valley or Bight of Benin Supply Zones. Spencer's slave may also have originated among the slaves at the French Fort at Albreda in the Senegambian Supply Zone.

Musa, owned by Timothy Reed from Annapolis, was "From the Guiney Country, speaks French but not much English." He was most likely from the Sierra Leone Supply Zone, where many Muslim families lived in the eighteenth century, or possibly the Windward Coast Zone. Mr. Reed sought his slave's return in the October 23, 1760, edition of the *Maryland Gazette*.[939] Musa, of course, is the Islamic name for Moses.

Another Maryland runaway slave named Amos was advertised by his owner, Colonel William Hopper of Queen Anne's County, in the May 31, 1746, edition of the *Pennsylvania Gazette*. Col. Hopper tells us that Amos "is about thirty years old, five foot six and comes from the Guiney Country." This would indicate that Amos was most likely from the Sierra Leone Supply Zone, or the Windward Coast Zone.[940] Both of these zones had a significant number of Muslims by the mid-eighteenth century.

The runaway slave of Jeremiah Stone was named Lewis. In the *City Gazette and Advertiser*, Mr. Stone stated:

> He is 24 or 25 years old, he speaks French and he used to be a hair dresser. He ran away on April 1, 1799.[941]

Again, the French-speaking implies the Gold Coast or the Wind-

---

938 Ibid. David Harris came to Upper Marlboro, Prince George's County, Maryland, from England in the early eighteenth century. "Harris Creek" there is named after him.

939 Ibid., September 20, 1793. Dr. Stephen Spencer owned a tobacco farm in Catonsville, Baltimore County, at the close of the eighteenth century.

940 Ibid., October 23, 1760.

941 Ibid., May 31, 1746. Col. William Hopper (1743–1806) was a tobacco planter in Queen Anne's County, Maryland.

ward Coast regarding Mr. Stone's runaway slave, or possibly from the French Fort at Albreda, or the one at Fort Saint Joseph in the Senegambian Supply Zone. In addition, in the opening chapter of this study, it was indicated that Ayyub Diallo, Lamine Joy and Kunta Kinte, all from the Senegambian Supply Zone, spoke Arabic. Yarrow Mamout, as well, from Guinea also spoke Arabic.

Thus, between nineteen and twenty-two of our Maryland slaves spoke a language other than English. At least four and as many as ten spoke Arabic, eleven spoke French, three spoke Dutch, and one German.

On May 18, 1789, George P. Keeporte offered eighty dollars reward for the recovery of his slave Elenor. She was five foot three, and thus the second shortest of the suspected Muslim runaway slaves in Maryland. Elenor was twenty years old, and "could easily pass as a Free Negro." She could also speak German. This latter point suggests that Elenor was from Namibia, a German colony on the southwest coast of Africa, and thus from the South African Supply Zone.[942] Mr. Keeporte also indicated that Elenor has a "scar on her right hand," an indication she may have been a member of the Fulbe Tribe, or, more probably, a member of the Wolof Tribe of the Senegambian Supply Zone. The Wolof Tribe seems most likely the origin of Mr. Keeporte's captive.

The tribal scars of several other Maryland runaways can also be identified. Earlier we spoke of a slave named Sobett who has scars above both breasts. The scars indicate she was, most likely, a member of the Yoruba Tribe of the Niger Valley Supply Zone, or the Bight of Benin Zone.[943]

---

942 City Gazette, April 1, 1799.

943 Maryland Gazette, May 18, 1789. George P. Keeports was another Revolutionary War hero. His papers are published by the National Archives of the Revolutionary Army. In the 1790s, he had an extensive cor-

Similarly, a slave named Dick Oblebe, owned by Isaac Cooke of Pikesville, has a "tribal scar over his right eye." This would indicate he was probably from the Niger Valley Supply Zone, or possibly the Bight of Benin, as well.[944] The name "Oblebe" is a fairly common one among the Yoruban Tribe of Nigeria. Dick also may have been a member of the Ibibio Tribe of the Bight of Benin.

It is likely Dick came from one of the northern states of Nigeria, such as Sokoto, Zamfara, Jigawat or Kano. All of these are more than ninety-five percent Muslim, even today. At any rate, Dick Oblebe was clearly from the Niger Valley Supply Zone, or the Bight of Benin Zone, as discussed in Chapter Two of this study.

Another slave named Bewdly is "a twenty-four-year-old woman, born in Africa, with Guiney marks on her forehead." The mark in question is one long horizontal mark across the entire forehead. This indicates that Bewdly was a member of the Fula, or Fulbe Tribe of the Senegambian Supply Zone, or possibly from the Sierra Leone Zone, like the Temne or Mende Tribes there.

Bewdly was accompanied by another slave named Esther, "a Negro girl of about sixteen, also with marks on the sides of her face that look like this I." That is, three vertical strokes beneath each eye.[945] If Bewdly was a Fula, she probably spoke Arabic.

In the May 8, 1787, edition of the *Baltimore Advertiser*, W. H. Jenifer sought the return of his escaped slave Jenny. She was a five foot four, light Mulatto woman with bad teeth and an aquiline nose. She also has "tribal marks above both breasts." This latter point suggests that Jenny was a member of the Wolof Tribe of the Senegambian Supply Zone, or the Yoruba Tribe in the Niger Valley Zone, or possibly a tribe from the Sierra Leone Supply Zone, like the Krobo.[946] Both were mostly Islamic by that point. Most of the Wolof Tribe in the area spoke

respondence with George Washington. The French fort at Albreda, on the North Bank of the Gambia River, was built by the French sometime in the mid-seventeenth century. The British took control of the fort in 1857.

944 Ibid.

945 Baltimore Sun, July 25, 1849. The Cooke Brothers, Ebenezer and Isaac, owned substantial property in Pikesville, Maryland, in the eighteenth and nineteenth centuries.

946 Maryland Gazette, July 28, 1849.

Arabic at that point in their history.

A slave named Jem, who was owned by Samuel Williams of Prince George's County, has "Three vertical lines on each cheek," an indication that he was from the Senegambian Supply Zone. Mr. Williams tells us about his escaped slave:

> He was born in Africa. He is twenty-eight years old, slender with a thin face. He sometimes pretends to be a Methodist Minister.[947]

The Methodism suggests that Jem lived during the Second Great Awakening in America from 1760 until the end of the century described in Chapter Eight. The tribal marks, on the other hand, suggest Jem may have come from the Muslim regions of the Niger Valley Supply Zone, among the Igbo, or possible from the Bight of Benin.

In Saint Mary's County, Michael Christian's Sambo, who his owner advertised for in the October 27, 1769, edition of the *Maryland Gazette*, "is about five foot nine and has a scar on one side of his face."[948] The scar in question was on the right side of the face, above the eye. This would indicate he is most likely a member of the Wolof Tribe in the Senegambia Supply Zone. At the time, the Wolof Tribe spoke Arabic as their first language. They also marked their warriors above the right eye, in the middle of the eighteenth century.

Mr. Williams advertised in the January 4, 1798, edition of the *Maryland Gazette*. Another slave who claims to be a Methodist preacher was named Sambo and owned by Charles Gosnell. In the *Baltimore Telegraph* of June 6, 1793, Mr. Gosnell reveals about his Sambo:

> He claims to be a Methodist Preacher, is about five foot eight. He left with a cloth jacket with a red under jacket.[949]

947 Baltimore Advertiser, May 8, 1787. W. H. Jenifer was a colonel in the Confederate Army. He also owned a thousand-acre farm in Charles County in Southern Maryland.

948 Maryland Gazette, August 12, 1773. The Williams Family, George, Jonas and Samuel owned substantial property in Prince George's County, Maryland, in the late eighteenth century.

949 Ibid., October 27, 1769. Also see: "Slaves as Advertised by Their Masters," in The Journal of Negro History 1, no. 2 (1916), pp. 163–216. Michael Christian offered forty dollars reward for his slave, Sambo.

These two slaves described as Methodist preachers were part of the Second Great Awakening, a religious movement that swarmed across the south beginning in the 1760s, converting followers, first to the Baptist faith in the 1720s and then to the Methodists from the 1760s until the turn of the century. Again, we have discussed these movements in Chapter Eight.

Concerning the use of Arabic and Islamic names in colonial Maryland and elsewhere, Michael Gomez states the following:

> With regard to Muslims in early America, these advertisements occasionally provide names that are clearly Muslim, but rarely identified as such. Names such as "Bullaly," or Bilali, "Mustapha," "Sambo," "Bocarrey," "Bubacar," from Abu Bakr, and "Mamado," (Mamadu) are regularly observed in the advertisements for runaway slaves. Unless slave owners clearly understood the origin of these names, they would not necessarily associate them with Islam.[950]

Professor Gomez goes on with an illustration of the phenomenon of Muslim names, he says:

> A good example is the name "Sambo," a corruption of the name Samba meaning "Second Son," in the language of the Fulbe, an ethnically spread people throughout The West-African Savannah.[951]

Gomez quoted from a May 24, 1775, issue of the *Georgia Gazette* that mentions the absconding of three slaves, "including a twenty-two-year-old Sambo of the Moorish Country," a term that signifies "North Africa," or the wearing Islamic dress.[952] In Maryland, around the same time, the *Maryland Gazette* advertised for a slave of Thomas Morgain of Calvert County.

He searches for, "A Negro named Sambo, born in Africa and who has a down look and is about five feet high, and has the appearance

---

950 Ibid., January 4, 1798.

951 Gomez, p. 688.

952 Ibid.

of a Moor."[953] This latter comment about Mr. Morgain's slave indicates he was from the North African Supply Zone, Tunisia, Algeria, or Morocco, and, therefore, most likely spoke Arabic. Among the Maryland runaway slaves who had obvious Muslim names, we can point to about twenty that are incontrovertible. Maryam, a woman who refused to change her name to Mary, was owned by Thomas Turton of Prince George's County. She was eighteen years old and escaped on March 14, 1807, or so the *Maryland Gazette* tells us.[954] The name Maryam, of course, is the Arabic version of the mother of Isa, or Jesus. Maryam has been a very popular female name in Islam from its beginning in the seventh century.

Ishaq, a slave owned by G. T. Greenwood of Prince George's County, is "thirty-one years old." The *National Intelligencer* of October 8, 1810, offers a two-pound reward for the escaped captive of Mr. Greenwood's, so he offered his reward in British money.[955] Again, *Ishaq* is the Arabic version of Isaac. In Islam, he is the second son born to Ibrahim, by his wife Sarah. But unlike Judaism and Christianity, where the son of sacrifice is Isaac, in Islam it is Ismail, or Ishmael, who, at least in Islam is Ibrahim's first-born son, or *Ibn*, by Hagar.

Yusuf, a slave owned by Andrew Barnett of Baltimore County, ran away on August 22, 1851, making him one of the latest or most recent Muslim runaways in this study. Mr. Barnett took out an advertisement in the *Baltimore Sun* on that date.[956] Another slave named Bood, who was owned by Wilson Hunt of Baltimore County, is described this way by Mr. Hunt:

> He is thirty-eight years old, about five foot ten. He has a yellow complexion and was African born.[957]

The name "Bood," or *Ma-Bood,* is used as both a first and family

---

953 Maryland Gazette, May 24, 1775.

954 Ibid., April 11, 1790. Thomas Morgain, or Morgan, (1724–1763) was a Calvert County tobacco farmer.

955 Ibid., March 14, 1807.

956 Ibid., October 8, 1810. G. T. Greenwood owned a tobacco farm in Prince George's County in the early nineteenth century. He also owned Greenwood Mines.

957 Ibid., August 22, 1851.

name in the Arabic-speaking world. It means "worshipped" or "adored" in Semitic languages. In the United States, these names more often appear in New York, Pennsylvania, Wisconsin, and in North Carolina.

Sheriff George Scott of Prince George's County advertised in the *Maryland Gazette* from September 12, 1763, for a runaway slave named Sambo. He is "Tall and wore an Osnabrig shirt and trousers when he escaped."[958] This points to another phenomenon in regard to slave auctions.

In the second phase discussed in Chapter Seven on auctions, the job of auctions was given to hotels and taverns. As we see here, the job also was taken over by sheriffs and their deputies at times by the late eighteenth century. Eventually slave auctions were conducted in the Chesapeake region by the major slave traders by the 1820s, as seen earlier in Chapter Eight.

Another Sambo escaped with his wife, Hagar. They were both owned by Thomas Todd of Patapsco Neck in Baltimore County. He was forty-five years old and escaped on June 5, 1783, or so the *Maryland Gazette* tells us. His wife, Hagar, was "Thirty-five years old. They are supposed to have thirty or forty dollars with them. Both easily could pass for Free Negroes."[959]

The fact that both husband and wife had Muslim names suggests even more that they were members of the Islamic faith. The mention of money stolen from the master's household, in addition to the mistress's clothing, were the most common items stolen by female runaway slaves in Maryland. It is likely, then, that Hagar absconded with

---

958 Baltimore Sun, August 24, 1851. The African name "Bood" comes from the Arabic name Ma'Book, that is usually a male name used in West Africa. In Arabic, the name means adored or worshipped.

959 Maryland Gazette, September 12, 1763. George Scott was the sheriff of Prince George's County, Maryland, from 1766 until 1768.

the cash of her mistress.

The Biblical name Hagar is spelled *Hajar* in Arabic and Islam. She is the concubine of Ibrahim and the mother of Ishmael, or Ismail in Arabic, the progenitor of the Muslim faith, according to Islam.

Notley Madox, a Prince George's County planter, in the August 28, 1842, edition of the *Daily International Intelligencer*, sought the return of his slave Sambo, who was twenty years old and had a large scar over one eye. The tribal mark suggests this Sambo was from Gambia and the Mandinka Tribe, the scar being over the right eye.[960] The primary language of the Mandinka Tribe in the Senegambian Region was Arabic.

Joseph Nicholson of Queen Anne's County, in the August 13, 1773, edition of the *Maryland Gazette,* sought the return of his runaway slave, Hagar. She had been arrested after striking a fellow slave with a hoe. When she finally recovered, she was pardoned for her felony charge on September 22, 1773.[961] Mr. Nicholson also stated that Hagar was "from the Eboe Country," most likely from the Niger Valley Supply Zone, or the Bight of Benin Zone.

This runaway slave is significant because she points to another important source for identifying Muslim runaway slaves in the Chesapeake Bay region—court and prison records in the seventeenth to nineteenth centuries. These records are sometimes enormously helpful in identifying suspected Muslim runaway slaves, as in this case.

In this regard, Joseph Durding of Kent County, at least according to court records there, sought the return of his runaway slave named Mingo in the January 16, 1742, edition of the *Maryland Gazette*. Mingo was born in Africa and has "Country marks under his eyes." The marks in question were three vertical strokes beneath each eye. The name Mingo, as we have pointed out earlier, was given to males born on Sunday in several clans and tribes in West Africa in the eighteenth

---

960 Ibid., June 5, 1783. Thomas Todd and his family have lived on the east side of 9000 Old North Point Road, near Fort Howard, since 1664. Thomas Todd built a new house on the location in 1816.

961 Daily International Intelligencer, August 28, 1842. The original Notley Maddox (1698–1757) bought substantial land in Prince George's County. His grandson is the Notley Maddox mentioned here.

century. Mr. Durdin informs us that his Mingo was a "Bite Negro," a reference to the Bight of Benin Supply Zone.

This Mingo of Mr. Durding absconded because he was convicted of a felony. He was recovered a few weeks later and hanged on February 3, 1742, "in front of the County Court House."[962] This is another example of the many services that took place at county courthouses—executions—from the mid-eighteenth century on in the Chesapeake Bay region.

Indeed, these two examples of convicts, and many like them, point to another source for identifying Muslim captives in the early Chesapeake—county court and prison records. Mingo's tribal marks under both eyes suggest the Muslim Igbo, from the Niger Valley Supply Zone, or the Bights of Biafra or Benin. The "Eboes," or Igbo, in all three locations marked their warriors with three vertical scars beneath both eyes.

A slave named Walle, owned by a planter in Charlestown named Edward Worrell, was five foot eight to five foot ten. Mr. Worrell advertised for Walle in the February 19, 1775, edition of the *Maryland Gazette*. It is likely that the slave's name was originally *Wali*, an honorific title in Islam that means, "learned scholar."

Walle was described in the *Maryland Gazette* as being "African born and about twenty years old." He formerly was owned by Timothy Perkins, who sought Wali's return on a November 27, 1760, edition of the *Maryland Gazette*, and where Mr. Worrell believes his slave may

---

962 Maryland Gazette, September 22, 1773. Joseph Hooper Nicholson (1770–1817) was born in Chestertown, Maryland, in Kent County. He was an American attorney and judge in Queen Anne's County, Maryland. Captain John Nicholson (1756–1803) was born in Chestertown and later owned a tobacco farm in Kent County.

have gone.[963]

Again, it is likely that this Walle was named Wali, back in West Africa. Wali's owner fears he may have escaped north to Delaware, so he took out an ad in the *Pennsylvania Gazette*, on that same date, so that he might be recovered there, as well.

Similarly, a slave named Alley, owned by Elizabeth Dare on the Eastern Shore of Maryland, was described as being "Eighteen years old and not very black." Mrs. Dare advertised for her slave in the *Annapolis Gazette* from February 19, 1775. It is likely that the slave's original name back in Africa was Ali.

The name "Ali" means "elevated" or "high" in Arabic. It was first employed in naming Ali Ibn Abi Talib, the cousin of the Prophet Muhammad. Ali was the leader, or Caliph, of early Islam from 656 until 661.[964] After that time, "Ali" became a popular name in Islam of both males and females.

Another woman named Hagar ran away with Dinah and appeared in a 1765 edition of the *Maryland Gazette*. Their owner was James Round of Worcester County. Both were "African born."[965] Another married couple, Mingo and Hagar, ran away from the farm of Jonathan Cathell on April 29, 1771, according to the *Maryland Gazette* of that date.[966] Again the fact that both Mingo and Hagar had Muslim names is quite indicative. The name for Hagar in Arabic is *Hajar*. She is the mother of Ismail, and in Islam, she is sometimes called the "Matriarch of Monotheism."

Another slave named Mingo was owned by the lighthouse keep-

---

963 Ibid., January 16, 1742. Also see: Governor and Council (Commission Records, State of Maryland, 1726–1786), p. 215. Also see: C. Ansley Ellefson, Seven Hangmen of Colonial Maryland (Courtland, 2009), p. 19. One of whom is Mr. Durdin's Mingo's execution.

964 Ibid., November 27, 1760. Elizabeth and Robert Dare, brother and sister, were the owners of a large plantation in Calvert County, Maryland, on the Eastern Shore.

965 Annapolis Gazette, February 19, 1775. James Round was a Worcester County, Maryland, commissioner in the 1760s and 1770s. Ali Ibn Abi Talib was the cousin of the Prophet Muhammad and one of the first Caliphs of the faith.

966 Maryland Gazette, May 17, 1764.

er at the Old Plains Flats in Cecil County in southern Maryland. The keeper was a man named William Gunther who kept the lighthouse from 1839 on.[967] Gunther says his Mingo, "prayed several times a day and would not eat pork, nor touch a drop of Spirits." The Muslim Holy Book, the Qur'an, has provisions against the consumption of pork and of alcohol, as well.

Gunther is referring to Muslim dietary laws and its provisions against consuming pork and alcohol, as well as the provision of *Salaat* or praying five times a day in the Islamic faith.[968] There is no doubt that the lighthouse keeper's slave was a believer in the Islamic faith. The Islamic prohibition against eating pork is to be found at Qur'an 5:3, which says, "Forbidden to you is the flesh of the swine." At Qur'an 2:219 tells about wine and alcohol, "In it is a great sin as well as some profit for people, but the sin is greater than the profit."

Five other Maryland runaway slaves also had Muslim or Arabic names. The first of these is "Hagar, a new Negro Wench from the Guiney Country." Thus, she was most likely from the Sierra Leone Supply Zone, or the Windward Coast Zone. She ran away from Goose Neck, Maryland, with "a new Osnabrig coat and wrapper and a black striped handkerchief around her head."[969] Again, the "Guiney Country" implies that Hagar either came from the Gold Coast, the Windward Coast or the Sierra Leone Zone. Many Muslims lived in these regions by the late eighteenth century, particularly in Guinea, Guinea Bissau, Ghana and the Ivory Coast.

Another Sambo was "Twenty years old and came on the British ship *Savage*," or so the *Maryland Gazette* from April 12, 1781, tells us. Sambo is described as being "stout and healthy."[970] The same British ship would be involved in the escape of seventeen of George Washington's slaves from Mount Vernon, fourteen of whom eventually were returned to the first president's estate in Fairfax County, including Sambo Anderson.

---

967 Maryland Gazette, April 29, 1771.

968 Ibid., April 22, 1771.

969 Ibid., May 14, 1785.

970 Ibid., April 12, 1781. Gooseneck, Maryland, is near Hyattstown, Maryland.

An advertisement from the *Baltimore Advertiser* from April 15, 1787, speaks of a slave named Mingo who appeared in Annapolis in "the appearance of a Moor."[971] In the late eighteenth century, this meant dressed in traditional Islamic costume with kaftan, trousers, and a curved blade to the side of one's waist. This advertisement suggests this Mingo is from the North African Supply Zone, from Tunisia, Algeria or possibly from Morocco. If these facts were true, then one of the Maryland suspected runaway slaves was from the North African Supply Zone outlined in Chapter Two of this study.

Two other escaped Maryland slaves, who may well have been Muslims, are Ishmael or Ismail, and Sarah. The former appears in an advertisement from the *Maryland Gazette* from February 19, 1765, one of the few Maryland runaways who escaped in the winter months. His owner tells us, "He is a Cooper by trade" learned "back in Africa."[972]

The other slave, a woman named Sarah, was owned by Isaiah Smith of Talbot County. In the January 27, 1778, edition of the *Maryland Gazette*, Mr. Smith relates that Sarah, "Is African born, speaks Dutch and is from the Guiney Country."[973] Most likely, Sarah was either from the Gold Coast, or the Sierra Leone Supply Zone, or possibly the Windward Coast, where many Muslims could be found at the end of the eighteenth century.

Three other Maryland runaway slaves were also most likely Muslims. Their names were Hagar, Mingo and Sambo. Hagar is described in the *Maryland Gazette* on August 24, 1759, as "escaping with child, Fanny. She is a Mustee."[974] A Mustee is a term to designate children who have African and Native American parents.

Jack D. Forbes, in his book *African-Americans and Native Americans: Mustees, Half- Breeds, and Zambos*, lists several slaves as Mustees, including a slim Mustee fellow named Mingo, who may have been

971 Baltimore Advertiser, April 15, 1787. The HMS Savage was a sixteen-gun sloop in the Royal Navy. In the spring of 1781, seventeen of George Washington's slaves boarded the ship while docked at Mount Vernon. Among these escapees was a young Sambo Anderson.

972 Maryland Gazette, February 19, 1765.

973 Ibid., January 27, 1778. Isaiah Smith (born 1683) was a tobacco planter in Talbot County, Maryland.

974 Ibid., August 24, 1759.

a member of the Choctaw Tribe.[975] Another slave listed by Forbes is "A mulatto Mustee man named Toney, who appears as an Indian in both hair and complexion."[976]

The Mingo mentioned above was a twenty-five-year-old slave owned by Richard Brown of Baltimore County. Mr. Brown sought Mingo's return in a May 17, 1721, edition of the *Maryland Gazette*. Mr. Brown tells us that Mingo was "a blacksmith by trade."[977] Mr. William Digges of Charles County sought the return of his slave Sambo in a February 27, 1755, advertisement of the *Maryland Gazette*. Sambo is "African born and a Carpenter by trade."[978]

Another Maryland slave with a decidedly Muslim name is Sulayman, a saltwater Negro, twenty to twenty-two years of age. His owner Thomas Perkins from Anne Arundel County advertised for him in the *Maryland Gazette* on June 23, 1774.[979] Mr. Perkins' slave is a good example of the fact that watermen and mariners were often the occupation or skill set of many Maryland runaway slaves, as indicated earlier. At any rate, Sulayman is the Arabic version of Solomon. He is the youngest son of *Nabi* Dawud or "Prophet David." Sulayman is a very popular male name in Sunni Islam.

Allah gave Sulayman the ability to converse with the animals. At Qur'an 27:16, for example, that says, "He has been taught the language of the Tair," and elsewhere in the Holy Book that says he understood the communication of ants.[980]

Another slave whose homeland can be identified is Jamie, "an

975 Jack D. Forbes, African Americans and Native Americans (Champaign: University of Illinois Press, 1993), p. 101. Jack D. Forbes (1934–2011) was an American writer, scholar and political activist who specialized in Native American issues.

976 Ibid.

977 Maryland Gazette, May 17, 1721.

978 Ibid., February 27, 1755.

979 Ibid., June 23, 1774. Thomas Perkins owned a tobacco plantation and a mill in the late eighteenth century in Anne Arundel County, Maryland. William Digges (1651–1697) was born in Charles County, Maryland, but he became a tobacco farmer in St. Mary's County in Southern Maryland.

980 The Holy Qur'an, 27:16 (Author's translation).

Eboe Negro about 35 to 40 years old." His owner, a man named Isaiah Stewart, sought his return in the *Maryland Gazette* from July 17, 1762.[981] "Eboe," of course, is the Igbo Tribe that sent a remarkable number of slaves to the Commonwealth of Virginia. Some estimates suggest that between 1662 and 1700, 58,000 Igbo came to Virginia and from 1701 until 1750, another 218,000 from that tribe.

Between 1751 and 1810, as many as 750,000 Igbo came to Virginia. All tolled, from 1662 to 1810, that is slightly over one million Igbos came to the Virginia colony/state, and many were members of the Islamic faith at that time.[982]

Igbo slaves came to Virginia from both the Niger Valley Zone and the Bights of Benin and Biafra. To Virginia planters, they were known as "Ibo," "Eboe," or those from Biafra and Benin, as "Bites." Some scholars estimate that by the 1770s, thirty percent of the Virginia slave population were Igbo.

Perhaps the most famous Igbos in Virginia at that time were a group of Africans accused of the murder of Ambrose Madison, the grandfather of the future President James Madison. Douglas B. Chambers, in his *Murder at Montpelier*, published by the University Press of Mississippi in 2005, catalogs the murder and its repercussions.[983]

The "Guiney," likely referred to in many of the advertisements cited above, is a reference to what was formerly called "French Guinea" and "Dutch Guinea." The former was a predominantly Muslim area established around 1730 in West Africa. The major language was French in businesses, schools, in government industries, and the media. More than two dozen other indigenous languages also were spoken there.

Even today, French is still the predominant language in the Ivory Coast. Dutch Guinea, on the other hand, was mostly identified with the Sierra Leone Supply Zone, or the Windward Coast Zone, and many of these captives spoke Dutch.

Much of West Africa began to speak French in the seventeenth

981 Maryland Gazette, July 17, 1762.

982 Douglas B. Chambers, Murder at Montpelier (Jackson: University Press of Mississippi, 2005). Chambers teaches in the history department of Southern Mississippi University in Hattiesburg.

983 Ibid.

century. A distinction is generally made between the "First Colonial Empire," that existed until 1814, and the "Second Colonial Empire, which began with the conquest of Algeria by France in 1830, and came to an end, for the most part, when Algeria declared its independence from France in 1962.

Mookinga and Sambo, two of the earliest Maryland runaway slaves with Muslim names and both African-born, were advertised for in the *Easton News*. They escaped from the farm of John Hollins on July 24, 1692.[984] Mr. Hollins called them "Mandingos," meaning they were most likely from the Senegambian Supply Zone, a Fulbe, a Wolof, or a Mandingo that seems most likely.

The slave of James George on the Eastern Shore of Maryland, a man named Pero, is the tallest of our suspected Muslim runaways. Mr. George tells us in the June 22, 1797, edition of the *Maryland Gazette* that Pero was:

> Six foot six. He has lost some of his fingernails from frost bite and was African born.[985]

The name Pero was very popular in the mid-eighteenth century in the Portuguese colony of Mozambique among the Bantu people there. Thus, the tall Pero most likely was from the East African Supply Zone. Again, Pero may have originated in the East African Supply Zone and then traveled by land on an Arab slave coffle to Angola, by way of one of the six major Arab caravan routes across Africa, east to west.

Walter Beall's slave, a Mulatto man named James, is about five foot ten and has short black hair. "He has a pair of buckles on his shoes and is a sensible and artful fellow. He was born in Africa and he may probably forged a pass, or bought one from a white indentured servant. Whoever takes him to a jail shall receive five pounds reward." This is consistent with early runaway slave rewards expressed in British currency.

Walter Beall offers his reward for James in British currency, he

984 Easton News, July 24, 1692. James George owned a tobacco farm in Calvert County, Maryland, on the Eastern Shore.

985 Maryland Gazette, June 22, 1797. Dr. John Hollins (1683–1739) was a British-born physician. He came with his family to America in the early 1790s. His father, John Hollins, is the slave owner mentioned here.

suggests James may have forged a pass, and it is possible he was aided by white indentured servants. At any rate, Beall offers a "five-pound reward" for the recovery of James. Another slave named Sambo was owned by Benjamin Brookes of Marlboro. Mr. Brookes' Sambo is:

> A clean made Fellow, between thirty and forty years old, has rather long hair, being of an East India breed. He was formerly the slave of Mr. Isaac Simmons, near Pig Point, in Anne Arundel County.[986]

The "East Indian" implies that Mr. Brooke's Sambo originated in the East African Supply Zone, which did regular commerce with India in the eighteenth century. Thus, this Sambo may have been another traveler across Africa, east to west, by way of an Arab slave coffle. It is also possible that Sambo originally came to the Caribbean before his eventual landing in Maryland.

Mr. Brookes purchased this advertisement for the recovery of his Sambo on May 25, 1775. The same slave occasionally goes by the name Sam Locker, or so Mr. Brooks indicates in his runaway Virginia advertisement.[987] He also may have originated from the Old Fort in Stone Town, Zanzibar, where another large slave prison existed in the late eighteenth century.

Mr. John Ashton offered six pounds reward for the capture of his mulatto slave named Tom, who is described by his owner as being:

> A Shoe maker by trade, about twenty-one years old, and five foot nine or ten inches high. He stoops naturally and has fair skin for a Negro, but he has a remarkable beard when he lets it grow. He was born in Africa and has a great deal of impudence in his conversation.[988]

Mr. Ashton indicates his slave Sambo is African born, a shoemak-

986 Ibid., May 25, 1775. Benjamin Brooks of Upper Marlboro was the brother of Joseph Brooks, who owned a shipyard in Annapolis in the mid-eighteenth century.

987 Ibid., June 15, 1775. Walter T. G. Beall and his son Walter T.G. Beall, Jr. (1817–1842) owned a tobacco farm in Montgomery County, Maryland.

988 Ibid.

er by trade, and is often impudent in his conversations. Ashton also mentions the fact that his Sambo "stoops naturally." He also indicates that Sambo has a remarkable beard when he lets it grow. This is one of the few runaway advertisements in Maryland that mention facial hair.

This is one of the few male suspected Muslim slaves in Maryland that refer to facial hair. Mr. Ashton purchased the advertisement for his absconded slave in the June 15, 1775, edition of the *Maryland Gazette*. "He may be living near Bellair, on the Patuxent, in Prince George's County, where he formerly lived with some white people," and that is precisely where Mr. Ashton believes he is headed.[989]

A young slave named Sarah belonged to George Somerville near Dr. Stevenson's copper mine. "She took with her a Mulatto boy, about six or seven years old, and a number of garments she has stolen." Mr. Somerville adds in his January 27, 1778, announcement of the *Maryland Journal and Baltimore Advertiser:*

> She is supposed to have one or more horses with her, and may possibly attempt to pose as a white wife. She is a lusty Wench that speaks good English and Dutch.[990]

More than likely, the clothes she absconded with were those of her mistress and the horses from the master. This is one of the rare cases where a female slave left with horses belonging to her master. More often, horses and guns were taken by male runaways. Mr. Somerville also indicates his slave could easily pass as a white woman. The expression "Lusty Wench" refers to the fact that she was a comely negro. Perhaps she was a "Fancy Girl," the name applied to female slaves in the sex business.

Again, Mr. Somerville's Sarah may have been from Dutch Guinea, and thus the Sierra Leone Zone, or the Windward Coast Zone, and quite possibly could also have been a Muslim. The same could be said for another married couple who ran away from the farm of John Chapple.

The woman of the pair was named Peg, who is about seventeen years old. She carried with her a young child. Her husband is a man

---

989 Maryland Journal and Baltimore Advertiser, January 27, 1778.

990 Maryland Gazette, February 19, 1779. George Clark Somerville (1757–1791) was a Revolutionary War hero and tobacco planter in Maryland.

named Ibrahim. He is about five foot six and "has an impediment in his speech." It is also significant that the husband's name was Ibrahim, not Abraham.

Mr. Chapple adds:

> He is about twenty-five years old, African-born, and a very artfull Fellow. He formerly belonged to Alexander Lawson in Baltimore Town. Whoever secures these two Negroes will be given a reward of twenty dollars.[991]

Again, given the name of the husband of this couple, they very well may have been members of the Muslim faith. The advertisement from Mr. Chapple mentions Ibrahim's personality, his former owner, and a reward given in American currency, something odd for the very late eighteenth century.

Similarly, the slave of John Hanson, whom he calls "Ned Barnes," is African born, "about thirty-five years old, and five feet six or eight high. He wears shoes with silver buckles, and he may attempt to join the British troops. He likely went off on a roan horse."[992]

The scar over the right eye indicates Mr. Barnes was most likely a member of the Mandinka Tribe from the Senegambian Supply Zone. Again, the mention of an absconded horse was accomplished by a male runaway slave, as was usual in Maryland.

Mr. Hanson took out this advertisement in the *Frederick Times*, from July 12, 1781. In an ad in the *Maryland Gazette* from November 13, 1783, Robert Darnall wished for the return of his mulatto wench named Phillis. "She has a large scar on one of her cheeks, and she will attempt to pass as a free woman."[993] This slave may have been Phillis Wheatley, who went on to become a famous African American poet during the colonial period in the Maryland colony. Wheatley is discussed in Chapter One of this study.

The tribal mark of this slave suggests she was a member of the

991 Ibid.

992 Ibid. Dr. Stevenson's copper mine was located in Frederick County, Maryland.

993 Ibid., July 12, 1781, and November 13, 1783. Alexander Lawson owned a tobacco farm in Baltimore County near the Harford County line in the eighteenth century.

Fulani Tribe, and thus the Senegambian Supply Zone, or the Yoruban Tribe in the Niger Valley Supply Zone, or the Bight of Benin. If she was a Fulani, then she most likely spoke Arabic.

A slave named Billy ran away from the farm of John Horrell in Saint Mary's County. Mr. Horrell tells us about his absconded slave:

> He is African born, about five foot ten inches high, a lusty well-made Fellow, and when he walks his right knee bends much toward his left, and his wool grows very low on his temples. He is about twenty years old and has a mother living in Alexandria.[994]

Mr. Horrell mentions his slave's hairstyle, his body type, and where he may have settled after his escape. The name of Billy back in Africa may well have been Bilali. Mr. Horrell also tells us about Billy that he has "one scar over his right eye," which indicates that he was a Mandinka, and probably spoke Arabic.

Another slave named Nace was owned by Samuel Abell when he ran away sometime around May 29, 1788, or so the *Maryland Gazette* tells us. Mr. Abell relates:

> He was born in Africa. About twenty-five years old and of a dark complexion, about five nine inches high, and has a scar over his right eye. He formerly belonged to Robert Abell, who lately has moved to Kentucky. When I purchased him he thought it a sham sale and now has run off accordingly. I offer six dollars reward.[995]

Nace is a Swahili male name. Thus, it is likely that Mr. Abell's slave was from the East African Supply Zone, as outlined in Chapter Two of this study. Most probably, Nace was a member of the Bantu

---

994 Ibid. John Francis Horrell was a tobacco planter in Saint Mary's County. John Hanson (1721–1783) was born on a tobacco farm called Mulberry Hill, also called Mulberry Grove in Port Tobacco, Maryland. In November of 1781, Hanson was elected to be president of the United States by the First Continental Congress. Thus, George Washington was not the first president of the US. Washington was elected seven years later in 1789.

995 Ibid., May 29, 1788. Samuel Abell (1755–1801) was a tobacco farmer in St. Mary's County in southern Maryland.

Tribe of Mozambique and Madagascar, one of the largest peoples in East Africa, and may have traveled on an inland coffle from West to East Africa.

Many Bantu, in the late eighteenth century, also had a tribal scar over the right eye. Again, if this is true, then Nace is one of the few East African slaves in this study, perhaps traded by Arab agents from Yemen or Oman, or maybe the Old Fort in Zanzibar.

What we have said here is also true of another female slave named Nacy, who was owned by Elizabeth Warring of Prince George's County. In the July 27, 1820, edition of the *National Intelligencer*, Mrs. Warring advertised for Nacy's return. She tells us that the slave "has a brother and sister living in Nottingham, Maryland, and Mrs Warring seems to think that is where Nacy was headed."[996] "Nacey" is the female version of Nace. It was another common female name in East Africa in the eighteenth century, among the Bantu peoples of the area. If Nacey was East African, then she may have traveled to West Africa by way of an in-land slave coffle conducted by Omanis or Yemenis.

Two final Maryland slaves who were both African-born were Malvina and Emmanuel. The latter was a twenty-five-year-old male owned by Thomas Early of Prince George's County. On March 16, 1855, Mr. Early took out an advertisement to recover Emmanuel. He says, "He has a mother and brother in Montgomery County and three horizontal scars beneath both eyes."[997]

The tribal scars suggest Mr. Early's captive was either a Mandingo, of the Senegambian Zone, or a Krio of the Sierra Leone Supply Zone, or possibly a member of the Mende Tribe. All three of these zones had pockets of Muslims by the mid-eighteenth century.

One of the most interesting of possible Maryland Muslim runaway slaves is a man named "Antonio," who came to Maryland in 1621 as an indentured servant. He survived an Indian massacre in 1622, was married to a slave named Mary in 1623 and received his freedom some-

996 National Intelligencer, July 27, 1820.

997 Maryland Gazette, March 16, 1855. The Elder Samuel Abell (1677–1762) first settled in Maryland. His son, Samuel (1755–1801) is the Samuel Abell mentioned here.

time around 1635. Later, he changed his name to Anthony Johnson. It appears he was born in Angola and was sold there by Arab slave traders.

It is likely that he converted before his sale. At any rate, later, Anthony Johnson became a tobacco farmer himself and owned several slaves in both Virginia and Maryland. He is discussed at length in the opening chapter of this study.

Even today, the largest tribes in Angola are all Bantu tribes. The largest is the Ovimbundu, which account for 37 percent of the population, the Kimbundu have 25 percent of Angola's population, and the Bakongo make up thirteen percent of the population of the Southwest African nation. If Antonio was indeed a convert to Islam, then he most likely was Ovimbundu.

Finally, Mr. James Duckett of Prince George's County advertised in the January 24, 1855, edition of the *Maryland Gazette* for the return of his slave called Malvina. She was born in Africa, speaks French and a little Dutch. "She has relations at the farm of John T. Berry of Nottingham, and a husband who belongs to Benjamin J. Hodges of Upper Marlboro," in Maryland.

The African-born and the ability to speak Dutch, also suggest the Sierra Leone Supply Zone.[998] The 1855 date makes Malvina one of the most recent suspected Muslim runaway slaves in the Chesapeake Bay region.

From this discussion of suspected Muslim runaway slaves in Maryland, we may make the following conclusions. First, in the two thousand advertisements for Maryland escaped slaves, we have discovered fifty-five suspected Muslims. This fifty-five includes forty men and fifteen women. Second, these suspected Muslim runaways came from a number of the Supply Zones outlined in the second chapter of this study.

Among these supply zones, we have indicated the Senegambian Zone, the Niger Valley Zone, the Gold Coast Zone, the Sierra Leone Zone, the Windward Coast Zone, the Angolan Zone, the Bight of Benin, the East African Supply Zone, the North African Zone, and one

998 Ibid., January 24, 1855. James Moore Duckett (1787–1850) was a tobacco planter in southern Maryland. Benjamin J. Hodges owned the property known as Pentland Hills in Upper Marlboro, Maryland. The historic house is on Danenhower Road. Pentland Hills was named after a group of hills in southwest Scotland, from which Duckett's ancestors came.

from South Africa, in Namibia.

Of the suspected fifty-five Muslim runaway slaves, thirty-nine may be identified in terms of their origins. At least twelve were from Senegambia, six from the Niger Valley Zone, seven from the Sierra Leone Supply Zone, ten from the Windward and Gold Coasts, one from Angola, and three from the East African Zone.

A third conclusion we may make about the fifty-five suspected Muslim runaways is that at least a dozen of these slaves may be identified from the tribal marks they received back in Africa. These twelve came primarily from Senegambia and the Niger River Valley, or the Bight of Benin Zone, much like what we saw in the suspected Muslim slaves in Virginia in Chapter Eight.

Many of the African tribes of the fifty-five suspected Muslim escaped slaves also can be identified. We have seen in our analysis members of the Wolof, Fulbe, or Fulani, the Tureg, Yoruba, Igbo, Krio, Mende, Temne, Bantu, Pungo, Mandingo, Krobo, and a number of other tribes in our analysis. Some of these identifications, as we have seen, come from biographical information provided by the owners of these slaves and some from their tribal marks, three fewer in Maryland than Virginia. In fact, we have suggested that a dozen of the suspected Maryland Muslim runaway slaves may be identified by the tribal marks alone, while there were fifteen in Virginia.

A fourth conclusion that may be made about the fifty-five suspected Muslim runaway slaves is that many of them may be identified by the languages, other than English, that the slaves were capable of speaking. These languages, as we have seen, include Arabic, French and Dutch. The Arabic speakers, most likely, came from the Senegambian Zone, the French speakers from the Windward or Gold Coasts, or the French Forts of Albreda and Fort Saint Joseph in the Senegambian Supply Zone.

The Dutch speakers from the Sierra Leone Supply Zone, and the German speaker most likely from Namibia, in Southwest Africa, where there was a German colony in the early twentieth century, and who may be identified simply by her Wolof Tribal mark on her right hand.

We also have suggested that biographical clues provided from the owners of many of these escaped Maryland slaves may be an aid in identifying the Muslim slaves. Slaves from the Senegambian Zone spoke Arabic, the Gold and Windward Coast captives often spoke French, and those from the Sierra Leone Zone many times spoke Dutch, and these facts may aid us in identifying Muslim slaves.

This information may say, "He is from the Guiney Country," or "He is a Mandingo," or "He is an Igbo." Finally, we have argued that many of the suspected Muslim runaways have Arabic and Islamic names that may aid in their identification as Moslems, particularly in the cases where multiple family members all have Arabic or Muslim names, or where there are many Arabic names in the same location. Indeed, more than eighty percent of the Maryland suspected Muslim runaway slaves had Muslim or Arabic names.

Indeed, of the fifty-five suspected Muslims, forty-five had Islamic names. This brings us to one more section of this chapter on pieces of art that embodied Maryland Muslim runaway slaves, the topic of the next section of this ninth chapter.

Muslim Runaway Slaves in Art

One final source of Maryland runaway slaves is several pieces of art that depict the phenomenon of escaped slaves. In this final section of Chapter Nine, we will discuss ten important pieces of art that may serve as aids for understanding Maryland runaway slaves. One piece is entitled *The Fugitive's Joy*. It shows a black slave dressed in a striped shirt and white pants. He carries his belongings, which are attached to a staff, much like a hobo. He appears to be headed for freedom. The caption beneath the depiction implies it may be Frederick Douglass on his journey to freedom. The watercolor and ink painting was completed around 1935 by African American artist Bernarda Bryson. The National Underground Railroad Network to Freedom published this image.[999]

The second image of runaway slaves was painted by Eastman Johnson in 1862 during the American Civil War. Johnson, who was born in 1824 and died in 1906, was an American painter from New York City. His painting, *A Ride for Liberty: The Fugitive Slaves*, shows a galloping horse on whose back ride a slave family: father,

---

999 Bernard Bryson, "The Fugitive Joy," in University of Ottawa Review.

mother and child. Johnson claims the inspiration for the painting was a scene he saw at the Battle of Manassas on March 2, 1862, during the Civil War.

Mr. Johnson's painting is a poignant and evocative image that tells the story of a runaway slave family, moving to their freedom.[1000] The Brooklyn Museum in New York owns this oil on paperboard painting.

The third image of runaway slaves is a more contemporary one. It is entitled *Charles Wright: The Runaway Slave Who Saved the Union*. It is a mixed-media creation on canvas, full of bright colors and hues. A well-dressed African slave stands in the center of the image. He wears a dark hat, and his arms are crossed at the hips. In the background are obvious signs of the American Civil War from which he seems to have escaped.[1001]

A fourth image that shows runaway slaves in the south was completed by German-born caricaturist Thomas Nast (1840–1902). Nast entitled this collection of images *Runaway Slaves*, one of which is called *Southern Exiles on Their Way North*. The painting is filled with huddled black slaves and a number of white sympathizers who appear to be helping the slave family to their freedom. A frightened and huddled family looks at an approaching storm. Lightning is seen in the background.

The storm in Mr. Nast's image appears to grow worse as it approaches. This painting was originally a leaf from an edition of *Harper's Weekly* in 1863. Nast's depiction is a stunning image of a slave family on the run.[1002] He regularly drew for *Harpers* in the mid-nine-

---

1000 Ibid.

1001 Eastman Johnson, A Ride for Liberty—The Fugitive Slaves, Johnson (1824–1906) was an American painter, born in Maine, and co-founder of the Metropolitan Museum of Art in New York City. Nottingham is an unincorporated town in Prince George's County, Maryland. The town of Upper Marlboro is the county seat of Prince George's County, Maryland.

1002 Charles Wright: The Runaway Slave Who Saved the Union by Bernarda Bryson Shahn (1903–2004), an American painter. The painting is a mixed media and acrylic creation on canvas approximately fifty-three inches by forty-one inches. Wright was a Virginia slave from Culpepper. He arrived at the Union lines in June of 1863, complete with copious information about General Lee's troops and their positions. Charles Wright was one

teenth century.

Another contemporary African American painter named Glenn Ligon in 1993 painted a series of images he calls *Runaways*. In the series, Ligor reproduces several runaway slave advertisements from the mid-nineteenth century. One of these is a twelve-inch by sixteen-inch lithograph on paper depicting a runaway slave who appears to be leaving his well-dressed master in the center of the image.[1003] Another image is also a replica of a mid-nineteenth-century Maryland runaway slave advertisement.

The *Runaways* is a series of ten lithographs based on nineteenth-century advertisements published by slave owners, wishing to recover their property. The series is owned by the Museum of Modern Art in New York City.[1004]

The Historical Hudson Valley Association, in their Center for Arts Education, own several pieces of art inspired by runaway slave advertisement from the colonial period. One image, in particular, is entitled *Night Journey*. It was completed by contemporary Chinese American artist Sisi Li. She was inspired by a runaway slave advertisement from April 23, 1753. In Li's painting, a female slave, dressed in a striped skirt, white blouse, and brown jacket, tugs at her waistline with her left hand.[1005]

Another painting from the same show by American painter Dara Illowsky shows a young African slave named Adonia. He is shackled by chains on his right arm, and blood is visible on his chest and abdomen. Ms. Illowsky calls the painting *The Last Time*. She says she was inspired by a runaway slave advertisement from September 30,

---

of the Civil War's greatest Union spies.

1003 Thomas Nast, Southern Exiles on Their Way North, in Harpers Weekly. Nast (1840–1902) was a German-born caricaturist and cartoonist. He is sometimes called The Father of the American Cartoon.

1004 Glenn Ligor, Runaways, Museum of Modern Art, New York City. See: Huey Copeland, "Glenn Ligor and Other Runaway Subjects," in Representations 113, (Winter, 2011), pp. 73–110. Charles H. Wright (1918–2002) was born to slave parents in Alabama. Eventually, he became a physician and founded the museum in his name.

1005 Sisi Li, Night Journey, the Historical Hudson Valley Association. Sissi Li is an abstract, Chinese American artist.

1761.[1006]

In Sisi Li's painting, a farm is seen in the background, at some distance, above which a full moon shines brightly. Li's creation is another evocative image of a young slave searching for her freedom.[1007]

An 1863 painting entitled *Fugitive Slaves Fleeing From the Eastern Shore of Maryland to an Underground Railroad Depot in Delaware* is produced by "Shutterstock."[1008] It shows a band of about a dozen slaves, with their belongings in hand, moving to freedom in the north. The black and white etching is thirteen and a half inches by nine and a half inches. It is produced by Alamay Images, Ltd.[1009]

Finally, an 1861 painting entitled *The Hunted Slaves* by English painter Richard Ansdell (1815–1885) shows a couple of runaway slaves beating off vicious dogs with an ax. The slaves in the painting are a man and a woman who appear to be very frightened by the presence of the dogs. Ansdell was born in Liverpool and painted animal and genre scenes. He was also an engraver.[1010]

This brings us to the conclusions of this chapter, followed by the notes of the same. Chapter Ten, the final chapter of this study, is a review of the general conclusions we have made in our analysis, or a general summary of the highlights of this study.

Conclusions

We began this ninth chapter with some general remarks about the phenomenon of runaway slave advertisements in the colony/state of Maryland from colonial times up until the Civil War. In this opening section, we described the twenty-five newspapers from which two thousand Maryland runaway slaves could be found. Those escaped slaves, as we have shown, primarily came from ten or eleven Maryland counties from central Maryland to the Eastern Shore and southern Maryland.

1006 Dara Illowsky, "The Last Time," Historic Hudson Valley Association. Illowsky, who was educated at Brown University, is now an environmental educator for city parks in Brooklyn, New York.

1007 Fugitive Slaves Fleeing the Eastern Shore of Maryland to an Underground Railroad Depot in Delaware. Alamay Images, Ltd.

1008 Ibid.

1009 Ibid.

1010 Ibid.

This section of the chapter was followed by an introduction, as well as an analysis of fifty-five runaway Maryland slaves whom we suspect were believers in the Islamic faith. From our analysis, we have shown that the forty men and fifteen women most likely came from the following African Supply Zones, from the seventeenth to the nineteenth centuries: Senegambia, the Niger River Valley, the Sierra Leone Supply Zone, the Gold Coast Zone, the Windward Coast Supply Zone, from Angola, the Bight of Biafra, from North Africa and Mozambique or Madagascar, of the East African Zone, as well as one slave from southwest Africa, in Namibia, and thus from the South African Supply Zone.

Along the way, we identified the African origins of thirty of the fifty-five suspected Muslim slaves. Also identified were the various tribes to which these slaves belonged and identified the tribal marks acquired in Africa of about a dozen of the escaped slaves in Maryland made from various tribes back in Africa. This is slightly fewer than the number we saw in the suspected Virginia Muslim runaways, where we saw fifteen.

Altogether, we introduced fifty-five suspected Maryland runaway slaves who may have been members of the Islamic faith. Forty are men and fifteen women. The average age of these suspected members of the Islamic faith was twenty-seven years and five months, about the same average of the Virginia Muslim runaways in the previous chapter. The shortest of these slaves was four foot three and the tallest six foot six. The average height was five foot eight, about the same average as our Virginia Muslim runaways in Chapter Eight.

Of the fifty-five, the origins of thirty-five can be fairly accurately identified: eight were from Senegambia; five from the Windward Coast, ten from the Gold Coast, and six from the Niger Valley Supply Zone, three from the East African Supply Zone, one from North Africa, one from Angola, one from southwest Africa in Namibia or the South African Zone, and the remainder are unknown.

Of the fifty-five suspected Moslems, at least four spoke Arabic and as many as ten, ten knew French, and another four spoke or understood some Dutch. The Arabic speakers were most likely from Senegal and Gambia, the French from the Windward or Gold Coasts, or the Sierra Leone Supply Zone, and the Dutch speakers from the Windward

Coast, or the Sierra Leone Supply Zone, as well.

Thirty of the fifty-five suspected Muslim slaves are identified in terms of the eleven Maryland counties from which they absconded. These were:

Baltimore County 10 Slaves

Prince George's County 2

Anne Arundel County 3

Montgomery County 1

Saint Mary's County 2

Saint Anne's County 2

Charles County 2

Cecil County 1

Worcester County 4

Queen Anne's County 2

Talbot County 1

In the closing section of this chapter, we explored ten different artistic depictions of runaway slaves in early America. Some of these images were produced in the nineteenth century or early twentieth century, and contemporary American artists constructed three of them.[1011]

In many ways, the conclusions made in this chapter are embodied by these pieces of art from the nineteenth and twentieth centuries. This brings us to Chapter Ten, an analysis of the major conclusions we have made in this study. It is best to see Chapter Ten as an analysis of the "Highlights" of this study.

1011 Ibid.

Chapter Ten: Some Major Conclusions of This Study

> He was sweating as much as I ever did while in Slavery on the Montserrat Beach... I had never seen Divines exert themselves in this manner.
>
> —Olaudah Equiano, *The Interesting Narrative of the Life of Olaudah Equiano*

> Everything in Africa, indeed, inclines the mind to thought, to meditation, to reflection, to comparison, to remark...it is a land much talked about and so little known
>
> —Francis Moore, *Travels into the Inland Parts of Africa*[1012]

> We made some of you the means of trying the others. So, will you persevere and be patient. Your Lord is always watching you.
>
> —The Holy Qur'an 25:20 (Author's translation)[1013]

Introduction

The overall purpose of this final chapter is to catalog the major conclusions found in this study on suspected Muslim slaves in the Chesapeake Bay region from colonial times to the end of the Civil War period. In that regard, it is best to see this study as having four major parts, the first of which begins in Maryland and Virginia, and consists of the

1012 Francis Moore (1708–1757) was a British travel writer and abolitionist. He worked for the Royal Africa Company in Gambia for many years. Monserrat Beach refers to an island in the Lesser Antilles where Gardo Baquàqua was taken before coming to Brazil.

1013 All the use of Arabic in Chapter Ten are the translations of the author.

opening chapter of this study. We will sketch out those four parts here, and then discuss them one at a time, in separate sections of this chapter.

These four sections of this study are the following:

> Part One: Introduction to Muslim Slaves in the Chesapeake. Chapter 1, in America
>
> Part Two: Slave Supply Zones and the Middle Passage. Chapters 2 and 3, in Africa
>
> Part Three: Coffles, Slave Traders, Slave Jails and Auctions. Chapters 4 to 7, in America
>
> Part Four: Runaway Slaves in Virginia and Maryland. Chapters 8–10, in America)

Also included in this final chapter are nine images that depict the material of this study, as well as four appendices providing the raw material of the suspected Muslim slaves in Maryland and Virginia, outlined in Chapters Eight and Nine (Appendices A and B), as well as a summary of the tribal scars and markings of twenty-seven of these suspected Muslim runaway slaves in the Chesapeake region (Appendix C), and a summary of other prominent Muslim American slaves (Appendix D).

In the first part of this study, we have attempted to give an introduction to the study of Muslim slaves in the Chesapeake Bay region. Here we shall begin this chapter with a general analysis of the material in the first part of this study on Muslim slaves in the Chesapeake Bay region in the seventeenth to nineteenth centuries. We then will explore subsequent sections in this chapter on parts two, three and four.

Part One: Introduction to Muslim Slaves in the Chesapeake Region.

In the first part of this study, we began by making some very general remarks on the history of West African slavery in relation to the Chesapeake Bay region. In this opening section of the first chapter, we also have introduced and discussed various laws both in Maryland and Virginia regarding the practice of slavery there. We also introduced and discussed the first known African man to set foot in the colony of Maryland, Mattheus de Sousa, who may well have been a Muslim slave from the Portuguese colony of Mozambique, and thus from the East African Supply Zone.

Indeed, we have suggested that Mr. de Sousa is significant for a number of reasons, including the fact that he came to Maryland, along with Father Andrew White, S. J., aboard the ship the *Ark*. Second, he came as an indentured servant. Third, he was of mixed African and European descent and thus was called a "Molato." Fourth, he was elected to the Maryland General Assembly in 1641. Fifth, after his manumission in 1646, de Sousa worked as a ship's captain, while trading among Native Americans. And sixth, de Sousa may well have been from the Portuguese province of Mozambique and thus from the East African Supply Zone, as outlined in Chapter Two of this study.[1014] de Sousa had a Portuguese surname and may have been brought to Mozambique by Arab traders from Muscat, Oman, or Aden in Yemen. If these suppositions are true, then Mattheus de Sousa may very well have been the first black man in Maryland, as well as the first Muslim man in the colony. Indeed, this may be why there is nothing in the de Sousa record about his religious views, if he had any.

In the opening section of the first chapter of this study, we also have introduced a black man named "Antonio," who may well have been one of the twenty Africans who first came to the colony of Virginia in 1619. Like Mattheus de Sousa, Antonio appears to have been an indentured servant, and like de Sousa, Antonio was set free after his required service. We also have pointed out that Antonio changed his name to Anthony Johnson, and then later owned slaves of his own in

1014 There are a variety of materials extant on the life of Mattheus de Sousa. The two best sources remain the Maryland State Archives document SC 3520-2810 and the essay by David S. Bogden, entitled, "Matheus de Sousa, Maryland's First Colonist of African-American Descent," in Maryland Historical Society Magazine 96, no. 1 (2002). The word "Molato" was a seventeenth century version of "Mulatto." Andrew White, S. J. (1579–1656) was a London-born Jesuit missionary who was one of the earliest chroniclers of the Maryland colony.

both Virginia and then in Maryland.[1015] Again, like de Sousa, Antonio originally had a Portuguese name before he decided in the New World that he wanted to sound more American. There is some evidence that Antonio was from the Angola Supply Zone, as discussed in the second chapter of this study. Angola, of course, was also a Portuguese colony for much of the seventeenth to nineteenth centuries. If Antonio came from Mozambique, then he could have traveled to the Angola Zone in an overland Arab slave coffle in one of the six major trading routes from East to West Africa, much like Matteus de Sousa.

As we have shown, Mr. Johnson also was involved in one of the earliest lawsuits in the colonies, when his slave named John Casor sued him because he claimed that Johnson had treated him cruelly.[1016] Mr. Johnson prevailed in this suit and lived out his life growing tobacco on his farms in Virginia and then in Maryland.

In the opening section of part one, we pointed out that by the 1680s, white European indentured servitude in the Chesapeake Bay region was on the wane, and slavery was on the rise. Indeed, we have introduced a series of laws in the two colonies that aided in the regu-

---

1015 The two best accounts of the life of Antonio, or Anthony Johnson, are T. H. Breen and Stephen Innes, Myne Owne Ground: Race and Freedom on Virginia's Eastern Shore, 1646–1676 (New York: Oxford University Press, 2004); and Peter Ward, Strange New Land: Africans in Colonial America (New York: Oxford University Press, 2003). The "Twenty and odd Negroes" to which we refer here is related to a comment made by John Smith in his General History of Virginia (London, 1642) in which he observes, "About the last August came in a Dutch man-of-Warre that sold us twenty Negars." Some more recent work on this issue comes from Engel Sluiter's article, "New Light on the Twenty and Odd Negroes Arriving in Virginia, August 1619." This essay was published in The William and Mary Quarterly 54, no. 1, (April 1997), pp. 395–398.

1016 There are a number of accounts of the life and legal case of John Castor and his relationship to Anthony Johnson. Among those are Michael Walsh, White Cargo (New York: NYU Press, 2008); John Anderson Russell, The Free Negro in Virginia (Baltimore: Johns Hopkins University Press, 1913), particularly pp. 29–32; Philip S. Foner, History of Black Americans (New York: Oxford University Press, 1980); and Edgar Toppin, The Black American in the United States (New York: Allyn& Bacon, 1973), particularly pp. 46–50.

lation of slave ownership. In fact, we have pointed out that the legal status of black people in the Chesapeake Bay colonies was not always crystal clear, in the seventeenth and eighteenth centuries, and stayed that way up until the close of the Civil War.

In the second section of part one of this study, we began by pointing out that the three most famous Maryland slaves—Harriet Tubman, Frederick Douglass and Kunta Kinte, the ancestor of Alex Haley—all had Muslim ancestors. Additionally, we have explored the lives and times of three other prominent Muslim slaves in Maryland—Job Diallo, Loumein Yoas and Yarrow Mamout, who was born in Guinea and thus was from the Sierra Leone Supply Zone. Mamout was quite possibly a member of the Krio Tribe, or Krobo Tribe, as was Sambo Anderson, George Washington's slave.[1017] Job and Loumein, of course, were both from the Senegambian Supply Zone and members of the Mandinka or Wolof Tribes.

In this second section of this opening chapter, we have argued that Harriet Tubman's Muslim ancestors were members of the Asante Tribe; Frederick Douglass' family name "Bailey" may have been derived from the common Muslim name, Belali, or Ben Ali; and that Kunta Kinte was a member of the Islamic faith from the Senegambian Supply Zone.

As we have shown, each of these three—Job, Loumein, and Yarrow—early on, were manumitted by their owners in Maryland. Each paid taxes, and two of the three—Job and Loumein—were returned to Africa. We also indicated that two of the three—Job and Yarrow—were the subjects of three Anglo-American painters. Kunta Kinte's life, of course, was the focus of the television series and film *Roots*. We have provided descriptions of those portraits by Peale, Hoare, and Simpson, at the close of Chapter One.[1018]

1017 James H. Johnson's From Slave Ship to Harvard is the best biography of Yarrow Mamout. It was published by Fordham University Press in 2012. Thomas Bluett's biography of Job Diallo, entitled Some Memories of the Life of Job, was originally published in the eighteenth century. Nabu Press in Charleston, South Carolina, published an edition of Bluett's work in 2014. For this study, we employed the copy of Bluett's narrative owned by the Maryland Historical Society.

1018 As indicated in Chapter One, Yarrow Mamout was painted by both

In a separate section of part one of this study on Chesapeake Bay Muslims, we have introduced what we know of a number of prominent Virginia Muslim slaves. Among these we discussed Captain Moses Osman of the Dismal Swamp, Bampett Muhamad, Selim the Algerian, George Washington's slave Sambo Anderson, as well as other Continental Army soldiers, such as Peter Salem, Yusuf Ben Ali, and brothers Francis and Joseph Saba, who were from the North African Supply Zone as outlined in Chapter Two.[1019]

We also introduced in part one of this study the work of scholar Mary V. Thompson who suggests that at least three other female slaves at Washington's Mount Vernon estate may well have been Muslims. Their names were Fatimer, Little Fatimer and Nila. Thompson suggests the latter is a version of the Arabic name *Nahilah*.[1020] She also suggests the name means, "Someone who acquires something," or "Someone who gets what she wants," when in fact it means, "Someone who is successful." Fatima, of course, is the name of the Prophet Muhammad's favorite daughter.

Along the way, in the first part of this study, we introduced several major figures we explored in the remainder of this study. Indeed, in the chapters on runaway slaves in Maryland (Chapter Nine), as well as runaway slaves in Virginia (Chapter Eight), we returned to an exploration of many of these major and prominent figures.

This brings us to a summary of the major conclusions of part two

Charles Wilson Peale and James Alexander Simpson. The former work is owned by the Philadelphia Museum of Art. The latter is owned by the Georgetown branch of the District of Columbia Library.

1019 There are a number of extant pieces of information about Sambo Anderson, including two sketches about him in the Alexandria Gazette from January 18 and 22, 1876. A list of Tithibles of George Washington from 1760, and entries in Washington's Diary, like one on January 8, 1760. Little information can be verified about the alleged Muslim slaves in the Continental Army, except Yusuf Ben Ali, also called Joseph Benhaley. He served as a corporal from 1775 until 1783, and Peter Salem, who supposedly fired the shot that killed General Pitcairn at the Battle of Concord.

1020 See Mary V. Thompson, "Islam at Mount Vernon," in Digital Encyclopedia of George Washington. Also see Thompson's "Religious Practices in the Slave Quarters at Mount Vernon," in Colonial Williamsburg Interpreter 21, no. 1 (Spring, 2000).

of this study on Muslim slaves in the Chesapeake Bay region, the subject matter of the next section of this concluding chapter.

Part Two: Slave Supply Zones and the Middle Passage

In the two chapters of part two, Chapters Two and Three of this study, we have shifted the focus from the Chesapeake in part one to Africa in part two. We will do this by looking first at Chapter Two on slave supply zones in Africa and the Middle Passage, or the route by which European slave ships most often traveled across the Atlantic to the New World. What then followed was an examination of slave forts and castles, mostly on the two coasts of Africa, from the fifteenth to the nineteenth century (Chapter Three) where we examined sixty or so slave forts and castles throughout Africa, mostly on both coasts of Africa, east and west.

We began Chapter Two with an introduction to the nine principal supply zones that existed in Africa during the Atlantic slave trade. These include the Senegambian Zone, the Niger Valley Supply Zone, the Windward Coast Zone, the Gold Coast Zone, the Bight of Benin Zone, the Sierra Leone Supply Zone, the Bight of Biafra Zone, the Angolan Supply Zone, and Mozambique and the East African Zone.

After introducing each of these nine supply zones and sketching out their geographical parameters, we then described the estimates that Professor Michael A. Gomez and others suggested for the percentages that each of the nine zones sent to the New World in general and to the Chesapeake Bay region in particular. Gomez's figures were the following:

Senegambian Zone, 13.3 percent
Niger Valley Zone, 7.0 percent
Sierra Leone Supply Zone, 5.5 percent
The Windward Coast Zone, 11.4 percent
The Gold Coast Supply Zone, 15.9 percent
The Bight of Benin Zone, 4.3 percent
The Bight of Biafra Zone, 23.3 percent
The Angolan Supply Zone, 1.0 percent

Mozambique and the East Africa Zone, less than 1 percent.[1021]

In addition to these nine supply zones outlined above, we also introduced two separate or supplemental supply zones for this study. The first of these was North Africa, from which Selim the Algerian and a few other Muslim slaves came to the Chesapeake Bay region in the late eighteenth century to the Civil War period. Figures like Peter Selim, Yusuf Ben Ali and Francis and Joseph Saba were all Virginian Africans from this North African Supply Zone.

The most important places in North Africa significant for our purposes are Algeria and Morocco. Selim, the Algerian, was obviously from the former, and Morocco was the first nation to recognize the independence of the United States from Great Britain in 1777.

Other soldiers with Muslim names in colonial America to the Civil War period include John Hamin, who was a corporal in the Fourth Company of the Virginia Militia; W. B. Osman, who died in 1865, and is buried in Poplar Grove National Cemetery in Petersburg, Virginia; and Yusuf ben Ali, who was born in Mali, Guinea, in 1756 and served in the US Army as an aide to General Sumter. Ben Ali died in 1861, at the age of one hundred and five years old.[1022] Peter Salem fought in the Revolutionary Army at the Battle of Concord. Many of these colonial Muslim slaves may well have been from the North African Supply Zone.

Joseph Saba, mentioned above, was born in Mali in 1756. He, too, served in the Revolutionary Army, as did his brother Joseph who is listed as a "Fifer" in the Continental Troop Roll number 132. Joseph Saba is listed in the same troop roll that covers the years 1775 to 1783. Thus, Saba was from the Bight of Benin, or the Niger Valley Supply Zones. In regard to the Civil War period, Captain Moses Osman (1822–1893) was the highest-ranking Muslim in the Union

1021 Michael A. Gomez, "Muslims in Early America," in Journal of Southern History 60, no. 4 (November 1994), p. 682.

1022 The best description of the Goree stick and its history can be found in the article called "The Middle Passage," https://www.ushistory.org/us/6b.asp. Sylviane Diouf and other scholars also give clear descriptions and functions of the device. See her Servants of Allah (New York: NYU Press, 1998), p. 43; and Douglas Grant, The Fortunate Slave (Oxford: Oxford University Press, 1968), p. 139.

Army. He was commissioned a First Lieutenant in the 104th of Illinois and promoted to Captain on September 29, 1864.[1023] Captain Osman was born in Dauphin County, Pennsylvania. He was the son of Robert Osman. Captain Osman's wife's name was Zilpha, and they had one daughter. Captain Osman is buried in the Ottawa Avenue Cemetery in Lasalle County, Illinois. Although he has a Muslim family name, he was born in the United States. The fact that his wife had an Arabic name is further evidence that Captain Osman was a member of the Islamic faith.

The eleventh supply zone we also have introduced was that of South Africa and specifically the nation of Namibia, where there were three different slave forts built by the Germans in the early years of the twentieth century. Most of the slaves who came from this area also spoke German. The slave forts in Namibia, including the Duwisib Castle there, were built by Baron Hans Heinrich von Wolf. The three slave forts in Namibia were built between 1908 and 1912, as well.[1024]

Indeed, a female slave named Elinor, one of the suspected Maryland runaway slaves, had a tribal scar on her right hand that indicates she was most likely a member of the Wolof Tribe in the Senegambian Supply Zone. She was likely captured or kidnapped in Senegal or Gambia and then sold to slave traders in Namibia.

The earliest references to Islam in Namibia come from the early twentieth century. It remains the third most popular religion in the country, after Christianity and local tribal faiths. The Islamic center in today's Namibia is the Windhoek Islamic Center. Moslems in Namibia are almost exclusively Sunni Muslims, many of whom speak tribal languages, German and Arabic.

Thus, if we add our two supplemental supply zones to our list, we

1023 Continental Troop Roll, Number 132, 1775–1783. The Fourth Company of the Virginia Militia was formed during the War of 1812 by Lt. Col. Henry Beatty. The 104th Illinois Volunteer Infantry Regiment served in the Union troops of the American Civil War.

1024 The two best short works on the Middle Passage are Charles Johnson, The Middle Passage (New York: Scribners, 1998); and John A. Clarke, The Middle Passage (New York: Dial Books, 1995). Hans Heinrich Von Wolf (1896–1944) was a German police official, politician and served in the Prussian Parliament from 1924 until 1928.

get the following:

Senegambian—13.3%

Niger Valley Zone—7.0%

Sierra Leone Zone—5.5%

Windward Coast—11.4%

The Gold Coast Zone—15.9%

The Bight of Benin—4.3%

The Bight of Biafra—23.3%

The Angolan Zone—less than 1%

Mozambique and East—less than 1%

North Africa Zone—less than 1 %

South African Zone—less than 1 %

In the second section of Chapter Two, we explored the phenomenon of the Middle Passage, the route by which most Africans from the fifteenth to the nineteenth centuries came to the New World. In this second section, we have included many descriptions of artistic depictions of the Middle Passage, mostly in eighteenth and nineteenth-century publications. Additionally, we also made some very general comments about slave coffles as they were conducted in Africa. As we have shown, for the most part, slaves were moved in African coffles by the employing of Goree sticks, a Y-shaped device made of hardwood with overseers in Africa carrying spears and swords. Indeed, at the close of the first section of Chapter Three, we included descriptions of five artistic depictions of Goree sticks and slave coffles in Africa.[1025]

1025 See Gomez, pp. 677–67; Douglas, pp. 44–45; and Diouf, p. 195. The Wolof are an ethnic group in Senegal, Gambia and Mauritania. They make up half of the population of Senegal, 20 percent of Gambia and 45 percent of Mauritania. The Krio people of Sierra Leone are the Creole people who were descendants of African American slaves, West Indians and freed blacks who settled in the western portion of Sierra Leone. The Ibibio people are a tribe in Southeast Nigeria. They are related to the Efik, the Anaagt and the Igbo. The Mandinga are also a West African tribe with a global popula-

In African slave coffles only the hands of males were bound, and punishment on the march consisted of adding weight to the end of the Goree stick. Whereas, in America, male slaves, as we have shown, were hand-cuffed, and the main punitive consequence was the dragging of a ball and chain or being subject to the lash.

First-person narratives of the Middle Passage was the subject matter of the third section of Chapter Two. All together, we have introduced the comments on the Middle Passage of three Africans and five white members of the African slave trade. Among these are Nigerian slave, Olaudah Equiano (1745–1797), Captain John Newton (1725–1807), Captain Thomas Trotter (1760–1832), and ship surgeon Dr. Alexander Falconbridge (1760–1792). Each of these men, as well as many others, in their narratives have provided their readers with a poignant understanding of the Middle Passage and the miseries, hardships, and even joys sometimes found on these voyages.[1026]

In the fourth section of this second chapter on supply zones and the Middle Passage, we described and discussed several observations that Chesapeake Bay planters made about slaves coming from the various supply zones. In particular, the labor of Mandingos, members of the Fulbe and Wolof Tribes, and slaves coming from the Sierra Leone Supply Zone, like the Krio Tribe, for example, was highly praised. George Washington's slave Sambo Anderson most likely was a member of the Krio or Krobo Tribes. Similarly, the Chesapeake Bay region planters highly prized the Akan Tribe of the Gold Coast. At the same time, Igbo and Ibibio tribe members, from the Niger Valley Supply Zone and the Bights of Biafra and Benin, were

---

tion of eleven million.

1026 On "Tight-packing," see images in Chapter Two in the section on the Middle Passage and the images at the end of the chapter. The English established Bunce Island and its slave fort in 1670. It is in Free Town Harbor of the Sierra Leone Supply Zone. John Newton (1725–1807) was an Anglican pastor and former slave ship captain. He also wrote the hymn "Amazing Grace." Thomas Trotter (1760–1832) was a Scot naval physician. Authors Brian Vale and Griffith Edwards recently published a biography of Trotter called Physician to the Fleet published by Boydell Books in 2011. Alexander Falconbridge (1760–1792) was a British surgeon who sailed on four British slave ship voyages between 1780 and 1787.

seen as surly and arrogant, and thus were not desired by those in the Chesapeake Bay region.[1027] Indeed, they were often seen as being aloof and suicidal.

Professor Gomez speaks of these preferences among the Chesapeake Bay planters. He tells us:

> Some Africans, such as the Igbo and Ibibio of Southeastern Nigeria, were reputed to be rebellious, unruly, and suicidal, and were not highly prized in some North American areas. In contrast, Akan speakers from the Gold Coast were regarded as more industrious and manageable.[1028]

Gomez goes on to say that slaves from the Senegambian and Sierra Leone Supply Zones were collectively called "Mandingoes" by white planters. This term became synonymous with "Muslim" by the beginning of the nineteenth century. Gomez reveals:

> Senegambian and Sierra Leone...were generally viewed by their owners as preferable to others[1029]

Thus, Chesapeake Bay farmers were partial to acquiring slaves from the Wolof, Fulbe, Mandinka, Krio, Krobo, and Akan Tribes. They were not fond of captives coming from the Bights of Biafra and Benin, as well as the Niger Valley Supply Zones because they were thought to be unruly, uncooperative, and suicidal, by North American

1027 Two good general works on African slave castles are James Pope-Hennessey, Sins of the Fathers (London: Castle Books, 2000); and William St. Clair, Door of No Return (Jackson, TN, Blue Bridge Books, 2007). Antonio, alias Anthony Johnson, (1600–1670) was an Angolan indentured servant turned tobacco farmer and then slave master in both Virginia and Maryland.

1028 At its height in the sixteenth century, Timbuktu, in present-day Mali, was a gateway of ideas, people and trade goods, linking the cities of North Africa to West Africa by way of the six principal trade routes that crossed the Sahara Desert. Bunce Island, in the Free Town Harbor of the Sierra Leone Supply Zone, was settled by the English in 1670. In its early history, the castle there was run by two London based companies. See Gomez, "Muslims in Early America," p. 685.

1029 Ibid.

farmers.

Another reason that Senegambian Muslim slaves may have been attractive to Chesapeake Bay planters is that they tended to be literate and erudite in their religious tastes. Kunta Kinte, Job Diallo and Yarrow Mamout all could read and write Arabic, a valuable tool among American slaves. This also was true of many slaves from the Muslim portions of West Africa in general.

At the close of Chapter Two of this study, we have introduced and discussed twelve pieces of mostly nineteenth-century art that depicts or illustrates the nine supply zones, the two supplemental zones, and the Middle Passage voyages. Some of these images, as we have seen, came from British and French artists, while some came from Americans. The final three of these images in Chapter Two are of the "Tight-Packing: Technique," used by ships' captains to store slaves on the Middle Passage, and an illustration of the *Speculum Orum*, the device by which slaves were sometimes forced-fed on trans-Atlantic voyages when they had been rebellious during a voyage of the Middle Passage.[1030]

Indeed, at the close of the first section of Chapter Three, we included five artistic depictions of Goree sticks and slave coffles in Africa. Later, in part three of this study, we did the same for slave coffles in the Chesapeake Bay region, from slave ships to slave jails and by land, rail and sea from the Chesapeake region to the Deep South.

In a subsequent and main section of Chapter Three, we introduced the phenomena of slave forts and castles, mostly from the fifteenth century to the eighteenth century. We began this section by describing five slave forts/castles in the Senbegambian Supply Zone: Fort James in Gambia; Fort Louis in Senegal; Fort Bayona, the Dutch settlement on the Gambia River; Fort Saint Louis on the Gambia River; and the French trading post and slave pen at Albreda, on the Gambian River. We also indicated that the French built another structure, Fort Saint Joseph, in the Senegambian Supply Zone.

Next, we examined several trading posts and forts in the Niger Valley Zone, including the facility at Badgary, from which it is probable that Olaudah Equiano most likely left Africa. Followed by intro-

1030 Fort Loboko was a fortress stockade controlled by the infamous pirate Pedro Blanco (1795–1854) on the coast of Sierra Leone.

ducing two slave castles from the Sierra Leone Supply Zone, one on Bunce Island and the other at Fort Loboko, the Spanish fort established by Pedro Blanco on the Gallinas River near Sulima on the Gallinas coast. This was followed by more analysis of slave forts at Timbuktu in Mali in the Niger Valley Zone. In that discussion, we have shown that slaves in Timbuktu were treated much better than most other places in West Africa.[1031]

The Angolan Supply Zones and its slave castles at Luanda and Benguela were the focus of the next part of this section of Chapter Three. The city of Cabinda, on the mouth of the Congo River, from the sixteenth century to 1836 when slavery was abolished in Angola, also sent thousands of slaves to the New World. "Antonio" or Anthony Johnson came from this zone, and possibly Mattheus de Sousa, as well, the first recorded black man in Maryland. This was followed by a discussion of slave forts and castles in Ghana, or the Gold Coast.

In this section, we described twenty-four separate facilities in Ghana, many of which still stand today. Included in these comments were the Elmina Castle and the Cape Coast Castle, perhaps the two most famous slave castles in West Africa.[1032]

All tolled, Ghana and the Gold Coast had over fifty slave forts and castles built on their coast by European powers in the fifteenth to nineteenth centuries, more than half of these in Ghana. There were also

1031 Two good works on the Cape Coast Castle are Telward Bowdich, Mission from Cape Coast Castle (London: Forgotten Books, 2012); and William St. Clair, The Grand Slave Emporium, originally published in London in the nineteenth century, reprinted by Profile Books in 2007. The Old Fort at Zanzibar was constructed in 1700 by Seyyid Said on the site of a ruined Portuguese church.

1032 Altogether, we have examined nearly sixty separate slave forts and castles in Africa. Half of those are/were on the Gold Coast and the others spread out over the eight or so other supply zones. The British India Office did slave business in Aden in the 1840s. The French were the first Europeans to do slave trading with Muscat in Oman. One French engraving, dated in the 1840s, shows Arab merchants selling boys at the Muscat Slave Market, see: http://bit.ly/2uJutLV. Among these trade routes across the Sahara was Cairo to the west; North Africa, like the city of Marakesh, south and west; Zaria in northern Nigeria west; the Berber people and south and west, as well as others.

nearly one hundred such facilities built in Africa altogether in that period, mostly on the east and west coasts of the continent.

We also have shown in our discussion of slave forts and castles in Ghana, or the Gold Coast, the following nations all had built slave facilities in that supply zone: Spain, Britain, Germany, Sweden-Norway, France, Portugal, Denmark, and the Dutch Republic.

In the next section of Chapter Three, we explored a number of other slave forts, castles and trading posts elsewhere in Africa. This included facilities in the Bight of Benin, the Bight of Biafra, in South Africa, in Southwest Africa, in Namibia, as well as several facilities in the East African Supply Zone. There we have seen castles and forts in Ethiopia, Egypt, Mozambique, and Madagascar, among other places, like Somalia and Tanzania.[1033]

There are also the ruins of two other slave forts in Zanzibar on two small islands near the coast. The first is called Kilwa. They traded in gold, silver, perfumes, Arab crockery and slaves. The other fort was called Songo Mnara, on a small island in the south of Tanzania. From the fourteenth to the sixteenth centuries, it existed as a stone town, complete with slave castle. When Europeans arrived in the fifteenth century, it had become a Swahili trading city, complete with Arab slave traders from Oman and Yemen. Arab crockery and other goods came from these two places in Arabia.

Arabic slave ships mostly left the port of Aden in Yemen and Muscat in Oman, to ports in Mozambique, Madagascar, to Zanzibar in Tanzania, and to Mogadishu, a port in Somalia. Many of these locations had slave forts that were utilized by the Arabs to send their slaves to the New World. The old fort at Zanzibar, for example, was built by the Omanis in the seventeenth century. Traders in Mogadishu, to cite another example, exchanged gold, livestock, leather and ivory for slaves coming from the interior of Africa. Then many of these slaves were sent by the Portuguese east to India or west to the New World, or overland across the Sahara to the west coast, perhaps including both Mattheus de Sousa and Antonio or

1033 Saint Anthony's at Axim was built in 1515 by the Portuguese. It was the second fortress built there by them after Elmina. Saint Sebastien at Shama is the third oldest of the fortresses built in Ghana. It was constructed between 1520 and 1526.

Anthony Johnson, discussed in the opening chapter of this study.

Arabic slave traders also marched slave coffles across the continent, using the six major trade routes across the Sahara Desert that existed from early on. These routes ultimately were a way of linking East Africa to West Africa, as well as North Africa, to ports in West Africa. One of these major slave trade routes went from Mozambique, across Africa to Luanda and Cabinda in Angola. Others went from the East African Supply Zone to the Sierra Leone, Senegambian, and Gold and Windward Coasts Supply Zones.

At the close of Chapter Three, we introduced five artistic depictions of African slave forts and castles in art. These were artistic renderings of Fort James Island, Saint Anthony's at Axim, Fort Saint Sebastien, a sketch of the Castle of Good Hope in South Africa, and the Annamaboe Castle on the Gold Coast on the Coast of Ghana.[1034] This brings us to a summary of the third part of this study on Muslim slaves in the Chesapeake Bay region, the topic of the next section of this concluding chapter.

Part Three: Slave Traders in Baltimore, Washington and Virginia

With the opening section of Chapter Four on slave coffles in America, we once again have shifted the venue from Chapters Two and Three in Africa, back to America in Chapter Four. In Chapter Four, we explored the phenomenon of slave coffles and chain gangs in America. After introducing the phenomenon in the opening section of the fourth chapter, we outlined the major similarities of coffles in Africa and in the Chesapeake Bay region, as well as the differences. This was followed by the presentation of a number of first-person narratives of slave coffles from slaves, white visitors, and even two fictional characters.[1035]

1034 The notes for these structures are in the body of the text. Kilwa Kisiwani, on the south coast of Tanzania, was called Husuni Kubai or "Great Fort" by local people. The fort exported spices, coconut, ivory and gold, as well as slaves. The ruins of the fort can still be seen there. Songo Mnara, another fort in South Tanzania, participated heavily in Indian Ocean commerce in the fifteenth and sixteenth centuries. They also traded with the Persian Gulf, the Red Sea, and the western portions of India.

1035 See Winifred Conkling, Passenger on the Pearl (Algonquin Books, 2015); and Sherri Hayes, Finding Anna (Sherri Hayes Books, 2016).

At the close of Chapter Four, as in all of the other chapters of this study, we provided several descriptions of art illustrations and depictions of slave coffles and chain gangs in America. We then ended the chapter, as we have with all the chapters of this study, with the major conclusions found therein.

In Chapter Five, which was devoted to Baltimore merchant ships and slave traders, we opened the chapter with some general remarks on slave merchant ships, both built in and sailed from the ports of Baltimore, from the early nineteenth century on.

After our discussion of these merchant ships in Baltimore, we devoted the remainder of Chapter Five to an exploration of thirteen slave-trading firms listed in the *Baltimore Directory* of 1850, as well as a variety of other slave dealers in Maryland. We saw in Chapter Five that the major slave traders in Baltimore were: Hope Slatter; the Campbell brothers, Bernard and his brother Walter; as well as Isaac Franklin, James Purvis, and Joseph N. Donavan. There were another half a dozen minor slave traders operating in Baltimore as well in the same period, as we have shown.[1036]

Among the other places in Maryland where we have shown there were slave traders in the nineteenth century were Cambridge, Fred-

Thomas Pringle (1789–1834) was a Scottish poet, writer and abolitionist. He first came to South Africa to do slave trading in 1820. Isaac Franklin (1789–1846) was partner in the firm of Armfield & Franklin and owner of the plantation called Fairvue. McCandliss Tavern was at M. Street and Wisconsin Avenue in Washington. It was the first home of Judge James Dunlop. Lloyd's Tavern was founded by John Lloyd (1835–1892), bricklayer and police officer. He was arrested because it was believed that he was part of the conspiracy to kill Abraham Lincoln.

1036 William F. Korff, The History and Development of Shipbuilding in Baltimore (College Park: Special Collections of University of Maryland Library, 1936). In addition to the slave traders elsewhere in Virginia, there were also four major traders in the city of Norfolk. Their names were W. T. Forster, R. L. Marsh, R. H. Banks, and Bernard Raux. The latter's slave-trading papers from 1828 to 1836 are owned by the Harvard University Library. Thomas Pringle was a slave trader between Alexandria and South Africa. See: H. E. Voss, "The Slaves Must Be Heard: Thomas Pringle and the Dialogue of South African Servitude," in English in Africa 17, no. 1 (May 1990), pp. 61–81.

erick, Annapolis, Easton, St. Mary's City, Denton, Hagerstown, Port Tobacco, and Queen Anne's County on the Eastern Shore of Maryland.

In the opening of Chapter Six, we examined slave ships owned by Washington, DC, and Virginia slave traders. There we saw that Franklin and Armfield of Alexandria owned a number of ships, and eventually, they sold two of them to Washington, DC, trader William H. Williams, the owner of the Yellow House on the Mall in Washington. Another ship was sold to George Kephart, a Frederick County, Maryland, slave trader, who was sometimes the agent of Franklin and Armfield in the mid-nineteenth century.

We also examined a number of slave dealers in Norfolk, Alexandria and Richmond in the first sixty-five years of the nineteenth century. We pointed out that many slave traders in those years captained their own ships. This was true of W. T. Forster, R. H. Banks and R. L. Marsh in Norfolk. It was also true of Thomas Pringle and Isaac Franklin, both of Alexandria.

In the second section of Chapter Six, we examined the major and minor slave traders in Washington, DC, in the same period. There we suggested that William H. Williams, W. Robey, Joseph Neal and John Gadsby were the most important traders there. But we also have seen that Washington had at least five other minor slave traders in the nineteenth century. Those include John Beattie of Georgetown, the George McCandliss Tavern and his slave jail in the city, the Miller Tavern at 13th and F Streets, Lloyd's Tavern on Seventh and Pennsylvania Avenue, and the slave pen at Potomac Park, where there is now a slave memorial.[1037]

We also have shown in Chapter Six that at least five significant white abolitionists visited a number of the facilities listed above and then reported what they had found. Their comments were always pejorative and negative of the Washington slave-trading businesses and thus were not supportive of what they found there.[1038]

1037 Creole: American Slave Ship Revolt (Washington: Niles National Register, 1842); and Tingba Apidta, The Hidden History of Washington (Washington: Reclamation Project, 2014). Also see: Hank Trent, The Secret Life of Bacon Tait (Baton Rouge: LSU Press, 2017).

1038 Ibid. Bacon Tait was a Virginian slave trader. He also served in the Continental Army in the War of 1812. For Rice Ballard, see: Papers of the American Slave Trade: The Papers of Rice Ballard (Chapel Hill: University

In the next section of Chapter Six, we examined the major and minor slave traders found in the city of Richmond in the first sixty-five years of the nineteenth century. We have seen in this section that the major traders in Richmond were Bacon Tait, Robert Lumpkin, R. H. Dickerson and Rice Ballard.[1039] And there were at least twenty-five other minor slave traders in the city of Richmond between 1820 and 1865.

Among the many minor slave traders in Richmond we introduced in Chapter Six were Samuel Alsop, Silas Omohundro, Jordan M. Saunders and David Burford, as well as David Pulliam and Hector Davis.[1040] We have shown that many other gentlemen also were engaged in the slave-trading business in Richmond in the middle of the nineteenth century. Among these figures were John Toler; John B. Davis; S. Grady; R. Faundron; W. Abrahams, a Jewish slave trader; and Robert Alvis.[1041]

At the time, the city of Richmond also included William Gouldin, William Dupree, William Martin, Edwards Matthews, Charles McMurray and many other traders of slaves in that Virginia city. There were more slave traders in Richmond than those combined in Norfolk, Alexandria and other locations elsewhere in Virginia combined.[1042] In fact, Richmond, from 1820 until 1865, was the hub of slave trading activity in the Upper South, as we have shown in Chapter Six of this study.

In the final section of Chapter Six, we introduced and discussed six pieces of art that depict slave traders in Washington, DC, and the

---

of North Carolina Library, 2002).

1039 Jack Trammel, The Richmond Slave Trade (Washington: History Press, 2012); and Kari Winter, The American Dream of John B. Prentis (Athens: University of Georgia Press, 2011). John B. Prentis (1788–1848) was outraged by slavery in his youth in Virginia, but he became a slave trader that transported thousands of slaves from Georgia to the Deep South.

1040 See Trammel, Note 21A. Jordan M Saunders, who died in 1886, was the largest slave trader in Warrenton, Fauquier County, for most of the first sixty-five years of the nineteenth century.

1041 Ibid. Eyre Crowe (1824–1910) was a London-born diplomat and painter of mostly historical scenes.

1042 Apidta, pp. 73–80.

Commonwealth of Virginia. The earliest of these six images were produced around 1800, with the majority of the images made in the mid-nineteenth century. These include paintings by Eyre Crowe, illustrations of Lumpkin's jail, Joseph Neal's place of business in Washington, and a photograph of Price, Birch, and Company about the time of the American Civil War.[1043]

Among the more prominent slave traders in the city of Baltimore in the nineteenth century were Austin Woolfolk, Hope Slatter, James Franklin Purvis, Joseph Donovan, Bernard and Walter Campbell, and John N. Denning. Among the minor nineteenth-century slave traders in Baltimore were Moody & Downs, James Bates, William Harker, Jonathan Wilson, and John Woods.

In the final chapter of part three of this study, Chapter Seven, we have introduced the phenomena of slave auctions and slave auction blocks and stones in the Chesapeake Bay region in the nineteenth century, leading up to the American Civil War. We opened Chapter Seven with a history of slave auctions in the Chesapeake Bay region. There we suggested three separate stages or phases of the phenomenon. In the first of these phases, from the 1660s to the 1720s, slave auctions in the Chesapeake mostly took place in county courthouses and town squares and central market places in both states.[1044]

In the second phase of the history we have proposed, the transition period from the 1720s to 1799, the place of slave auctions in the Chesapeake had moved to county jails, private hotels and taverns. Indeed, we introduced a number of hotels and taverns in DC, Maryland and Virginia, where slave auctions were frequently conducted in the first sixty-five years of the nineteenth century. We have seen several examples in Baltimore, Washington and Virginia in the mid-nineteenth century, where the job of slave auctions was taken over by taverns and hotels in these areas. We have seen slave auctions going on in a tavern

1043 This three-part history of slave auctions was devised by the author of this study.

1044 Two fine books on American abolitionism are Ronald Walters, The Anti-Slavery Appeal (New York: W. W. Norton, 1984); and Aileen S. Fraditor, Means and Ends in American Abolitionism (Washington: Ivan R. Dee Edition, 1989). The Sotterley Plantation is the only remaining Tidewater plantation in the Chesapeake still open to the public.

in Upper Marlboro, in the McCandliss Tavern in the District of Columbia, and in John Gadsby's hotel in Baltimore called the Indian Queen, to cite three examples.

In the second section of Chapter Seven, we introduced many first-person narratives of slave auctions in the Chesapeake Bay region. Slaves from the Chesapeake Bay area wrote the first eight of these narratives. We also introduced the first-person descriptions of slave auctions of a number of white people. Included in this second group were the narrative of one Virginia slave dealer, a poster from an American abolitionist society, and the first-person descriptions of a number of white abolitionists in mid-nineteenth century, who had experienced the phenomenon of slave auctions first hand.[1045]

In fact, Eyre Crowe completed a number of sketches, and eventually paintings, of slave-trading firms in Richmond just before the Civil War years, and they were later exhibited in London in the mid-1850s.

In a subsequent section of Chapter Seven, we examined twelve different surviving slave auction blocks and stones in the Chesapeake Bay region. As we have seen, two of these surviving blocks and stones were in the District of Columbia, five are in Maryland, and five can still be found in the Commonwealth of Virginia. The DC auction blocks were at Decatur House at 1610 H Street and at the city courthouse where slave auctions were conducted by the sheriff and his deputies in the nineteenth century.[1046]

As we have seen, the Virginia auction blocks and stones can be found in Luray in Page County, at Inn Lawn Park in Fredericksburg, at the town of Warrenton, and in the city of Blacksburg. In Maryland, we have examined slave auction blocks and stones at the old jail on Jonathan Street in Hagerstown, a slave block at the corner of Main and Sharpe Streets in Sharpsburg, and at a hotel in Upper Marlboro. We also have shown there is extant a slave auction block that exists at

1045 See Apidta, pp. 100–110.

1046 Theodore R. Davis (1840–1894) was an American artist who made numerous drawings of significant military and political events before, during, and after the American Civil War. Lewis Miller (1796–1882) was born in Pennsylvania, worked for many years as a carpenter, and then turned to painting. His Sketch Book of Landscapes in the State of Virginia watercolors completed in the 1850s, have become famous.

the Sotterley Plantation in Hollywood in southern Maryland near the famous slave cabin there.[1047]

In addition, we have shown that a slave auction block existed in the slave jail of Hope H. Slatter on the west side of his slave yard in Baltimore. Presumably, the block was destroyed when the building was razed in the 1870s. A gasoline station now sits where the yard used to be in the mid-nineteenth century.[1048]

In the closing section of Chapter Seven, as well as the final section of part three of this study, we examined a number of illustrations and depictions of Chesapeake Bay slave auctions and slave blocks and stones in the nineteenth century. In all, we have included eleven different images at the close of Chapter Seven. One was a piece by David Claypoole Johnstone; a second, a slave auction in Christianburg, Virginia, from the 1850s by Lewis Miller; and a third, a painting by Theodore R. Davis of a *Slave Auction in the South.*[1049]

Additionally, at the end of Chapter Seven, we have included a description of a painting by LeFevre J. Cranstone of a *Slave Auction in Virginia*, as well as photographs of auction blocks and stones from various places mentioned in the chapter. We also described and discussed photographs of the auction stone in Fredericksburg, an illustration that accompanies an edition of Henry Bibb's autobiography owned by the University of North Carolina, as well as two more modern pieces that depict the same phenomena.[1050]

We have suggested that the auction blocks in Luray and Fredericksburg, Virginia, both have occasioned some controversy about

---

1047 David Claypoole Johnston (1799–1865) was a nineteenth-century American cartoonist, printmaker and actor in Boston. For LeFevre James Cranstone, see Donald L. Smith's LeFevre James Cranstone: His Life and Art (Richmond: Brandylane Books, 2004). Henry Bibb (1815–1854), was a Kentucky slave, author and abolitionist. See his Narrative of the Life and Adventures of Henry Bibb: An American Slave, originally published in 1849.

1048 Jeanne K. Pirtle, The Sotterley Plantation (Glenside, PA: Arcadia Books, 2013); and David G. Brown, Sotterley: Her People and Their Worlds (Chambersburg: Chesapeake Book Company, 2010).

1049 See Trammel, chapters two and three.

1050 The notes on these pieces of art are in the body of the text.

whether these blocks were employed for auctioning slaves in the nineteenth century, or they simply were used to mount horses and carriages. Differences of opinion about the purposes and uses of these stones remain until the present day.

Part Four: Runaway Muslim Slaves in the Chesapeake Bay Region

The major focus of part four of this study has been the detecting of suspected runaway Muslim slaves in Virginia and Maryland. To that end, Chapter Eight was devoted to suspected Virginia Muslim slaves, and Chapter Nine to suspected Maryland runaway Muslim slaves. In our analyses in these two chapters, we have seen a host of similarities in the two states, as well as a number of important differences.

In terms of the similarities of suspected runaway Muslim slaves in the two states of the Chesapeake Bay region, we have found fifty-five in Maryland and fifty-one in Virginia. In both places, the men outnumber the women about four or five to one. The average age of the escaped Muslims in both locales was twenty-eight years old. The youngest slave in Maryland was fourteen and fifteen in Virginia. The oldest suspected Muslim runaway slave, in both states, was sixty years old. There were very few slaves in both states over the age of forty.[1051]

The shortest Muslim runaway slaves in both states were four feet three (Maryland) and five feet three (Virginia), while the tallest was six feet six in Maryland and six foot three in Virginia. The shortest was a woman and the tallest a man. The average height in both states was five feet eight. In both locales, thirteen of the total numbers in Maryland and fourteen in Virginia could be identified by their tribal scars or markings alone.[1052] A summary of these may be found in Appendix C at the close of this final chapter.

The suspected Muslim runaways in both states were garnered from twenty-four different local newspapers and other national publi-

1051 Henry Bibb gives a first-person narration in his autobiography, Narrative of the Life of Henry Bibb (New York: Create Space, 2016). The Krobo Tribe are known for their beads. They live mostly in Southern Ghana in the Odumase region of the country. The Kano Kingdom was a Hausa Kingdom formed in northwest Nigeria in the late eighteenth century.

1052 See the five appendices to this chapter.

cations. In both places, more than seventy percent were in the *Maryland Gazette* and the *Virginia Gazette*.

Nearly half in both states were also found from only three of the supply zones outlined in Chapter Two—Senegambia, the Niger Valley Zone, and the Sierra Leone Supply Zone. Twenty- five of fifty-five in Maryland and twenty-four of fifty-one in the Commonwealth of Virginia were from those zones.

The suspected Muslim runaway slaves in both states came primarily from the same twelve African tribes. These were the Wolof, the Pungo, the Fula or Fulbe, the Mandinka, the Yoruba, the Igbo, the Ibibio, the Krio, the Bantu, the Krobo, the Toureg, and the Kano. Additionally, we have discovered Mustee slaves, the offspring of an African and a Native American, in both locations, one in Maryland and two in Virginia.[1053] In both Maryland and Virginia, the overwhelming number of suspected Muslim runaways escaped in the spring or summer months, with very few in the fall or winter times in either locale.

In both Maryland and Virginia, the reward for the recovery of a runaway slave was lower if apprehended in the county, higher if found in the colony, and still higher if found elsewhere, beyond the colony/state. In both places, we discovered suspected Muslim runaway slaves speak languages other than English. Those languages included Arabic, French and Dutch, but the Maryland runaways included one who spoke German, as well.[1054]

By and large, the same items were stolen from the masters of our suspected runaway Muslim slaves. In general, female slaves stole items of clothing that belonged to their mistresses or cash. Men, on the other hand, most often absconded with firearms, boats, money or horses owned by their masters.

Another similarity between the two colonies/states and their suspected runaway Muslim slaves is that both groups seem to have

1053 The two best works on tribal scars are D. B. Singh, "Sex Differences in Anatomical Location of Human Scarification," in Evolution and Human Behavior 8, no. 6, pp. 403–416; and Enid Schildkrout, "Inscribing the Body," in Annual Review of Anthropology 33, no. 1 (2004).

1054 The two best accounts of Mustee culture are Lance Homer, Mustee (New York: Fawcett Books, 1967); and B. F. Presbury, The Mustee: Or Love of Glory (New York: Hard Book Press, 2013).

been affected by the Great Awakening, the eighteenth and early nineteenth-century religious movement that spread across the south beginning around 1720. The southern Tidewater region in Virginia and the Low Country there were influenced by white northern preachers, who converted blacks and whites to Baptism and then later on to Methodism.[1055] The oldest African American Baptist church, for example, in Baltimore was the Bethel African-American Methodist Episcopal Church, or Bethel AME Baptists and Methodist Church, built in 1785. Construction continued steadily for the next one hundred years. The Leadenhall Street Baptist Church, another example, was constructed beginning in 1873. The oldest African American Baptist churches, in both Virginia and Maryland, were built in the 1770s and 1780s.

One effect of the two Great Awakenings was that the first black Baptist churches were opened in southern Virginia, two, for example, in Petersburg alone, early on. The Great Awakening and the development of Baptism and then Methodism were also quite popular on the Eastern Shore of Maryland among slaves in the mid-eighteenth century. Some saw the new religious movement as a reaction against the Enlightenment and its emphasis on reason. In its stead, the new preachers and churches substituted their central emphasis on ecstatic religious, mystical experience, or the experience of being "born-again."[1056] This effect can be seen in seven slaves in this study who identify with the Great Awakening, with the Baptists, or the Methodists, who called themselves Baptist or Methodist preachers.

In Maryland, the effect of the Great Awakening was not as strong. In the period from 1800 to the Civil War, the influence of the Great Awakening can be seen strongest in places like Talbot and Queen Anne's Counties on the Eastern Shore, and not in the larger urban areas like Baltimore, Annapolis and Frederick. In 1740, Anglican priest George Whitefield published an open letter to southern slave owners,

1055 See Chapter Nine on Maryland runaway slaves.

1056 The best account of Methodism in America's Second Great Awakening remains Ben F. Lehmberg, A New Awakening for Methodism (Boston: Methodist Evangelical Materials, 1963). Franklin knew Whitefield through the Quakers.

including those in Virginia and Maryland, and many southern slaves responded to his message.[1057]

At the time, Benjamin Franklin was instrumental in publishing Whitefield's letter in his *Three Letters From the Reverend George Whitefield.*[1058] Although the Great Awakening seems to have a profound effect on the religiosity of blacks in the south in the first sixty-five years of the nineteenth century, not all the responses to the movement were positive ones. Olaudah Equiano, for example, writes of encountering George Whitefield in his autobiography.[1059]

Mr. Equiano says of Whitefield in an epigram to this chapter, he was:

> sweating as much as I ever did while in Slavery on the Montserrat Beach... I had never seen Divines exert themselves in this manner.[1060]

Clearly, Olaudah Equiano did not know what to make of Whitefield and his ecstatic religion, nor, apparently, did he identify with the message of the preacher, which he refers to as a "divine," a term used in eighteenth and nineteenth-century English to designate a theologian or religious scholar.

Perhaps by far, the most significant aspect of the similarity of the

1057 Three important works on George Whitefield are J. C. Ryle, A Sketch of the Life and Labor of George Whitefield (New York: Amazon Digital Services, 2011); Thomas S. Kidd, George Whitefield: America's Spiritual Founding Father (New Haven: Yale University Press, 2016); and a small biography by Arnold Dallimore called George Whitefield, published in 2010 by Crossway reprints. Whitefield (1714–1770) was an English Anglican clergyman who was one of the founders of the Great Awakening in America.

1058 Ibid. The "Montserrat Beach" to which Equiano refers is an island in the Lesser Antilles.

1059 Benjamin Franklin, Three Letters from the Rev. George Whitefield, originally published in Philadelphia in 1801. Reprinted by Ecco Gale in 2010.

1060 Carolyn A. Haynes speaks of the encounter of George Whitefield by Olaudah Equiano in the fall of 1766, in her book From Conquering to Conquer (Jackson: University Press of Mississippi, 1998). The entire first chapter is devoted to the encounter. See pp. 1–27.

suspected Muslim slaves in both Maryland and Virginia is that in these runaway slave advertisements, we only get the perspective of the owners/planters. In none of the advertisements, in both places, is anything to be found from the perspectives of the slaves, in either Maryland or Virginia, about why they left, nor where they believed they were going.

Perhaps the final and most significant similarity between the Virginia and the Maryland suspected Muslim runaways is that in our analyses, we have employed the same five variables in judging that a particular slave was a member of the Islamic faith. The first of those variables is if he or she was born in Africa and now speaks very little English. A second factor was biographical information provided by the slave owners in their advertisements. They may say, "He is from the Guiney Country," "She is from Gambia" or "He is a Bight Negro."

A third factor, as we have maintained, are tribal marks and scars that slaves received back in their homelands. Comments from the slave masters may say, "He has Country marks," "He has a scar across his entire forehead" or "He has three strokes beneath both eyes he got back in Africa." Indeed, of the one hundred and six suspected Muslim runaway slaves, twenty-seven may be identified solely by the scars and tribal marks acquired in Africa. These tribal marks are listed in Appendix C at the end of this final chapter.

A fourth factor had to do with whether a slave spoke another language besides English, usually Arabic, French, Dutch or even German. As we have shown, these languages are sometimes helpful in identifying the African origins of some slaves. Those who speak Arabic, for example, often can be identified as coming from the Senegambian Supply Zone in the eighteenth and nineteenth centuries. French was spoken in the Gold and Windward Coasts Zones, as well as at Albreda and Fort Saint Joseph in Senegambia, and Dutch in the Sierra Leone Supply Zones.

A fifth and final factor was whether a slave had an Arabic or Islamic name, including those who were their companions in the escape. Indeed, as we have shown, more than sixty percent of our suspected Muslim slaves from both states had Arabic names. The most popular of these Arabic and Muslim names in this sudy were Sambo, Cuffee, Mingo, Jem or Jemima, Bewdley, and Hagar.

In our analyses of the materials in both states, we have not suggested that a particular slave was a Muslim if he or she did not fit at least three of the five variables or factors listed. In some rare cases, the judgment seems appropriate with fewer factors present, as when the tribal marks as a Muslim group may indicate the judgment, or where several members of the same family all have Arabic or Muslim names, such as the Jacob Aba family where eleven family members all had Islamic names. At any rate, we have presented our one hundred and six suspected Muslim slaves in the Chesapeake colonies/states of Virginia and Maryland—fifty-one in Virginia and fifty-five in Maryland—and the vast majority had Arabic or Muslim names.

In addition to all these similarities in the suspected Muslim slaves from Maryland and Virginia we have outlined here, there also were a significant number of differences between the two colonies/states. One big difference is that the suspected Maryland Muslim runaway came from only ten counties of the state. In Virginia, however, they came from twenty-four different counties, but mainly from ten, as well. Another big difference is that the number of runaway slave ads in Maryland, around fifteen hundred to two thousand, was only half of the three thousand ads examined in Virginia. A third important difference has to do with the concentration of suspected Muslim runaways, as we shall see next.

In Maryland, the highest concentration of suspected Muslim runaways came in the period from the first half of the eighteenth century, while in the Commonwealth of Virginia, that concentration is in the second half of the eighteenth century. Another difference is that Maryland has one suspected Muslim runaway who spoke German, while Virginia did not. We have seen that this German-speaking slave in Maryland also had a tribal scar that suggests she was a Wolof, and quite possibly a Muslim. This point is related to another significant difference.

The German-speaking slave in Maryland most likely came from the nation of Namibia, a German colony in Southwest Africa. Thus, Maryland had slaves from the nine supply zones outlined in Chapter Two, plus southern Africa, for a total of ten.

On the other hand, we saw in our analysis of suspected Muslim runaways in Virginia that one man was described as wearing "Moorish dress."[1061] This suggests that at least one of the Virginia slaves, then, was from North Africa. There were a number of other Virginia Muslim slaves who served in the Revolutionary Army, including Yusuf ben Ali, Bampett Mohamad, Peter Salem and the Saba brothers who were also from North Africa. Thus, like Maryland, the Virginia suspected Muslim slaves came from ten separate African supply zones, as well.

A final significant difference between the two groups of suspected Muslim runaway slaves has to do with the reward offered for their recovery. Both states increase the amount depending on whether the recovery is in the county, in the colony, or elsewhere, outside the colony or state. But the two locations are significantly different when it comes to the period from 1800 until the Civil War. In Maryland, in that final period, the reward for a suspected Muslim runaway in that state was $278, while in Virginia, in the same period, it was $378.[1062] Why the reward was significantly higher in the Commonwealth of Virginia, however, is not entirely clear.

Some scholars have recently suggested that the bounty for a runaway slave in the nineteenth century is directly proportional to how close the slave was to the Mason-Dixon Line. The farther away, the higher the ransom.[1063]

We have in mind here the work of Fogel and Engerman, as well as more recently, Connor Lennon, who gives the following example from the mid-nineteenth century state reward:

Maryland $278
Virginia $378
North Carolina $ 410
South Carolina $420
Georgia $470
Mississippi $520
Louisiana $540[1064]

1061 Ibid., pp. 11–13.

1062 Ibid., pp. 17–20. Henry John Steadman (1845–1915) had a long career in the Indian Service. Later, he served as a Liberal MP.

1063 Ibid.

1064 Michael A. Gomez speaks of this Muslim runaway slave in Virginia in his Black Crescent: The Experience and Legacy of African Muslims in

In this example, Louisiana is the most distant from the Mason-Dixon Line and thus has the heftiest price for the recovery of a runaway slave. Maryland, on the other hand, is closest to the line, and the price for a runaway is only half of that in Louisiana. Virginia, on average, is a hundred dollars more than Maryland, and North and South Carolina, a hundred and thirty-five, and a hundred and forty-five dollars more.

In addition to the material outlined in the above analyses, along the way in this study on suspected Muslim slaves in the Chesapeake Bay region, we also provided a description of a wealth of artistic depictions and embodiments of various issues discussed in the body of this study. To that end, in total, we have provided copies of, and discussions of, fifty separate depictions contained in the ten chapters of this study.

This brings us to the notes of this tenth and final chapter, followed by four appendices on the Muslim runaway slaves discussed in Chapters Eight and Nine (Appendices A and B), as well as the tribal marks of twenty-seven of our suspected Muslim slaves (Appendix C), and a final appendix on "Other Prominent Muslim Slaves in Early America" (Appendix D).

Since this is a concluding chapter, we will end with nine other artistic depictions, one for each of the nine previous chapters. Before moving to those images, however, we will add one short section that discusses a number of common traits that appear to have been present among the suspected Muslim runaway slaves.

Common Characteristics of Muslim Slaves in the Chesapeake Region

In the course of research for this study, we found twelve core characteristics that the suspected Muslim slaves appeared to have had in common. First, a significantly greater number of them were literate compared to the general slave population. In this regard, a significant number of pieces of writing by Muslim slaves are extant in this country, many written in Arabic, or transliterated from Arabic to English.

Job Diallo recited the Qur'an from memory when in London. Salih Bilali, who was born around 1770 in Mali and then settled on

the Americas (Cambridge: Cambridge University Press, 2005), p. 149.

Sapelo Island in America, wrote a thirteen-page manual of Islam.[1065] Muhammad Ali Ibn Said, kidnapped in northern Nigeria, later wrote an autobiography in English. Abu Bakr as-Saddiq kept plantation records in both Arabic and English. Phillis Wheatley (1753–1784) was the first published African American poet in America.[1066] Olaudah Equiano also wrote an autobiography, and several other early Muslims in America were clearly literate.

Secondly, in countless cases throughout North America, early Muslims came from royalty or had a very high station back in Africa. One was called a king, another a prince. A female slave in Maryland from the Gold Coast was known as "Queen Nanny." A Moor on the Mississippi was said to be the "son of a Prince," and many other Muslim captives appear to have been of a high station back in Africa.[1067]

Third, the suspected Muslim slaves in the Chesapeake region were often thought to be or were described by other slaves as being aloof or disconnected from the other slaves. Charles Ball's description of his Muslim grandfather, as well as other Muslims he encountered in his slavery in Maryland and Georgia, is a prime example of this phenomenon. Similarly, S'Quash, who was a slave in South Carolina, was said to be "aloof from other Negros." Indeed, many reports about Muslim slaves in the eighteenth and nineteenth centuries exist that suggest that the Muslim slaves saw themselves as being better than other captives.

1065 A list of these other prominent Muslim slaves in America can be seen in Appendix D of Chapter 10.

1066 The author of this study did these calculations by using the runaway slave advertisements discussed in Chapters Eight and Nine. John Gabriel Steadman (1744–1797), British-Dutch soldier, began his military service as an ensign in 1760 at the age of sixteen. Phillis Wheatley was a pioneer African American poet. She was born in the Senegambian Supply Zone, was kidnapped there at age eight, and brought across the Middle Passage to Boston. Later, she became a servant to her master John Wheatley who taught her to read and write.

1067 A Senegambian by Henry J. Frey (Paris, 1890). Frey also completed a portrait of Don Pio Pico (1801–1894), California rancher and politician. Dr. John Whitridge (1793–1878) was a Baltimore physician and trader of slaves. For more on the "Moor of the Mississippi" see Allan D. Austin's African Muslims in Antebellum America (London: Routledge, 1984), pp. 16, 24, 35, and 43–46.

A fifth characteristic that the Muslim slaves, at least the ones in the Chesapeake region, seem to have had in common is that they often were not suited for manual labor. Indeed, there is lots of evidence that the Muslim captives were more suited to housework or to the tending of cattle than to manual labor. This factor was true of Job Diallo, Lamine Joy, Yarrow Mamout, and many other African Muslims who came to the New World. Dr. James Collins, in his *Practical Rules for the Management and Medical Treatment of Negro Slaves*, also points to the abilities of Muslim slaves from the Senegambian Supply Zone, when he observes, "Many of them converse in the Arabic language and some of them are sufficiently instructed even to write it. They are excellent for the care of cattle and horses and for domestic service, though little qualified for the ruder labors of the field." In his analysis, Collins mentions the first commonality of literacy, as well as the fifth, that Muslim slaves in the Chesapeake were not suited for tobacco farming.

Another characteristic that the Muslim slaves of the Chesapeake Bay region had in common is that they generally were manumitted or set free after only a few years. This is particularly true of early Muslim slaves in the Chesapeake, like Antonio, Job Diallo, Matteus de Sousa, and Yarrow Mamout, to cite four examples. This is also related to another core element—that Muslim slaves on Chesapeake Bay tobacco farms, as well as farms in Georgia and South Carolina, often were given positions of some authority over other captives on the farm.

Indeed, at least six Muslim slaves in early America became the plantation managers, including Ab ar-Rahman in Natchez, Mississippi, Salih Bilali, S'Quash of South Carolina, and Abu Bakr, who managed his plantation in Jamaica.

A ninth characteristic that the suspected Muslim slaves often appear to have in common is that a number of the more prominent Chesapeake Bay Muslims, or others early Muslims in North America, returned to Africa, a very rare occurrence among the general slave population. Examples of this ninth similarity of prominent early American Muslims who returned to Africa were Job Diallo, Lamine Yaos, Abu Bakr, Lamine Kebe and Abd Ar-Rahman, who returned to Africa after being freed in Natchez, Mississippi.

Tenth, many times, the suspected Muslim slaves appear to have had an ambivalent relationship to Christianity. Although the vast majority of slaves converted to the Christian faith, there apparently were many Muslims who identified Allah with the God of the Judeo-Christian tradition and Muhammad with the life of Jesus Christ and that sometimes appears to have created an ambivalence among some of the suspected Muslim slaves in this study.

Nevertheless, there is copious evidence that several of the prominent Muslim slaves in America appear to have maintained their observations of Islamic laws. Yarrow Mamout prayed in the streets of Washington and Job Diallo left his animal-tending duties to pray in the woods. The slave of a lighthouse keeper in Maryland is reported to "have prayed five times a day, and did not eat pork, nor touch a drop of spirits."

An eleventh item that many prominent Muslim slaves in America had in common is that at least a dozen of them had their portraits painted or drawn by European or American artists. These include Job Diallo (twice), Yarrow Mamout (twice), Umar Ibn Said, Ibrahim ar-Rahman, Nicholas Said, Mohomah Baquaqua, Salih Bilali, and Osman of the Dismal Swamp.

Finally, the Muslim slaves, particularly the prominent ones in this study, had acquaintances or friendships with a variety of famous people in England and America. These notable individuals include President John Quincy Adams; James Oglethorpe, the founder of the Georgia colony; members of British royalty, such as Sir Hans Sloane and Queen Christina; George Sale, the great Qur'an translator; Mark Twain; Henry Clay; George Washington; Thomas Jefferson; Theodore Dwight; and many others.

This brings us to the final artistic images that depict some of the materials in this study, the subject matter of the next section of this tenth, and final chapter.

More Images of Chesapeake Muslim Slaves

In this final section of this tenth chapter, we shall examine nine additional artistic images that depict the material in this study, one image that shows an aspect of each of the nine previous chapters. The first image comes from an illustration of John Steadman's *Narratives of a*

Five Year Expedition in Surinam, 1772–1777.[1068] In the image a group of ten bare-chested adult female slaves are overseen by one European with a whip. Two of the women have small children, one an infant and the other a toddler. A white dog wanders around the scene.

The second image is an aerial photograph of Elmina Castle in Ghana on the Gold Coast. It shows the various buildings of the compound in the center, the Atlantic Ocean in the background, and palm trees and a modern road in the foreground. The photograph was taken in the late twentieth century.[1069]

The third image, which is related to the Middle Passage, shows a slave about to be thrown over the starboard side of a European ship by two white sailors. Behind the three, stands another slave being guarded by a third sailor with a long sword waiting to be dealt with. The image is produced by www.haikudeck.com./the-middle passage.[1070]

Image four is an illustration of a "Senegambian," by Henri Frey, published in Paris in 1890. It shows a young African man, not with very dark skin, seated and wearing a black robe and a white turban. The man has a serene look on his visage. He looks like many of the slaves brought to the Chesapeake Bay region from the Senegambian Supply Zone.[1071]

The fifth image is a tintype of Dr. John Whitbridge's slave Patty, who holds one of the family's children, a girl, on her lap. It is a tender photo, owned by the Maryland Historical Society, in Baltimore. The Whitbridge family was so fond of Patty that she is buried in the family plot.[1072]

A sixth image is entitled *Introduction to Slavery in Virginia.* It shows two gentlemen, presumably a European and a Virginian, who are haggling over the price of a slave family: man, woman, and two

1068 Tintype of Dr. John Whitridge's slave, Patty, owned by the Maryland Historical Society in Baltimore.

1069 Anonymous, Introduction to Slavery in Virginia. The illustration is owned by the New York Public Library.

1070 Image can be found at www.knowla.org.

1071 Image can be found at https://www.nps.gov/ethnography.

1072 Illustration of Mahommah Gardo Baquaqua in Muslim Freedmen in the Atlantic World by Paul E. Lovejoy, pp. 233–262. Image on p. 249, http://bit.ly/2t9Ppv3. Mahomah Gardo Baquaqua (1824–1857) was a native of Zoogoo in West Africa. He became a slave in Brazil.

children. The image is included to depict a Virginian slave trader in the nineteenth century.[1073]

A slave dealer sits at an auction table with gavel raised above his head in his right hand. On the auction platform stands a young male slave dressed all in white. Around the auction table stand many planters. Behind the slave on the platform is a female slave with a white Moslem-looking headdress.[1074]

The image of a slave coffle in Africa shows twenty-five slaves held together by Goree sticks. They are accompanied by three guards who carry spears. A black dog wanders in the scene. It can be found at www.nps.gov/ethnography/aah/slaveCaravan.[1075]

Finally, an illustration of Mahommah Gardo Baquaqua is found in an essay by Paul E. Lovejoy entitled, "Muslim Freedom in the Atlantic World." Baquaqua is seated and dressed in Africa garb. A look of serenity is across his face.[1076]

This brings us to the conclusions of this tenth chapter, followed by the notes of the same. These will be followed by four separate appendices. The first two of these, A and B, are on the suspected Muslim slaves in Virginia, and then Maryland. The third, Appendix C, is a summary of the tribal scars of twenty-seven of the Chesapeake captives. Appendix D is a catalog of other prominent Muslim slaves brought to the New World during the Atlantic slave trade.

Conclusions

In this concluding chapter, we argued that it is best to see this study on Muslim slaves in the Chesapeake Bay region as having four parts. In

---

1073 Hagar Williams (1842–1925) was a Maryland slave who married Joseph Collier. They had four children. Later they moved to Georgia, where she died.

1074 These twelve slaves, and their tribal marks, are identified in the body of the text.

1075 Although we have said that seven slaves spoke Arabic, that number could be as many as twelve.

1076 Jean St. Malo, who died June 19, 1784, also known as Juan St. Malo in Spanish, was the leader of the group of runaway slaves called "Maroons," who inhabited parts of the Dismal Swamp from the late eighteenth century to the 1860s.

the first of these, which amounts to Chapter One, is a general introduction to the phenomenon of Muslim slaves in Virginia and Maryland. This was followed by part two, consisting of Chapters Two and Three, and dealing with African supply zones and the Middle Passage—the route by which most Africans in the fifteenth to nineteenth centuries came to the New World.

The third part of this study, which includes Chapters Four, Five, Six and Seven, was an analysis of slave coffles, slave traders in Baltimore and Maryland, slave traders in the District of Columbia, and slave traders in the Commonwealth of Virginia. In the third part of this study, in Chapter Seven, we also introduced the phenomena of slave jails and slave auctions, auction blocks and stones in the Chesapeake Bay region in the first sixty-five years of the nineteenth century.

In the fourth part of this study, Chapters Eight to Ten, we introduced fifty-one suspected Muslim slaves in the state of Virginia, as well as fifty-five in Maryland, from the seventeenth century to the Civil War period. In both of these chapters, we identified the 106 suspected Muslim slaves by depending on the five variables discussed earlier. By attending to tribal marks, languages other than English, being born in Africa and knowing very little English, biographical information garnered from the owners of the slaves and having an Arabic or Islamic name. We then introduced the 106 suspected Muslim slaves in the Chesapeake Bay region, in that time period, in Chapters Eight and Nine.[1077]

In the fifth section of this final chapter, we gave a summary of twelve core characteristics that the suspected Muslim slaves in this study seem to have shared. These characteristics may be summarized this way:

1. Literacy
2. Royalty or high station
3. Aloofness, especially in relation to other slaves
4. Thought themselves better than other slaves
5. Not good at manual labor. More suited for animal tending

1077 Hagar Jumper was born around 1750. She received her freedom from Stephen Dance of Dinwiddie County, Virginia, in a court case based on her ethnicity. Because she was descendant of American Indians, she was declared free by the Virginia court.

6. Often given positions of authority over other slaves
7. Manumitted or freed early
8. Observed Islamic law and life
9. Returned to Africa
10. Ambivalence about Christianity
11. Subjects of portraits or film
12. Knew famous people in Britain or America

After exploring those five parts in this chapter, we then introduced nine final artistic depictions that have aided us in displaying the one hundred and six slaves we have discussed. These images were followed by five appendices that provide the raw data in regard to the suspected Muslim slaves from both states.

This brings us to the four appendices: Muslim Slaves in Virginia (Appendix A), Muslim Slaves in Maryland (Appendix B), a Catalog of Slave Tribal Marks from Africa (Appendix C), and a list of Other Prominent Muslim Slaves in Early America (Appendix D), as well as a discussion of each of these prominent Muslim slaves.[1078]

1078 Osman was an African man who escaped slavery and went to live in the Dismal Swamp, where he too became a leader of the Maroons there. Yaqob Aba was an American slave in Virginia of Mr. J. Reed of Accomack County. His wife, as well as his nine children, all had Muslim or Arabic names.

Appendix A: Muslim Runaway Slaves in Maryland

Of the fifty-five suspected Muslim slaves in Maryland, forty were males and fifteen were females. Among that fifty-five, there were:

9 Sambo

3 Hagar

2 Wali

2 Cuffee

3 Musa

2 Ali

2 Ayyub or Job

Among the prominent Muslim runaway slaves, we have discussed:

Job Diallo

Lamine Joy

Kunta Kinte

Yarrow Mamout

In terms of the century in which the fifty-five escaped, one was from the seventeenth century, forty-one from the eighteenth century, and thirteen from the nineteenth century. The fifty-five slaves range from fourteen years old to sixty years old, with the average age being twenty-seven and a half. The majority of the fifty-five were found in seven different newspapers and periodicals. These were:

Maryland Gazette 41

National intelligencer 2

Baltimore Sun 3

Annapolis Gazette 3

City Gazette and Advertiser 2

Baltimore Telegraph 2

Baltimore Advertiser 2

The height of the suspected Maryland Muslim ranged from five foot three to six foot six, with the average of five foot eight. Of the fifty-five, thirteen may be identified by their tribal scars. In terms of their origins in Africa, twenty may be identified, including five from Senegambia, five from the Niger Valley Zone, and ten from the Gold and Windward Coasts. Of languages spoken, other than English, at least six spoke Arabic, and as many as ten; ten French, two Dutch, and one German. In terms of the Maryland counties from which they escaped. These may be summarized this way:

Baltimore County 18

Prince George's County 4

Anne Arundel County 11

Montgomery County 2

Saint Mary's County 2

Saint Anne's County 3

Charles County 2

Cecil County 2

Worcester County 7

Talbot County 2

St. Anne's County 2

Catalog of Suspected Maryland Muslim Runaway Slaves

Name	Owner	County	Periodical
Sambo	J. S. Stevens	Anne Arundel	*Maryland Gazette* 4/12/1781

Mingo	J. Smith	Anne Arundel	*Maryland Gazette* 7/7/1759
Dinah	J. Smith	Anne Arundel	*Maryland Gazette* 7/7/1759
Esther	J. Round	Worcester	*Maryland Gazette* 9/8/1765
Sarah	I. Smith	Talbot	*Maryland Gazette* 1/27/1778
Ismail	J. Baker	Baltimore	*Maryland Gazette* 2/19/1765
Musa	M. Forestell	Baltimore	*Maryland Gazette* 10/23/1760
Mingo	R. J. Stevens	St. Anne's	*Baltimore Advertiser* 4/15/1787
Charles Thomas	Henry Thomas	Talbot	*Denton News* 2/29/1803
Hagar Williams	T. Berry	Baltimore	*Maryland Gazette* 10/3/1761
Hagar	W. Payne	Baltimore	*Maryland Gazett* 9/7/1766
Hagar	J. Smith	Baltimore	*Maryland Gazette* 7/7/1759
Hagar	W. P. Jones	Charles	*Maryland Gazette* 9/8/1765
Maryam	T. Turton	Prince George's	*Maryland Gazette* 9/12/1801
Ishaq	G. T. Greenwood	Prince George's	*National Intelligencer* 10/8/1810
P. G. Yusuf	A. Barnett	Baltimore	*Baltimore Sun* 8/22/1851
Minty	B. Hawkins	Baltimore	*Baltimore Sun* 10/6/1852
Dan	W. Risteau	Baltimore	*Maryland Gazette* 6/30/1850
Dick Oblebe	I. Cooke	Baltimore	*Maryland Gazette* 7/25/1849

Mingo	R. Brown	Baltimore	*Maryland Gazette* 6/6/1721
Bood	W. Hunt	Anne Arundel	*Maryland Gazette* 12/20/1766
Mingo	Savoy. J. Edwards	Anne Arundel	*Annapolis Gazette* 7/7/1753
Jack	A. Byrnes	St. Anne's	*Maryland Gazette* 7/20/1779
Mingo	W. Gunther	St. Mary's	*Maryland Gazette* 5/19/1793
Mingo	W. Bull	Anne Arundel	*Annapolis Gazette* 6/21/1801
Sambo	unknown	Anne Arundel	*Annapolis Gazette* 9/1/1768
Sambo	W. Sharpe	Worcester	*Maryland Gazette* 6/17/1744
Hagar	J. Round	Worcester	*Maryland Gazette* 7/23/1765
Mingo	J. Cathell	Worcester	*Maryland Gazette* 6/16/1772
Sambo	T. May	Cecil	*Maryland Gazette* 8/12/1784
Sue	S. Worthington	Baltimore	*Maryland Gazette* 9/27/1802
Sambo	G. Scott	Prince George's	*Maryland Gazette* 9/12/1763
Jem	G. Scott	Prince George's	*Maryland Gazette* 9/12/1763
Sambo	T. Todd	Baltimore	*Maryland Gazette* 6/5/1783
Hagar	T. Todd	Baltimore	*Maryland Gazette* 6/5/1783
Walle	E. Worrell	Charles	*Maryland Gazette* 2/19/1775

Ali	E. Dare	Anne Arundel	*Annapolis Gazette* 2/19/1875
Joe	D. Owens	Anne Arundel	*Annapolis Gazette* 6/26/1791
Charles	D. Owens	Anne Arundel	*Annapolis Gazette* 6/26/1791
Hagar	A. Philips	Worcester	*Easton News* 7/19/1686
Pero	J. George	Worcester	*Easton News* 7/19/1686
Sambo	C. Gosnell	Baltimore	*Baltimore Telegraph* 6/6/1793
Sambo	D. Damcourt	Baltimore	*Maryland Gazette* 10/18/1796
Sobett	J. Thompson	Anne Arundel	*Maryland Gazette* 1/17/1801
Jem	S. Williams	Prince George's	*Maryland Gazette* 1/4/1798
Will	J. H. Stevens	Baltimore	*Maryland Gazette* 1/4/1798
Jack	T. Stone	Charles	*Maryland Gazette* 1/4/1798
Jack	C. Beverly	Worcester	*Denton News* 4/23/1700
Sambo	M. Christian	St. Mary's	*St. Mary's Journal* 10/27/1769
Tower	D. Harris	Baltimore	*Baltimore Sun* 1/29/1841
Sambo	W. Digges	Charles	*Maryland Gazette* 2/27/1755
Nanny	S. T. Smithson	Baltimore	*Maryland Gazette* 7/17/1686

Lewis	J.M. Stone	Baltimore	*City Gazette and Adver.* *4/1/1799*
Tower	D. Harris	Baltimore	*Maryland Gazette* 2/16/1801
Sambo	W. Digges	Charles	Maryland Gazette 2/27/1755

In terms of tribal scars, the following numbers of suspected Maryland Muslim runaways may be identified: numbers 2, 4, 9, 10, 11, 13, 22, 30, 36, 40, 41, and 45. In these cases, the slaves' origins may be identified simply by the tribal marks alone. More is said of these tribal scars and marks in Appendix C of this final chapter. Before that, however, we move to Appendix B, a summary of the fifty-one suspected Virginia Muslim runaway slaves.

Appendix B: Virginia Runaway Muslim Slaves

In the Commonwealth of Virginia, we have found fifty-one suspected Muslim runaway slaves. Forty-one of these were men, and ten women. The age range of these slaves is fifteen to sixty, with the average being twenty-eight years. Of the fifty-one, two were from the seventeenth century, forty in the eighteenth century, and nine in the nineteenth century. The earliest Virginia Muslim runaway was in 1673, the most recent in 1864.

Fifteen of the fifty-one could speak a language other than English. Among these seven spoke Arabic (and possibly as many as ten). Two spoke Dutch, and six knew French. Among the Arabic and Islamic names there were:

Ten Sambo

Three Hagar

Six Mingo

Five Cuffee

One Musa

Two Ali

One Ayyub

Two Fatima

One Quash

One Nila

The suspected Virginia Muslim runaway slaves came from the following counties of Virginia:

Orange 10

Charles City 2

Fairfax 7

Chesterfield 9

Mecklenburg 5

Prince William 2

Henrico 6

Accomack 5

Dismal Swamp 2

Yorktown 1

Farrowsville 1

Mustee 1

Catalog of Suspected Virginia Muslim Runaway Slaves

Name	Owner	County	Periodical
Sambo	Purdie and Dixon	Richmond	*Virginia Gazette* 11/2/1779
Sambo	W. Holbourne	Richmond	*Virginia Herald* 6/61793
Sambo	W. Hunter	Orange	*Virginia Gazette* 5/16/ 1745
Sambo	A. Marshall	Orange	*Virginia Gazette* 11/4/1763
Jean St. Malo		Dismal Swamp Fairfax	Unknown
Hagar	W. Smith	Henrico	*Virginia Gazette* 5/13/1750
David	George J. Bryan	Henrico	*Virginia Gazette* 11/19/1853
Jack	M. Arburtnott	Chesterfield	*Virginia Gazette* 10/10/1765
Stephen	A. Trueheart	Orange	*Virginia Gazette* 5/15/1746

Sambo	Gibson & Gran-berry	Fairfax	*Virgina Gazette* 6/17/1768
Sambo	J. Buchanan	Fairfax	*Virginia Gazette* 12/12/1770
Step	G. Robinson	Chesterfield	*Virginia Gazette* 9/ 12/1771
Bonaund	R. Booker	Richmond	*Virginia Gazette* 12/24/1772
Bacchus	J. A. Finnie	Charles City	*Virginia Gazette* 9/30/1773
Jem	Gilchrest & Taylor	Orange	*Virginia Gazette* 9/12/1773
Nick	B. Harrison	Fairfax	*Virginia Gazette* 1/14/1775
Tom Binford	S. A. Dilliard	Charles City	*Virginia Gazette* 2/19/1864
Sambo	G. Jones	Chesterfield	*Virginia Gazette* 6/16/1775
George	T. Smith	Prince William	*Virginia Gazette* 1/14/1773
Hagar Jumper	S. Davis	Mustee	*Virginia Gazette* 8/14/1800
Osman		Dismal Swamp Fairfax	Unknown
Sambo	Anderson Geo. Washington	Fairfax	*Virginia Gazette* 5/13/1763
Job	T. T. Smithson	Orange	*Virginia Gazette* 6/ 29/1785
Ali	J. Russell	Mecklenburg	*Virginia Gazette* 6/1/1790
George	Thom Jones	Orange	*Virginia Gazette* 4/19/1784
Bewdley	J. Walker	Accomack	*Virginia Gazette* 1/18/1771
Fatimar	Geo. Washing-ton	Fairfax	*Virginia Gazette* 5/13/1763

Little Fatimar	Geo. Washington	Fairfax	*Virginia Gazette* 5/13/1763
Sambo	J. Walker	Accomack	*Virginia Gazette* 1/10/1771
Sambo	J. Stone	Chesterfield	*Virginia Gazette* 3/7/1771
Mingo	M. Selkin	Mecklenburg	*Virginia Gazette* 1/5/1782
Mingo	J. Walker	Accomack	*Virginia Gazette* 9/5/1755
Mingo	M. Phillips	Chesterfield	*Virginia Gazette* 5/12/1774
Mingo	A. Allen	Orange	*Virginia Gazette* 3/ 12/ 1673
Mingo	J. Stone	Chesterfield	*Chesterfield News* 6/27/1649
Yaqob	Aba J. Reed	Accomack	*Virginia Gazette* 5/15/1821
Sambo	T. Williams	Orange	*Virginia Gazette* 1/25/1815
Quash	W. Neffen	Orange	*Virginia Gazette* 12/19/1736
Cuff	H. Skipwith	Chesterfield	*Virginia Gazette* 4/23/1753
Cuffey	R. Munford	Yorktown	*Virginia Gazette* 5/30/1772
Cuffey	J. McLaughlin	Mecklenburg	*Virginia Gazette* 3/12/1772
Cuffe	L. Holstead	Orange	*Virginia Gazette* 10/13/1796
Cuffe	A. Emmenton	Chesterfield	*Virginia Gazette* 9/8/1801

Musa	E. Carter	Prince William	*National Intel* 5/30/1837
Ephraim	M. Jett	Farrowsville	*Virginia Gazette* 5/30/1837
Ali	J. W. Peters	Mecklenburg	*Virginia Gazette* 1/21/1790
Job	M. Tolsey	Chesterfield	*Virginia Gazette* 7/7/1785
Jibril	M. Sheppard	Henrico	*Harper's Weekly* 7/2/1864
Obidiah	J. Wise	Accomack	*Virginia Gazette* 11/29/1864
Nila	G. Washington	Fairfax	*Virginia Gazette* 5/13/1763

The Virginia suspected Muslim runaway slaves who can be identified by their tribal marks are numbers: 1, 8, 9, 12, 14, 15, 16, 17, 19, 21, 26, 38, 43, 45, and 46. We say more about these in Appendix C of this chapter. Thirty-three of the fifty-one suspected Muslim slaves in Virginia had Arabic or Muslim names. Forty six of the fifty-one were found in the *Virginia Gazette*.

Appendix C:
Tribal Scars in Africa

In our analysis of one hundred and six suspected Muslim runaway slaves, twenty-seven of them may be identified solely by their tribal marks back in Africa. Twenty of these slaves were male and seven were females. Fourteen of the twenty-seven were in Virginia, and thirteen in Maryland.

The Virginia slaves with tribal scars were the following:

Name	Tribe	Marks
Billy	Wolof	Scar over right eye
Jack	Mandinka	Three parallel strokes
Sambo	Wolof	Both cheeks
Sambo	Mandinka	Scar across forehead
Bounard	Wolof	Both cheeks
Sambo	Mandinka	Three parallel strokes
Stephen	Mandinka	Three parallel strokes
Step	Yoruba	Three vertical strokes
Jem	Makonde	Right hand
Tom.	Fulani	Scar across forehead
Bewdley	Fulani	Scar across forehead
Sambo	Wolof	Scar over right eye and hand
Bacchus	Fulani	Right hand
Nick	Wolof	Over right eye
Sambo Anderson	Yoruba	Vertical parallel lines over face

The thirteen slaves with tribal marks in Maryland were the following:

Name	Tribe	Marks
Nanny	Krobo	Left hand
Cudjoe	Krobo	Right hand

Joe	Mandinka	One horizontal mark on forehead
Sobett	Pungo	Above both breasts
Dick Oblebe	Yoruba	Over right eye
Bewdley	Fulani	One horizontal line on forehead
Esther	Mandinka	Three parallel strokes under both eyes
Jenny	Pungo	Above both breasts
Jem	Mandinka	Three parallel strokes under both eyes
Anonymous	Wolof	Three vertical strokes under both eyes
Jem	Fulani	Over right eye
Sambo	Wolof	Over left eye
Elenor	Wolof	Scar on right hand

Appendix D: Other Prominent Muslim Slaves in Early America and the New World

In this fourth appendix, we shall list a number of other prominent Muslim slaves in early America and the New World. This list comes primarily from Allan Austin's *African Muslims in Antebellum America.* Those additional Muslim slaves on this list made themselves prominent, in one way or another, after arriving in the New World.

Ibrahim Abd ar-Rahman (1762–1829), born in Guinea.
Abu Bakr as-Saddiq (1790–1841), born in Timbuktu.
Salih Bilali (1772–1855), born in present-day Mali.
Lamine Kebe (1775–1835), born in Senegambian Supply Zone.
Man Who Prayed Five Times a Day (born ca. 1800), born in Niger Valley Supply Zone.
The Moor on the Mississippi (?). Discussed pp. 43–46 of Austin.
Mohammed Ali Ibn Said (1833–1882), born in Kingdom of Borneo.
Umar Ibn Said (1770–1864), born in Senegal.
Phillis Wheatley (1753–1784), born in Senegambia.
Selim Aga (1826–1875), born in Sudan.
Bilali Muhammad (1770–1857), born in Guinea.
Boyrereau Brinch, aka Jeffrey Brace (1742–1827), born in Mali in Niger Valley Zone.
S'Quash (?)
Samba Makumbo (?), born in Senegal.
Muhammad Sinei (1788–1838).
Dorugu Kwage Adamu (born ca. 1820).
Hamet Abdul, Tennessee slave mid-nineteenth century.
Charles Ball's South Carolina Muslim.
The Moorish Slave. Mohammad Abdula. Fulbe from Kano. Slave in Bahia, Brazil.
Anna Muusa, a.k.a., Benjamin Cochrane. Jamaican slave in late eighteenth century.

Abd ar-Rahman was born in Guinea. He was captured on the Gambia River and placed in the hold of the slave ship *Africa*. He was brought to the British West Indies and subsequently shipped to New Orleans, and then by riverboat to Natchez, Mississippi, where he became a slave. After more than forty years of slavery in America, Abd ar-Rahman returned to Africa.

Abu Bakr as-Saddiq was born in Timbuktu, in present-day Mali. He became a slave in Jamaica, where he wrote a sixteen-page autobiography in Arabic, in 1831. He later became a slave in Charleston, South Carolina, until he ran away to Fayettesville, North Carolina.

Salih Bilali was also born in present-day Mali. He became a slave of William Brown Hodgson. He also worked as a plantation overseer. Later, Salih became the slave of James Hamilton Couper who wrote several descriptions of Bilali and his work, on his plantation on St. Simons Island in Georgia.

Lamine Kebe was born in Senegal. In America, he was known as "Old Paul." He befriended Theodore Dwight who suggested he was "a great source for information about Africa." For a while Kebe worked for the American Colonization Society in New York. In Africa, before his abduction, Kebe taught Qur'anic studies, to both men and a few women.

The Man Who Prayed Five Times a Day was born around 1800 in either Nigeria or the Bight of Biafra. He became a slave in South Carolina, where he was also described as being "aloof." Nothing else is known of his biography. Similarly, the Moor on the Mississippi, was said to pray openly on his voyage down the Mississippi, but little else is known about him.

Mohammed Ali Ibn Said, also known as Nicholas Said, was born in the Kingdom of Borneo. He became a slave in the Deep South in America, and he traveled to five different continents in his lifetime. Omar Ibn Said also was born in Senegal. Eventually, he became a slave in Charleston, South Carolina, where he became an overseer of other slaves.

Phillis Wheatley was born in Senegal, kidnapped at age eight, and brought across the Middle Passage to Boston, where she became a slave. Later, she became the first African American poet in New England. Selim Aga was a native of Sudan. At the age of eight he was kidnapped and brought to Scotland where he received a first-class education. Later, he returned to Africa, where he also was killed in 1875.

Bilali Muhammad was born in Guinea, in the Sierra Leone Supply Zone. He became a slave on Sapelo Island. He was also the author of the "Bilali Document," a sixteen-page summary of the tenets of the faith of Islam. Boyrereau Brinch, also known as Jeffrey Brace, was born in Mali. Later, after becoming a slave in America, he served in the Continental Army of George Washington. Samba Makumbo was born in Senegal. After his voyage on the Middle Passage, he was brought to Trinidad, where he was made a slave. Later, he gained his freedom there.

Muhammed Sinei was a Mandingo Gambian, born near the Gambia River. He was first taken to a French Fort on Goree Island and then transported to Trinidad. Later, Sinei was involved in the manumitting of other Mandingoes there, by buying them back from their owners. Several contemporary scholars have written accounts of the life of Sisei, including Carl Campbell, as well as an article in the 1838 edition of the *Journal of British African Geographical Society of London*.

Dorogu Kawag Adamu, of Central Sudan, was abducted near his home in 1839. He was purchased by a German diplomat named Adolf Overweg in 1851 and taken to Europe. Later, Adamu was freed and then returned to Central Sudan in 1864.

Tennessee slave, Hamet Abdul was obviously a captive who insisted on retaining his African and Muslim name. He was first noted in 1834, when he sought to raise money, so he could return to Africa. Charles Ball, in his autobiography, supplies a nineteen-page narrative from a Muslim slave he discovered in South Carolina. Ball's Muslim was most likely a member of the Tuareg Tribe, in present-day Mali. Ball says he was captured on the Gambia River and was brought to Charleston, South Carolina, around 1807.

A Mississippi slave known only as the "Moor," was brought to the Mississippi River around the year 1812. He was interviewed by a white American. He claims to have been a Muslim prince from the Niger River Valley. He was captured there by a rival clan and placed on a Spanish ship, whereupon he was brought to New Orleans. The Moor was forced to eat pork there for survival, but he never touched spirits in his time in America.

Mohammad Abdullah, a slave from Kano, was enslaved in Bahia, Brazil, sometime in the 1840s. By then, Abdullah had fulfilled his obligation of the *Hajj,* or pilgrimage to Mecca, and he appears to have been a Fula in Nigeria. Anna Mousa, or Benjamin Cochrane, was the son of a Mandinka priest, as well as a skilled physician in Kingston, Jamaica. Mousa also appears to be a native Arabic speaker and was familiar with Richard Robert Madden (1798–1886), Irish writer, physician and abolitionist historian. Madden first arrived in Jamaica in November of 1833.

Finally, a slave known only as “S’Quash,” was brought to Charleston, South Carolina, in the late eighteenth century where he became a slave. Again, little else is known of this man’s biography. Sylviane Diouf suggests that S’Quah could read and write Arabic and Greek, and that he had been to Cairo. He may be related, however, to a married couple who were slaves of George Washington—Deborah and her husband Henry Squash. The couple escaped Mount Vernon in 1781 and joined the British in New York, where they were declared free in 1783.

Acknowledgements

The writing of any book brings certain kinds of debts. For this one, I am indebted to my wife Sandra and our son, Jack. Also, my dear friends Marguerite Villa Santa, Rick Armiger, John Fitzpatrick, Ray Alsalka, and Sarah Ferris, who helped me with the Arabic. I also am indebted to my in-laws, Tom and Mary Lee Parsons, and to James McPartland, and all the others who have done blurbs for this book. None of this would be possible without the wonderful publishing folks at Calumet Editions, who all deserve medals! Any and all errors to be found in this book are entirely my own.

About the Author

Before his retirement in 2016, Stephen Vicchio taught for more than forty years at the University of Maryland, Johns Hopkins University, St. Mary's Seminary in Baltimore, and other universities in Britain and the United States. He has authored over two dozen books, as well as essays and plays, mostly about the Bible, philosophy and theology. Among his books since 2000 is his interpretation of the Book of Job: *The Antichrist: A History, Biblical Figures in the Islamic Faith*, and books about the religions of American presidents George Washington, Thomas Jefferson, Abraham Lincoln and the forthcoming *Ronald Reagan's Religious Beliefs*.

www.ingramcontent.com/pod-product-compliance
Lightning Source LLC
Chambersburg PA
CBHW032145080426
42735CB00008B/590